ECONOMICS
Its Nature and Importance

G. CARL WIEGAND

Professor of Economics
Southern Illinois University
Carbondale, Illinois

Barron's Educational Series, Inc.
Woodbury, New York

All inquiries should be addressed to:
Barron's Educational Series, Inc.
113 Crossways Park Drive
Woodbury, New York 11797

Library of Congress Catalog Card No. 67–26023

PRINTED IN THE UNITED STATES OF AMERICA

Preface

If every college student, irrespective of his field of specialization, were permitted to practice medicine, the health and welfare of the public would probably be in a rather sad state. Yet not only every college graduate, but every American, educated or illiterate, can and does "practice" economics, even though he may not know more about monetary and fiscal theory, business cycles, and price formation than he knows about removing an infected appendix or setting a broken leg.

This is the problem which faces every modern nation, and particularly every democracy where people are free to express their desires. Every man who borrows money to buy a house or a car, every woman who trades in her old refrigerator for a later model, every student who cuts down on his meals to buy a fancy sports jacket, all of them make economic decisions. Millions and millions of these decisions — some arrived at after careful consideration, others on the spur of the moment — determine the day-to-day course of the nation's economy.

More far-reaching decisions are made at the polls, where millions of Americans vote for candidates who either promise more government spending or a balanced budget, more or less foreign aid, "full employment" or price stability.

This Outline is not designed to turn the reader into a professional economist or into a future manager of the nation's economy. It is not intended to "cover" the whole involved and often highly technical field of economics, but to "uncover" its importance and its basic problems. The country needs highly trained economists. But the need is even greater for a broad understanding by the general public of the basic economic forces which help to shape the nature of our society.

The Outline is addressed not primarily to the economic expert, but to the student who, in his first course in economics, is confronted with a formidable 7–800 page text and who seeks a more compact summary of "what it is all about." It is addressed to the high school teacher who teaches a social studies course, to the college student who takes a general education course in economics or in the general field of social studies, and to the layman who likes to know more about the forces which shape the world in which he lives.

It is an attempt to make a difficult subject more readily understandable, although it is not the intention to make economics "easy" by omitting the many unsolved complexities.

The text is divided into four parts. In the first chapter the much debated question of "What is Economics?" will be discussed.

Chapters 2–8 provide material on the changing cultural and institutional framework within which the "Economy" functions which the economist tries to understand.

Part III (Chapters 9–19) deals with macroeconomics, the basic issues, institutions (such as the monetary and fiscal system), the theories and policies which affect the economic development of the nation as a whole.

In Part IV (Chapters 20–26) microeconomics is discussed: What determines the prices of goods and services? How does the structure of the market affect prices? How do the individual factors of production which cooperate in the production of goods share in the proceeds of the final product?

Reading Guide

TO SIX WIDELY USED TEXTBOOKS

The first column shows the chapter numbers in this Outline. Read across to find the corresponding chapter numbers in six widely used textbooks, where you will find in detail the same material discussed in the Outline.

Chapters in this Outline	*Alchian & Allen*	*Bach 4th Ed.*	*Hailstone & Dodd 5th Ed.*	*Lipsey & Steiner*	*McConnel 3rd Ed.*	*Samuelson 6th Ed.*
1,2	1	1,4	2	1,2,3	1,2	1,2
3	—	11,44	—	—	—	2,35
4	24	27	—	—	6,9	—
5	18	23	33	—	35	20
6	23	17,20,43	4,30	16,18, 19,20	8	5
7	20,21	29,30,31	31,32	35	36	7,27
8	18	18,42	17,34	—	7,37,38	6
9,10	9	3	—	43,58	6	3
11	29,30, 31	7,8	18,19, 20,21	52,53,54	16,17,18	14,15,16
12	28	36	22,23,24	51	15	8,9
13	25	6,13	26	49	11	13
14	38	11,12, 34,44	27,38	56,57	20,21,41	35,36

Chapters in this Outline	Alchian & Allen	Bach 4th Ed.	Hailstone & Dodd 5th Ed.	Lipsey & Steiner	McConnel 3rd Ed.	Samuelson 6th Ed.
15	36,37	38,40	36	38	39	31,34,37
16	34,35	37,39	35	38,39,40	39,40	32,33
17	26	5	25	45	10	10
18,19	27,32	9,10,14, 15,16,35	26,27, 28,29	45,46,48, 55	12,13,14, 19	11,12,17, 18
20,21	3,5,6	19,21,22, 24,25,26	6,7,8, 9,10,11	6,7,8,9,10	22,23,24, 25,26,27, 28,29	19,20,21, 22,23
22	19	27,28	13	31,32,33, 34,37	—	25,26
23	20	29	13	35	31	27
24	22	32	15	36	32	28
25	7	32	14	34	32	26
26	15	33,34	16	17	32	29

Contents

PART I
What is Economics?

1 The Nature and Scope of Economics 2

PART II
The Cultural and Institutional Framework

2 The Cultural Framework 18

3 Population Trends 33

4 Economics and Politics 42

5 Agriculture 50

6 The Organization for Production 66

7 Labor and the Union Movement 90

8 The Consumer 110

PART III
Macroeconomics: Institutions, Theories and Policies

9 Four Macroeconomic Objectives 131

10 Free Enterprise and Economic Planning 140

11 The Monetary and Banking System 155

12 The Fiscal System 182

13 Cyclical Fluctuations 209

14 Economic Growth 229

15 The Balance of Payments 246

16 International Trade 259

17 National Income Accounts 283

18 The Theory of Macroeconomic Intervention 297

19 The Tools of Economic Intervention 322

PART IV
Microeconomics: Price, Value and Distribution

20 Price, the Basic Issue of Microeconomics 345

21 Supply, Demand and Price 361

22 The Theories of Production and Distribution 384

23 Wage Theories 392

24 The Changing Role of Interest 407

25 The Theory of Rent 416

26 Profit as a Dynamic Force 423

GLOSSARY 440

STUDY QUESTIONS 483

SOURCES OF STATISTICAL AND OTHER CURRENT INFORMATION 507

BIBLIOGRAPHY 509

INDEX 519

PART I
What is Economics?

Chapter 1

THE NATURE AND SCOPE OF ECONOMICS

THE BASIC FACTS

Economists have not yet agreed upon a definition of economics which is satisfactory to the majority of them or to the general public. Is economics a science *which permits reasonably reliable business forecasts, or is it an* art *which depends upon the skill and intuition of the economist? This is a vitally important question today, since economic planning rests to a large extent upon the ability of economists to predict future developments.*

One must distinguish clearly between the Economy, *an empirical reality which we can observe, and* Economics, *a system of abstractions and theories designed to explain the operation of the Economy. A study of the Economy is largely descriptive. It deals with "what is." Economics, on the other hand, deals with the — invisible — forces which shape the real-life economy. It deals with "why is it."*

One can look upon economics in three ways: (1) as an analytical discipline *(either an "art" or a "science"), which attempts to discover the underlying forces, the so-called "economic laws" which determine the operation of the economy; (2) as a* normative discipline, *a system of applied socio-*

economic ethics designed to govern the operation of the economy; and (3) as a pragmatic discipline, a tool of practical politics, which is used to achieve the economic, social and political goals of a given period.

Virtually all textbooks treat economics, at least by implication, as an analytical discipline. This has been the predominant approach for the past 150–200 years. Government policy makers, on the other hand, are less interested in abstract analytical studies. They tend to look upon economics as a means of achieving politically or socially desirable goals. Normative economics, finally, which characterized medieval economic thought, is far from dead. It finds its reflection in the economic philosophy of the Catholic Church. In reality, therefore, three distinct types of economic thought exist side by side, and it is important to know whether an economic doctrine is the result of an objective scientific analysis, or whether it represents a rationalization of an economic policy which may have been adopted for social or political, rather than purely economic, reasons.

Just as economists find it difficult to agree on the nature of economics, they hold widely differing views regarding the proper scope of the discipline. Should — and can — economists confine themselves to the study of economic forces in the narrow sense, such as the forces of supply and demand? Or must they, in order to obtain a realistic picture of the economy as it exists in everyday life, take into consideration the changing economic, social and political institutions which affect the impact of economic forces? And if the economist takes into consideration the institutional framework, must he not also consider cultural forces which produce the changing institutions? In other words, can the economist really understand the ever-changing real-life economy, if he functions as a narrow specialist interested solely in the strictly "economic" forces?

Or must he be a "generalist," a social scientist in the widest sense? Few economists agree on these questions.

What is Economics?

The first unpleasant surprise which awaits the student of economics is the fact that it seems all but impossible to formulate a definition of economics which would be acceptable to the great majority of economists, let alone the general public.

"Economics" and *the* "Economy"

We must distinguish clearly between *the Economy,* an empirical reality which we can observe and measure, and *Economics,* a system of abstract theories which attempts to explain the forces which govern the production, distribution and consumption of goods and services. Economics and the Economy are related but they are by no means the same. A study of the Economy is largely descriptive. We observe the operations of the banking system, the stock exchange, the wholesale and retail trade, the money and capital markets, the transportation and communication systems, labor relations, etc. All these activities and institutions can be studied by direct observation or by means of more or less reliable statistics. But knowing all about the real-life economy does not make us economists. That wheat sells for $2 a bushel; that 9 million cars were produced in a given year; that a certain stock sells for $58 a share; that according to government statistics, 2.5 million unemployed were looking for work are "economic facts." The economist, however, is not satisfied with these purely descriptive data. His work merely begins at this point. He wants to find out why wheat sells for $2; why the U.S. produced 9 million instead of 8 million or 10 million cars; why stocks sell at certain prices; why there are millions of unemployed in one country, yet an acute labor shortage in another. In short, economics does not deal with "what is," but "why is it."

A Definition of Economics

The classic definition of economics was given by the famous English economist Alfred Marshall (1842–1924). He defined economics as "a systematic and organized method of reasoning . . . about mankind in its ordinary business of life. . . . It is on the one hand a study of wealth; and on the other, and more important side, a part of the study of man." Economics deals with man's material needs and desires, which seemingly can never be fully satisfied; in other words, with the problem of scarcity. And it deals with man's changing ways of trying to solve or adjust to this problem.

How man reacts to the socio-economic problem of scarcity depends largely upon the cultural environment in which he lives. He can look for a solution through divine guidance; he may search for natural laws which he assumes will best determine his action; or he may feel that he can solve the problems directly, by himself, without reference to divine guidance or natural laws. Depending upon the prevailing intellectual and cultural climate, economics can thus be regarded (1) as a form of applied ethics, a *normative discipline,* as it was during the Middle Ages; (2) as an *analytical science,* which has been the predominant view of the past 150–200 years; or (3) as a *pragmatic discipline,* an approach which is becoming increasingly important today. While all three types of economic thought deal with the same problem of scarcity, their approach is basically different.

Normative Economics

Normative economics starts with the assumption that every phase of man's life, including the all-important aspect of making a living, is, or should be, governed by a system of ethical norms which are known and universally accepted. The task of the normative economist, during the Middle Ages as today, thus consists of studying the prevailing business practices in order to ascertain whether they follow the basic principles of the universally accepted ethical norms. To defraud your neighbor by selling him adulterated merchandise is clearly immoral, but which price is "fair" to the seller and the buyer, which constitutes an overcharge, and hence an immoral act? What is a "just" wage? To exploit a worker is morally wrong, but it is equally wrong for the worker to try to get the biggest possible pay for the least amount of work. While there is nothing immoral in displaying merchandise, to mislead the potential customer is a form of fraud. "Usury," the lending of money on interest, has been regarded as an immoral practice since the days of the Old Testament. Yet wasn't there a difference, the medieval economists asked, between an emergency loan extended to a neighbor who was temporarily in need of help, and a business loan designed to enable the borrower to carry on a profitable business? To draw these dividing lines between morally acceptable and unacceptable business practices is the task of the normative economist. This, of course, presupposes that the great majority of the people accept a general code of ethics, which was the case during the Christian Middle Ages. It is no longer the case today in our age of ethical relativity. There is no agreement, based on ethical principles, whether maximum employment or price stability are more important, or to what extent private property rights and individual freedom should be subordinated to the public good. Yet the normative approach to economics is not dead. It is still the official approach of the Catholic Church, and thus influences the action of millions of people.

A modern economist, who does not believe in "eternal principles," will ask of course where the dividing line can be found between eternal norms and momentary expendiency. How should we classify, for instance, the modern doctrine that the state is responsible for providing a job for all who wish to work? Those who are critical of normative economics tend to see in the "norms" — which are presented as eternal and universal ethical principles — mere rationalizations of policies which favor the ruling class. Rather than rely on ethical norms which may have been invented by man for his own convenience, analytical economists strive to discover "in nature" the basic forces — similar to the laws of gravitation — which they assume are truly eternal and universal.

Analytical Economics

This analytical, or scientific, approach toward economic problems is relatively new. It developed gradually since the middle of the 18th Century and is based on two assumptions: (1) that the social world is governed by inherent "laws" similar to those which govern the physical universe; and (2) that economists can discover these laws just as Newton "discovered" the laws of gravitation. The normative and analytical economists thus start from radically different premises. The normative economist starts with a *known system* of *ethical laws* which he applies to everyday business practices. The analytical economist, on the other hand, starts with a study of the economy in the hope of *discovering* the innate *economic laws* which make the economy function. Normative economics deals with "what ought to be" according to the accepted ethical norms; analytical economics with the "what is" — or at least the "what seems to be" — on the basis of real-life economic developments.

The analytical approach is the most widely accepted today,

and virtually all textbooks assume that it is the task of the student of economics to learn about the "economic laws" which govern the economic life of society.

Empirical Approach

In order to discover these laws the economist employs two scientific methods: (1) He attempts to observe economic developments, just as the astronomer observes distant stars; and (2) he reasons from seemingly "self-evident truths," as did Einstein in discovering the Theory of Relativity. Unfortunately, both approaches involve serious methodological difficulties. The economist cannot, like most natural scientists, "observe" empirical reality. He can watch Mrs. Jones buy a dozen eggs at 50¢ and refuse to buy a box of strawberries at 65¢. But the economist is not only interested in what Mrs. Jones is buying, he is far more interested in the total sales of eggs or strawberries throughout an area at a given price. And these totals or, as the economist calls them, these "aggregates," cannot be "observed." They can only be studied by means of statistics, and some of the most important statistical aggregates, such as unemployment, national income, and balance of payments data, are subject to large errors and to widely varying interpretations.

The Rational Approach

Nor can the economist safely reason from what seems "self-evident" at the moment. The history of economic thought knows of only too many "self-evident truths" on which elaborate economic theories and policies were built, and which proved wrong within a few decades.

The Malthusian Theory

Toward the end of the 18th Century, for instance, after many decades of rapid population growth, many people were worried (as they are today) that there would not be enough food for the steadily increasing number of people. Thomas Malthus (1766–1834) "proved" that there *couldn't be!* He showed "mathematically" (his statistics were very bad by modern standards but perfectly acceptable by the standards of his own time) that the population would always grow faster than the food supply. Poverty was thus a basic law of nature.

Starting with this "Law of Poverty" as a "self-evident truth" — all intelligent people knew that the population had been increasing rapidly and all were aware of the poverty in the city slums — the economists of the early 19th Century proclaimed the "iron law of wages." Wages, they argued, could never rise for any length of time above the subsistence level, because if they did the workers would have larger families, which would increase the number of workers faster than the food supply and would thus reduce them again to or below the subsistence level. All this was, of course, a very convenient theory for employers who wished to keep wages as low as possible. Actually, despite Malthus' "Law of Poverty" wages have risen way above the subsistence level without causing a world-wide famine.

The Keynesian Theory

Just as 19th-Century economists based some of their arguments on Malthusian assumptions, modern economists start with the "self-evident truth" presented by Lord Keynes (1883–1946) during the 1930's. The world was in the throes of a great depression. With millions unemployed there was not enough demand for the goods which industry could produce. At the same time idle savings were piling up. All this was "self-evident," and John Maynard Keynes provided a seemingly logical explanation. Britain and the United States, he argued, were "mature economies." Their populations were increasing only very slowly; their industries were fully developed; and since a large segment of the consuming public had acquired all the needed goods — houses, furniture, a car, etc. — there was little reason to expect per capita consumption to increase sharply. Hence there was little need for additional factories. At the same time, however, the wealthy minority continued to save as it had done in previous decades, when the economy still needed large amounts of investment capital for new plants. With no outlet for the savings, these accumulated in idle hoards.

The solution thus seemed obvious. Steps had to be taken to increase the consumption of the masses and to curtail excessive savings. This, in turn, could be accomplished through government intervention, through public works, deficit spending, steeply progressive income taxes, reduced interest rates, and curtailed dividend payments. Keynes himself, it should be emphasized, did not draw all these conclusions. In fact he argued that one of the most effective means of stimulating employment was an increase in the rate of profit, which could be accomplished by holding wages stable. But generally speaking, there seemed little doubt, during the 1930's, that the policy conclusions drawn from the "self-evident" fact of mass unemployment were perfectly logical.

With the outbreak of World War II in 1939, however, the situation changed completely. The premise of a "mature economy" which could not produce adequate investment outlets for the savings which were accumulating, ceased to be valid. The world stood at the threshold of several decades of an explosive population growth, of extremely rapid technological and industrial developments, and a seemingly unlimited demand for consumer goods throughout the world. All this required vast capital investments for which existing savings proved completely inadequate. In other words, since 1939, general economic conditions throughout the world have been the very opposite of the situation which appeared "self-evident" during the 1930's. People no longer save too much, but total savings are actually inadequate to meet the vastly increased demand for capital. In order to meet this demand, government agencies created money artificially, which in turn started a thirty year world-wide inflation. Prior to 1939, the problem of the world was deflation; since 1939 the problem has been inflation. Yet those economists who favor redistribution of income and government intervention continue to repeat the Keynesian arguments of oversaving and underconsumption which were actually developed to explain the depression of the 1930's.

Economics an Art or Science

The rapid socio-economic changes of the past half-century have produced a great deal of groping uncertainty among economists. Prior to World War I some of the best economists of the time felt that the basic truth about economics had been discovered. All that was left to do was to introduce certain minor refinements. This confident certainty seems extremely naive today. As two leading American economists and mathematicians, Oskar Morgenstern and John von Neumann, wrote: "There is at present no universal system of economic theory, and . . . if one should ever be developed, it will very probably not be during our lifetime." Neither statistics nor "self-evident truth" can be fully trusted as means of achieving a reliable knowledge of the economic forces. In addition to the widest possible knowledge of all factors which influence the economy, a good economist must have a sixth sense, a feeling for the implications of statistical evidence and the trustworthiness of what is presented as "self-evident truth."

The question whether economics is more an art or a science

has thus become a popular issue of the day. According to Professor Arthur F. Burns, one of America's leading economists and President Eisenhower's chief economic advisor, economics is "a branch of knowledge that is approaching very slowly, very gradually the status of an exact science." The English economist F. W. Paish, on the other hand, argues that "economics, or at least applied economics, is much more an art than a science." And even John Maynard Keynes, whose theories, as we have seen, form an essential aspect of modern economic policy, warned that he had not invented "a machine, or method of blind manipulation, which will furnish an infallible answer," but that he had tried to provide "an organized and orderly method of thinking out our particular problems."

Pragmatic Economics

Frustrated by the obvious difficulties of developing economics into a pure science, and confronted with the popular demand that government solve the multitude of economic problems which confront society, a new type of economists has developed since the 1930's. Seeking practical solutions for concrete current problems such as unemployment or inflation, these modern economists treat economics as a tool of practical politics, to be judged by its effectiveness in achieving social and economic goals.

Most Washington policy makers belong to this group. They are "pragmatists." As *Time* wrote in 1961, pragmatism "is the vogue word among economists today, the term that most of them use to label themselves and one another. When economists call themselves pragmatists, they mean that they are the opposite of dogmatists, that they are wary of broad theories, that they lean to the cut-and-dry approach to public problems, and that they believe it is possible to improve the functioning of the economy by tinkering with it."

The basic difference between an economic scientist and an economic pragmatist is fundamental. The former tries to discover the natural laws which govern a given economic situation, and then follows the blueprint of these laws, just as in constructing an airplane the designer applies the known laws of aerodynamics. A pragmatist, on the other hand, relies on a trial and error method. As President Franklin D. Roosevelt put it in explaining his monetary policies: If the approach we are trying now does not work, we shall try another. Once a policy has been decided upon as being likely to achieve a certain desired social, economic or political goal — for instance an increase in minimum wage rates — it then becomes the task of the modern pragmatic economist to furnish a logical theory to justify the policies to be adopted.

The Scope of Economics

Just as economists disagree regarding the nature of economics, they are in equal disagreement regarding the proper scope of the discipline.

Let us assume that economics is primarily an analytical science, and that its foremost goal consists in developing theories or models which illustrate, in a form comprehensible to the human mind, the interplay of forces which govern economic life. We have all seen models of molecules. Scientists do not claim that molecules actually look like the models, but they believe that the essential aspects of a molecule can be understood and explained with the help of these models. Economic models, or theories, serve the same purpose. Whether they take the form of involved equations, graphs or figures, the purpose is always the same: to picture, and thus understand, the *essential forces* which govern economic life.

Unfortunately, economists do not agree as to what constitutes these *essential forces.*

The level of wages and prices, and the rate of employment and output, are obviously economic problems. But can they be studied by themselves? Prior to the 1930's wages, prices, employment and production were governed largely by the forces of supply and demand. If demand declined, production was reduced, prices were cut, workers were laid off, and wages declined. Since the 1930's however, and especially since the end of World War II, the government has assumed the responsibility for maintaining "maximum employment," and the unions have grown sufficiently powerful to prevent a reduction of wages even in times of unemployment. Besides, the government has taken a direct hand in influencing prices.

In order to get a true picture of the economy, it would thus seem not enough to study the formation of wages and prices, of employment and of production in the abstract. We must relate them to the prevailing government policy, the institutional framework, within which the economy functions. We must take into consideration the "full employment" policies of the government, the relative power of the unions, government policies regarding price changes, the availability of credit (which has a bearing on the ability of the manufacturer to expand his plant), and the operation of the unemployment insurance system (which makes unemployed workers reluctant to take a job "at any price").

But these socio-economic institutions, in turn, do not develop in a vacuum. They change as the general mood of the country changes. During the 19th Century, when the United States was still a predominantly rural country, the people felt that they could look after their own affairs. They preferred to trust the forces of supply and demand rather than the intervention of the government. During the 1930's, however, the forces of the market seemed to have broken down and, feeling helpless in the general chaos of the Depression, the people turned to the government. The result was the creation of the unemployment insurance system and, after the war, the adoption of the "full employment" policy; the evergrowing regulation of the economy by government agencies and the overall planning by the government to achieve "full employment" and "maximum economic growth." The change in the general attitude of the people, and their social and political philosophy, thus produced changes in the institutional framework, which in turn affected the actual functioning of the economic forces.

Three Levels of Economic Facts

The economist is thus confronted with three types, or levels, of "essential facts": (1) economic data and economic forces, (2) the institutional framework which influences the functioning of the economic forces, and (3) the cultural framework which determines the development of social and economic institutions.

Should the economist confine himself to the study of the economic forces in the narrow sense, or should he take into consideration the changing institutional and cultural framework? There are good arguments in favor of either approach. According to the basic premise of economics as a science, "economic laws" are universally valid irrespective of the institutional framework within which they function, just as the "law of gravitation" is valid everywhere even though its effects may be suspended temporarily while we are riding in an airplane. Besides, the economy involves so many factors that the economist must always strive to prevent a further proliferation of variables, especially of the type which are difficult to predict, such as institutional and cultural changes. Most analytical economists, therefore, are inclined to treat the institutional and cultural framework as given. This approach is reasonable so long as we think in terms of very short time spans, certainly of not more than 3–5 years. In fact, in our fast-moving world, we often experience sufficiently important institutional changes from one year to the next that these changes have to be taken into consideration in building a realistic model of the economy as it exists.

The trouble with too many economic theories is not that they were originally false, but that they have become obsolete. The obsolescence occurred because the "pure scientist" had lost touch with the rapidly changing reality. A theory which had been startlingly new and helpful a few years earlier developed into conventional wisdom and was reprinted faithfully in every new textbook, even though the original premise no longer coincided with the actual conditions of the economy which the model was intended to explain.

To escape from the necessity of having to adjust their ideas to an everchanging reality, the pragmatic economist, as we have seen, tends to be less and less concerned with abstract theory and to concentrate instead on changing the economic life to the prevailing socio-economic ideas. The pure economic scientist, on the other hand, retreats farther and farther into purely abstract models which have less and less to do with reality. In doing so he runs the risk of which the English economist Roy Harrod warned, that "it is useless to refine and refine when there are no basic ideas present at all."

Economics has never been an easy subject, because it requires the ability to grasp and evaluate logically a very large number of variables. It is a particularly difficult subject today, because the very nature of economics is undergoing a fundamental change, and because economists are in general disagreement regarding methods and premises. However, in spite of these basic difficulties which plague the experts, the novice can acquire a great deal of economic knowledge which is generally accepted and which will enable him to gain a better understanding of the world in which he lives.

PART II
The Cultural and Institutional Framework

Chapter 2

THE CULTURAL FRAMEWORK

THE BASIC FACTS

The basic philosophic attitudes of a nation have a great deal to do with the development of economic institutions, the general character of the economy, and the way in which the public and the experts reason about economic issues. Economic theories are ultimately determined by their explicit or implicit premises, and those premises, in turn, are largely a reflection of the general intellectual and ethical climate.

In this chapter we shall discuss the four basic questions which every society must answer: (1) how much to produce; (2) what to produce; (3) how to produce; and (4) for whom to produce. The answers to these questions determine to a large extent the character of the economy. But the answers are not to be found in pure economic reasoning. They are ultimately determined by ethical, political, social and technological considerations.

Economists must thus be familiar not only with economic theories and with what happens in the economy; they must also keep an eye on important technological, political, and social developments, and be aware of possible changes in the cultural framework.

As we shall show in this chapter, the far-reaching changes which have occurred in American economic thought and policies since the 1930's were largely the result of basic changes in the prevailing social philosophy, which affect the three issues of (1) what should be the relationship between the individual and society, (2) what is the inherent nature of man, and (3) what is the nature and basis of private property.

Four Basic Socio-Economic Questions

In the preceding chapter we showed that economics can be treated either in a narrow sense as a study of the basic and universal forces which determine the production, distribution and consumption of goods and services, or in a wider sense, in which case we have to take into consideration the cultural and institutional factors which condition the economic forces. In this chapter we shall discuss some of these forces.

Every society has to answer four basic questions: (1) how much to produce; (2) what to produce; (3) how to produce; and (4) for whom to produce. Different civilizations will answer these questions differently, and the character of the economy, in turn, depends largely upon how these questions are answered.

How Much to Produce

With the modern emphasis upon maximum economic growth and the elimination of poverty, one would assume that all individuals and all societies would strive to maximize their output in order to increase the supply of goods and services. This, however, is by no means the case. Throughout history man has rarely tried, except during periods of emergency, to achieve the greatest possible production of material goods. And the same is true today. This is not surprising. To most human beings, the "good life," which all men strive to attain, is based on a combination of material possessions and leisure. While the Middle Ages held with St. Thomas Aquinas (1225–74) that a minimum of comfort is necessary for the efficient practice of virtue, and that man's income should be adequate to meet the necessary expenditures of the station of life into which it had pleased God to call him, the production and consumption of goods was never an end in itself. The ultimate purpose and goal of man's earthly existence was the attainment of salvation. Not until the 16th Century, under the impact of Protestanism and especially Calvinism, did conscientious and productive work in itself acquire a stamp of ethical approbation. "Seest thou a man diligent at his business," Benjamin Franklin's Puritan father drummed into his son's mind. "He shall stand before Kings." Obviously, in a society in which diligent work is held to be not only a social virtue but a religious duty, economic development is likely to be more rapid than in another society, which stresses meditation and leisure.

The emphasis on meditation and leisure is one of the problems which faces many underdeveloped countries, as for example India, and which explains the fact that the output of goods and services is increasing only slowly. Even in the United States and Western Europe, where maximum production and consumption are stressed as a national goal, and where the people are perturbed by the seemingly rapid growth of the Russian economy, most people approve of the fact that the work week has been reduced to 40 hours, and some union leaders call for a 35- or even 30-hour week. With larger pensions and an earlier retirement age, more people retire at a time when they could still contribute a great deal to the output of goods and services. Leisure, in the form of early retirement, a shorter work week, longer vacations and extended coffee breaks, reduces total production. Leisure thus has a value, equal to the goods which have not been produced. In the language of the economist, leisure is an "economic good," just as is a car or a machine tool.

The character of a civilization and its emphasis upon maximum economic production, or upon religious meditation, aesthetic enjoyment, or plain "leisure," thus has a great deal to do with the "how much to produce."

Economic theory, however, has its own answer. The individual producer, and whole industries, are assumed to increase their output so long as each addition to the output can still be sold at a profit. The volume of production is thus determined by (1) the cost of production and (2) the prevailing prices. If the production cost rises due, let us say, to higher wages, and prices remain the same, marginal plants will no longer be able to operate at a profit and the total output will decline. The question of "how much to produce" is thus determined, like most socio-economic developments, by cultural factors on the one hand, and purely economic ones on the other.

What to Produce

What percentage of our national income should be spent on armaments; public welfare; durable consumer goods such as cars, television sets, or washing machines; national parks; education; suburban housing; or slum clearance? The answer can be either economic or political. Either those goods will be turned out which result in the greatest profit to the producer, or production will be influenced or determined by the government in order to achieve certain political or social objectives.

Social critics like to point out that the United States spends five times as much on dog food as on college textbooks; considerably more on cosmetics and personal care than on religious and welfare activities; and more on tobacco than on doctors or hospitals.

Professor John Kenneth Galbraith's well-known book, *The Affluent Society*, deals with this problem. The average American, the author contends, is well provided with food, clothing and shelter, and other goods and services, such as education, public parks, and highways "must be paid for collectively or they cannot be had at all." He therefore suggests that the government should play a more important role in determining the types of goods and services which are to be produced. Rather than permit the individual to spend his money on liquor, cigarettes and gadget-laden cars, the government should tax away a larger share of the individual's income and use the money for education, research, slum clearance, public parks, etc.

How to Produce

In order to produce goods and services, we need four "factors of production": (1) manpower (which the economist refers to as "labor"); (2) land and raw materials (which the economist calls simply "land"); (3) factories, machinery and transportation equipment (referred to as "capital," "capital goods" or "production goods"); and (4) managerial skills. How are these factors to be combined? When will machines be used in place of labor? When will land be worked either intensively or extensively? The answers differ, depending on whether they are given by an economist, an engineer or a social planner. From the point of view of the economist, the factors of production will be combined in such a way as to produce the greatest profit. As a rule, those factors will be used which are most plentiful and thus relatively cheap. Per acre production in American agriculture is lower than in Western Europe, and especially in Japan, because land is more plentiful in the United States and labor much more costly. On the other hand, an American farmer produces many times as much during a day as a European or Japanese farmer, because the high-priced American worker uses a great deal of farm machinery which could not be used equally efficiently in Europe and Japan, where the farms are much smaller because of the relative scarcity of land.

As the cost of one factor of production increases, other factors are likely to be used in its place. If wages rise beyond a certain level, labor-saving machinery is installed. If the price of farm land increases, farmers will use more fertilizer ("capital") to increase the total output. The ultimate aim is always to combine the factors of production in such a way as to produce the greatest possible profit.

Such a combination of factors, however, need not result in the largest possible output. If the maximization of the output is the goal, as it was during the war, the engineer rather than the economist will determine the most effective combination of factors.

Finally, social and political factors enter into the picture, determining the mode of production. It may be profitable to replace labor by machinery, but if this results in increased unemployment, the government and unions may object. Throughout history, labor-replacing machinery has been attacked by workers and government agencies. Modern unions as a rule do not object to the installation of more efficient machinery, but they insist that the number of workers should not be reduced and that the major portion of the increase in profits he used for higher wages. This in turn may make the installation of new machinery not worthwhile, and industry will thus not be able to use the available factors of production — namely, the more efficient machines — to the fullest extent.

For Whom to Produce

According to the philosophy of free enterprise capitalism and the traditional 19th-Century economic theory of distribution, financial rewards in the form of wages, rent, interest and profits should correspond to the relative contribution which each factor has made to the final product. This in turn determines which individuals and which economic classes will have the greatest purchasing power and which the least.

Socialist and modern welfare state advocates do not agree with this capitalistic notion that purchasing power should be based exclusively on the relative productivity. They hold, instead, that income, and hence the ability to buy goods, should be distributed "according to needs." Even though a worker produces very little or nothing, because he cannot find a job or because he is sick, too old or too young, society should nevertheless see to it that he has an adequate income to meet his needs. And what these needs are is determined by society, not economic theory. This notion underlies the goal of President Johnson's "Great Society" of providing every American family with a minimum income of about $3000.

The question of the distribution of income, the "for whom to produce," is one of the basic points of conflict between normative and analytical economics. Normative economics holds that the distribution should be based on ethical considerations, while analytical economics postulates that it be governed by the "natural laws" of production: to each according to his productivity.

Basic Social Philosophies

The four seemingly purely economic questions which we have just discussed are influenced by broader considerations of social philosophy. We shall now discuss three of the basic issues of social philosophy: What should be the relation between the individual and society? What is the nature of man as a social being? And what is the basis and nature of private property? The nature of the economy and the character of the entire social system depend to a large extent upon the answers we give these questions.

The Relationship of the Individual and Society

There are two basic social philosophies which deal with the relationship between the individual and society: the atomistic and the organic. The former compares the individual with a grain of sand, a self-contained unit, which the winds shift according to the laws of nature. The grains of sand are independent of each other. If one vanishes the others are in no way affected. The individual grain may be blown to the top or shifted to the bottom; it would make virtually no difference to the nature of the sand dune, since all grains of sand are essentially more or less alike. According to the atomistic philosophy of society the individual is a self-contained unit and society a mere agglomoration of individuals. Some decades ago people used to say: "There is no America; there are 100 million Americans."

The organic concept of society, on the other hand, compares the individual to a cell in a living organism. The health of the entire body can be affected if the individual cell becomes ill; and the cell in turn can survive only as long as the whole organism survives. Moreover, each individual cell has to perform its own specific function. The cells of the brain are different from those of the stomach, and one cannot perform the function of the other. The organic concept of society shifts the emphasis from the individual to the society as a whole. Each individual must perform his duties so that the society can prosper, and society in turn, in its own interest, must see to it that the individual cell, the individual citizen, remains healthy and productive.

A society with an essentially atomistic philosophy, which believes the individual to be all-important, is likely to emphasize the protection of private property and freedom of private enterprise, even though this may occasionally involve excesses which have a detrimental effect on society as a whole.

If, on the other hand, a civilization looks upon its social structure as a living organism, as did the Christian Middle Ages, the welfare of the community will be stressed at the expense of the freedom of the individual and of private property rights.

The change from the laissez faire philosophy of the 19th Century to the modern welfare state philosophy, with its emphasis on the public as against the private sector, would not have been possible without the gradual change in the American social philosophy from a predominantly atomistic-individualistic approach to an organic-social one.

The Nature of the Individual

The philosophy which governs the relationship of the individual to society is paralleled by the prevailing popular estimate of the capacities and the nature of man as an individual. Is man inherently good and a social creature, or is he predominantly selfish and asocial? Does man as an individual have the capacity to manage his own affairs better than anyone else, or does he need the strong hand and wise guidance of a powerful government?

The relationship of the individual and society has undergone drastic changes during the past 400 years. During the 16th and 17th Centuries the state grew ever more powerful while the influence of organized religion gradually declined. It was a period of great unrest. As Thomas Hobbes (1588–1679), the philosophical exponent of English Absolutism, put it: "Continual fear and danger of violent death" dominated the lives of the people, unless there was a strong state to keep order. Man was regarded as an inherently weak and asocial creature.

In order to enforce law and order at home and build overseas empires, the nations needed strong armies and navies and a large bureaucracy to collect taxes and run the government, and since in the 16th and 17th Centuries gold and silver were virtually the only acceptable forms of money, exports had to be increased and imports reduced so that a nation could collect the difference in specie, the so-called "sinews of war." This in turn required that the production cost, which meant wages, be kept low; and in order to make it possible for the workers to survive on small wages, food prices also had to be kept as low as possible.

Gradually, by the late 17th and early 18th Centuries, the general unrest had quieted down, and the great scientific discoveries and radically new philosophic ideas of the 17th Century strengthened man's faith in his own abilities. Instead of "by the grace of God," the rulers were gradually assumed to govern "by the consent of the people." John Locke (1632–1704) proclaimed "life, liberty and property" as the "inherent rights" of the individual, which no government could violate. The Earl of Shaftesbury (1671–1713) argued that far from being asocial, as Hobbes had assumed, man was basically guided by a "moral sense," by "benevolence," and by an awareness that "every vicious action must be self-injurious and ill." And Jean-Jacques Rousseau (1712–1778) went so far as to say that evil was the product of society, of the state, which had corrupted the originally good human beings.

While the Age of Absolutism (16th–18th Centuries) had conceived man as inherently asocial and in need of a strong government, the Age of Enlightenment (18th Century) regarded him as an inherently social being and better able to manage his own affairs than was any government.

Quite logically, a period which does not believe that the individual can manage his own affairs will tend toward a regulated or planned economy, such as the system of Mercantilism against which the American Colonists revolted in 1776. On the other hand, an age which believes in the individual and his ability to look after himself, will give the individual maximum freedom and restrict the powers of the state. This was the case in the United States during the 19th Century and down to World War I and the Great Depression of the 1930's. As President Wilson wrote: "I believe, as I believe in nothing else, in the average integrity and the average intelligence of the American people."

A multitude of factors have combined to undermine this faith in the inherent goodness and ability of man to look after his own affairs. Urbanization and industrialization have deprived millions of individuals of the possibility of sustaining themselves during difficult times. Yesterday's farmer, if not threatened by a maturing mortgage, had a roof over his head and was able to feed himself and his family. Today's apartment dweller in a big city, on the other hand, cannot raise the food he needs if he loses his job. And in periods of mass unemployment many workers are unable to find any kind of remunerative work. Modern man has thus come to look to society for his everyday needs. The cruelties of two world wars, moreover, and of the Russian Revolution and the Nazi concentration camps, have severely shaken the 18th-Century belief that man is inherently a good and social creature. And just as the writers of the 16th and 17th Centuries, we are again calling for a powerful state so that "peace may not perish, and trade and society may not be utterly destroyed."

The modern statism, including the welfare-statism in the United States, which has altered fundamentally the nature of the American economy, is a clear reflection of the declining faith in the inherent self-sufficiency and goodness of man as an individual.

The Changing Status of Private Property

The changing relationship between the individual and society is well illustrated by the changing status of private property during the past 50 years.

Different writers have expounded a variety of ideas regarding the nature and basis of private property. The French socialist Pierre Joseph Proudhon (1809–65) proclaimed that "property is theft," and many philosophic socialists still incline to this view. In the Middle Ages (and this is still the official philosophy of the Catholic Church) private property was regarded not as an inherent right of the individual, but as a "necessary institution in a sinful world," which existed for the benefit of the individual as well as society. There were no "property rights" which were not balanced by "social obligations," and the welfare of the society always ranked above the advantages of the individual.

Against this medieval tradition, John Locke (1632–1704), the great philosophic proponent of English Liberalism, asserted the notion that private property is an "inherent right" of the individual, equal in importance to life and liberty, and no government and no majority has the right to abridge the individual's rights. It was this notion of absolute property rights which predominated especially during the second half of the 19th Century.

Since then the situation has changed drastically. According to modern social philosophy, private property is no longer an inherent right of the individual. It is regarded today as a socioeconomic institution created by society for its own benefit, hence subject to change at the will of society. Congress, it is assumed, has the virtually unlimited power to determine the property rights of the individual. And since Congress is dominated by the non-propertied majority, the rights of the propertied minority have been progressively abridged during the past 50 years, a change which has profoundly altered the character of the American economy.

Declining Economic Freedom

In 1905, for instance, the Supreme Court held that the attempt of the State of New York to regulate the working hours of bakers was "an illegal interference with the rights of individuals, both employers and employees, to make contracts." [1] Nor could the government authorities fix minimum wages, as the Court held as late as 1923 when it declared the District of Columbia Minimum Wage Act unconstitutional.[2] With the growth of the welfare state during the 1930's, however, the Supreme Court changed its views. By 1937 the Court upheld the right of the State of Washington to fix minimum wages,[3] and in 1941 the Court sanctioned the power of the Federal Government to regulate wages and hours throughout the country under the Fair Labor Standards Act by prohibiting the shipment of any goods in interstate commerce "produced under substandard labor conditions." [4]

Freedom to Form Unions In 1908,[5] and again in 1915,[6] the Supreme Court denied that either the Federal Government or the states had a right to prevent an employer from discharging a worker because he joined a union. But during the Great Depression, the belief in the unfettered freedom of the market gave way to a growing philosophy of government regulation, and by 1937,[7] Chief Justice Hughes upheld the National Labor

[1] Lochner vs. New York
[2] Adkins vs. Children's Hospital
[3] West Coast Hotel Company vs. Parrish
[4] United States vs. F. W. Darby Lumber Co.
[5] Adair vs. United States
[6] Coppage vs. Kansas
[7] National Labor Relations Board vs. Jones & Laughlin Steel

Relations Act of 1935, holding that "employees have their correlative right to organize for the purpose of securing the redress of grievances and to promote agreements with employers relating to rate of pay and conditions of work."

The Gold Clause Cases The Supreme Court will go a long way in limiting private contracts and private property rights in general, if it considers such limitations in the public interest. In the famous Gold Clause cases which came before the Supreme Court in January, 1935, the Court had to rule on the power of the Federal Government to set aside valid and legal private contracts and to repudiate its own written promises. Since the value of the paper dollar had fluctuated widely during the 19th Century, it had become customary to specify in most private contracts, such as mortgages and railroad bonds, that payment was to be made in dollars equal to a certain quantity of gold. But when President Roosevelt, in 1933, raised the price of gold and some bondholders demanded payment in gold or in paper dollars at the new and higher gold price in accordance with the original contract, the Court held that the government had the power to invalidate the gold clause in private contracts, since it interfered with the government's constitutional power to regulate the value of money. In the case of the government's own bonds, which like private contracts contained a gold clause, the Supreme Court held unanimously[8] that the refusal of the government to pay its obligations in gold was unconstitutional. But constitutional or not, the plaintiff could collect no damages because, as the Court held, he had "not shown or attempted to show that in relation to buying power he has sustained any loss whatsoever."

The New York rent law which freezes rents at artifically low levels clearly transfers "property" from the landlord to the tenants. A government policy of maintaining artifically low inter-

[8] Perry vs. United States

est rates reduces the income of the lender, including the small bondholder, for the benefit of the borrower, which may be a large corporation. The fixing of farm prices transfers income, i.e. private property, from the consumer to the farmer. The decisions of the Interstate Commerce Commission, which force railroads to maintain services on which they lose money, deprive the owners of the railroad of part of their property.

All these transfers of income, made possible through the change in property rights by Congress, government agencies or the courts, result in a far-reaching redistribution of income and thus a substantial change in the nature of the economy.

Chapter 3

POPULATION TRENDS

THE BASIC FACTS

Population trends are among the most important aspects of man's material existence. However, contrary to a popular misconception, neither the rate of population growth nor the absolute density of population determine the standard of living of a nation. It is determined by the size (and quality) of the labor force in relation to the supply of the other factors of production: raw materials, machinery and managerial skills.

A flexible economic system can usually adjust itself to changes in the rate of population growth. "Overpopulation" exists only in those countries which lack raw materials, machinery or skills, which is the case at present in many of the underdeveloped countries, whose mortality rate has been reduced sharply through modern health methods but whose birth rate continues close to the theoretical upper limit.

Since many of the countries lack the necessary socio-economic adaptability, they are unable to match the increase in the labor force with a corresponding increase in machines and skills. As a result, production growth cannot keep pace with the increase in population, and the actual standard of living of the masses declines.

The "population problem" in the United States is due to the wide fluctuations in the birth rate in recent decades resulting in the "hollow generation" of the 1930's and the "bulging generation" of the 1940's and 1950's. During the late 1940's and 1950's, when the postwar demand for homes, cars and other durable consumer goods was particularly great, the labor force increased much more slowly than the non-working portion of the population. This temporary scarcity of labor explains in part the sharp wage increases, which in turn led to automation and the replacement of large numbers of highly-paid workers by machines. During the 1960's and 1970's the population as a whole will increase more slowly than the labor force. In order to avoid chronic unemployment it will be necessary (1) to invest heavily in new machinery (which in turn calls for a high rate of savings), (2) to keep prices down in order to expand markets, and (3) to provide workers with greater skills.

Population Trends and Economic Prosperity

Since economics deals above all with human beings, population trends are of far-reaching importance. The poverty in India and China, and in a number of other countries, is often blamed on "overpopulation." Yet in the United States a rising standard of living and economic growth have usually been associated with periods of rapid population increase, whether due to heavy immigration, as after the War between the States, or to a high birth rate, as after World War II. Densely populated Belgium has a far higher standard of living than much more thinly populated Brazil. Japan had a greater population density 100 years ago than India has today, yet this did not prevent Japan's rapid economic development.

The Size of the Labor Force in Relation to Other Factors of Production

The mere size of the population per square mile and the rate of population growth are not the decisive factors. This should be perfectly obvious, if we remember that there are four factors which determine the output of goods and services: manpower, raw materials, machinery and managerial and technological skills. Manpower, the size of the labor force (which in turn is largely determined by the size of the population), is only one factor. There may be many millions of potential workers, but if the nation lacks raw materials, machinery and managerial skills, the workers will be unemployed, or at best earn only a small wage. The rate of economic growth and the standard of living thus depend upon the proper relationship of the four factors of production.

The "Scarcity" of Labor in the U.S.

A flexible economic system will tend to adjust itself to the relative abundance or scarcity of the various factors. In the United States, capital and managerial skills are most plentiful, and the supply of raw materials is larger than in Western Europe. Labor, on the other hand, while not "scarce," is definitely less abundant than in many other countries. American prosperity is thus based upon the maximum use of machinery in place of the relatively scarce labor. On the other hand, since labor is relatively scarce and must therefore be supplemented with highly efficient machinery, the per capita output of the American worker far exceeds that of workers in the rest of the world, and his wages are correspondingly much higher.

"Scarcity" of Labor and Chronic Unemployment

However, this basic relative scarcity of labor — as compared with other countries — does not eliminate the problem of unemployment, even chronic unemployment. In order to find a job in America's highly mechanized and organized economy, a worker has to possess skills and adaptability. And many workers, especially young people, lack the skills and proper attitude to meet the needs of modern business. Another reason for chronic unemployment is the fact that, because of the very high average wage level, some workers do not "earn their keep." A businessman will not pay a worker indefinitely $50 a week if the worker produces only $45 or $50 worth of goods; nor can he reasonably be expected to do so. It is thus quite possible for a country to suffer chronic unemployment, even though labor is relatively the scarcest of the four factors of production.

Abundance of Labor, Average Productivity and Wage Levels

In countries where the potential labor force is large but machinery is scarce, labor will be used more extensively, the per capita production of the worker will be lower, and so will be the wages. An American earth-moving machine does the work of about 50 to 100 Indian coolies, whose earnings may be as low as 35¢ to 50¢ a day, while the man who operates an earth-moving machine in the United States may earn $20 to $30 a day. Yet despite the high wages he receives, the American worker may actually be "cheaper," if his wages are compared with the amount of earth he has moved during the day, than those of the 50 or 100 Indian workers. Why then doesn't India replace its coolies with modern machinery? With some 30 million of her workers wholly or partially unemployed, it would be very unwise for India to replace workers with machinery, even if she had enough dollars to buy the machines and enough skilled workers to operate and maintain them. Mechanization is not a panacea. It raises the standard of living if the labor force is relatively scarce; it can further depress the standard of living if labor is overabundant.

The Problem of "Overpopulation"

Towards the end of the 18th Century the widespread fear of overpopulation influenced economic theory and policy for decades. Thomas Malthus, for instance, claimed in his famous *Essay on the Principle of Population* (1798) that the population always tended to increase more rapidly than the production of food, and unless there was a check on the population increase, the standard of living would continue to decline until the people perished from mass-starvation. After being regarded as false for decades, the Malthusian Theory is again extremely popular today because of the rapid increase in population in recent decades. Again we are told that very soon there will be "standing room only" on this earth, and our daily diet will have to consist largely of seaweed. Much is said about the need of spreading the gospel of birth control, especially in the underdeveloped countries where the birth rate is particularly high. The Indian Fourth Five Year Plan (1966–71), for instance, provided for an increase in the number of family planning centers from 11,000 to 48,000.

Overpopulation and Economic Growth

In some parts of the world, especially in Latin America and India, the rapid increase in population is undoubtedly complicating the task of raising the standard of living of the masses. There is a theoretical upper limit of the birth rate, 4½ –5%, and in nations which traditionally have had a high mortality rate, the birth rate has been high because a healthy society, like a healthy individual, has an innate sense of self-preservation. In order not to vanish in the course of time, a nation with a high mortality rate must have a high birth rate. This equilibrium was disturbed in recent decades through the advance of modern hygiene and medicine into the less developed parts of the world. It took Western Europe more than a hundred years to reduce the mortality rate from 3% to 1½% . In many of the underdeveloped countries, on the other hand, such a decrease has been achieved in barely twenty-five years, and since the birth rate did not decline simultaneously, the population has been increasing by 2½ to 3½% a year, and in some countries by 4%. In order to feed and clothe these millions of potential consumers and in addition raise the standard of living of all the people, the output of goods and services would have to be increased by 5–6% each year. To accomplish this, a corresponding increase in the supply of the three other factors of production — raw materials (including food), machinery, and managerial and technological skills — are needed, and as Malthus had predicted a century and a half ago, this increase lags behind in many countries, thus resulting in more poverty and social unrest.

In due course, as the mortality rate continues to decline, the birth rate is likely to decline also, as it did in Western Europe and the United States in decades past. But this requires a gradual change in the cultural pattern. In most of the developing countries a man is still proud of having begotten a dozen or more children — even though he may be unable to feed and clothe them. The growing urbanization will undoubtedly change this attitude. On the farm, where children can make themselves useful at an early age, they constitute to some extent an economic asset. In urban areas, on the other hand, where there is little work for youngsters, they represent obvious economic liabilities.

Until the birth rate begins to decline, however, the rapid population increase throughout the world will continue, in the decades ahead, to have an adverse effect on the standard of living of the masses, and on the economic development in general, and will hence increase the demand for birth control.

Population Problems in the U.S.

The United States also has a "population problem," although of a different nature from the one which plagues India and other "overpopulated" countries.

During the past 50 years the rate of population growth and the birth rate have fluctuated widely in the United States, while the mortality rate has declined fairly steadily by more than 40%. The population increased by only 7.3% during the 1930's, but by 14.5% during the 1940's and by 18.5% during the 1950's.

In 1915 the birth rate was 25 per 1000; by 1935 it had declined to 16.9, and it stayed below 20 per 1000 until the end of World War II. Beginning in 1947, the "baby boom" hit the United States, and the birth rate climbed to 25.2 in 1954 and again in 1957, only to decline anew to 19.4 by 1965. These wide fluctuations in the birth rate naturally affect the distribution of the population by age groups.

During the boom years of the 1950's, the portion of the population of working age (20 to 64 years) grew by only 7%, while the total population increased by 18.5%, and the number of the young and the old by about 35%. In other words, the consuming but non-producing segments of the population increased far more rapidly than the producing-age groups. The population structure thus added to the relative shortage of labor during the postwar years, when pent-up demand for houses and durable consumer goods was at its peak and large wartime savings and ample credit facilities were available to finance the purchases.

This relative labor shortage resulted in a sharp increase in wages. Average weekly earnings in manufacturing industries increased from $44 to about $108 between 1945 and 1965, or by more than 145%. Since consumer prices advanced by only 75%, the purchase power, and hence the standard of living of the wage earners, rose sharply. However, as a result of the shortage of workers and the rising wages, employers found it necessary, or at least more economical, to replace high-priced workers by more and more efficient machinery. The process came to be known as "automation."

Growing Labor Force During the 1960's and 1970's

Conditions changed during the 1960's. By the late 1950's the replacement of workers by machines had resulted in a slow rise in unemployment, and while the Kennedy and Johnson Administrations were able to create a record number of new jobs through a vast expansion of public spending and credit, little could be done about the flood of postwar babies which began to enter the labor market. The age groups between 20 and 64 increased much faster than the total population. While there was a growing shortage of seasoned and mature workers (as a result of the low birth rate of the late 1920's and 1930's), young and unskilled workers (born during the postwar baby-boom years) faced increasing difficulties in finding jobs.

The Need for Increased Capital Investments A sharp increase in one factor of production can be turned into an advantage only if it is matched by a corresponding increase in the other factors. The sharp growth in the number of workers thus calls for a corresponding increase in capital investments. More machines are needed to provide jobs for the additional workers. The resulting increase in production in turn calls for a corresponding expansion in sales. This can be achieved if technological advances and increased productivity are used to lower prices and thus capture additional consumer markets at home and abroad.

The changing structure of the population resulting from the fact that the "hollow generation" of the 1930's is gradually being replaced by the "bulging generation" of the 1940's and 1950's, thus calls for a careful adjustment of employment, investment, price, wage and tax policies in order to avoid chronic large unemployment.

Chapter 4

ECONOMICS AND POLITICS

THE BASIC FACTS

Most economic policies (and the theories designed to explain them) are conditioned by political developments.

Between the two extremes of anarchism ("no government") and modern totalitarianism can be found various combinations of individual freedom and social restraints, each in turn producing a different type of economic order. Anarchism and laissez faire emphasize the freedom of the individual; the regulatory and the welfare state the security of the individual; and socialism and totalitarianism the power of society, as personified by the state. The political and economic order of the United States has gradually changed during the past century from a laissez faire system to a regulatory one, and since the 1930's to a welfare state. The individual surrendered personal freedoms, chiefly of an economic nature, in return for increased social security. This in turn has produced a different economic order, often referred to as a "mixed economy," consisting of a government-regulated private sector and a growing public sector.

Economics and the Political Power Structure

Throughout history, economics has been regarded, as we saw in Chapter 1, as a form of applied ethics or as a subdivision of politics. Not until the 18th Century did economics begin to emerge as an independent analytical discipline, separate and distinct from both ethics and politics, and it is a moot question whether the isolation of economics from the other social sciences was a fortunate development. To this day economics is referred to in Europe and some American universities as "political economy," indicating the close ties between economics and politics. While certain highly technical areas in economics can be studied without reference to the prevailing ethical and social climate, most economic theories and policies are conditioned by the political and ethical framework within which the economy functions.

The Individual and Society

One of the most important aspects of political philosophy, and the one which is probably most important so far as the economist is concerned, deals with the relationship between the individual and the state. This relationship can range from extreme individual freedom and a minimum of governmental controls, (anarchism — "no government") to a maximum of governmental controls and a minimum of individual freedom (totalitarianism). Between these two extremes are various combinations of individual freedom and social restraints as shown in Figure 1.

Anarchism is often regarded as a form of left-wing radicalism, similar to Communism. Actually the philosophy of anarchism constitutes the very opposite of Communist totalitarianism. It means literally "no government." Anarchists argue that any form of government restricts the freedom of the individual: the more government, the greater the restrictions and the loss of freedom.

Laissez Faire Liberalism rests upon the philosophic assumption of the 18th Century that God has created an orderly

FIGURE 1 Society and the Individual
The Increasing Power of the State

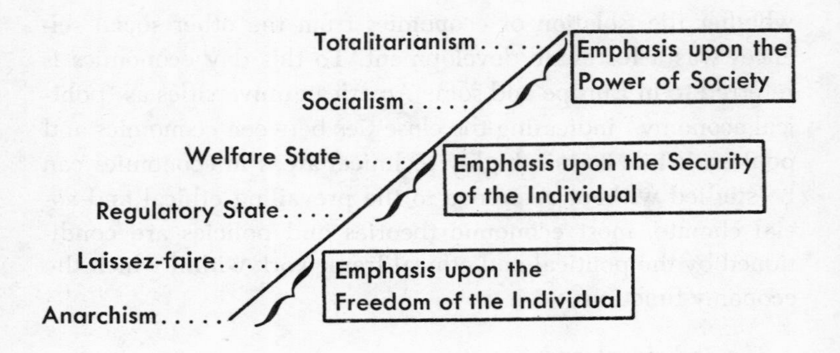

self-equilibrating social universe. As the French philosopher-economist Victor Mirabeau (1715–1789) put it: "The world runs by itself." Whatever is wrong with the world is due to the interference by the government bureaucracy with the divinely ordained order. Eighteenth Century laissez faire represented a natural reaction against the administrative chaos resulting from a government which had grown in size and oppressiveness for more than two centuries. The least-governed country, the people came to argue, is the best-governed country.

Parallel with the notion of natural laws governing the economic life of a nation ran the age-old concept — going back to Greek and Roman Law — of a natural moral law which could be set down in the form of a constitution for all men to understand and binding on all government agencies. In the United States the people were so concerned that the government might exceed its powers, that within a few years after the Constitution had been adopted, they added ten amendments, the so-called Bill of Rights, stressing that "The powers not delegated to the

United States by the Constitution, nor prohibited by it to the States, are reserved to the States respectively or to the people."

The United States started with a philosophy of limited governmental powers and of a high degree of individual freedom. Congress could collect taxes to provide for the common defense and "general welfare," [1] but the authors of the Constitution did not expect the government, in the name of "general welfare," to regulate the economy and provide for the "personal welfare" of individuals. Congress could "regulate the commerce with foreign nations, and among the several States," [2] but in 1787 nobody would have thought it possible that this clause might be interpreted as giving the Federal Government the power to fix minimum wages and maximum working hours, and regulate the relationship between employers and employees.

In the spirit of the 18th Century, the laissez faire state of the American Constitution evisaged a social order and an economy in which the citizen looked after his own business and his own welfare, largely free from government controls and without government aid. The government confined itself to the maintenance of law and order within the country, the protection of the country against foreign enemies, and the performance of a limited number of services such as the creation of the necessary currency.[3]

Regulatory State In the course of the second half of the 19th Century, conditions changed. While during the 18th Century the slogan "laissez faire" had stood for the freeing of the people from an oppressive state, by the middle of the 19th Century, and certainly after the War between the States, laissez faire developed more and more into a doctrine which

[1] Art. I, Sect. 8, Par. 1
[2] Art. I, Sect. 8, Par. 3
[3] Art. I, Sect. 8, Par. 7

paralyzed the power of the government to protect the weak against abuses and exploitation by the strong. At the Frontier a horse thief or a cheat at the card game was hanged. The people of New York and Chicago could not do likewise with the meat packer who put spoiled meat and refuse into cans, the maker of fake drugs, or the manager of a trust who artificially raised prices. The people thus came to look to the government for protection. The result has been the development of literally hundreds of regulatory agencies: the Federal Trade Commission (which administers the various Pure Food and Drug Acts), the Interstate Commerce Commission, the Federal Communications Commission, the Securities and Exchange Commission, and many more.

Welfare State The change from a combination laissez faire and regulatory state, which had characterized the socio-economic order of the United States for about half a century, to a welfare state came during the Depression of the 1930's. Millions of unemployed city dwellers lacked the basic necessities of life, tens of thousands of farmers lost their land, and the individual seemed unable to cope with the cataclysmic forces of the Depression.

The Welfare State is based on the assumption that in our modern complex society the individual is no longer able to secure for himself the degree of economic security to which he is, or the government feels he should be, entitled. In the past, in a predominantly rural economy, the family or private charity could look after those in need. An old-time farmer who owned his land could survive a depression. He could always raise enough food to feed his family, he had a roof over his head, he could gather wood for heating and cooking, and he could make a patched pair of trousers go a few months longer. A factory worker, on the other hand, who lives in a large apartment house, or in a suburban home on which he has paid down barely 10%, and who owes heavily on his car (and he has come to depend upon the car to get to work, to get the children to school, and to do the shopping) cannot raise the necessary food to feed his family. And if unemployment is widespread, the chances of his finding any kind of a job are not good. Hence the need to rely on outside help.

The three major uncertainties which threaten all individuals are the insecurity of old age, the lack of protection against sickness, and the threat of unemployment. As far back as 1881, von Bismarck, the founder and Chancellor of the new German Reich, and the leader of the Conservative Party, began to introduce social welfare legislation in Germany, which gradually comprised workmen's compensation, health insurance, and a limited old age security. Unemployment insurance was added by the Weimar Republic after World War I. In the United States, old age and unemployment protection was introduced during the 1930's as part of the New Deal reforms, and after World War II Mississippi became the last state to provide for workmen's compensation. Health insurance remains one of the controversial issues in American politics even though the introduction of medicare in 1966 now provides a fair amount of medical care for oldsters and the handicapped.

The modern welfare state, however, goes beyond protecting the individual against the three great risks of life, sickness, old age and unemployment. It attempts to create a social and economic order in which the vicissitudes of life are minimized, where poverty and unemployment are largely abolished. To the three great traditional freedoms — freedom of speech, of religion and of the press — President Franklin D. Roosevelt added the fourth freedom: "freedom from want." And President Johnson declared "War against Poverty."

Modern welfare statism calls for a big and powerful state

with centralized authority, the very opposite of the laissez faire state which characterized the first 100 years of American history.

Socialism as a philosophic goal goes back thousands of years. It is based on the assumption that private ownership of the means of production entails economic inequality, which produces social and political inequality, and results in the exploitation of the non-propertied classes. Socialism, in whatever form (and there are many), thus calls for public ownership of the means of production. Modern socialism developed largely as an ethical protest against the injustices of early-day capitalism which even middle-class writers such as Charles Dickens attacked. But even though most of these injustices — sweatshops, fraudulent goods, monopolistic exploitation — have largely been eliminated during the past 30 to 50 years in Europe and the United States, socialism continues to be advocated by intellectuals and special interest groups. After World War II, the British Labor Government nationalized all means of transportation, the coal mines, the public utilities and the steel mills. In Germany and France public ownership of substantial segments of the economy has long been the accepted practice. In this country, private enterprise still accounts for more than 80% of all the goods and services produced and consumed, and the American system relies more on rigid controls of private enterprise than on outright public ownership. But public ownership is increasing, especially in the field of public utilities — TVA being the outstanding example.

Totalitarianism goes a step further. It involves not only a rigid centralized planning and public ownership of the means of production; it assumes quite logically that if the government is to manage successfully the details of the nation's economy, it must also regulate and manage all other aspects of the social system. If the individual is free to work or not to work, to pick one occupation or another, to spend or save his money freely, to travel abroad or buy foreign goods, the government cannot achieve its economic goals. Totalitarianism, whether of the Russian Communist or the German National Socialist variety, thus means total control by the state of virtually every aspect of the individual's life. Freedom is not divisible. The individual cannot surrender his economic freedom and hope to retain in the long run his political and personal freedom. But even in Russia, after half a century of totalitarian socialism, private enterprise has not vanished completely. In 1959, one third of the beef cattle, one half of the milk cows, and four fifths of the goats were still owned by individual peasants, although since then great efforts have been made by the Russian Government to reduce the dependence of the people on private producers.

Chapter 5

AGRICULTURE

THE BASIC FACTS

Agriculture is the most basic and oldest occupation of man. Industry cannot develop nor civilization progress unless the farmer produces the necessary surplus to feed the non-farming portion of the population. The fact that some 60% of the people of the world suffer from nutritional deficiencies is due not to "overpopulation" but to the fact that in large parts of the world farming methods are hopelessly inadequate, and the governments of most underdeveloped countries tend to neglect agriculture.

The problem of agriculture in the United States is the opposite from that of most underdeveloped countries. American agriculture suffers from overproduction because of the tremendous productive capacity of modern large-scale scientific farming. While there is "potential" demand for American farm surpluses, the hungry people of the world lack the necessary dollars to purchase American products, and a substantial portion of the farm surpluses has to be shipped abroad as part of the foreign aid program. Even those nations which have the necessary dollar purchasing power tend to buy in other markets, because Congress has been trying to keep American farm prices above world market levels in order to assure a higher income to the American farmer.

While its beginnings go back to World War I, the farm aid program became important during the great Depression and especially since the end of World War II. At first the government provided easy and relatively cheap credit. This was followed by attempts to "stabilize" farm prices by limiting output and introducing the philosophy of "parity prices," designed to assure the farmer of a purchasing power somewhat equal to that of the non-farming population.

In the meantime, however, American agriculture experienced revolutionary scientific and technological changes. In the late 1930's one farmer could provide the necessary food and fibre for 10 non-farmers. Twenty years later, he produced enough for 30. This tremendous increase in productivity was made possible through very heavy capital investments which, in turn, spelled the end of the small family farm. Half of today's farm population is no longer needed to produce the food and fibres required by the American economy. Yet political, economic and social obstacles render it extremely difficult to transfer the underemployed subsistence farmers into other occupations.

Agriculture, the Oldest Occupation of Man

Agriculture — the production of food and fibres — is the most basic and oldest occupation of man. Civilization began as man gradually changed from a hunter and food-gatherer into a food producer. Since the non-farming population depends ultimately upon the farmer for their sustenance, handicraft and industry cannot develop until the farmers produce more than they consume themselves, thus providing a surplus for the non-farming occupations.

Modern Neglect of Agriculture

The principle is as true today as it was in the neolithic age 15-20,000 years ago. Yet modern politicians and economic planners tend to disregard the basic relationship between the food supply and economic development. Since the United States, Western Europe and Japan are the most heavily industrialized regions of the world and at the same time enjoy the highest standard of living, underdeveloped countries tend to jump to the conclusion that rapid industrial development provides the key to economic growth. They forget that the industrial revolution, which began in England during the second half of the 18th Century and in the United States during the first half of the 19th Century, was preceded by a rapid increase in agricultural production. What we would call today "scientific farming" was the great fashion in England during the latter part of the 18th Century. Without the resulting increase in the output of food and fibre, the population growth and the rapid industrialization and urbanization of Western Europe and the United States could not have been sustained. The fact that today about 60% of the world's population go hungry is due not to the inability of man to produce an adequate sustenance, but to the fact that in most parts of the world farming methods are hopelessly inadequate.

Overpopulation and Mass Starvation

Time and again throughout man's history, the population has threatened to outrun the food supply. During the 18th Century Europe's food production increased rapidly, but since the population grew even faster, many well-informed people at the end of the 18th Century were convinced that mankind would always be faced with an inadequate food supply.

The subsequent decades proved this theory to be wrong.

Through the application of modern science and technology, food production increased more rapidly during the 19th Century than did the population. But today, the old spectre has arisen again and there are many neo-Malthusians who again "prove mathematically" that the world is headed for disastrous food shortages. Statistics seem to justify their belief. While there are actual or potential surpluses in a number of important staples, including cotton, wheat, sugar, coffee and cocoa, more than half the people of the world suffer from malnutrition. But — as we should emphasize again — this is due not to the inability of man to produce enough food for the ill-fed millions, but to ignorance and poor economic planning.

The Problem of Overproduction in the United States

While more than half the people of the world do not have enough to eat, the great problem of American agriculture has long been "overproduction." The farm problem involves three distinct elements: (1) the tremendous productive capacity of large-scale scientific farming, (2) the limited purchasing power of the great majority of the people throughout the world who could otherwise consume the American surpluses, and (3) the politically determined high price level for American farm products.

The "potential" demand for American farm products — measured in terms of the world's need for food and staples — exceeds by far the productive capacity of American agriculture, but the people who need American farm products are too poor to buy them. And those countries which could buy the American surpluses find it cheaper to buy what they need in other countries, since most American farm prices have been fixed by the government at well above world market levels. The European nations, moreover, levy tariffs against American farm products to protect their own farmers, whose production cost is as a rule higher than in the United States (despite much lower wages), because the much smaller land holdings in Europe hamper mechanization and scientific farming. Since the 1920's, and especially since the end of World War II, the American Government has thus been faced with the unpleasant dilemma of either subsidizing the farmer at the expense of the American taxpayer and consumer, or of letting farm prices drop to world market levels, which would have had adverse economic and social effects, and would have been politically inexpedient for those Congressmen who depend on the farm vote.

The price support picture is as follows: (1) The average income of farm families is about 40% below that of non-farm families, because of the large number of impoverished marginal farmers who derive little benefit from the farm aid program. (2) The price support program costs the American taxpayer and consumer many billions of dollars each year (how much has not been calculated), thus adding to the inflationary pressure, lowering the average standard of living, and slowing economic growth. (3) The farm program has an unfavorable effect on the American balance of payments, thus speeding the loss of gold.

The History of American Farm Aid Policy

Poverty has long been the lot of many American farmers. Of the pioneers who streamed westward in search of free land, the majority gathered no riches through farming, because farm prices tended downward during much of the 19th Century. Farm "profits" were derived to a large extent from rising land values rather than profitable farm operations. Time and again in American history, the rebellious mood of the farmers flared up, from Shays's Rebellion in 1786–87 to the Granger movement of the 1870's and the physical violence directed against farm foreclosures during the 1930's. Long before the idea of the "welfare state" was thought of, the American government extended special help to the farmers, for instance, through the creation of land grant colleges designed to train farmers and improve farm operations. Until World War I, however, government farm aid was small and indirect. In the spirit of 19th Century laissez faire, the farmer was expected to assume personally the risks of his occupation.

Changing Attitude During the 1920's The attitude began to change during World War I, as the farmers were called upon to produce "food for victory." Farm prices rose sharply (wheat, for instance, from 79¢ a bushel in 1914 to $2.16 in 1918, and cotton from 7.35¢ a pound to 35.34¢) and the prices of farm land advanced even more rapidly. Millions of acres, including much semi-arid land in the West, were brought under cultivation to meet the temporary demand and to take advantage of the temporary possibilities for profit.

With the end of the war, the demand collapsed and the prices of basic staples including cotton, wheat, wool and corn dropped as much as 50% in two years. As the 1920's wore on without a marked improvement in the farm situation, Congress decided to act. The farm aid program, like any form of government intervention, began with what seemed a perfectly logical measure of indirect help by providing low-cost credit for farmers. As this form of indirect help did not achieve the desired results, more direct measures were taken, and within less than 20 years farming became subject to rigid and costly government controls — without producing a solution for the farm problem.

Easy Credit for Farmers American agriculture had suffered from a shortage of credit for almost a century. Since few people at the Frontier had enough income to accumulate substantial savings, capital was scarce, the risk was great, and interest rates were correspondingly high. It is thus not surprising that Congress first decided to help the farmer by providing relatively cheap and ample credit. In 1917 the Federal Land Bank System was created, followed in 1923 by the Federal Intermediate Credit Bank System, and ultimately by the Banks for Cooperatives. The Land Bank and the Intermediate Credit Bank systems have grown into huge organizations. As of January 1966, the former had $4.8 billion and the latter $2.7 billion in loans outstanding.

Basic Economic Forces and the Farm Support Program

By 1929, before the Depression had actually set in, Congress went a step further and decided to "stabilize" farm prices. It was the first timid step in a futile battle against elementary economic forces which is still going on. Congress did not plunge into this policy between one day and the next, but slipped into it slowly step by step. In 1929, it created the Federal Farm Board whose task it was to minimize price fluctuations and provide for an orderly marketing of farm products by buying up surpluses in the hopeful belief that these surpluses could be sold without a loss during the "seven lean years." Unfortunately, Congress did not succeed in duplicating the feat of economic planning which Joseph had accomplished in Egypt in Biblical times. By 1932 farm prices had dropped another 50%, and the Federal Farm Board had lost $345 million of its original $500 million revolving fund.

New Deal Farm Policy To cope with the disastrous price decline and the widespread poverty and unrest in the farm districts, the New Deal added crop controls as the logical counterpart to the futile efforts of the Hoover administration to stabilize prices. While the government spends many millions of dollars every year to prevent businessmen from getting together to reduce production in order to raise prices and profits, the same principle, Congress decided, should not apply to the farmer. Since there were too many farmers to agree on a policy of raising prices through an artificial restriction of output, the government assumed the task.

Production Controls The Agricultural Adjustment Act of 1933, designed to raise farm prices and curtail production, was held unconstitutional in 1936 because the Federal Government apparently could not, under the Constitution, regulate agricul-ural production which at that time was still regarded as an intra-state business. The Aministration immediately attempted to achieve the same goals through the Soil Conservation Act of 1936 and the Second Agricultural Adjustment Act of 1938, which made the enforcement of the crop restrictions subject to the approval of the individual states. At the same time, the constitutional philosophy of the Supreme Court changed. What had been declared unconstitutional in 1936 was held constitutional in 1942. In the famous Wickard vs. Filburn case, the Supreme Court argued that even if a farmer raises his surplus wheat only to feed his hogs, and consumes the pork and hams himself, the "home-consumed wheat would have a substantial influence on price and market conditions," which in turn affects interstate commerce. And since Congress has the constitutional powers to regulate interstate commerce, it hence can regulate also what a farmer produces for his own consumption.

Parity Prices Next to the crop control policy, the most characteristic notion of the New Deal farm aid program was the "parity price" idea. Congress decided that the farmers' ability to purchase non-farm goods should be kept at par with the purchase power of other economic groups. If the average price of the goods a farmer purchased for his own consumption and to operate his farm had risen from 100 in 1909–14 to 313 in 1964, and the average price of wheat in 1909–14 had been 88¢, the "parity price" for wheat was $2.76 (88 times 3.13). Actually, the government did not guaranty the farmers the full "parity price," but only a percentage, e.g., 85–90% of parity, which is fixed periodically by Congress.

The basic philosophy of the "parity price" is economically and socially unsound, and has lost much of its political appeal in recent years, although it remains, with some adjustments, a part of the basic American farm aid philosophy.

The Technological Revolution on the Farm

While Washington is still talking in terms of the depressed farm conditions of the 1920's and 1930's, life on the farm has undergone a revolutionary change — probably more revolutionary than the changes brought about by automation in industry. And the end is not yet in sight. The scientific and technological developments of the past 25 years — hybridization, new fertilizers and pest controls, improved breeding methods and new farm machinery — represent the most important advances in agriculture since Jean Baptist Boussingault and Justus von Liebig discovered soil chemistry in the 1840's. During the 1950's alone, per acre production increased by 30%, and the production per farm animal by 20%. While the population of the United States grew by about 1.8% a year during the 1950's, the farm output increased by 2.5%. Between 1940 and 1960, the American farmer was able to increase the output of wheat per acre by 35%, of corn by 55%, of cotton by 70%, and of tobacco by 60%. The cows give 35% more milk, the chickens lay 50% more eggs, and beef cattle provide 30% more meat.

Increased Farm Labor Productivity

During much of the 19th Century, the average American farmer was able to feed and clothe about five non-farmers. By 1900 the figure had risen to about seven, and by the outbreak of World War II to about ten. Then came the great technological and scientific breakthrough of the 1940's and especially the 1950's, and by the 1960's only one farmer was needed to supply 30 non-farmers. While man-hour productivity in agriculture increased by about 50% during the 30 years from 1910 to 1940, it rose by 62% during the 1940's alone and by another 68% during the 1950's. Between the early 1930's, when the farm support policy was adopted, and the early 1960's, wheat production per farm worker increased 4½ times, cotton production 2½ times and sugar production almost 5 times. The yield per acre for all crops combined rose by 51% between 1945 and 1965, and livestock production per breeding unit by 39%.

Changing Nature of American Agriculture

The revolutionary changes of the past 25 years have altered the basic character of American agriculture. The traditional American family farm, which constituted "a way of life," is rapidly giving way to the scientifically operated agrobusiness employing a large amount of capital and equipment and a small number of skilled workers. About nine per cent of the farms, the largest ones, account for about half of the total agricultural production. Huge amounts of capital are needed to operate a modern agrobusiness. Highly mechanized grain farms, for example, require capital investments of well over $100,000 per worker, about five times as much as is needed to provide a job in industry. These huge capital investments in turn are making possible the tremendous increase in man-hour productivity. It should be noted, however, that while the production *per farm worker* is by far the highest in the United States, the production *per acre* is only about half as large as that of Western Europe and Japan, which illustrates a basic economic tendency: Each economy makes most extensive use of those factors of production, such as land or labor, which are most plentiful and hence relatively the cheapest. In the United States land and capital are relatively plentiful, while cheap labor is scarce; hence the reliance on extensive farming and a high degree of mechanization. In Europe and Japan, on the other hand, land is far less plentiful than manpower, and agricultural production is therefore intensive and relies less on capital-consuming machinery.

Declining Farm Population

The mechanization of agriculture has made possible a large-scale migration from the farm to the city without an impairment of the nation's food supply. Changes in government statistics becloud to some extent the depopulation of the farms. Prior to 1959 all farms of three acres or more, as well as smaller farms with annual sales of $150, were included in the government statistics. Since 1959, a farm is defined for statistical purposes as a place of 10 acres, or of less than 10 acres but with annual sales of $250. As a result of this change of definition, some 232,000 farms disappeared from the statistical records. But even without this statistical adjustment, it is obvious that the number of farms and farm workers is declining rapidly.

While the total population of the United States increased by 18.5% during the 1950's, more than half the counties, chiefly in the thinly populated rural areas, lost population.

Rural "Under-Employment"

Yet, even this large migration is not enough, and the rural labor force continues to be much larger than can be used effectively. In the terminology of the economist, agriculture suffers from "under-employment." Well over 90% of the food and fiber sold commercially are produced by 45–50% of the farm enterprises. Since the government for some years has acquired about 8% of the farm output, it would appear that half the farms now under cultivation, namely the agrobusinesses and the large family farms, could meet all the present needs; and the increase in production which can by expected is likely to take care of any rise in domestic demand which will occur during the next 20 years.

The Failure of the Farm Aid Program

The farm aid program has been extremely costly to the economy as a whole without solving the farm problem. But after a generation of experimenting, the system has become an integral part of the country's social, political and economic structure, so that a drastic change would require a great deal of political courage on the part of the government, and maturity of economic thought on the part of the electorate. Actually, the majority of the American people are only vaguely familiar with the basic technical details of the farm support program.

American farmers produce some 250 farm commodities, but only 12 enjoy price supports at fixed levels; and of these 12, five — wheat, cotton, corn, sorghum and dairy products — receive 80–90% of all price support help, even though they account for only 40% of the total farm production. In return for restricting the acreage under cultivation, the farmers are permitted to turn over their crops to the government against crop loans based on prices fixed by Congress. If market prices rise above the loan values, the farmers can reclaim their crops and sell them in the open market. If prices stay below the loan values, the farmers need not repay the loan, and the government holds the surpluses, which in recent years have repeatedly reached a total value of $9 billion. The situation changed, at least temporarily, in 1965 and 1966, when crop failures in various parts of the world, especially in India, enabled the American government to dispose of a large part of its surpluses.

Aid Beneficiaries Since the amount of aid received by the individual farmer depends upon the volume of production, most of the farm aid goes to the large commercial enterprises, many of which could operate profitably without the subsidies. Among the "farmers" who in recent years received government subsidies for not raising corn or cotton were the Ford Motor Co.; Libby, McNeill & Libby; the Mississippi State Penitentiary; the Arkansas State Penal Institute; and the Kansas State University Endowment Association. On the other hand, the State of Ohio was fined $28,000 because its mental and penal institutions grew more wheat than their federal quota permitted, and individual farmers had their farm machinery seized and their bank accounts blocked by the government.

Sugar Subsidies In fighting the sugar subsidy system, under which sugar imports are rigidly restricted in order to raise domestic prices, Senator Douglas of Illinois quoted the following figures for 1962: world market price, 2.7 cents per pound; price to the American consumer for sugar produced outside the United States 6.4 cents. Between 1948 and 1962, the American consumer paid $5 billion for sugar alone, in excess of existing world prices.

Butter Price Support Higher prices tend to reduce consumption while stimulating production. Between 1940 and 1963 the per capita consumption of butter in the United States declined from about 17 pounds per year to 6–7 pounds, which was less than the per capita consumption in Russia and less than the amount of butter consumed by relief recipients in the United States, who received about 10 pounds of butter free from the government. While the American consumer switched from price-supported butter to cheaper margarine (for which the raw materials have to be imported, thus burdening the American balance of payments), the government lost $519 million between 1933 and 1960 in its attempt to support butter prices, and ended up in 1960 with 105 million pounds of butter in cold storage.

Various suggestions have been made to abandon the price support program and to pay direct subsidies to needy farmers. At one time, Senator Douglas of Illinois campaigned to limit the government subsidy, so that a farm family's total income would be equal to (but not in excess of) the average family income in America, or about $7500. Others have suggested limiting farm subsidies to $15,000 to $25,000 per farm. All these suggestions, however, have never advanced beyond the suggestion stage.

Reasons for the Failure of the Farm Aid Program

The failure of the American farm aid program illustrates strikingly that even the richest government in the world cannot in the long run disregard basic economic forces. The farm support program has been a failure because:

1. Artificially raised prices stimulate production while curtailing demand in the United States and especially in world markets;
2. The program has failed to allow for the fact that, because of technological and scientific changes, the 40-acre-homestead farmer can no longer produce efficiently;
3. It provides large subsidies for the large, efficient, low-cost

producers, but little help for the needy marginal farmer.

4. It has done little to ease the movement of marginal farmers into other occupations;
5. It has raised the cost of living, and has swallowed vast sums of taxpayers' money, thus increasing the inflationary pressure of the postwar years; and finally
6. By raising domestic support prices above world market prices, it has hampered commercial exports and thus aggravated the American balance of payments problem.

Obstacles to the Development of a Sounder Farm Policy

Yet, while all these facts are well known, it is extremely difficult, for political, economic and social reasons, to develop an economically sound farm policy.

Political Reasons Congressmen from rural areas are not likely to vote themselves out of a job by supporting a farm policy which will result in a further population decline in their electoral districts. They advocate instead government subsidies to bring industries to marginal farmers. Some of these industrial development schemes are no doubt sound. Others constitute merely a movement of plants from high-wage to low-wage areas without adding to the total national output. Instead of underemployed marginal farmers in Alabama, there will be unemployed industrial workers, who were formerly employed in Massachusetts textile mills. Some of the subsidized industries, moreover, may never become self-supporting.

Economic Reasons Thirty-five years of farm subsidies, as well as other economic forces, have produced an artificial price and cost structure which cannot be altered without far-reaching repercussions. Farm real estate prices have sky-rocketed since 1940. They rose 115% during the 1940's and another 110% between 1950 and 1965. Several factors have contributed to this sharp rise: the necessity of increasing the size of the farm in order to take advantage of mechanized equipment; the large amounts of farm land taken for super highways, airports, and especially surburban developments; the belief of many non-farmers that farm real estate constitutes a sound hedge against a further decline in the purchasing power of the dollar; and finally, the farm price support program itself. If the price support policy were to be abandoned, as it should be from a purely economic point of view, many farmers would find it difficult to earn a fair return on their inflated investments. Having paid a high, and possibly an excessive price for their land, partly in expectation of a continued rise in farm real estate values, farmers tend to favor more inflation rather than lower prices.

Social Reasons While it may seem economically logical to move marginal farmers who cannot earn an adequate income on the farm into other occupations, few of the subsistence farmers possess the necessary skills to obtain and hold jobs in industry. Only too many marginal farmers are functionally illiterate (even though they may be able to read and write) so far as modern industry is concerned, and if moved to the city they would only swell the ranks of the unemployed and relief recipients.

Chapter 6

THE ORGANIZATION FOR PRODUCTION

THE BASIC FACTS

The productive capacity of a nation, and hence its standard of living, depends to a large extent on the development of a suitable organizational structure of business. There are more than 4 million business enterprises in the United States. Seventy-five percent of all the business is done by corporations.

A modern free enterprise economy could not exist without corporations, nor without well-functioning securities markets. No other country in the world has as many ways of financing corporations as does the United States, which is one explanation for the dynamic strength of the American economy.

Securities markets serve a duel purpose: (1) they provide the intermediary mechanism between the individuals (who accumulate savings) and the corporations (which need capital); and (2) they provide facilities for the public to buy and sell securities, thus providing for the liquidity of investments.

For technological and economic reasons, businesses tend to grow and swallow their competitors until only a few large firms control the market. The concentration of economic power is not a development of modern capitalism. The tendency, however, is reinforced by the modern dependence on mass pro-

duction methods. Modern oligopolistic competition usually attempts to avoid price-cutting because of the danger of destructive price wars. While there are many individual instances of price fixing and trade restraints, generally speaking the American economy has long enjoyed a considerable degree of freedom from such restraints. This is due to (1) reasonably effective antitrust laws, and (2) a rapidly changing technology which renders the allocation of markets difficult.

Despite the concentration of power, the fluidity of the American economy — the ability of newcomers to rise to the top — has been largely preserved.

The dual problem which faces all businessmen is the question of optimum location and optimum size. There is no general rule by which this problem can be solved.

The Importance of "Business"

Many Americans today disapprove of the philosophy of life reflected in the remark which President Coolidge made in 1925 that "America's business is business." Yet, the standard of living of a nation and its position in the world depend to a large extent upon the volume of goods and services the nation produces, and this maximization of production depends in turn, on the development of an organizational framework best suited to the social and political system of the country. A free enterprise economy has a different organization of production than a planned totalitarian state. Our modern age of mass production calls for economic institutions different from those of the Middle Ages, which was characterized by handicraft.

Business Organizations

There are well over 4 million private business enterprises in the United States, ranging from small farms and corner grocery stores to corporate giants such as General Motors and American Telephone and Telegraph. By far the largest number of business ventures consist of individual proprietorships, a much smaller number of partnerships, and the remainder of corporations, but the latter account for about 75% of all the business conducted in the United States.

Proprietorships and Partnerships An individual proprietorship is a one-man or one-woman business, in which the sole owner makes all decisions, gets all the profits and assumes all the risk. Most of the small farms are individual proprietorships, as are corner groceries and drugstores. There is little expense and red tape in setting up a proprietorship, the overhead is relatively small, and in the case of a small enterprise the taxes are less burdensome than they would be if the business were organized as a corporation. The chief disadvantage of a proprietorship is the fact that the owner assumes "unlimited liability," and the creditors can seize his non-business assets — his home, furniture and car — if the buiness assets are inadequate to cover all obligations.

Partnerships are created through written or oral agreements, when two or more individuals get together to conduct jointly a business, assume jointly all responsibilities, and share in the profits according to a previously agreed-upon key. Partners incur "unlimited liability," just as the owners of proprietorships. They are liable for all obligations contracted by one partner, and unless the partnership agreements are limited in time, one or the other partner can soon prove a liability to the business rather than an asset, and it may be difficult to get rid of him.

A limited partnership is a partnership in which some partners, known as general partners, assume full responsibility, while the liability of one or more partners, the limited partners, is limited to the amount they have contributed, and thus does not extend to their non-business assets. If a partner dies and the partnership finds it difficult to pay to the widow the partner's share in the business, the widow is often induced to become a limited partner. She has no voice in the conduct of the business, but shares in the profits.

Corporations A corporation, according to the famous definition of Chief Justice Marshall in the Dartmouth Case of 1819, is "an artificial being, invisible, intangible and existing only in the contemplation of the law." It is a legal fiction created by the state. As a legal form, corporations were fully developed under Roman Law 2000 years ago; they were used throughout the Middle Ages (monasteries, for instance, were corporations, just as Harvard and other private universities are today); but it was not until the middle of the 19th Century that the corporate form came to be widely used as a business organization. Today the capitalistic system could not function without the modern corporation, just as the business of the Middle Ages could not have been conducted without guilds. A corporation enjoys all the privileges and obligations of a natural person. It can hire workers, borrow money, own property, manufacture goods and provide services; it can sue and be sued. Since a corporation is an artificial being, created by the state, the latter can impose special burdens, such as a heavy corporate income tax. However, despite these special burdens and a certain amount of red tape involved in setting up a corporation, the advantages usually outweigh the disadvantages. The liability of the owners, known as shareholders or stockholders, is limited to the amount they have paid in (even though the corporation itself might go into bankruptcy). The corporation has, as a rule, perpetual life (while a partnership comes to an end when one of the partners dies, goes bankrupt or becomes insane); it can attract vast funds far beyond the resources of even the richest men; and it enables the owners to dispose of their investment freely.

Creation of Corporations Corporations can be created either by a special act of Congress or of the state legislatures. The Federal Reserve System, for instance, the Tennessee Valley Authority, and the Federal Deposit Insurance Corp. operate on the basis of special charters granted by Congress. Or — and this is usually the case — corporations can be set up simply by meeting the requirements of federal or state general incorporation laws. National banks are set up under federal law, but most other corporations are organized under the laws of one of the 50 states. (The first general incorporation act was adopted by the State of New York in 1811.) Some states, especially New Jersey and Delaware, have particularly favorable laws of incorporation, and many corporations which do business in other states are organized under the laws of New Jersey and Delaware. One distinguishes between private corporations (such as U.S. Steel) and public corporations (TVA); between stock corporations (such as the companies listed on the stock exchanges) and non-stock corporations (such as private universities).

The Financing of a Corporation

No country in the world has developed as many means of financing a corporation as the United States, or to put it differently, there is no country with so many different types of securities. (For a breakdown of the major types of securities see Table 1.)

Common Stock Common stockholders are called the "residual owners" of the business, because they own all the assets of a corporation which remain after all obligations and prior claims

TABLE 1

Main Types of Securities

Equity Capital:	Common stocks
	Preferred stocks
Borrowed Capital:	Bonds (secured long-term obligations)
	Debentures (unsecured long-term obligations)
	Notes and Certificates (medium or short-term obligations which can be secured or unsecured)

have been paid, including the claims of the preferred stockholders and bondholders. As a rule they have the exclusive right to determine and supervise the day-by-day operations. Occasionally, a company has voting and non-voting common stock, with the power of governing the corporation resting with the former group.

Preferred Stock There are many types of preferred stock, but the principle is always the same: Preferred stockholders have to be paid a fixed dividend before the common stockholders can receive anything, and the preferred stockholders have a prior claim to assets in case the company is dissolved. In turn, the earnings of preferred stockholders are usually limited. Let us assume that a company has 100,000 shares of $6 preferred (with a par value of $100) and 100,000 shares of common stock (with no par value) outstanding. If earnings amount to $800,000, the preferred stockholders get $6 each (or $600,000), which leaves only $200,000, or $2 per share, for the common stockholders. If earnings increase by 50% to $1,200,000, preferred stockholders still get only $6, but the residual earnings available for the common stockholders are now $600,000, or $6 per share, an increase of 200% . On the other hand, if the earnings were to drop to $600,000, the preferred stockholders would continue to get their full dividend, but the common stockholders would get nothing. Some preferred shares *participate,* that means they share with the common stockholders in the earnings after preferred dividends have been paid. The basis on which the preferred stockholders share in additional earnings differs with the various issues. The terms are specified when the preferred stock is first sold to the public. One also distinguishes between cumulative and non-cumulative preferred stock. If a preferred stock is cumulative no dividend may be paid to the common stockholders until all dividend arrears owed to the preferred stockholders have been paid. In the case of a non-cumulative stock, the preferred stockholders have no further claim, if the company fails to earn the preferred dividend payable in a given year, or the management does not declare the dividend. As an added protection for the preferred stockholders the terms of issue usually provide that in case the preferred dividend has not been paid a number of times (usually if five quarterly payments are in arrears), the preferred stockholders are to elect the majority of the board of directors and thus assume control of the company. It should be emphasized, however, that preferred stockholders are owners, not creditors, so that they cannot seize the assets of the company, even if no dividends have been paid for a long time.

Obligations The situation is different in the case of bonds, debentures, notes and certificates, whose owners are creditors. If interest or principal are not paid when due, the creditors can, and as a rule do, demand that the company be put in the hands of a receiver. In other words, the non-payment of bond-interest usually leads to a declaration of bankruptcy.

A bond agreement consists of two instruments: (1) the promise of the company to pay interest and principal at specified times, and (2) a pledge of certain assets. Each bondholder holds the company's promise to pay, the bond. The assets, however, are pledged to a trustee, usually a trust company, which holds the pledge on behalf of the bondholders. In case the company fails to live up to its promise the trustee moves to foreclose on the pledged property. The latter may consist of real property (in which case one usually speaks of mortgage bonds), chattel (movable property) or intangibles (stocks and bonds). The security is no better, of course, than the value of the pledged property. If a railroad pledges its main terminal as security for a bond issue, the latter is probably well secured. If, on the other hand, the pledge consists of a first mortgage on a sideline which is operated at a loss, the security would be of little value in case of bankruptcy. Yet both issues are properly called "First Mortgage Bonds." The value of a bond thus depends first of all on the ability of the company to earn the interest charges, and secondly on the relative value of the assets pledged, which requires a careful analysis.

Bonds as against Debentures If the same company had a bond and a debenture issue outstanding the former would be more desirable because it enjoys the pledge of special assets, which the bondholders can attach in case of bankruptcy. The debenture holders, on the other hand, have only an unsecured claim and in case of bankruptcy can look only to those assets which have not been taken by creditors with prior claims. Yet, it is completely misleading to assume that "mortgage bonds are always better than debentures." Among the very highest type of obligations available are the American Telephone and Telegraph debentures, which rank only a fraction below the obligations of the United States government; yet these AT&T debentures do not enjoy any special security. In fact, AT&T is such a sound business that it can borrow freely without pledging any assets.

A typical example of medium-term secured obligations are

the so-called equipment trust certificates, which are used to finance the purchase of rolling stock by the railroads and of busses by the bus companies. One can often see on railroad cars a brass plaque indicating that the car is owned by a trust company and leased to the railroad. In this case, the railroad does not acquire title to the car until the equipment trust certificates, through which the purchase of the car was financed, have been paid off in full.

Securities Markets

Just as the modern capitalistic system could not function well without corporations, a free economic system cannot operate efficiently without well-organized securities markets. One of the weaknesses of the postwar Western European boom has been the lack of an adequate system of financing the expanding economy, and the situation is far worse in underdeveloped countries.

Securities markets perform a dual function: (1) they provide the facilities for the public to buy and sell stocks and bonds thus making these investments more liquid, and (2) they operate as an intermediary mechanism between the individual who accumulates savings and the corporations and governments which need funds. The banking system performs a similar function in that it uses the money which the public deposits in the form of checking and savings accounts to make loans. However, banks are severely restricted if it comes to providing equity capital. Banks can make loans (as a rule only medium- and short-term loans), but in order to provide the economy with adequate equity (or risk) capital securities markets are needed. If the facilities to convert savings into investments (either into loans or equities) are inadequate, savings tend to lie idle or be invested non-productively in gold and silver hoards (as in India), or in vast land holdings which remain uncultivated (as in Latin America). At the same time, industry could not develop for lack of investment capital.

Investment Bankers

The distribution of new securities is the task of investment bankers. Either individually, or as underwriting syndicates, they purchase a whole new bond or stock issue from a corporation which needs new capital, and then sell the bonds and shares retail to the general public. They assume the risk that something might happen after they have taken over the issue which could make it difficult for them to "distribute" (sell) the securities to the ultimate investors at a profit. In other words, they "underwrite" the risk of distribution, and are hence called "securities underwriters." Securities dealers are highly skilled experts who operate in an extremely competitive market. They must know what securities can be sold at what price, and they must then reconcile the demands of the market with the needs of the corporation. The business of a corporation, for instance, may be subject to wide fluctuations, showing large profits in one year and small profits or even losses in others. It would thus be dangerous for such a corporation to assume fixed charges in the form of interest payments which have to be met whether business is good or not. The corporation should thus rely chiefly on common and preferred stock to meet its capital requirements (since dividend payments can be suspended in bad years) rather than on bonds and debentures.

But this raises a problem if the stock market is weak and common stocks are hard to sell. In such a case, the underwriter may offer a cumulative preferred stock, which provides the investor with the assurance that he will receive eventually the contractual rate of return (even though payments may be deferred during bad years), and frees the corporation of the threat of bankruptcy if it cannot meet payments during a given year.

Effect of Taxation Tax-wise, it is usually more advantageous for corporations to operate with borrowed capital (bonds and debentures) because interest charges can be deducted from profits before taxes are calculated. On basis of a 50% corporate income tax, a 6% bond issue thus does not cost the corporation more than a stock issue which is sold on a 3% yield basis. And from the point of view of the investor, a share of stock yielding 3% may seem more attractive than a bond yielding 6%, provided the investor assumes continued inflation, which would result in a steady increase in corporate earnings.

Registration Statements Once the corporation and the underwriters have agreed on the terms of the new issue, the latter helps the corporation in preparing the Registration Statement which has to be filed with the Securities and Exchange Commission before the new securities can be sold. The SEC never "approves" a new issue, but if it does not raise an objection within thirty days after the Registration Statement has been filed, the issue can be offered publicly. The fact that the SEC has raised no objection does not mean that the new issue is "good" and will prove profitable to the investor. It merely means that the corporation has provided all the information necessary for the investor to get a complete picture of the risks involved and the profit possibilities. Actually, very few small investors have the time and expert knowledge to study a registration statement in detail, which as a rule consists of 50 to 100 pages of legal and technical language. But at least the experts, the securities salesmen and customers men, can get the necessary information, and they in turn are expected to advise their clients, just as lawyers explain to their clients the fine points of the law and doctors the results of an X-ray picture. During the past 30 years the high-pressure securities salesman, who knew how to sell but often knew distressingly little about what he sold, has given way to the well-trained and closely supervised professional customers man and securities salesman, who must pass stiff examinations before they can deal with the public.

Stock Markets

While the underwriters deal in newly issued securities, the stock markets, chiefly the New York Stock Exchange, provide facilities to buy and sell securities already in the hands of the public. A stock exchange is an auction market, where most brokers buy and sell securities for their clients on a commission basis — although some brokers also act as dealers and buy and sell for their own account. Without securities markets, investments would lack the necessary liquidity, and investors would be reluctant to tie up their funds for fear that they might need their money in an emergency but be unable to sell their securities.

Securities prices fluctuate, on the one hand, with existing business conditions (if corporate earnings decline, stock prices tend to go down) and, on the other, with public sentiment, which is often irrational and unpredictable. When President Eisenhower suffered a heart attack, securities prices dropped sharply, even though there was neither an economic nor political justification for the decline. As a rule investors tend to be over-optimistic during boom periods (such as the late 1920's), and over-pessimistic during periods of depression (such as the early 1930's). To "play the market" requires a great deal of intimate knowledge, constant attention to market conditions, a sixth sense, and above all a great deal of courage. Great fortunes are made by those who have the wisdom — or courage —

to "swim against the stream," who buy during a depression and sell during a boom.

Listed and Unlisted Securities All important stock and bond issues (important in the sense that they are held by a large number of investors) are "listed," i.e., officially admitted for trading at one of the stock exchanges. The great majority of all stock and bond issues, however, (those which are held by only a small number of investors, or which are not frequently traded) are "unlisted" and are traded "over-the-counter," in a nationwide market which is maintained by several thousand securities dealers who buy and sell unlisted securities for their own account. Their income is derived from the spread between the buying and selling price, while the income of a broker who is admitted to a stock exchange consists in a commission which he earns by buying or selling securities for his clients. Between 80% and 85% of all listed securities are traded on the New York Stock Exchange. The second most important market is the American Stock Exchange (formerly known as the Curb Exchange) which is also in New York. The Midwest Exchange in Chicago is the third largest market.

The number of stockholders has increased rapidly since the 1950's, from fewer than 6½ million in 1952 to about 22 million in 1967. While only about 2% of the American families own securities worth $25,000 or more, more and more middle-income families own stocks. About 50% of the share-owners have an income of less than $10,000. This "people's capitalism" enables even the relatively small investor to share in the growth of the economy and to protect himself against the depreciation of his savings as a result of inflation. A danger of this development lies in the fact that small investors usually cannot afford a major decline in the stock market, which occurs from time to time despite rigid government supervision. The wealthy investor can weather storms of this type. Small investors, on the other hand, who may be forced to sell when prices are low because of personal needs (such as temporary unemployment) can suffer permanent losses. Whoever buys stocks should realize the amount of risk involved; and the small investor should keep at least part of his savings in the form of bonds and savings deposits to be prepared for an emergency, even though the return on these investments may be very small as a result of the chronic inflation.

The Dangers of Bigness

"Power corrupts, and absolute power corrupts absolutely," warned Lord Acton (1834–1902). This applies not only to an all-powerful church and a big government, but to Big Business and Big Unions as well.

Why Monopoly?

But just as people will continue to smoke even though they know it may adversely affect their health, monopolistic restraints have continued throughout the centuries despite their undesirable social and economic effects, and the efforts of the authorities to control economic power. The reasons are twofold: (1) Like all human beings, only too many businessmen are inclined to take the short-range point of view by trying to earn an extra profit through monopolistic restraints irrespective of the long-range effect; and (2) modern technology tends to restrict the number of competing producers. It would be highly inconvenient and costly to have a city served by a number of competing telephone companies. And the same is true of water, power, and gas companies. The governmental authorities thus grant a monopoly to a single company, and in turn closely regulate operations and prices in order to prevent abuses. The situation is far more difficult in the case of "oligopolies" (a few sellers), as for instance in the automobile, steel, cigarette, aluminum, copper and many other similar industries. Modern mass production methods require vast capital investments and large markets. But since all markets are limited, society is faced with the alternative of having either many small and relatively high-priced producers (because they cannot take full advantage of the savings derived from mass production methods), or a few large and low-cost producers. The latter, however, raises the danger of the few producers getting together to raise prices, which they could not do if there were a large number of small producers, as there are in farming. It has been estimated that about one third of all the privately produced goods and service in the United States are produced under monopolistic or clearly oligopolistic conditions.

Corporate Concentration In 1932 Adolf A. Berle and Gardner C. Means in their widely read book *The Modern Corporation and Private Property* stressed two facts: (1) that the 200 largest corporations in America owned 50% of the total assets of non-financial corporations, and (2) that these corporations were controlled by a relatively small number of directors, while the great mass of stockholders, who "owned" the corporations according to the law, actually had very little influence on the management. And shortly before the outbreak of World War II the Temporary National Economic Committee (TNEC) published a report on the concentration of economic power and came to the conclusion that the 19th Century concepts of "free enterprise" and "competition" had largely lost their meaning in a changing world. The Berle and Means book and the TNEC study served for many years as a basis for attacks on "Big Business," because both studies seemed to indicate a progressive concentration of economic power to the detriment of the consumer and the country as a whole.

Two Aspects of the Problem The problem of "bigness" has two aspects: (1) the weakening of competition, and (2) the elimination of effective control by the stockholders. The latter continues to be a very real problem, although the government has not been particularly concerned about it. Many of the major corporations are controlled by self-perpetuating boards of directors who actually own only a very small percentage of the stock — often less than 5%. As long as they can convince the stockholders that the board produces the best possible results, enough stockholders will give the management their proxies to enable the latter to control the annual meetings. It is obviously impossible for about 2 ½ million American Telephone and Telegraph stockholders to get together and determine the policy of the company.

The place of the 19th Century entrepreneur is thus being taken, in the case of most of the large corporations, by a class of professional managers. About one third of the directorships of the 250 largest corporations are held by 400 men. This change in the nature of managerial power has affected the character of the economy. An individual entrepreneur may be willing and able to take a long chance, because if the gamble works out he is the chief beneficiary. The modern managerial bureaucracy is more likely to play safe and avoid extreme risks, for the very human reason that if the gamble works out the benefits go chiefly to the stockholders, not to the managers, and if it fails, the management is likely to be replaced by irate stockholders. On the other hand, it is often pointed out that large corporations with diversified interests are far better able than small entrepreneurs to assume the often great risk of developing a new product. Without the great concentration of economic power, research financed by business would be severely curtailed, and this in turn would hamper economic development. While it is not difficult to find instances over the years where management pursued policies which favored their own personal interests rather than those of the stockholders, whatever one may say about the corporate bureaucracy — the "gray flannel suit" mentality — American corporations on an average are by far the most efficiently operated business enterprises in the world.

Concentration of Economic Power In 1964, 55 companies had sales of more than a billion dollars each and total sales of the 100 largest manufacturing corporations amounted to well over $180 billion. One out of every 9 employees in manufacturing industries worked for these 100 largest corporations, which had invested an average of $26,000 per worker. The investment was highest in the petroleum industry amounting to $73,000 per worker, followed by $53,000 in the public utilities and $47,000 in transportation. The 100 corporations listed more than 13 million stockholders. Sixty-six of the top 100 corporations had more stockholders than workers.

This obvious concentration of economic power, however, thus far has not prevented newcomers from rising to the top. Nor has it diminished the spirit of enterprise on the part of the very big, even though scientific management has largely replaced individual risk-taking. Every year 170–190,000 new corporations are formed, and some of them make it to the top. Of the 100 largest corporations in 1900, almost two thirds had disappeared from the top list by 1958. Between 1945 and 1958 no fewer than 13 new corporations reached the list of the top 100.

The Dangers of "Monopoly" Bigness produces power, and power can be abused. This is as true of corporations as it is of governments. Yet just as big governments need not abuse their power, neither must big corporations.

In an industry which is dominated by less than half a dozen large firms it may seem simple to reach agreements to restrict production or allocate sales territories in order to raise prices. The bid-rigging and price-fixing conspiracies of 29 electrical equipment makers which were widely publicized in the early 1960's gave big business in general a black eye, and drew attention to a situation which can readily develop to the detriment of the consumer and the economy as a whole. Politicians and union leaders, moreover, seized upon the indictments to claim that the post-war inflation was not the result of large government deficits, an easy credit policy, and large wage increases, but of "administered prices," i.e., the ability of big business to raise prices through oligopolistic restraints.

Oligopolistic Competition While the pricing policy of American business may have been economically unwise during the postwar years, there is no evidence to confirm the popular charges. The character of competition has undoubtedly changed. General Motors and Ford do not try to undersell each other, but to increase their sales by pointing to actual or imaginary advantages of their products. Most cigarettes sell for about the same price, and the "quality competition" is counting more often than not on the simple-mindedness of the buyer. A cigarette is not necessarily better because a scantily-dressed female star is shown in the advertisement. But, as we shall see in Chapter 20, an oligopolistic market structure renders price competition usually destructive, a fact which many politicians and the general public often fail to realize. Price cutting leads to price wars, which as a rule do not produce a corresponding increase in sales. In the end they are likely to eliminate the weakest industry members, thus resulting in a further concentration of economic power.

As is often pointed out, government agencies at times receive identical bids from a number of supposedly competing firms, which would seem to indicate that the terms were previously, and illegally, agreed upon by the bidding firms. Actually the sealed bids are usually identical with the listed prices which are generally known. The law requires that the terms of the contract must be published by the government upon accepting the offer, so that it becomes common knowledge if one company has made a bid below the list price. The next time, the competitors are likely to undercut the list price themselves, and a price war is on.

It is quite possible that while the government receives half a dozen identical bids, a private concern may actually receive a lower bid, and that the same firm may demand a higher price from the government (namely the list price) than from a private customer. The explanation is simple: The private customer does not have to publish the price which he accepts, and the price cutting is thus concealed and not likely to lead to a price war. In short, the whole problem of oligopolistic restraints of trade — a danger which undoubtedly exists — is far more complex than is generally assumed.

Antitrust Laws

Whatever the dangers of monopolistic restraints may be at this time, there is no doubt that the closing decades of the 19th Century witnessed many flagrant abuses of economic power to the detriment of the public and of small competitors, which led to the passage of two important antitrust laws, the Sherman Antitrust Act of 1890 and the Clayton Act of 1914. The laws prohibit collusion of competing firms in order to raise prices and restrain trade. According to Article I of the Sherman Act "every contract, combination . . . or conspiracy in restraint of trade or commerce among the several States, or with foreign nations, is illegal." All agreements among competitors regarding the raising or lowering of prices, the volume of output, changes in plant capacity, or the allocation of markets constitute a violation of the law, subject to fines of up to $50,000 and jail sentences for guilty officials of up to one year. It does not matter whether the illegal conspiracy resulted in higher or lower prices, or even indirectly benefited the public and the country; as long as the government can prove collusive action, the courts will hold the defendents guilty. If the case does not justify criminal action, the government may institute civil proceedings asking the court to issue an injunction prohibiting the practices which the government regards as illegal. In the case of criminal convictions, the companies involved can be sued for damages, which in the case of the electrical manufacturing companies convicted in 1961 ran into many millions of dollars.

The Sherman Act also prohibits the exclusion of potential competitors. According to Article II "every person who shall monopolize, or attempt to monopolize . . . any part of the trade or commerce among the several States or with foreign nations, shall be deemed guilty of a misdemeanor . . ." It was under this anti-exclusion provision of the Sherman Act that the old Standard Oil and American Tobacco trusts were broken up in 1911. Three years later, in 1914, the provisions were extended through the Clayton Act which lists various illegal practices, such as price discrimination and "tying contracts." (Movie producers, for example, forced movie theaters to take second rate pictures in order to get the big hits.) And the 1950 amendment to the Clayton Act prohibits mergers if the effect "may be substantially to lessen competition." The standards "may" and "substantially" are obviously vague and thus leave much room for court interpretations, and this, in turn, has resulted in considerable legal uncertainty. Thus it has happened repeatedly that one agency of the government, e.g., the Comptroller of the Currency or the Interstate Commerce Commission, approved of a merger while the Antitrust Division of the Department of Justice challenged it.

In 1920 the Supreme Court held that "mere size is no offense" and that the United States Steel Company did not violate the law even though it accounted for about half of the country's steel production. And in 1945, in the Aluminum Company of America decision, the Court was still reluctant to regard the mere fact that the company occupied a dominant position in the industry (it accounted for almost 90% of the output) as a justification for a forced dissolution. Since then, however, there has been a growing tendency to regard mere size as cause for suspicion. Neither the Antitrust Division of the Department of Justice nor the Federal Trade Commission (which was created in 1914 under the Clayton Act "to prevent unfair methods of competition in commerce") can eliminate all restraints of trade, especially since Congress has more or less exempted agriculture and labor unions from the antitrust provisions. Patent laws, which stimulate research and technological progress, at the same time represent a restraint of trade and tend to favor large companies which have the funds needed to carry on advanced research.

European Cartels

While America has been fortunate in controlling monopolistic abuses (in fact, some economists and many businessmen feel that in its zeal to prevent restraints of trade by business firms, government agencies may actually weaken business in general), this has not been the case in other countries. Until after World War II hundreds of legalized cartels controlled output and prices throughout Europe, and hampered economic progress. Not until the early 1950's, especially under the pressure of the Common Market authorities, did Western Europe adopt the American philosophy toward monopolistic restraints and the European cartels lose their power.

Methods of Restraining Competition

There are various ways in which competition can be and has been reduced or eliminated; most of them are now either illegal in the United States or subject to rigid controls by the authorities. It is still possible for competing firms to merge, although the Antitrust Division has prohibited many mergers in recent years if there were merely a possibility that the combination would materially affect competition. Other methods which were widely used in the United States before the antitrust laws came into effect have now been largely abandoned. It is no longer legal for the shareholders of competing companies to transfer their stock to a trustee (against issuance of voting trust certificates) thus giving the trustee effective control of the companies. Also outlawed are interlocking directorates which enabled the same persons to sit on the boards of competing companies and thus correlate their policies, or to transfer the voting stock of competing companies to a holding company.

Size and Location of Industries

Some outstanding economists and management experts have devoted a great deal of time to the dual problem of the optimum location and optimum size of a business enterprise. The location of some industries is determined by soil and climate. Saw mills are located near forests; cotton gins near the cotton fields; grain mills near grain fields; ore and oil refineries near the mines and oil fields. But in many cases, other factors enter into the picture. Tin ore is not smelted in Bolivia, but in England or Texas, because the political and labor situation in Bolivia has always been such that it would not be wise to operate a smelter there The availability of power is another important factor. Water power is cheap in Norway, making it possible for that country to produce aluminum. The coal-producing German Ruhr has an advantage in the production of steel over the iron-ore-producing Lorraine region of France, because it is cheaper to ship one ton of French iron ore down the Rhine than two tons of German coal upstream. The availability of labor is often a vital factor, and some of the southern states have tried to attract industries by advertising their ample supply of willing workers. Some products are best produced near the markets where they are sold, which is the reason for the clothing industry, especially women's fashions, being concentrated in New York and, more recently, in California. For some industries, transportation facilities to obtain the raw materials and to ship the finished product are the decisive factors. To these basic factors which determine the location of an industry have come in recent years two artificial factors: favorable tax provisions and public subsidies. Industries developed rapidly in Puerto Rico because the plants did not have to pay corporate income taxes. Distressed areas in the United States try to attract industries by offering to build and lease at a low rental the necessary plant facilities.

Optimum Size Even more complex than the problem of the optimum location of a plant is the problem of the optimum size. Production is limited by the size of the market. Small countries with a limited market cannot successfully produce automobiles, and it is doubtful whether the more than a dozen underdeveloped countries which have built steel mills since the war have in the foreseeable future a large enough domestic market for steel products to justify the heavy investment. On the other hand, large-scale production permits greater specialization of equipment, a spreading of the overhead, economics derived from purchasing in large quantities, and additional revenues resulting from the utilization of by-products. However, there are definite limits. As a plant and a firm grow, the managerial overhead increases, the top management finds it more and more difficult to attend to details, and production becomes increasingly inflexible.

There is no simple formula to determine where the disadvantages of bigness begin to outweigh the advantages.

Chapter 7

LABOR AND THE UNION MOVEMENT

THE BASIC FACTS

Labor is the most basic and, in many respects, the most important "factor of production." The development and maintenance of an effective economic system depend to a large extent upon appropriate labor supply and labor relations.

Modern unionism in the United States dates back to the post-Civil War decades, but unions did not acquire their present position of power until the 1930's. The numerous anti-union measures employed in the past have largely been outlawed, and since the 1930's government agencies and courts have tended to favor labor (just as they had previously sided with employers).

In a rapidly changing world, unions are confronted with many new problems, and experts do not agree as to what constitutes "sound" union policy. While some experts credit the influence of unions for the substantial improvement in the average standard of living, others blame the high wages and fringe benefits for the relatively high rate of unemployment, the creeping inflation and the balance of payments deficit which have plagued the country since the 1950's.

Labor relations are further complicated by the impact of

(1) automation (which has resulted in fairly heavy unemployment among semi- and unskilled workers), (2) the problem of "featherbedding," and (3) the demand of unions for "job security" measures.

The philosophy of union security, which involves the problem of compulsory unionism (closed, union, and agency shops); the special position which unions enjoy under the law; the attempt of unions to regulate production methods; and the very size and power of some unions, are leading to a gradual change of public attitude toward the union movement, which calls for added statesmanship on the part of the union leaders.

The Importance of Labor

Of the four basic factors of production — natural resources (older textbooks speak of "Land"); labor; man-made resources, such as factories and machinery ("Capital"); and technological and managerial skills — labor is the most basic and in many respects the most important. This does not mean, as Karl Marx claimed, that the total output is the product of labor, but it is probably true that no economy can develop and prosper without an adequate supply of skilled workers, effectively organized, and with a constructive attitude toward their work.

The Importance of Skills and Attitudes The mere number of workers, however, is not the only factor. (If this were the case, India would outproduce the United States.) Far more important than the mere number of workers is the general education level and the skill of the workers.

Equally important as skills and general education is the attitude of the workers. A nation cannot prosper if its laboring masses lethargically accept poverty and disease as the unavoidable fate of man in the hope that a future life will bring a better fate. On the other hand, if the ethos of a society stresses the importance of constructive and faithful labor as a form of divine duty, as was the case with the Calvinists, Puritans and Methodists in the 17th and 18th Centuries, the chances of economic progress are greatly improved.

Nor should one underestimate the problem of labor relations: the attitude of the employers and the general public toward labor, and the attitude of labor toward work and its overall responsibility toward society. Flourishing industries and great nations have been weakened through bad labor relations.

Labor Relations

The problem of labor relations is as old as organized society. It involves psychological, ethical, political and economic issues. As Adam Smith, the "Father of Modern Economics," pointed out, the relationship between management and labor — like all economic relationships — must be governed by two basic impulses: egoism and altruism. Man's desire to improve his economic status provides the dynamic force which makes for progress, while man's sense of social responsibility prevents egoism from destroying society. In the spirit of the Enlightenment Adam Smith believed that the equilibrating force between egoism and altruism is to be found in the heart and mind of man as a rational being. The 19th Century saw the balancing mechanism in the "economic laws" of supply and demand, while our own 20th Century has rejected both the ethical approach of the 18th and the mechanistic approach of the 19th Century. The 20th Century balances the centrifugal forces of individual initiative and the need for social cohesion through an appropriate institutional framework, such as labor unions, labor legislation, and government agencies to prevent the "egoism" of either employers or labor from destroying society.

The Institutional Framework

It is therefore vital for modern society to develop an institutional framework which will assure a smooth and effective functioning of labor relations; and it is extremely important for an understanding of the modern economy in action to know about the character of existing labor relations. The exploitation of labor can easily lead to a political explosion; the exploitation of the employer to economic stagnation. History is familiar with both developments.

Present-day labor relations in the United States and in most parts of the free world represent a mixture of often conflicting forces: the need of industry to operate profitably, the desire of unions for power, and the demands of workers who are interested in "bread and butter issues" — wages, job security, and working hours. Psychological elements complicate matters, such as the demand of modern labor for "co-determination," i.e., the right of labor to be treated by the employer as a partner whose wishes are to be considered, rather than as an inarticulate "factor of production." The free world, and to some extent even the Communist world, attempts to solve the issues partly in the spirit of free enterprise — "to each according to his productivity," and partly according to ideals of 19th Century socialism — "to each according to his needs," with many vital issues being decided not on an ideological basis but according to political expediency.

Unionism in the United States

While there were labor organizations of one kind or another in Europe since the 12th Century and in the United States since the 18th Century, modern unionism developed in England during the late 18th Century, and in the United States during the post-Civil War decades, more or less as a by-product of the industrial revolution. During the Middle Ages the employer had definite social and legal obligations to look after the welfare of his workers and their families. The workers in turn owed loyalty to the employer. This paternalistic relationship gradually vanished after the Renaissance as a result of the growing individualism. It was never characteristic of the typical mill town of the 18th and 19th Centuries. The relationship between employer and worker was no longer based on tradition and mutual obligations which extended even beyond the working hours. It was now based on the legal fiction of a "contract" between the employer and the "free wage earner," who hired himself out for a certain wage, but owed no further obligation to the employer. Nor was the latter obligated to worry about the welfare of the worker. The "free wage earner" was a "factor of production" similar to raw materials and machinery, and was treated accordingly in practice and in economic theory.

Psychological Aspects In reality, of course, workers are not only "factors of production," as economic theory assumes. They are also free-willing human beings, and above all a political power. This threefold nature of labor leads to conflicts. The employer looks upon labor basically as a factor to maximize production at the lowest possible cost. If machines prove cheaper than labor, he will replace workers with machines. If he acted differently he would soon be out of business. And if many employers neglected to minimize cost, the nation's economy as a whole would suffer. Workers, on the other hand, rebel against being mere "factors of production." As thinking human beings, they demand a voice concerning the conditions under which they work, and as voters they use their power to enforce their wishes. Very often the demands of workers as human beings and as voters conflict with economic rationality: the need to maximize production at the lowest possible cost. The results are labor conflicts, which may lead to a shrinking demand for labor and thus unemployment. When the labor cost in Detroit rises too rapidly, General Motors and Ford shift part of their production to foreign countries, and the American public begins to buy foreign-made cars.

Knights of Labor The first attempt to organize American labor was made by the Knights of Labor in the 1870's, who tried to combine skilled and unskilled workers, regardless of trade, into one large industrial union. The attempt failed because the United States was still a predominantly agricultural country with vast areas of free land available to those who tried to escape the pressure of factory jobs, and because the heavy influx of immigrants complicated the task of organizing the workers. Besides, the legal status of organized labor was far from clear. It was not until 1825 that English unions were no longer regarded as criminal conspiracies, and the old common law tradition against restraints of trade continued to affect American court decisions throughout the 19th Century. As late as 1908, in the famous Danbury Hatters Case, a union was held guilty of "conspiracies and contracts in restraint of trade" in violation of the Sherman Antitrust Act. Only in 1914, under the Clayton Act, were labor unions specifically exempt from the prohibition of restraints of trade.

American Federation of Labor The oldest and largest American labor organization, the American Federation of Labor (AFL), was founded in 1881 under the leadership of Samuel Gompers, who guided its destinies for many decades. The AFL constitutes a loose federation of independent craft unions. Local unions are united into city councils, state groups, and eventually national or international (with locals in Canada) unions, which combine to form the AFL. In the tradition established by Gompers that a union should be interested primarily in "bread and butter" problems, in wages and in working conditions, the AFL did not follow the pattern of European unions which took an active part in the political life of their countries. In Britain, for instance, the Trades Union Congress was the main support of the Labour Party, and on the Continent the unions were closely allied with the Socialist parties and generally opposed to the existing social and political order.

Anti-union Measures Progress was slow for organized labor in the United States, since not only the legal tradition, but above all the existing socio-political climate, were essentially hostile to unions. Industry developed a whole arsenal of weapons against union organizers. Workers known to be active in the union were fired and *blacklisted*, so that they could not get another job. As a condition of employment, workers had to sign so-called *"yellow-dog contracts,"* pledging themselves not to join a union while holding their job. Courts could be relied upon to grant *injunctions* enjoining unions from picketing and many other activities designed to make strikes more effective, and under the protection of the courts and the local police force, employers could hire *strikebreakers* when the regular workers went on strike. Slow-downs and unrest were answered by *lock-outs,* and cases of physical violence by police against workers were not infrequent.

Until well into the 20th Century, labor was clearly the underdog. At the turn of the century, a 60-hour work week was the rule. There were no paid holidays or vacations, no unemployment or old age security. By modern standards, working conditions were generally bad and often hazardous. Sanitary conditions were often poor. Wages, though higher than in Europe, were often barely adequate to sustain the usually large immigrant families crowded into the dingy slums of the great cities and industrial areas. As late as the 1930's some New York companies laid off $18-a-week employees for two or three weeks in order to avoid having to pay them for a 1–2 week vacation.

While conditions have changed radically during the past 60 and especially during the past 35 years, the mental attitude created through the poor labor relations of the pre-1930's era still affect public opinion and poison the relationship between management and labor. The public still thinks of labor as the underdog in need of protection, and labor still thinks of management as the potential exploiter. These deeply ingrained attitudes continue to complicate a sound labor-management relationship and endanger the economic development of the nation.

Changing Position of Labor

The change set in gradually. Intellectuals, shocked by the description of poor working and living conditions, came to look upon unions as a necessary protection of the working men. Moreover, as the immigrants of yesteryear were gradually replaced by the first-generation Americans who were more aware of their rights, the labor vote began to develop into a political factor which politicians had to take into consideration.

Labor under the New Deal

As the Depression spread during the 1930's, and public opinion began to hold "Business" responsible for the national disaster, the restraints upon union activities fell one after another. The Norris-La Guardia Act of 1932 drastically limited the right of courts to grant injunctions, and outlawed "yellow-dog contracts." The National Labor Relations Act of 1935 set up the

National Labor Relations Board, which was directed to compel employers to bargain in good faith with the unions which the NLRB had certified as the bargaining units to represent the workers. This Act also prohibited a number of so-called "unfair labor practices" on the part of the employer, which interfered with union activities. While for more than 60 years the power of the state and of the courts had been on the side of the employer, under the New Deal, and ever since, Washington with few exceptions, has tended to favor unions against management, a policy which would not have been possible had it not met with the approval of the majority of the American voters.

Congress of Industrial Organizations

The result was a rapid increase in union membership from 3,200,000 in 1932 to 8,980,000 in 1939. But as more and more workers were organized, a basic organizational problem arose. The AFL was a federation of craft unions: carpenters, bricklayers, plumbers, typesetters, photoengravers, etc. This made it necessary for a large industrial plant to have contracts with many unions, while there was really no room in the traditional unions for the large number of semi-skilled workers at the assembly line. Thus the conflict arose between the old craft unions and the new industry unions, which attempted to organize all workers, whatever their skills or work, as long as they were employed in a certain plant or industry. In 1936 the industrial unions, under the leadership of John L. Lewis of the United Mineworkers, broke away from the AFL and combined into the Congress of Industrial Organizations (CIO). While the AFL was inclined to be conservative and non-political, the CIO was "progressive," and stressed political and ideological activities. In 1955 the AFL and CIO reunited, even though their different characteristics continue to make themselves felt. This leaves only the Railroad Brotherhoods, the United Mineworkers, and the militant and controversial Teamsters Union as the major units of organized labor outside the fold of the main organization.

Size of Union Movement There are some 200 autonomous unions in the United States, with about 78,000 locals and more than 18 million members. The unions reached the peak of their power in the middle of 1950's, when about 33% of the non-agricultural workers were union members. Since then the labor force has increased steadily, but the number of union members has increased far more slowly, so that by the middle 1960's union membership accounted for only about 30% of the non-agricultural labor force.

This development is due in part to a structural change in the labor market. As automation progresses, fewer workers are needed at the assembly lines, and more in clerical and administrative jobs as well as in service industries. In the auto industry, for instance, the number of hourly workers dropped between 1948 and 1962 from 82.9% of the total number of employees to 70%. And American unions have had little success thus far in organizing white-collar workers. Ten unions account for about half the total union membership, namely, the Teamsters, Steelworkers, Autoworkers, Carpenters, Machinists, Mineworkers, the International Brotherhood of Electrical Workers, Ladies Garment Workers, Hod Carriers and Hotel Workers. Thirty-three other unions had more than 100,000 members in 1960. About half the total union membership is concentrated in five states: New York, Pennsylvania, California, Illinois and Ohio.

The Major Issues of Modern Unionism

In speaking of modern unionism in the United States, the distinction is often made between issues which affect primarily the welfare of the workers (either workers in general or union members) and those which concern primarily the unions as socio-economic institutions and the union hierarchy. In the popular mind there is a tendency to equate union strength with the immediate or at least long-range welfare of the workers. The thesis is hard to prove. The social and economic position of labor improved slowly but steadily during the 19th Century and the first three decades of the 20th Century, even though unions had little power. There was no immediate improvement in the economic position of labor when the unions were given large powers during the 1930's. Some economists believe that the rapid progress of American labor since the 1940's has been more the result of the war and the postwar inflation than the growing power of the union movement (although the latter undoubtedly played an important role). During the postwar decade, when American workers made their greatest economic gains, union power had actually been somewhat curtailed through the Taft-Hartley and Landrum-Griffin Acts. In short, it seems wise to distinguish between the welfare of (1) the nation, (2) the unions and their leadership, (3) the union members and (4) American labor in general, since the interests of the four parties may not always be identical.

Principal Demands of Workers

Whether union members or not, workers are interested primarily in five major objectives: high wages; shorter working hours, including vacations; good working conditions (safety provisions, healthy and pleasant surroundings, no unreasonably exhausting speed-ups, etc.); job security; and "fringe benefits" (pensions, supplementary unemployment insurance, free health care, etc.). Most of these goals add to the cost of production, and hence must be offset by higher productivity, rising prices or lower profits, and may thus lead in the long run to inflation or a decline in job opportunities as industry replaces highly-paid workers by machines.

Some of the labor objectives, of course, are not only in the interest of labor, but of management as well, and should be pursued whether there are unions or not. Poor safety provisions, exhausting work, generally undesirable working conditions, lack of proper health care on the job, bad personal relationships between supervisors and workers, and fear of the workers for their jobs reduce efficiency and make for sabotage.

Far more difficult to solve are the issues which involve an increase in the overall cost of production: wages, production schedules, working hours and fringe benefits. Here the interest of unions and union leaders, workers, employers and the economy at large may come into direct conflict. Workers pay union dues to "get results," i.e., more benefits for shorter hours, and the power, if not the very existence, of unions depends upon their ability to deliver the goods. But the ability of the employer to pay has definite limits. No employer will pay a worker for more than he produces for any length of time.

Conflicting Wage Theories

As we shall see in more detail in Chapter 23, different economists hold different wage theories. "Inadequate" wages, as modern economists emphasize, will result in inadequate demand and thus unemployment. This is the old Marxian argument, presented in a new and more scholarly form by John Maynard Keynes. On the other hand, "above equilibrium" wages (wages which are higher than the value of the goods which the worker produces) will result in either higher prices (and thus a decline in domestic demand and in exports) or in lower profits (which will reduce investments). Either result will reduce job opportunities. The determination of the wage level is thus one of the key problems in an economy, whether it is left to the natural and unimpeded forces of supply and demand, or whether an attempt is made to achieve the proper level through government intervention. Unfortunately, there is no way of determining whether a certain wage rate is "inadequate" or "above equilibrium." It is not possible, in practice, to say that an hourly wage of $3.30 will promote jobs, while a $3.60 rate will make for inflation or rising unemployment.

"Guideline" Theory An economist can say that "in theory" wages can be increased by 3%, without the need of raising prices, if productivity increases by 3%. But it can be dangerous to generalize this self-evident theoretical truth, as President Kennedy's and President Johnson's economic advisors did in promoting the so-called "guidelines" for wage increases.

Over a long span of years the man-hour productivity in the American economy has increased by about 3.2%. (Other government estimates placed the increase at 3% or even 2.8%, an indication of how difficult it is to arrive at such highly abstract averages.) Wage increases which did not exceed 3.2%, according to the "guideline" reasoning, would thus not be inflationary. The opponents of the scheme argued that it confused abstract theory and hard, everyday reality. While the productivity of farm workers has increased much faster than 3.2% a year since the end of the war, it has increased by no more than 1–2% in service industries, and even less among professionals. Wage increases based on "productivity" would thus mean small increases for school teachers, and very large increases for workers who tend the new automated machines. If wages and salaries were increased uniformly by 3% or some other fixed percentage, there would be every reason to expect the prices in service industries and for professional services (including medical care and education) to increase steadily (as they did since the end of World War II). To offset these increases, the prices in automated industries (where productivity increased faster than the national average) were expected to decline according to the "guideline" theory, so that the cost of living in general remained more or less stable. The critics of the theory argued from the outset that the scheme was based on wishful thinking, and the union leaders in automated industries would never be satisfied with "average" wage increases, if the productivity in their particular industries grew faster than the national average. And within a few years the critics were proved correct, and the scheme was abandoned in 1967. To achieve wage and price stability under conditions of near-full employment probably requires government controls, as the original advocates of a full employment policy recognized as early as the 1940's.

Stable Wages and Declining Prices From a purely economic point of view, it would probably have been much wiser in the 1950's and 1960's to pursue a policy of keeping wages more or less stable, while applying the gains achieved through increased productivity toward a gradual lowering of prices. This would have benefited the consumer at large, and enhanced the country's ability to compete in world markets. Such a policy of lowering prices as declining production cost permitted was characteristic of many American industries prior to the 1940's. In less than two decades, for instance, a sharp reduction in prices turned the automobile from a luxury of the few into a popular conveyance of the many.

During the past 25 years, however, conditions have changed. There has been a substantial increase in union power and a tremendous growth in public and private indebtedness. Union leaders are paid to get the most for their members rather than to accept a policy of wage stability. And only too many Americans whose debts have grown tremendously since the end of World War II (the mortgage debt on 1–4 family homes alone rose from $18 billion to $213 billion between 1945 and 1965) have come to expect annual wage increases in order to make it easier for them to pay their debts.

A government which depends heavily on union support and which appeals to the debtor class thus can ill afford to advocate a policy of wage stability and declining prices. Instead it has to find a logical justification for steadily rising wages without incurring the wrath of the consumers who would suffer from rising prices. The "guideline" scheme provided a seemingly plausible and in the short run politically expedient scheme for labor to get a steadily rising income without the general public paying for it in the form of higher prices. The scheme failed as prices began to rise and American industry found it increasingly difficult to compete in world markets.

Many union leaders were opposed to the scheme from the outset because they feared that "voluntary guidelines" would eventually harden into wage controls. And union leaders may also ponder another aspect of the scheme. If wages and fringe benefits were increased automatically every year at the same rate as the overall productivity of the nation increases, there would be little need for unions to negotiate wage increases, since they could ask no more nor less than the national average. All that would be needed would be for the Washington experts to calculate the increase in productivity during the preceding 12 months, and then all wages and salaries would automatically rise correspondingly. This would favor workers in occupations where the productivity had increased little. But how could the unions in highly mechanized industries, where productivity increased more than the national average, explain to their members that they would get less than they had "earned"? In short, the "guideline" approach involves profound dangers for the economy as a whole as well as for the unions. There just is no easy mechanical answer to the unions' and the nation's problem of finding a socially just and economically sound wage policy.

Unions in a Changing World

Since the 1930's, when the New Deal emancipated the unions from the traditional legal restraints and built the basis for their present power, the world has changed a great deal. Average yearly wages in manufacturing industries, not counting fringe benefits, rose from less than $900 in 1932 to about $5,500 in 1966. Even allowing for the fact that the 1966 dollar bought only about as much as 40¢ did in 1932, the real income of the American worker rose by almost 150% in 34 years. An ever-increasing number of workers have become part of the great suburban middle class, far removed from the slums of 50 or even 30 years ago. The position of the unions has also changed. In 1930 the AFL still struggled against heavy legal and political odds. Today the unions have accumulated financial reserves running into hundreds of millions, many union leaders are as highly paid as business executives, and their large and often luxurious offices in Washington testify to the fact that the unions have become one of the most powerful, if not *the* most powerful, political pressure groups in Washington.

Automation and "Featherbedding"

The new technological revolution, known as "automation," makes it possible for industry to dispense with large numbers of semi- and unskilled workers. Labor leaders have reacted differently to the problem of automation. John L. Lewis, of the United Mine Workers, favored mechanization provided the increase in productivity was used in part to provide the workers with higher and higher wages and benefits. Walter Reuther, of the United Automobile Workers, likewise favored technological progress which leads to greater productivity. Like Lewis, he also demanded that the higher productivity must result in greater benefits to the workers, but, somewhat illogically,

Reuther insisted in addition that automation should not result in a decline in job opportunities.

"Featherbedding" and the Railroads The basic conflict between technological progress and job security is not new. The problem has existed for centuries, but it promises to become particularly acute in the years to come because of the heavy influx of new workers into the labor market and the large number of workers which can be replaced through automation. The conflict reached a dramatic peak in 1963 in the great battle between the railroads and the railway brotherhoods concerning the problem of "featherbedding," the insistence of unions to preserve jobs which were no longer needed. The railroads, many of them in financial difficulties, claimed that under existing work rules they had to pay almost $600 million annually for "work" which was not needed, or was actually not even performed, and a government commission which had investigated the problem recommended that 60,000 "superfluous" jobs be eliminated.

There is a growing tendency in the labor movement to demand that labor should have a decisive voice in the change of production methods. While this does not mean that labor will necessarily oppose technological innovations, it may permit changes only under conditions which may prove too burdensome for industry. Technological progress, vital to the future growth of the American economy, would thus be determined in part by the policies adopted by union leaders.

Spreading the Work One "solution" to the problem of automation suggested by some union leaders is a reduction of the work week, without a corresponding reduction in the weekly take-home pay. Such a policy would result, of course, in a corresponding increase in hourly wages and total employment cost.

While the legal work week established by Congress under the Fair Labor Standards Act is 40 hours, the United Rubber Workers have a 36-hour week and some of the New York building trade workers an even shorter week. All time worked beyond the agreed-upon basic work week is paid for at the higher overtime rate fixed by Congress.

In 1957 President Lyndon B. Johnson, who at that time was a member of the Senate, pleaded for a lengthening of the 40-hour week to meet the Russian threat — "either we tighten the belt around our waist or the Communists will tighten the noose around our throat." Labor leaders, however, continue to promote a shorter work week. AFL-CIO President George Meany called for a 30-hour week, and former United Steel Workers President David McDonald wanted Congress to amend the Fair Labor Standard Act in order to establish a 32-hour work week.

If the work week were reduced and the total weekly take-home pay were not reduced, the effect would be a sharp increase in production cost and prices, and the nation's ability to compete in world markets would be further impaired. Nor is it at all certain that a 10% reduction in the work week would result in a 10% increase in the number employed. Even on the basis of a 40-hour week, more than 3½ million workers in 1966 held two jobs and worked on an average more than 12 additional hours. During the boom of the mid-sixties about 8% of industrial production was turned out with the help of overtime.

Union Security

To retain their power in the face of increasing automation and declining factory employment, the unions have striven for "union security" and have attempted to organize the growing number of white-collar workers.

American white-collar workers, and especially public employees, have been slow in joining labor unions. This is not so in other countries. In West Germany about 40% of the industrial workers, 25% of the office employees and 75% of the civil servants are organized into unions, despite the fact that West Germany's "Basic Law" (which takes the place of a constitution) specifically prohibits compulsory unionism as a violation of the principle of the freedom of association.

Compulsory Unionism Under the American system workers can be forced to join unions. There are various ways in which "union security" can be achieved in order to give the union as far as possible a monopoly over the supply of labor. Not wages and working conditions, but "union security," is often regarded as "the primary aim of any union."

Closed Shop The most effective way is a closed shop, under which the employer may hire only members of a given union, and the union has the right to determine who should become or remain a member. If a closed shop covers an entire industry, the union has complete power to determine whether and under what conditions any American citizen may work in this particular industry. Loss of union membership means permanent loss of a chance of employment in the closed shop industry. The Wagner Act of 1935 legalized the closed shop; the Taft-Hartley Act of 1947 specifically prohibited it.

Union Shop Almost as effective as the closed shop is the union shop, which quickly replaced the former after it was outlawed. By 1965 almost three fourths of the workers covered by collective bargaining agreements were subject to union shop provisions. An employer must negotiate with a union which has been certified to represent the workers, even though, let us say, only 55% of the workers have actually voted for the union. Under the Taft-Hartley Act an employer may (but need not) conclude a contract with the union which requires all workers (including the 45% who voted against the union) to join the union or be discharged from their job. The union shop is legal under Federal law, but as of 1965, had been banned by 19 states under so-called "right-to-work" laws, which the unions have been pressing Congress to outlaw.

Agency Shop Still another form of union security is the agency shop, which is banned in 18 states but permitted in Indiana (although that state bars the union shop). Under an agency shop a worker must not actually join the union, but in order to retain his job he must make regular payments to the union equal to the regular union dues. Union dues, and union contributions under an agency agreement, are usually deducted by the employer from the worker's pay and then transferred to the union. This "check-off" system makes it unnecessary for unions to prod reluctant members for their dues.

Changes in Public Attitudes

In addition to the economic changes which pose difficult problems, the American unions are faced with a possible change in the public attitude. Power produces abuses and public criticism, and the unions have had a great deal of power during the past 30 years.

While the majority of the American voters back the unions in principle, a reaction has set in, and the future of American unionism will depend to a large extent upon the ability of the union leadership to act as statesmen rather than union leaders, with the general welfare in mind. If the unions do not succeed in adjusting to their new roles, the government may eventually step in to regulate labor relations "in the interest of society."

Chapter 8

THE CONSUMER

THE BASIC FACTS

The character of an economy is strongly influenced by the volume and nature of consumer spending. The attitude toward consumer spending in the United States has undergone important changes in recent decades, from the 19th Century stress on "private consumption" (based on the notion of "consumer sovereignty") to the modern emphasis on "social consumption" (based on socio-economic planning).

The changing character of the American family has affected the nature and volume of consumption and of the relationship of private versus public consumption.

Consumer spending is determined by (1) the total disposable income of the entire population, (2) the distribution of income, (3) the inclination of the individual to consume or to save and (4) the rate of consumer borrowing. The postwar boom was made possible to a large extent by a 13-fold increase in consumer indebtedness.

During the past decades the government has been playing an increasingly important role in the life of the American consumer. A large number of regulatory agencies have been created to protect the public against malpractices, and since the 1930's efforts have been made to assure the individual of a minimum of income in case of unemployment, old age or the death of the breadwinner.

Whether the "poverty" which still exists in the United States (the most affluent society of all times) can best be banned through private initiative or government intervention involves important decisions which will have a far-reaching effect on the character of the American economy.

The American Consumer

The American "consumer," 200 million men, women and children, consumes about 65% of the goods and services produced by the economy. Government spending and private capital investments account for most of the balance. The purchases of the consumer determine to a large extent the character of an economy and the level of production and employment. Besides, through his power at the polls the consumer influences government economic policy.

Changes in Consumer Demand Changes in consumer spending can spell prosperity for one industry and difficulties for another. During the 1950's, for instance, consumer income rose sharply, and the demand for pleasure boats even more so. Yet at the same time there was a decline in the demand for liquor, which in the past had fluctuated fairly closely with the general level of prosperity.

Economic Aspects

As economists, we are concerned with a variety of factors which influence consumer demand, and thus in turn production, employment and profits: (1) the total amount of consumer income; (2) the distribution of income among the individual consumers; (3) the tendency of the consumer to spend more or less than his income (he can either save part of it, or use part of it to repay old debts. In either case, his consumption will be less than his income. Or he can go into debt in order to be able to buy more than his current income permits.); (4) the distribution of consumer spending among food, clothing, shelter, education, recreation, medical care, old age security, travel, etc.; (5) the methods employed by industry to stimulate consumer spending through advertising, planned obsolescence, and other means; (6) the attempt of the consumers to protect their interests by forming consumers' associations; and (7) the role of the government in shaping the consumption pattern of a nation. All these aspects are usually discussed under the heading "Consumer Economics." In this chapter we can consider only a few of them.

The New Role of the Consumer

Before discussing these traditional topics, we must mention the changes which are taking place from time to time in socio-economic theory regarding the role of the consumer. Back in the 17th and 18th Centuries during the Age of Absolutism and Mercantilism, consumer spending was controlled by the government and subordinated to the overall goal of strengthening the state.

It was against this statist philosophy of Mercantilism that the writers of the late 18th Century, including many leaders of the American Revolution, revolted. As Adam Smith put it: "Consumption is the sole end and purpose of all production; and the interest of the producer ought to be attended to only so far as it may be necessary for promoting that of the consumer . . ."[1]

[1] Adam Smith, *The Wealth of Nations*. New York: The Modern Library, (Random House Inc.) 1937, p. 625.

"Consumer Sovereignity" As the liberals of the 18th and 19th Centuries saw it: (1) The welfare of society is increased by increasing the welfare of the individual; (2) each individual, as a rational being, knows best what will add to his pleasures and welfare; (3) production should thus be geared toward meeting the ever-expanding demands of the individual; and (4) economic theory should be directed toward discovering the forces which will maximize the satisfaction of the individual. Traditional economic theory was based on the principle of "consumer sovereignty." The consumer was the key figure in determining production.

New Philosophy of Consumption

During the past 40 years, however, the social philosophy of the western world has undergone a profound change. The emphasis has shifted from the individual to society, and the assumption of the 19th Century liberalism that the welfare of society is equal to the sum total of the welfare of the individual citizens is being rejected by modern social philosophers. Society is assumed to exist in its own right, independent of and superior to the rights of the individuals who compose it. This new socio-political philosophy, or rather this reversion to the philosophy of the 17th and 18th Centuries, is reflected in a new theory of consumption of which the best-known (but by no means only) exponent is Professor John K. Galbraith, the author of the best-seller *The Affluent Society*. We have reached a stage of economic development, Galbraith argues, where all reasonable needs of the individual consumer have been met, or can be met, on the basis of our productive capacity. Production is no longer primarily designed to satisfy existing and obvious wants. In other words, we do not produce to satisfy the rational wants of the consumer (these have been largely filled). We produce, or should produce, to maintain full employment. And in order to get rid of the ever-widening stream of new goods which our economy, operating at full employment levels, produces, we have to create constantly new wants.

To break this seemingly stupid cycle, Professor Galbraith argues that our economy should produce more goods for social consumption, rather than create new wants in order to be able to produce more goods for private consumption.

The Family Structure

The most important of the social institutions which affect the pattern of consumption is the family. A change in the family structure has far-reaching effects on the patterns of consumption. In the United States a number of such important changes have occurred during the past 50–75 years: (1) Families have become smaller because there are fewer children; (2) the three-generation family (grandparents, parents, children) has become increasingly rare; (3) a substantial percentage of wives and mothers hold outside jobs; and (4) family life has been "externalized" — more and more people, especially young people and even children, seek their entertainment outside the home.

The Impact of Urbanization The shift from the reasonably spacious farm house, where grandfather and grandmother could help with many tasks, to the modern city apartments or the tight little suburban homes, leaves no room for the grandparents. They are being segregated into what Margaret Mead has called the "ghettos for the old." The wisdom, conservatism and time perspective of the older generation is thus often missing in the modern American family. This in turn tends to increase the restlessness and rapid changes in our mode of life. Households in which "the older generation" has an important voice are less likely, for instance, to trade furniture, household appliances, and even homes for "more modern" ones than would households in which the young husband and wife do not have a lifetime's attachment to their surroundings.

Loosening of Family Ties Thirty-five years ago a young man, at least if he belonged to a middle-class family, was expected to have a job enabling him to support a family before he married. Today young people marry on the expectation that either husband or wife will somehow find a job, or the families or the state will help them. Marriages are entered into more lightly — and terminated more freely. Modern society has created the isolated individual, freed from the bonds and deprived of the protection of the family and kinship group.

Social Security Where once the family looked after its sick, aged and unemployed, the task has now fallen more and more to society. Personal relationships have been institutionalized. Money which the family was formerly free to spend as it saw fit is now taken by the state in the form of taxes to provide certain services for the individual. The result is the shift of purchasing power from the consumer, both as an individual and as a family, to the state. While the free world rejects the Communist philosophy that the state should forcibly take over many functions of the family, we must realize that we are moving in the same direction, even though we travel along a different road.

Effect of Birth Rate on the Economy

The wide fluctuations in the birth rate affect the demand for many consumer goods, especially educational facilities. The population of Chicago increased by about 33% between 1920 and 1947; the number of school children, however, actually declined by 65,000 because of the low birth rate in the 1930's and 1940's. Five years later, as the "baby boom" generation of the postwar years began to reach school age, educational facilities proved inadequate, and a widespread demand for federal aid to education arose, the need for teachers became acute, and (following the law of supply and demand) teachers' salaries increased by 164% between 1946 and 1962. As the "baby boom" children of the late 1940's and 1950's entered the labor market, new problems arose, and again the Federal Government was called upon to provide the necessary training and jobs for the millions of young people.

Working Wives In the 19th Century a married woman with paid employment was a rare exception. By 1900, 6% of the married women had jobs; by 1940, 15%; by 1950, 25% and by 1960, 30%. In 1940, 5 million women held paid jobs; in 1960, 22 million. The effects are economic and social. A job held by a married woman may mean unemployment for a man who is the only breadwinner of his family. On the other hand, with two wage-earners in the family (and the husband often holding two jobs) the over-all spending power of the family is much greater. The rapid increase in consumer spending during the postwar years was due at least in part to the fact that more and more wives contributed to the family income.

Consumer Spending

Even though the economist does not deny that economic developments must be understood in the light of social change, he prefers to leave such aspects as the family structure, divorce, the changing birth rate, crime and illegitimacy to the sociologist. On the other hand the economist is very much interested in the factors which determine the income of the average consumer and his ability and willingness to consume. Consumption is determined by four major factors: (1) the total disposable income of all the people after payment of taxes; (2) the distribution of income; (3) the percentage of the income which is actually spent, (with the balance being saved); and (4) the volume of consumer borrowing.

Disposable Income Disposable Personal Income (the total income of individuals after payment of taxes) in the United States rose from $158.9 billion in 1946 to $508.8 billion in 1966. But this does not mean that the purchasing power of the average American increased by more than 200% in 21 years. The population increased from 141 million to about 198 million and consumer prices rose by about 80%. The actual increase in consumer purchasing power during the 20 postwar boom years was thus about 40%.

Distribution of Income Possibly even more important than changes in the total consumer income is the distribution of income. If 20% of the nation's families received 80% of the disposable income, while 80% of the people had to live on the remaining 20%, the rich would probably save a substantial portion of their income, and total consumption would be small. If, on the other hand, income were distributed more equally, the rich would have less income to save, while the rest of the people would use the bulk of their additional income to increase their consumption. It is a generally accepted economic rule that a wide disparity in income will result in large savings, and if these savings are invested wisely the economy will grow rapidly. A more even distribution of income, on the other hand, will tend to increase consumption and reduce savings and thus the rate of economic growth. The political ideal of a modern democracy — greater equality of income — may thus be in conflict with the economic necessity of increasing the rate of savings in order to speed the nation's economic development.

Consumption, Saving and Growth While the wider distribution of income has helped to boost consumption, has probably lowered social tension, and has proven politically expedient, the policy may have contributed also to the slower rate of economic growth, and thus to the relatively high rate of unemployment. All we know is that some countries, for instance Germany, pursued a different policy. Once the German currency was stabilized in 1948, wages (the income of the lower income brackets) were held down to stimulate profits (the income of the higher income groups). Instead of the German workers receiving higher wages, most of which would have been spent on consumer goods, a larger share of the income went to the stockholders, who converted a large portion of their income into factories and machinery which produced more goods and more jobs. Not until the late 1950's did Germany begin to work toward a more even distribution of income.

Poverty in the U.S.

Even though American policy has been directed toward greater equality during the past 30 years, and the average income in current dollars per "consumer unit" (47 million families and 9½ million unattached individuals) rose from $3,031 in 1949 to $6,569 in 1964,[2] the "poor" remain with us, although there is no agreed-upon definition as to what constitutes "poverty."

When President Johnson started his "War on Poverty" in 1964, the government classified 9.3 million families (with 20–25 million voters) as living in poverty, because their annual income was $3000 or less. The Twentieth Century Fund, a private research organization, figured that one in 10 American

[2] "Median money income of families in current dollars," see *Statistical Abstract of the United States, 1966*. Washington: U.S. Department of Commerce, 1966.

families lives in "abject poverty" on an income of $2,500 or less. Interpreting the same statistics in a somewhat different fashion, the Department of Commerce figured that one in seven families lived in poverty. In short, "poverty" is a relative concept, subject to widely differing interpretations.

The 1962 Conference on Economic Progress held that 70 million Americans were "poor and deprived." Statements of this type, as a rule, have more propagandistic than economic significance, but there is no doubt that while the standard of living of the American middle-class has risen rapidly since the war, there remain pockets of poverty, especially among marginal farmers, the aged and the functionally illiterate of our city slums, in other words among the groups which lack productive capacity. The solution lies either in continued public aid for these groups, which will tend to lower the average standard of living of the American people and probably retard economic growth, or in raising the economic productivity of the marginal producers by training or retraining the unemployed.

Rate of Saving

The third important factor which affects consumer spending is the rate of saving. In 1945, under the impact of the war, American consumers saved 19.1% of their income; by 1950, the figure had dropped to 6.1% and by 1966 to below 5%. In other words, the average American consumer spent in 1965 more than 95 cents out of every dollar he received, compared with 81 cents at the end of the war. Even a small change in the rate of savings can have an important effect on the economy. A 1% increase in consumer spending is equal to the purchase price of more than a million cars. This does not mean that increased saving must necessarily mean a decline in total spending. It is possible (and in underdeveloped countries very likely) that the increase in savings will lead to increased capital investments. As the consumer buys fewer shoes and suits and saves the difference, the entrepreneur can borrow more money to build an addition to his plant, thus providing more jobs and more goods. Increased savings become troublesome only if there are not enough investment outlets, or if the businessmen do not wish to borrow the increased savings in order to enlarge their plants because part of their present plants stand idle.

The rate of savings is determined not only by economic factors (the income of the consumer) but above all by psychological ones. If people worry about the possibility of a depression and widespread unemployment, they will spend less and save more, and this very action will tend to slow down the economy. If, on the other hand, the people are afraid of rising prices, they will increase their purchases and in doing so push up the prices further. There is some truth in the saying that people can "think" themselves into a depression and into an inflationary boom.

The rate of spending and saving is also influenced by institutional factors. If a worker knows that in case of unemployment he can count on unemployment insurance from the state and supplementary unemployment insurance from his company, he will be less concerned about setting aside savings for a rainy day. Private saving is, in effect, replaced by forced saving through the government. Instead of the individual worker setting aside a certain percentage of his income each month as a reserve for unemployment and old age, the state taxes the worker and in return pays him unemployment and old age benefits.

Rate of Consumer Borrowing

Not only the rate of saving, but also the rate of borrowing affects total consumer spending. The postwar boom was financed to a substantial degree by a rapid increase in the consumer debt. The rapid increase in consumer credit — between 1939 and 1965 — was due mainly to two factors: the changing American mores, and the rapid development of durable consumer goods (cars, TV sets, washing machines, air conditioners, etc.). Only 40 years ago public opinion still frowned on people who "lived beyond their means" by going into debt. Today consumer credit is regarded as a legitimate way of financing a high standard of living.

In 1965 the amount of "automobile paper" outstanding was equal to the purchase price of more than 7 million cars, or close to a year's production. Many of these cars would not have been sold, and hence would not have been produced, if it had not been for the tremendous expansion of consumer credit. The same applies to a good many other durable consumer goods, and a large part of the mushrooming suburban housing developments. In fact the great postwar boom was at least in part the result of the tremendous increase in consumer, corporate, state and local indebtedness. And with the consumer debts rising faster than consumer income, economists wonder what will happen to production and employment if the additional stimulus of increased consumer demand (based on steadily expanding credit) eventually reaches the limit where the average consumer cannot continue to mortgage future earnings.

While an increase in the supply of credit adds to the amount of goods and services which can be sold, it also leads as a rule to price increases and hence to losses for the millions of people whose savings consist of savings bonds, savings accounts, life insurance policies and old age annuities.

Public versus Private Consumption

While the volume of consumer spending is determined by the size of the individuals' income (after taxes) plus the amount of available credit, the *pattern* of consumer spending is subject to a multitude of social, technological, cultural and economic factors. One of the major issues of our time is the question whether the individual can be trusted to spend his income wisely, or whether a growing share of the individual's income should be taxed away to be spent by the government for the benefit of society as a whole. Many books like Professor Galbraith's *The Affluent Society* have been written in recent years pillorying the "irrationality" of the consumer. Americans spend more on tobacco, liquor and cosmetics than on education; more on chromium-laden cars than on public parks and operas. There is just enough truth in these arguments to convince many people. The same man who buys a gadget-laden car on credit expects society to look after the education of his children. Much of the consumer spending is obviously unwise (and similar complaints were voiced 200, and 2,000, years ago). The question is only: Unwise according to whose standards? Why should Professor Galbraith know better than Bill Jones what gives Jones the greatest pleasure? Keynes implied that the government knew better how to regulate capital investments than private businessmen. Galbraith claims that the government knows better than the consumer how the latter should spend his income.

Government Intervention

Government intervention on behalf of the consumer falls into two catagories: (1) The state takes action to protect the general public against fraud, inferior merchandise and malpractices in general and (2) the state takes positive action to help those in need. The "regulatory state" dates back to the 19th Century; the "welfare state" (so far as the United States is concerned) is largely a product of the past 35 years.

Government Regulatory Agencies

It is impossible to discuss or even to mention the thousands of government regulatory agencies designed to protect the public. The Interstate Commerce Commission regulates the railroads to prevent monopolistic restraints and to provide the public with adequate service. But the ICC is also responsible for the rate structure which prevents the railroads from lowering their tariff (which would help the consumer), because this would interfere with the profits of the trucking companies. Nor are the railroads allowed to replace trains which are no longer needed with cheaper bus services, because this would reduce the taxes which the local governments collect.

The Securities and Exchange Commission regulates the trading and selling of securities and the operation of the stock exchanges. The Federal Communications Commission has the power of life and death over all TV and radio stations whose programs it polices and whose licenses it can revoke. The Food and Drug Administration supervises the food sold to the public, and has to approve all new drugs before they can be marketed. The Federal Trade Commission is primarily concerned with preventing illegal restraints of trade. Yet, under the Robinson-Patman Act, the same Commission combats "unfair competition" by preventing retailers from selling trade-marked goods below the prices stipulated by the manufacturer, which is obviously a restraint of trade to the detriment of the consumer. (The law was adopted by Congress to protect small retailers against the powerful competition of chain and especially cut-rate stores.)

While the basic idea of regulatory agencies, namely the protection of the public, is obviously sound, there is a very real danger that a mushrooming bureaucracy, responsible in effect only unto itself, may in due course do more harm than good to the consumer, and to the nation's economy as a whole.

Welfare Measures

The regulatory activities of the government differ basically from the welfare activities. The former are intended to restrain malpractices, the latter to promote welfare. The difference implies a different philosophy of government. As far back as the 1870's, Bismarck's Germany began to adopt welfare measures by assuming the responsibility of protecting the public, and especially the rapidly growing masses of industrial workers, against the hazards of modern life. It was originally an attempt to combat the growth of socialism through a form of governmental paternalism. Under Bismarck, health, accident and old age security protection was provided by the government, to which unemployment insurance was added after World War I. In England the first old-age security system was started in 1908.

Workmen's Compensation

In the United States, workmen's compensation, designed to protect workers in case of accident on the job and against occupational diseases, began slowly before World War I. Federal workers on hazardous jobs were covered in 1908; by 1911, 10 states had adopted workmen's compensation laws; by 1920, 42; and in 1948 the last state, Mississippi, fell in line. The methods of insurance differ from state to state, but the effect — the protection of the worker — is fairly uniform. At the same time American industry has achieved a remarkable degree of plant safety, and has found that the money spent on accident prevention pays not only in humanitarian terms but in cold cash, by raising workers' morale and avoiding costly delays. Prior to the adoption of the workmen's compensation principle an injured workman had no automatic claim against his employer. He had to bring legal action, and the employer could resort to a variety of common law arguments to answer the worker's claim. Today the costs of workmen's compensation insurance and of an injury suffered by the worker on the job are regarded as part of the cost of production. Every year, some 2 million claims of this type are settled, usually without legal arguments.

Social Security Act

In 1935 Congress adopted the Social Security Act, providing for unemployment insurance and old age security, the latter on a very limited basis. Since then the law has been frequently amended, the coverage has been extended, and the benefits have been raised. The unemployment insurance system is not an "insurance" in the ordinary sense of the word, that premiums are collected on basis of the calculated risk, because the rate and duration of unemployment are unpredictable on an actuarial basis. The system is operated by the individual states, and the benefits differ widely from one state to the next, somewhat in line with the wage differentials in the various regions of the country. In 1964, for instance, average weekly payments amounted to $24.16 in Maine and $43.68 in California. The waiting periods and the duration of payments likewise vary from state to state. As the cost of living and the nation's prosperity increased, unemployment payments were raised. They averaged $10.88 in 1940 and $20.78 in 1950, and reached $35.96 in 1964.

Supplementary Unemployment Insurance

In addition to the state unemployment insurance, the workers in some industries receive supplementary unemployment insurance payments financed out of a fund set up by the employers. The auto workers, for instance, receive additional payments (up to $40 a week) until their total unemployment compensation equals 62% of their regular pay.

The logic behind the unemployment payments is twofold: They help to minimize personal hardships, and they tend to stabilize consumer purchasing power, thus reducing the danger of the unemployment in one sector spreading throughout the economy. However, as the experience of the early 1960's, for instance in Michigan, has shown, the present unemployment insurance provides no adequate protection against prolonged unemployment, and heavy relief expenditures, which may become necessary when unemployment protection has run out, can endanger the solvency of the state.

OASDI

The Old Age Survivor and Disability Insurance (OASDI) is financed through a payroll tax levied on employers and employees in covered industries. The tax rate started with 2% in 1936, reached 8¼% in 1966, and will increase to 11.3% in 1987. Half the tax is deducted from the workers' wages and salaries (thus reducing the take-home pay); the other half is paid directly by the employer (thus increasing the wage cost). Since 1951 self-employed persons in most occupations are likewise subject to Social Security taxes.

Private Pension Plans

Since the end of World War II private pension plans have grown far more rapidly than the three Federal systems. Between 1950 and 1960 the assets of private pension plans covering 22 million beneficiaries grew from $12 to $50 billion, while the total assets of the three Federal systems covering 76 million people amounted to only $37 billion in 1960.[3]

[3] To these should be added on the one hand state and local governmental pension funds which increased from $5 to $19 billion during the

No Vested Rights Since the contributors to OASDI have no vested right in the system they have no legal claim to benefits. As OASDI officials point out, Congress did not set up a retirement system, but merely attempted to provide partial protection against loss of income due to retirement. If a beneficiary continues to work and earns more than $140 a month (the figure was raised from the original $100 in January 1968) he loses part of his benefits for that month. Yet there are men and women whose skills are badly needed and who are penalized for continuing to work after they reach 65 by being deprived of their old age security payments.

Medical Care

About 60 countries, including all major industrialized nations of the world, have some form of government-sponsored health and accident insurance. Some of them date back well over half a century. Some function well, others less so. Until the Medicare bill was passed in 1966, the United States was the only major country which provided no public health insurance, and even Medicare is limited to the aged and the needy. About 75% of the American people rely on various types of private medical and hospital insurance schemes. In most instances, however, the coverage is inadequate in the case of a prolonged and serious illness. Older people, above 60, in the past have had difficulties in obtaining adequate coverage, and the rates for older people rise steeply so that adequate protection is beyond the reach of those who depend on old age security. The policies of individual companies vary widely. Many of them reserve the right to cancel policies, which the company

---

1950's, and on the other, the life insurance policies in force which rose from $115.5 billion in 1940 to $234.5 billion in 1950 and to $586.4 billion in 1960, thus providing, in effect, the largest amount for old age and survivor security.

may exercise in case of frequent illnesses or as the insured reaches a certain age, in which case it would be difficult for the insured to obtain other coverage. Other companies, including some of the largest, exclude from coverage a variety of diseases which may lead to future claims.

Another unfortunate tendency has been for physicians to hospitalize patients (even though hospitalization could have been avoided) because the insurance does not cover office calls. Preventive examinations or treatments are usually excluded from coverage, even though preventive medicine often eliminates much heavier expenditures afterwards and might, in the case of cancer, save lives. Then, too, the charges of physicians are often well in excess of the fees which the insurance companies agree to pay, because fees are often based on (1) the amount which the insurance company pays, which is known to the physician, plus (2) what the physician regards as the patient's ability to pay. Americans in the middle income brackets, as a rule, need two simultaneous policies to cover medical and hospital care, and some insurance companies refuse to pay claims if the same claim is covered by two policies. To this must be added a good deal of chiseling by probably millions of claimants.

Medicare As a result of these difficulties government health insurance had long been demanded by economic liberals and labor unions, and in 1966, as part of the Great Society scheme, Congress adopted Medicare to provide partial health insurance for the aged. The system provides two types of protection: Hospital Insurance and Medical Insurance. Virtually all Americans 65 or over (whether covered by Social Security or not) are automatically covered by Hospital Insurance. Medical Insurance, on the other hand, requires monthly premiums of $4 (with the Federal Government matching the individual payments). The benefits are far more limited than those provided by most of the European health insurance systems. In the case of hospital care, the beneficiary has to pay the first $40, with the government paying the cost for the next 60 days and $10 per day for an additional 30 days. No payments are made beyond 90 days, and there is a lifetime limitation of 190 days. On the other hand the government pays for 80% of the diagnostic services even if the patient is not hospitalized, as well as for post-hospital care. The medical insurance program pays 80% of the "reasonable costs or charges" for covered services, except for the first $50 in a calendar year. The services include those of physicians and surgeons at home, in the doctor's office, in a clinic, or in a hospital; diagnostic tests; X-ray and radiation treatments; surgical dressings, braces, artificial legs, arms and eyes; and the rental of medical equipment.

PART III
Macroeconomics: Institutions, Theories and Policies

Chapter 9

FOUR MACROECONOMIC OBJECTIVES

THE BASIC FACTS

Economic theory is generally divided into microeconomics (which deals with the problems of the individual firm and consumer) and macroeconomics (which deals with economic issues which concern the nation as a whole).

Macroeconomic theory developed largely since the 1930's. It reflects the change in social philosophy, and the increasing importance of the public sector. With the private sector (which accounts for about 80% of the economic activities) thinking chiefly in microeconomic terms, and government planners in macroeconomic terms, Washington and Main Street often look upon the same problem from different angles. Thus far no overall economic theory has been developed to coordinate micro- and macroeconomic notions.

Modern economic policy, based on macroeconomic theory, is designed to achieve four goals: (1) "full employment," (2) monetary stability, (3) a maximum rate of economic growth, and (4) a balance in international payments and receipts.

The four goals are interdependent, but more often than not are at least partially in conflict with each other. A policy of "full employment," for instance, may lead to rising prices and a deficit in the balance of payments. The art of macroeconomic policy is thus based on compromises, on achieving the best possible combination of four conflicting objectives. What constitutes the "best possible" compromise is a matter of judgment. There may be two quite different "best possible" solutions: one based on pure economic reasoning, the other based on political considerations.

If such a conflict arises government economic advisors will be called upon to develop logical economic arguments for economic policies which are essentially based on political decisions.

The public is thus often presented with two contradictory sets of economic theories, both seemingly perfectly logical: one based on economic reasoning, the other representing the rationalization of political decisions. This does not imply that the former is "good" or "sound," and the latter "bad" and "misleading."

The choice of economic objectives depends ultimately upon the subjective decisions of the political leaders who have no "scientific blueprints" on which to base their decisions, but who must follow their own wisdom or instinct.

Macro and Microeconomics

Macroeconomics looks at the economy as a whole. It is concerned with statistical abstractions, and with aggregates which reflect the developments in the nation's economy in its entirety, such as the rate of employment, the average price level, the flow of international payments, or the rate of economic growth.

Microeconomics, on the other hand, looks upon the economy from the point of view of the consumer and the individual firm, whether large or small. It deals with the forces which determine the actual price at which a firm or industry sells its goods, the volume of sales, the actual wages paid and the profits earned.

The forces which determine the price which the corner grocer charges for his cabbage are dealt with in microeconomics. The general price level, on the other hand, a statistical abstraction which reflects the cost of living of the people as a whole, belongs to macroeconomics. We shall discuss macroeconomics in Chapters 11–19 and microeconomics in Chapters 20–26.

Macroeconomics

Modern macroeconomic theory is essentially a relatively recent development. It goes back to the 1930's. At the end of World War II no elementary textbooks were yet available in the United States which included a detailed discussion of the theories which make up the major portion of macroeconomics today. Prior to the 1940's, and certainly prior to the 1930's, economics consisted almost entirely of what is called today microeconomics.

Changing Social Philosophy

This revolutionary change in the structure of economic theory, which occurred during the past generation, is a reflection of an equally drastic change in the social philosophy of the West and its politico-economic system. During the 19th Century, and in this country well into the 1930's, social philosophy was essentially atomistic. The nation was conceived as a sum total of millions of free individuals, and the economy was looked upon as a composite of millions of individual firms. To understand economic forces, the economist thus had to study the actions of the individuals and of individual firms.

Since the 1930's, however, our social philosophy has become increasingly organic. Individuals are now compared to the cells of a body, subordinate to the structure as a whole — namely, society. Their welfare depends upon the welfare of the nation. As a logical consequence of this shift in emphasis in social philosophy, modern economists are increasingly concerned with macroeconomic problems and the forces which affect the economy of the nation rather than the individual firm. As a result, microeconomics has lost the preeminence which it enjoyed prior to the 1930's — although it has not lost its importance.

Public versus Private Sector

Just as economic theory is being divided into macro- and microeconomics, the economy of a nation consists of two major sectors, the public and the private. We must be careful, however, not to equate macroeconomic theory with the public sector, and microeconomic theory with the private. In a very general way, it can be said that the Federal government is concerned primarily with economic problems which affect the nation as a whole, and thus tends to think in macroeconomic terms. Individual firms and industries, on the other hand, which make up the private sector, are primarily concerned with such microeconomic problems as the most profitable level of operation of the individual plant, production methods, and the prices of individual products.

Washington and Main Street The different approach of macro- and microeconomics raises an interesting — and perhaps critical — psychological problem. Washington economists tend to think in macroeconomic terms. They are interested in the total number of unemployed throughout the country, in the average cost of living and in the rate of growth of the economy as a whole. The private sector, on the other hand, thinks predominantly in microeconomic terms: how much to produce and what price to charge in order to achieve the largest net profit. At times the macroeconomic goals of the government — let us say "full employment" — and the microeconomic goals of business — the greatest possible profit — do not coincide, and economists have thus far been unable to develop an overall economic theory which includes and coordinates both macro- and microeconomic aspects.

Four Macroeconomic Goals

Modern economic planning (at the governmental level and the level of the individual firm) is directed primarily toward the production and distribution of goods and services, and in attempting to achieve the goal of the highest possible material standard of living the modern economy and economic planning must pursue four objectives:

1. A high rate of employment of the nation's resources, especially its manpower (popularly called "full employment").
2. A stable purchasing power of the currency, by avoiding a chronic rise in the cost of living (inflation) or a sharp decline in values (deflation).
3. A healthy rate of growth of the output of goods and services.
4. A balance between international payments and receipts.

The Interdependence of Economic Goals The four objectives are discussed in detail in Chapters 13–16. They are closely interrelated. If a government concentrates too much on one of them (let us say "full employment") and disregards the others (such as stable prices and a balance between international payments and receipts), disequilibria develop, which in the end may prevent the attainment of any one of the desired goals. The art of socio-economic planning thus consists, in part at least, in balancing the various desirable objectives against each other.

The Goal of "Full Employment"

"Full employment" is one of the great social aims of our time, and the chief goal of economic policy in the United States. Lord Beveridge, the father of the modern "full employment" philosophy, defined the term as meaning that there must always be "more vacant jobs than unemployed men." This goal has rarely been achieved for any length of time anywhere.

Causes of Unemployment

Unemployment is the result of a number of different forces, and economists often disagree regarding the specific cause which produces a certain level of unemployment at a given time and what steps should be taken to remedy the situation. There is no disagreement about frictional and seasonal unemployment and their causes. The former is the result of workers changing their jobs. Between half a million and a million of the American unemployed fall into this category. Seasonal unemployment (for instance in agriculture, the building trades and resort areas) is relatively less serious today than it was in the past due to the greater mobility of workers (resort workers, for example, work in New England in the summer and in Florida in the winter) and the efforts of business to reduce seasonal fluctuations.

Technological unemployment is caused by the replacement of workers by more efficient machinery. This has been a problem for hundreds of years and time and again workers have tried to prevent the installation of labor-saving devices. In the end, however, technological improvements have invariably created more jobs than they have destroyed. This is true even of modern automation. Cyclical unemployment is due to changes in the general level of business activities. (The causes of cyclical fluctuations will be discussed in detail in Chapter 13.) The large unemployment of the 1930's was due almost entirely to the Great Depression. At times more than 20% of the labor force was without regular employment.

Unemployment virtually disappeared during the War, because millions of workers were drafted into the armed forces. In 1940 14.6% of the workers were without a job; in 1945 only 1.9%. During the postwar years unemployment fluctuated between 3½% and 5% but increased slowly until it reached 6.7% in 1961. Economists offered two explanations for the gradual increase: inadequate demand and structural changes. Even though both forces were at work, individual economists stressed one or the other factor depending upon their socio-economic philosophy.

Unemployment due to inadequate demand calls for radically different remedies than structural unemployment. The former can be reduced by increasing the total demand for goods and services which can be accomplished through increased government spending, easy credit and wage increases. Holding that unemployment was due to inadequate demand, the Kennedy and Johnson Administrations from 1961 to 1966 concentrated on strengthening the overall demand. With Federal spending increasing by more than 40% between 1960 and 1966 and bank credit by more than 50%, unemployment was reduced to 4½–5%. By 1966, however, the undesirable side effects of the policy began to make themselves felt: The cost of living began to rise, and the country continued to have a substantial deficit in the balance of payments. (The details will be discussed in Chapter 15.) The result was a change in the official policy. The emphasis shifted to the elimination of structural unemployment by stressing the need of teaching the unskilled the necessary skills and providing them with a basic education. [At the same time, however, the Administration approved an increase in the minimum wage from $1.25 to $1.60 even though this increase made it more difficult for marginal workers (the structurally unemployed) to find a job, unless prices in general increased, which the government was trying to avoid.]

How can this seeming conflict between "full employment" and price stability be solved? (1) The government can try to prevent prices from rising by imposing wage and price controls; (2) the country can accept inflation as the price it has to pay for "full employment"; or (3) the country can be satisfied with less than the ideal of "always more vacant jobs than umemployed men." In other words, the choice is between either controls or the partial sacrifice of one of the two goals: price stability or "full employment." Modern economic policy represents a composite of the three possiblities.

Price and Wage Controls

Lord Beveridge suggested that if "full employment" should lead to inflation (and he quite readily admitted that this was likely to be the case), wages and prices should be frozen and the government should, if necessary, determine what, how, and for whom goods and services are to be produced. In short, Lord Beveridge was ready to replace free enterprise by a system of price and wage controls, and ultimately by some form of government allocation of resources, in order to achieve his goal of "always having more jobs than men to fill them."

Compromise Solution

Since this "solution" was clearly not acceptable to the great majority of the American people, the American "full employment" policy had to follow a line of compromises dictated by the domestic and international exigencies of the moment. Instead of rigid price and wage controls, the government relies on more or less forceful "persuasion" to prevent wages and prices from rising too rapidly. Washington policy makers no longer think in terms of "more jobs than job-seekers," but have accepted a certain amount of "frictional unemployment," equal to about 3% or even 4% of the labor force. Many economists, moreover, argue that absolute price stability is not necessary. A mild chronic inflation of 1–2% a year is supposedly not too high a price to pay for the maximum use of the nation's economic resources, including maximum employment.

The Role of Economic Advisor

This places the economist who acts as a government advisor in a peculiar position, which a student of economics must understand in order to appreciate the bewildering confusion of conflicting economic theories. The task of the economic advisor consists, obviously, in planning for the "best possible" combination of the four major goals: the lowest possible rate of unemployment, the greatest possible price stability, the most rapid rate of growth and a balance in international payments. Unfortunately there may be two quite different "best possible" solutions: one from the political, and one from the economic point of view. Long range economic rationality may call for a high degree of price stability and the avoidance of a deficit in the balance of payments in order to protect the international position of the dollar. The political situation, on the other hand, may call for drastic action to create a million additional jobs in order to reduce the rate of unemployment. In this case purely economic reasoning would call for a tightening of credit, for higher interest rates, and a balanced Federal budget, (as will be discussed in the subsequent chapters). The politically dictated goal of increased employment, on the other hand, calls for the very opposite: easier credit, lower interest rates and heavy deficit spending by the Federal Government.

Chapter 10

FREE ENTERPRISE AND ECONOMIC PLANNING

THE BASIC FACTS

A nation can use three different economic systems to achieve the four economic goals discussed in Chapter 9. It can rely (1) on free enterprise, (2) on centralized planning and direct economic controls, and (3) on more or less decentralized planning and indirect controls. The character of a society will be largely determined by the choice of its economic policy. The philosophic assumptions of free enterprise have their roots in the spirit of the 18th Century Enlightenment. Free enterprise rests on the belief that man, an inherently rational and social being, lives in a social universe governed by self-equilibrating forces, which can be understood by the human mind. The profit motive and competition (which provide the dynamic force and the equilibrating mechanism in a free enterprise society) must not be confused with Spencer's "survival of the fittest" doctrine. Even while striving to maximize profits and while competing with others, man remains, according to the philosophy of free enterprise, a rational and social creature aware of his being a part of the social organism.

This optimistic spirit of the Enlightenment, which provided the rationale for the theory of 19th Century free enterprise, has been largely lost as a result of two world wars and the great depression.

Modern man no longer believes in the self-equilibrating forces of the economy, nor in the inherent rationality and social conscience of man. He assumes, instead, that the socio-economic order can be improved through planning and government intervention.

Totalitarian regimes rely on centralized planning and direct controls; western democracies stress greater decentralization of planning and indirect controls.

Even though centralized planning appeals to many intellectuals as the inherently most rational economic system, the results have been far from satisfactory for three reasons: (1) the lack of the necessary statistical knowledge regarding existing resources and conditions, (2) the extreme difficulty of predicting future developments, and (3) the lack of standards by which to measure the efficiency of production. Most important, centralized planning and direct controls involve by necessity severe restrictions on the freedom of the individual.

The free nations of the West therefore rely primarily on decentralized planning and indirect economic controls in the form of monetary and fiscal measures.

Three Roads to Economic Progress

A nation can follow three different roads in trying to achieve the four macroeconomic goals discussed in the preceding chapter. The road it follows will be determined largely by its political system, and in turn will influence the character of its civilization. A nation can rely on the self-equilibrating forces of the market economy; it can adopt a system of centralized planning and direct controls; and it can rely chiefly on indirect controls.

During the 19th Century, and down to World War I, free

enterprise predominated throughout much of the world. Centralized economic planning and controls are most fully developed in Soviet Russia and mainland China. The reliance on indirect controls has been characteristic of the prevailing economic philosophy of the West, especially the United States since the 1930's.

The Philosophic Assumptions of Free Enterprise

The philosophy of free enterprise developed during the second half of the 18th Century. Economic and social conditions, and the whole intellectual climate, had changed since the 16th Century, when Absolutism and Mercantilism first developed. The strong states, which had promised protection to the defenseless individual, had come to be regarded as the enemy of personal freedom and as one of the chief causes of the prevailing economic chaos. While Thomas Hobbes (1588–1679) had defended the absolutistic-mercantilistic state, less than a hundred years later Jean Jacques Rousseau (1712–1778) argued that "man is naturally good and that it is by our [social and political] institutions alone that men become wicked." Order was not the result of government laws; it was inherent in nature. This notion of an orderly universe, following its own inherent universal and eternal laws, was not completely new, Greek philosophers had thought along these lines, but it had been almost completely lost during the Christian Middle Ages, since it seemed impossible to reconcile the idea of an all-powerful God with the notion of natural laws, which could not be changed by divine fiat. The attitude changed slowly, as Europe became more indifferent toward religious doctrine, and a long line of scientists — Copernicus, Galileo, Keppler — "discovered" the "laws" which seemingly govern the movement of the stars, until finally, after almost 200 years of gradual progress, Sir Isaac Newton (1642–1727) achieved the great synthesis by "proving" that the same forces — he called them "gravitation" — seemingly governed not only the fall of the apple, but also the movement of the stars.

Philosophic Implications of Newtonian Physics The philosophic implications of the Newtonian system changed the character of western civilization. For more than a century the greatest minds tried to reconcile the new world of Newton's *Principia Mathematica* with the traditional mode of thought: (1) the idea of the immutability of natural laws as against the notion of an all-powerful God who is free to change the material world; (2) the seeming conflict between the unchangeable forces of nature and the humanistic belief that man is free to shape the world in which he lives; and (3) the growing conviction that the laws of nature are eternal, impartial and predictable, while man-made laws are time-conditioned, biased and unpredictable. Out of this conflict of ideas developed the philosophic basis of free enterprise. If an all-powerful, all-wise and all-kind God had created an orderly physical universe, as Newton had "proved," it was only logical to assume that he had also provided for a socio-economic system of self-equilibrating forces similar to the centrifugal and centripedal forces of the Newtonian system. And this system, if not interfered with, would make for the best of all worlds, politically and economically speaking.

Man and the Forces of Nature Nor was man a slave to the "blind" forces of a vast socio-economic machine over which he had no power. The forces could be apprehended by man's mind — just as the laws of gravitation had been discovered by Newton — and man was then free to fit himself into the divinely created system and derive the greatest benefits from it.

Man's freedom consisted in accepting or rejecting the natural order.

Immutability of Natural Laws Neither the individual nor the government could disregard the natural laws with impunity. "It would be very singular," wrote Voltaire (1694–1778), "that all nature, all the planets, should obey eternal laws, and there should be a little animal, five feet high, who, in contempt of these laws, could act as he pleased, solely according to his caprice." De la Mettrie wrote of *L'Homme Machine,* Holbach of the *System of Nature,* and Quesnay (1694–1774) claimed that his *Tableau Economique* (freely translated: Economic Blueprint) disclosed the "laws" of economic life. His followers, a group of philosophers and economists who came to be known as the Physiocrats, believed that "physis" (nature) should govern the socio-economic order just as it governed the physical universe. Hence, the Physiocrats demanded: "Laissez faire, laissez passer; le monde va de lui même." (Freedom of production, freedom of trade; the world runs by itself.)

The Profit Motive

If we compare our economic system with a carefully balanced machine, we have to explain the forces which drive the machine — the gasoline, so to speak — as well as the mechanism which keeps it running smoothly. Nineteenth Century economists devoted much of their time to such an explanation of the dynamic forces and the balancing mechanism of free enterprise. They agreed that man's economic activities — whether he plows a field or trades in the market — can be the result of any one of three incentives. He may be driven by his master, working because he fears punishment. Or he may labor because of purely altruistic reasons, like the monks who went forth to convert and teach the heathens. And finally, man may work to obtain the essentials for survival or to gain affluence and power. Given this choice of three possible inducements for man's work, the philosophers of the late 18th and the 19th Centuries chose private initiative as the most likely and effective method of achieving economic progress. From a purely ethical standpoint, altruism is to be preferred to self-aggrandizement. In our accepted scale of values we rank Albert Schweitzer higher than John D. Rockefeller. And yet if we are to measure the two by the ultimate good — in material terms — which they have accomplished, we may very well conclude that the "selfishness" of Rockefeller, at least indirectly, did more to make this a better world than the "unselfishness" of Albert Schweitzer.

Misinterpretation of the Profit Motive The fact that free enterprise frankly accepts the "profit motive" as the driving force of human effort is regarded by many as one of the inherent weaknesses of the system. How can we build a civilization on "human greed?" This is a charge one hears frequently among devout Christians in America and among the intellectuals of India and other underdeveloped countries. The answer is threefold: (1) Is forced labor, either under the rule of a slavemaster or an all-powerful state, ethically to be preferred to a system under which man is driven only by his own needs and ambitions? (2) Given human nature, how many men would labor and do their best throughout the daily grind of routine work, merely to make this a better world? Finally (3), free enterprise, as conceived by Adam Smith and the classical economists of England such as John Stuart Mill, was not a struggle for survival among hungry jungle beasts.

The Role of Competition

Just as the "profit motive," the driving force of free enterprise, is often misunderstood, so is the idea of competition, the balancing mechanism. Competition, too, is regarded as something "immoral," reminiscent of the jungle. "Cut-throat competition," fought with all means, fair and foul, legal, quasi-legal and illegal, is no doubt destructive of social cohesion and human values. And some forms of competition may be wasteful. On the other hand, if competition is governed, as Adam Smith assumed, by the sense of social responsibility of moral beings, it provides not only the incentive for continuous progress, but also the necessary safeguards against monopolistic restraints.

Centralized and Decentralized Economic Planning

While free enterprise rests on the assumption that the forces of nature are so constituted that they make for the best possible world, economic planning subsitutes the wisdom and skill of human planners for the automatic forces inherent in the social order. The trend throughout the world is toward more government intervention and more controls.

In speaking of economic planning and government controls, we must distinguish between centralized and decentralized planning, and between direct and indirect controls. Centralized planning affects the economy as a whole. The four macroeconomic goals, for instance, which we discussed in the preceding chapter, involve centralized planning. Public housing and urban rehabilitation, on the other hand, and all the planning done by state and local governments, by semi-public and by private organizations, are still largely of a decentralized nature.

A system of price ceilings clearly constitutes direct controls, while the use of credit controls to achieve price stability represents a form of indirect controls.

Centralized Planning and Direct Controls

The economics of totalitarian countries, especially Russia

and mainland China, are characterized by a high degree of centralized planning and direct controls. In the democratic countries of the West, on the other hand, much of the planning is on a decentralized basis, carried on either by government agencies or private firms. And while there are a multitude of direct controls exercised by a large number of federal agencies (the FTC, ICC, CAB, and many others), by state agencies (e.g., the liquor boards) and by local governments (e.g., the enforcement of building codes), the major macroeconomic objectives, such as price stability and "full employment," are pursued primarily by indirect rather than direct means. This at least was the situation during the 1950's. Since the early 1960's there has been a definite tendency in the United States toward greater centralization of economic planning and toward direct controls through "guidelines" and "voluntary cooperation," which may have far-reaching long-range effects on the American economy and the character of the entire social order.

The greater the centralization of planning and the more a government relies on direct controls, the more limited is the area in which the individual can make his own decisions. The techniques of economic intervention thus have a great deal to do with the maintenance of personal freedom.

The Role of the American Consumer

While the amount of government planning and controls in the United States has increased tremendously since the 1930's, the basic character of the American economy continues to be determined by the decisions of millions of businessmen and tens of millions of consumers. Goods and services are produced because the consumers demand them, and because they provide a profit for the producer. The consumer is the ultimate judge. Some people argue that the consumer's judgment is not rational, that he is the victim of "hidden persuaders," and that he wastes his money on tail-finned cars and popular records, while he should spend it on furthering his education and listening to Brahms and Beethoven. Yet the fact remains that in a free society we must assume that a person who can be trusted to vote rationally on the most critical issues confronting the nation must also know best how he wishes to spend his wages.

Russian Economic Planning

This is not the case in Russia, where centralized planning has largely replaced the wishes of the ultimate consumer as the guiding force in the economy.

The Russian economic planners start with the analysis of the available national resources: manpower, machinery, power, transportation facilities, raw materials, etc. These constitute the potential "input." The planners then determine, in close cooperation with those experts who analyze the domestic and international situation, what should or must be produced during, let us say, the next 5–Year Plan.

From a purely theoretical point of view centralized planning and direct controls seem rational and "scientific." The approach promises to eliminate waste, thus assuring a rapid growth of the nation's productive capacity and a high standard of living for the consumer. In reality, the results of centralized planning have been far from satisfactory in Russia, as well as mainland China, because of three reasons: (1) like all human beings, the planners have made serious mistakes, (2) the system has led to an often fantastic waste; and (3) it has necessitated a drastic curtailment of the freedom of the individual as a producer and consumer.

"Maximum Efficiency" and "Profits" The very word "maximum efficiency" has a different meaning in a centrally planned economy than in a free enterprise system. In America "maxi-

mum efficiency" can be directed toward one of three possible objectives: the largest possible output, the lowest possible cost, or the greatest possible profit. That firm will be the most successful in the long run which can find the best possible combination between output, price and profit. In Russia, in the past, it was not a question of how cheaply goods could be produced, or how "profitably."

In fact, prices in a centrally planned economy have a completely different significance than in a free society. In the latter, the prices of all goods are determined by supply and demand. If there is a shortage of silver or copper, their prices will go up.

In Russia prices are determined by government fiat either to obtain revenue for the government or to regulate the demand. If the demand for shoes is higher than the government wishes it to be (because it does not have enough shoes to satisfy the demand), it merely raises the price, and people who could formerly afford a new pair will now have to defer the purchase until some future date.

Centralized Planning and Personal Freedom Since private property rights, and the freedom of the individual to pick his job and to spend his income as he sees fit, make "efficient" centralized planning impossible, these freedoms have to be curtailed or abolished. In the end, it is probably fair to say, effective centralized planning is possible only in a totalitarian state.

Centralized Planning in Underdeveloped Countries It may be argued, of course, that in many underdeveloped countries the great mass of the people are illiterate, apathetic and psychologically unprepared to develop the entrepreneurial prerequisites of a free economy. If a government is confronted with millions of semi-starved, illiterate and passive peasants or coolies, centralized planning and regimentation of the passive masses may seem the only way to achieve rapid economic progress. This is the argument of many intellectuals in underdeveloped countries, who admire the "Russian miracle."

The argument overlooks a number of important facts. Centralized planning requires, first of all, reliable statistics, which are usually lacking in underdeveloped countries. It requires further a large and well-trained staff of planners, which are hard to find even in more fully developed countries. An Indian who has just received an M.A. in Economics in some small American college is obviously ill equipped to plan a solution for the terrifyingly difficult problems of the Indian economy. Yet he would be one of the better qualified among his colleagues. Finally, the best plans are worthless unless they can be forced upon the hostile or at best passive population, and in underdeveloped countries only the totalitarian regimes possess the necessary ruthlessness and power to do so.

Centralized Economic Planning in Democratic Countries

Actually, in most underdeveloped countries outside the Iron Curtain, centralized planning does not follow the Russian pattern. In Latin America, for instance, the "Alliance for Progress" scheme provides that every nation should develop a plan setting forth the nation's needs during the years ahead. The "Alliance," however, says nothing about how these plans are to be implemented. What if the individual businessmen and the consumers do not follow the government blueprint? If they spend more on radios and cars, and save less than the government expected, will the government step in and by direct controls curtail the production of consumer goods and force savings by means of higher taxes?

Planning and Indirect Controls

Most people agree that centralized economic planning of the Russian type does not provide the answer for the economic problems of the West. Centralized planning has proved extremely wasteful, aside from depriving the individual of essential freedoms as producer and consumer. On the other hand, we find it hard to believe that the economic disequilibria which the world experienced during the past half-century are the result of man's failure to adjust to the inherent social and economic forces. The western world is thus confronted with the task of finding means of intervening in the economic process, in the hope of improving it, without doing violence to the freedom of the individual, which is one of the basic tenets of our civilization.

Economic Planning and Personal Freedom Since we reject both 19th Century laissez faire and 20th Century centralized planning, we have had to find a compromise solution. The result has been the development, during the past 30–40 years in Western Europe and the United States, of a system of monetary and fiscal measures designed to prevent cyclical fluctuations, stimulate economic growth and bring about social and political stability based on a substantial degree of economic equality.

The Tools of Indirect Intervention

The logic behind the system is quite simple, although there are many complications which we shall discuss in the subsequent chapters. A government cannot fix wages and prices, and regulate directly the volume of production of goods and services, without impairing the personal freedom of the consumer and producer. For more than 200 years freedom of production and consumption have been regarded as essential features of a free society. On the other hand, since the 1930's it has come to be generally accepted that (even in a free society) the government can regulate the supply of money and credit. By regulating the supply of money and credit the government can influence indirectly the output of goods and services, the general price level, the rate of employment and of economic growth, and the international flow of goods and capital. (How this is done will be discussed in detail in subsequent chapters.)

Economists generally agree that the supply of purchasing power (money and credit) has a bearing on the volume of sales and hence production and employment. An expansion of credit facilities as a rule will induce people to buy more, which in turn will call for an increase in production and employment. Economists also agree that the volume of money and credit in relation to the available goods and services affects the general price level. This relationship between the quantity of purchasing power (which represents the "demand"), the quantity of goods and services ("supply") and the general price level can be presented as $P = \frac{M}{G}$ where "P" stands for the general price level, "M" for money and credit and "G" for the supply of foods and services.

This presentation, however, does not represent a mathematical equation, but merely illustrates a basic functional relationship.

If the supply of money and credit is increased ("inflated") while the supply of goods and services remains constant, prices are likely to rise and the country will experience an "inflation." On the other hand, if the volume of credit declines, but the output of goods and services remains more or less constant, the demand will decline, prices will tend to go down, and the country will suffer from "deflation." By changing the supply of money and credit, the government thus can stimulate or retard economic activities.

While the scheme seems quite simple in theory, its application involves many complications. It is extremely difficult to determine with any degree of accuracy how much money and credit will be needed to achieve "full employment" without an increase in the general price level ("inflation"), especially since many other forces (in addition to the supply of money and credit) influence consumption, production and employment.

As long as the productive capacity of a country is not fully employed an increase in the supply of money and credit (which will enable the people to buy more) is likely to lead to an expansion of production and employment. On the other hand, if the economy is faced with a shortage of vital factors of production, such as skilled manpower and plant capacity, a further increase in the supply of money cannot lead to increased production, but will result in an increase in prices. And no government knows with certainty when the productive capacity of the country will be reached and a further expansion of credit will tend to raise prices.

Since economists disagree whether "a little inflation" is a smaller evil than "a little unemployment" or vice versa, opinions differ regarding specific policy measures and timing. Those who favor maximum employment tend to expand the supply of money and credit more freely than others who favor a high degree of monetary stability, and there is no "scientific" norm by which a government can determine the "right" amount of money and credit.

Nor should one assume that monetary and fiscal policies are the only forces which influence the level of business activities. It is quite possible for monetary and fiscal policies to be stymied by other forces which are beyond governmental control. During the 1930's, for instance, the government's efforts to stimulate the economy by increasing the supply of credit and reducing interest rates proved largely in vain because businessmen and consumers under the psychological impact of the depression were reluctant to go into debt. On the other hand, prices can rise suddenly and sharply (even without an increase in the supply of money and credit), if the people suddenly decide to use their savings to buy goods because they fear either rationing (as was the case at the outbreak of the Korean conflict in 1950) or rapidly rising prices. Neither a depression-bred pessimism nor sharp price increases resulting from a sudden panicky buying wave can be controlled through monetary and fiscal measures. And there are other situations in which indirect controls are of little help.

As a rule, however, governments have considerable leeway in stimulating consumption and production and in preventing major price increases without fixing wages and prices or regulating the output of goods and services. Despite its weakness and defects the system of fiscal and monetary policies has been more effective in the long run than the system of direct controls on which the totalitarian countries rely. Most important perhaps, the system of indirect controls assures a considerable degree of individual freedom for the producer as well as the consumer. The government attempts to influence the people in order to further certain economic and social objectives, but it does not force them into a rigid mold.

In the subsequent chapters we shall discuss the tools of monetary and fiscal policies, namely in Chapter 11, the monetary and credit system of the United States and in Chapter 12, the fiscal system. In Chapter 19, finally, we shall deal with the actual monetary and fiscal policies.

Chapter 11

THE MONETARY AND BANKING SYSTEM

THE BASIC FACTS

The Monetary System — "Money" is anything which is widely used and generally accepted as a medium of exchange and as a standard of value. In the United States, money consists almost entirely of credit instruments: paper money, and above all, checking accounts. Without an efficient monetary system a complex modern economy cannot function. Money, moreover, is regarded in modern economic theory as one of the most important tools in regulating the course of economic activities.

The Commercial Banking System — The American banking system is complex. There are some 13,000 commercial banks, subject to a variety of banking laws. The art of bank management consists above all in providing maximum security for the depositors, yet at the same time achieving the greatest possible profit for the stockholders, maintaining the necessary liquidity, and providing credit facilities for the community.

From a macroeconomic point of view, by far the most important role of the commercial banking system is its ability to expand credit, thus providing the necessary supply of "money" to finance the economy.

The Federal Reserve System — The System functions at three levels: (1) the Board of Governors in Washington, which determines overall policies; (2) the 12 regional Federal Reserve banks, which carry on most of the routine functions provided by the System; and (3) the approximately 6000 Member Banks which deal with the general public. The most important policy-making organ of the System is the Open Market Committee, which is controlled by the Board of Governors, although the individual Federal Reserve banks can press their own points of view.

The original task of the Federal Reserve consisted in providing the necessary flexibility in the supply of money, and in holding the legal reserves of the banking system. The "Fed" also supervises the member banks, operates the most efficient check clearing system in the world, and acts as the fiscal agent of the Federal Government.

Since World War II the Federal Reserve System has taken on the difficult and controversial task of trying to execute various economic policies of the government. It tries to manipulate the supply of credit in such a way as to achieve "full employment" and a maximum rate of economic growth. In doing so, the System has at times been forced to neglect the traditional central bank function of maintaining price stability and preventing a prolonged deficit in the balance of payments.

The Federal Reserve can use specific and general controls. The latter are the more important. They consist of (1) changes in reserve requirements, (2) changes in the discount rate and (3) open market operations.

The Role of Gold — Even though the gold standard no longer functions in the traditional, 19th Century mechanistic form, gold continues to play an important role in international finance. It is the only universally acceptable means of interna-

tional payment. The other traditional functions of the gold standard (to prevent the fluctuation of foreign exchange rates; to equalize world market prices; and to regulate the supply of money within a country) have been largely superseded by government intervention, thus removing a once effective barrier against chronic inflation.

What Is Money?

Money is *anything* that is widely used and generally accepted within an economic community as a medium of exchange and as a standard of value. In the olden days, money had to have intrinsic value, i.e., consist of gold or silver. Our modern money, however, is entirely based on faith and lacks the old prerequisite of having a value of its own.

Many things have been used as money. During the postwar period in Germany, cigarettes served as a medium of exchange and a standard of value. The beads of the Algonquins, wampum, could be used for a short time during the 17th Century for the payment of taxes in Massachusetts. Tobacco, rum, powder, skins, hides, knives, fishhooks, and many other things have been used as "money" in these United States. In Homer's *Iliad* we read that the armor of Diomedes cost only 9 oxen, but that of Glaucus cost 100 oxen; and we still speak of "pecuniary" problems, usually without remembering that the English word comes from the Latin "pecus," meaning cattle.

The Lydians in Asia Minor were the first to coin money, about 750–700 B.C., some 300 years after the destruction of Troy. King Croesus of Lydia was probably the first to produce gold coins. But for many centuries thereafter, the weight of metal, rather than an abstract monetary unit, continued as the measure of value.

Paper Money The Chinese were the first to introduce paper money at the time of Marco Polo in the 13th Century. Like virtually all governments after them, they promptly printed too much money, with the result that the paper became valueless. After a few years of false prosperity economic chaos ensued.

Until World War I, the majority of the people of the world preferred money which had intrinsic value, such as gold and silver coin, and only during the past 50 years has paper money come into almost universal use.

The Functions of Money

Money performs two major functions:

(1) It serves as a *medium of exchange*, as a token of power to command goods and services. The butcher exchanges his meat for money, and he can then exchange the money for shoes. In theory, of course, the butcher could have bartered his meat directly for the shoes — provided the shoemaker wanted the meat, but barter is based on a "coincidence of wants" (the butcher needs a $20 pair of shoes, while the shoemaker needs $20 worth of meat), a situation which rarely presents itself. In many areas of activities, and especially over long distances, barter is extremely cumbersome. Money thus provides the consumer with freedom of choice. Without money, mass production, based on the division of labor, would be all but impossible.

(2) Money provides a *standard of value*. We measure the weight of an article in pounds, its dimensions in inches, and its value in dollars and cents. Money thus performs the same function as any other standard of measurement.

In addition to its two major functions, money serves various other purposes. It provides a *standard of deferred payments*. If we borrow $100 today, and promise to repay the $100 in a year, both the debt and the repayment are measured in terms of dollars. This may be dangerous in times of rapidly rising prices, since the purchasing power of the dollar, by which the repayment of the debt is measured, decreases.

Traditionally, money was the most important *store of value.* Food and other supplies as a rule cannot be stored conveniently until needed, but people could store coins to be used as a medium of exchange at some later date.

Money serves as the only *guarantor of solvency.* A man may own land and jewels, but if there is nobody willing to buy either, and he cannot meet his obligations when due, he may be forced into bankruptcy. This happened to many American farmers during the early 1930's. They were "land rich," but since nobody was willing to buy their land, they were unable to meet their obligations and lost everything.

Finally, money is used as a *unit of account.* The books of all business enterprises as well as of the Federal government in Washington are expressed in terms of dollars and cents in order to have a uniform system of measurement.

Internationally, as we shall see later, there is ultimately only one type of "money" which meets the two basic requirements of being widely used and generally accepted as a medium of exchange and a standard of value — namely gold. If the American government were to refuse to redeem in gold the dollar balances which foreign central banks and international monetary institutions hold in this country, the dollar would cease to be universally acceptable.

Money in the United States

Within the United States we have three major types of money: coins, paper money and checking accounts. Table 2 shows the relative importance of the various types.

Table 2 indicates the significant changes which took place in the American monetary system. In six years, the supply of

TABLE 2

Money Outstanding in the United States (in Millions)

I. Currency in Circulation	(As of June 30) 1961	1967
Coins (Silver, Nickel and Copper)	$2,338	$4,641
Paper Money		
Silver Certificates (Blue Seal) are "warehouse receipts" certifying that for each one dollar Silver Certificate, "there is on deposit in the Treasury of the United States one dollar in silver payable to the bearer on demand." The Silver Certificates are being replaced by Federal Reserve Notes.	2,096	396
United States Notes (Red Seal) are a hang-over from Civil War days when Washington ran out of gold and silver and hence issued promissory notes, the so-called "greenbacks." These government I.O.U.'s are payable only in other paper money.	318	300
National Bank Notes and Federal Reserve National Bank Notes which are being redeemed from the General Fund of the Treasury.	147	87
Federal Reserve Notes (Green Seal) are the joint obligation of the United States Government, the entire Federal Reserve System, and the individual issuing Federal Reserve Bank (see the black seal showing which one of the 12 Federal Reserve Banks has issued the specific note). Until 1968 these notes were secured to the extent of at least 25% by "Gold Certificates" (which in turn are backed dollar for dollar by gold held by the U.S. Treasury).	27,353	39,289
Total Currency:	$32,252	$44,713
II. Bank Deposits		
Demand deposits (subject to transfer by check)	123,560	155,890
Total money supply	$155,812	$200,603
Time and Savings Deposits	116,220	231,320
Total Potential Money Supply	$272,032	$431,923

Source: Board of Governors of the Federal Reserve System, "Federal Reserve Bulletin," August 1961, September 1967.

money increased by almost 29%. If we include savings deposits (which can quickly be converted into money), the increase amounted to more than 58%. At the same time, due to the withdrawal of silver coins (made necessary by the silver shortage), the amount of Silver Certificates declined sharply.

"Checking Account" Money

By far the most important type of money in the United States is not the currency (coins and paper money), but checking accounts (demand deposits). Close to 90% of all payments (measured in terms of dollars) are made by check. Savings and other time deposits cannot be used directly as money, but they can be transferred to checking accounts and thus turned into "money" on very short notice. They are therefore often referred to as "near money."

Credit Money The American monetary system is based almost entirely on credit: the confidence that the man who writes a check will have an adequate deposit to cover the check; the confidence that the bank on which the check is drawn is solvent; the confidence that the next fellow will accept the little piece of paper supposedly worth $10 or $20 just because the government in Washington says it is "worth" that much, even though it has in itself no value whatever and the government will only give us other little pieces of paper in exchange for the one we hold.

The Importance of Money

Except for primitive barter systems, no economy can function without a suitable supply of money. The more intricate the economy, the greater the need for a well-functioning monetary system. If the system deteriorates, the economy as a whole declines. And in the end both the monetary system and the economy collapse. Modern urban life, mass production based on the division of labor and the mobilization of private savings, and above all the modern system of taxation, would be impossible without a reasonably orderly monetary system.

Money in Economic Theory

Strangely enough, economists in years past have tended to underestimate the importance of money. John Stuart Mill, for instance, the famous 19th Century English economist, regarded money as merely "a contrivance for sparing time and labour which does not interfere with the operation of any of the laws of value." Hence, he concluded, from the point of view of economic theory, "there cannot be intrinsically a more insignificant thing in the economy of society than money." Mill's point of view reflected a prejudice of the 19th Century, which looked upon money as "a mere veil" hiding the actual transactions, an attitude which represented a natural reaction to the mercantilistic view of the 16th to 18th Centuries which overemphasized the importance of money.

Today the pendulum has swung again in the opposite direction. Modern economists look upon money (1) as one, if not the most important, cause of inflationary booms and deflationary depressions, and (2) as the most effective tool of economic planning in a non-totalitarian society.

The Creation of Money

The most elementary — and today the least important — way of creating money is by mining or importing gold and silver, which is then used either for coinage or, more likely, for the issuance of paper money "backed" by the newly acquired metal.

The government cannot just "print money," as the saying goes. Of the two types of government paper money, Silver Cerificates and United States Notes, the former is being withdrawn from circulation because of the shortage of silver, while Congress has limited the issuance of United States Notes to the small amount of $347 million. Contrary to popular belief, the American government thus does not "print money."

In a complex modern economy, money is not created through coinage or the printing press, but through the creation of bank deposits, which, as we have seen, account for about 80% of the money supply of the United States. The creation of money requires the interaction of the government, the Federal Reserve System, the commercial banking system and the business community.

To understand how money is created through the banking system, we must first discuss the structure of the banking system.

The Commercial Banking System

The American banking system is complex. There are a large number of different types of banking institutions to serve different purposes. Saving and the financing of homes are facilitated through mutual savings banks, savings and loan associations, building and loan associations and Federal Home Loan Banks. The American farmers obtain credit through Federal Land Banks, Federal Intermediate Credit Banks and Banks for Cooperatives. The consumer can borrow from consumer credit institutions, including small loan companies, while business obtains funds with the help of investment houses. Private investors, finally, buy and sell stocks and bonds through brokers and investment dealers. By far the most important banking institutions, and the only ones which we can discuss here, are the commercial banks, which differ from other banking institutions in two ways: They provide checking accounts, and they can "create money."

Unit and Branch Banking A commercial banking system can be organized either as a unit or as a branch banking system. Most states of the Union restrict branch banking (the chief exception being California), which makes the United States the only major financial power whose commercial banking system consists of literally thousands of individual banks. In England 80–90% of all the commercial banking business is handled by five big banks, which have thousands of branches. And the situation is similar in most countries.

National and State Banks In the United States, on the other hand, there are more than 13,000 individual commercial banks, some organized under Federal law (national banks) and the majority under the laws of the 50 states (state banks). All national banks have to be members of the Federal Reserve System, and all the major state banks are members. However the majority of the smaller state banks find it advantageous not to become members and thus avoid the more rigid standards required from member banks.

Only about 45% of the commercial banks of the country are members of the Federal Reserve System, but these are by far the most important ones since they administer more than 80% of all bank deposits.

During the middle 1960's Federal banking provisions underwent minor but, from the point of view of the commercial banks, important changes. As a result, a number of commercial banks, including the Chase Manhattan Bank (the country's third largest), which had formerly operated under state laws, became national banks.

Federal Deposit Insurance Corporation

The deposits of all Member Banks (members of the Federal Reserve System) must be insured with the Federal Deposit Insurance Corporation (FDIC). Deposits are insured up to $15,-000 (prior to 1966 up to $10,000), for which the banks pay an annual premium of 1/12th of 1% of the total deposits, minus a rebate, which in recent years has run as high as 50% of the premium paid. Most of the non-member banks' deposits are likewise insured with the FDIC.

Assets and Liabilities of Commercial Banks

While the balance sheet of large commercial banks shows many accounts, these can be condensed into five groups of accounts:

TABLE 3

Chief Assets and Liabilities of Commercial Banks

Assets			*Liabilities*		
	Cash assets	18%		Deposits	91%
	Loans	51%		Capital accounts	9%
	Securities	31%			

The art of banking consists in manipulating these five groups of accounts to achieve the best possible combination of four objectives: (1) maximum security for the depositors; (2) the necessary liquidity to meet sudden demands for payment by the depositors; (3) an adequate profit for the stockholders of the bank; and (4) the best possible credit facilities for the community.

Lending Capacity

The lending capacity of the banking system depends upon the amount of loanable funds. Not all Cash Assets can be loaned out, since the banks need working balances and are required by law to maintain reserves against their deposits.

Cash Assets consist of: (1) Cash in the vault; (2) Balances with other banks; (3) Required Reserves with the Federal Reserve; and (4) Free Reserves with the Federal Reserve.

All commercial banks are required to maintain a certain percentage of their deposits in the form of liquid reserves, either as Cash in the Vault or (in the case of Member Banks) as deposits with the Federal Reserve. The size of the required reserves of the Member Banks is determined from time to time by the Board of Governors of the Federal Reserve System. The reserve requirements for the non-member banks are determined by the respective state banking authorities. In the case of the member-banks, the Federal Reserve distinguishes between Reserve City Banks (some 220 large banks in the major cities) and Country Banks. The reserves which the Reserve City Banks have to maintain against demand deposits can vary from 10% to 22%, those of the Country Banks from 7% to 14%. Reserve requirements against time deposits can vary from 3% to 6%.

Most banks maintain a minimum amount of cash in their vaults and in other banks. All extra cash is deposited with the Federal Reserve. If these deposits exceed the reserves which a bank has to maintain, it has "excess reserves," which it can use to make loans or buy securities. The "excess reserve" thus indicate the lending capacity of an individual bank.

Some banks occasionally fall short of the required reserves. If one deducts these shortages of some banks from the excess reserves of the other banks, one arrives at what is called "free reserves," which represent the immediate lending capacity of the banking system as a whole.

The Art of Commercial Banking

As banks are anxious to maximize their profits, they will try to attract as many deposits as possible in order to have a high ratio of deposits to capital accounts. The smaller the equity the greater the possibilities for profit. But there is a limit to the degree of leverage, since the capital accounts in effect represent a cushion against losses. In recent years about 9% of the funds of the commercial banks consisted of the banks' own capital and reserves, and 91% of checking accounts and time deposits. Thus, if the average value of the banks' loans and investments were to decline by 12%, the banks would face bankruptcy. The ratio of capital accounts to deposits can be called the "safety ratio" because it indicates by how much the value of the assets can decline before the deposits are endangered.

Liquidity and Profit Ratios

The banks' earnings are derived from loans and investments. Banks will therefore try to lend and/or invest as high a percentage of their assets as possible. However here again there are limits, because the banks have to maintain an adequate degree of liquidity to meet the demands of the depositors. We can therefore speak of the "liquidity ratio," namely the ratio of Cash Assets to Deposits. The banking system in 1967 had about $1.00 in cash (or its equivalent) for every $6.50 of deposits. Finally, we speak of the "profit ratio," namely the ratio of loans and investments (which produce income) to capital accounts. The banking system had invested about $9 in earning assets for every $1 provided by the stockholders.

The Creation of Money Through the Banking System

We are now ready to understand how a commercial bank — rather, how the commercial banking system as a whole — creates money. As we said before, checks drawn on the demand deposits of commercial banks are the most important form of money. The size of the demand deposits is thus a good indication of the money supply. Demand deposits, according to their creation, fall into two groups: (1) *Primary deposits,* resulting from a deposit of actual cash with the bank (in depositing money the client converts currency into demand deposits), and (2) *derived deposits,* which arise when the bank extends a loan to a client. Let us take a very simple case: The client gives the bank a promissory note for $1000, and the bank in return credits the checking account of the client with $1000.

XYZ — Commercial Bank

Assets		*Liabilities*	
Loans	$1000	Demand deposits	$1000

By making a loan to the client, the bank has created a demand deposit, in other words, "money." The individual bank must, of course, expect that the client will withdraw the credit balance, because if he did not need the money he would not have borrowed it. The individual bank thus must have enough cash assets to be prepared for such withdrawals. But the money withdrawn from bank "A," as a rule, is promptly deposited in bank "B," so that bank "B" now has additional funds to make a loan to one of its clients, who will use the loan to make a payment, as a result of which the funds will show up in bank "C," and so on. In other words the $1000 of actual cash assets originally held by Bank "A" have resulted in the creation of demand deposits in banks "A," "B," and "C," and the process can be continued. Each deposit represents an increase in the money supply.

This process of creating money through the commercial banking system is limited in two ways: (1) The banks' clients must be willing to borrow, and if business is slack, businessmen will not borrow money; and (2) every time a bank creates a demand deposit it must (as we have mentioned before) set up a legal reserve, involving, in the case of a member bank, an increase of its required reserve with the Federal Reserve.

Limits of Lending Capacity

The lending capacity of the banking system is thus determined by two factors:

1. the amount of free reserves available.
2. the legal reserve requirements.

Let us assume that free reserves of the banking system as a whole amount to $1 billion, and the average legal reserve requirements are 12%. Under these circumstances the banking system could increase its loans and investments by about $8.3 billion. [For every $1 billion of new credit $120 million of additional reserve have to be set aside, and since there are $1 billion of free reserves (which can be turned into legal reserves), this $1 billion divided by $120 million gives us the approximate lending capacity of the banking system.]

By creating and destroying free reserves, and by changing legal reserve requirements, the Federal Reserve can control the lending capacity of the banking system, and hence the total money supply. But — and this should be emphasized again — the mere fact that the banking system can extend credit and thus create additional money does not mean that the supply of money will actually be increased. It depends ultimately upon the willingness of businessmen and private individuals — or, as we shall see shortly, the government — to borrow money.

The Federal Reserve System

All major nations, and most of the smaller ones, have central banks. The oldest ones, the Riksbank of Sweden and the Bank of England, date back to the 16th and 17th Centuries. Others were created during the 19th Century. The United States was the last of the major countries to set up a central bank. The

Federal Reserve Act was adopted in 1913 after a bitter political struggle. It represented a compromise between those who strove for the centralization of financial powers in New York, and others who insisted on regional decentralization. The result was a system of 12 "independent" Federal Reserve Banks, locally owned, but tied together into a central banking system through what is known today as the Board of Governors of the Federal Reserve System, located in Washington.

Growing Government Influence During the past half-century the Federal Reserve System has undergone many changes. The power has shifted increasingly from the twelve decentralized regional banks to the Board of Governors in Washington. While the twelve banks continue to be privately owned by their member banks, and, in theory, the Board of Governors is supposedly free from political control, for all practical purposes the Federal Reserve System has become an arm of the government.

Hard or Soft Money This trend in the United States is paralleled by similar developments in other countries. It reflects the spirit of our time. During the 19th century, most people felt that governments could not be trusted with the creation of money, because, throughout the course of history, governments had almost always tried to "solve" their financial problems by inflating the amount of money in circulation and thus lowering its value. While government ownership of the central banks was advocated by the Marxian socialists in accordance with the principles of the "Communist Manifesto" of 1848, the middle class, in this country and Europe, felt that if the purchasing power of the currency was to remain reasonably stable, the control of the money supply had to be in the hands of those who lost most through a depreciation of the currency, meaning the creditors, of whom the bankers were the most important. Hence, the argument ran, control of the supply of money should rest with the privately owned banks.

The debtor classes, who are interested in cheapening the money in order to reduce the real burden of their debt, quite naturally opposed the "hard" money policy of the banking interests. This was particularly the case during times of declining prices. In fact the history of the United States could be written in terms of a never-ending struggle between those who believe in a stable dollar, and those who want "higher prices." The Constitution was originally designed, at least in part, to strengthen the dollar. Through Jackson's victory over the Second Bank of the United States, the "soft money" group gained a temporary upper hand. But from 1865 to 1932, the period which witnessed the rise of the United States to a world power, the emphasis was again upon a stable dollar, despite the attacks of the Silverites and of farm groups, and Bryan's "Cross of Gold" campaign. The situation changed during the Great Depression. President Roosevelt devalued the dollar to raise prices, and deficits in the Federal budget (which increase the supply of money and thus tend to lower its value) have come to be regarded as a tool of sound economic policy.

The world-wide trend toward "soft money" policies and the equally wide-spread tendency of giving the government more and more power over the economy, has resulted in a drastic change in central bank philosophy. During the 19th Century when it was assumed that governments should not have the power of regulating the supply of money, most central banks were private institutions and free from government control. Since the 1930's, on the other hand, the great majority of the central banks have been nationalized, and even those which remain nominally privately owned, such as the Federal Reserve, are largely controlled by the government. If the government is responsible for economic planning, so the argument runs, it must have the power to regulate the supply of money. There are only a few exceptions to this general trend. In Switzerland, Germany and Austria, government control over the policies of the central bank have been severely limited by constitutional and other legal provisions.

The Structure of the Federal Reserve System

The Federal Reserve System functions at three levels:

I. *The Board of Governors of the Federal Reserve System* consists of seven Governors appointed by the President of the United States, for a period of 14 years, with the consent and approval of the Senate. Every four years the President of the United States appoints one of the seven governors as Chairman of the Board. The chairman can be reappointed for another four years. His is the most powerful position in the system, and the fact that the President has a free choice in picking the man he wants from among the seven governors, without a check by either the Senate or any other authority, gives the White House a substantial power over the policies of the Board and thus the whole system.

II. Of the *Twelve Federal Reserve Banks,* (with their 24 branches) the Federal Reserve Bank of New York is by far the largest. Even though its relative importance has declined as the rest of the country developed, it still holds about 25% of the total assets of the system. Prior to the 1930's New York in effect controlled Federal Reserve policies. Since the 1935 Banking Act, however, the power has shifted to Washington, and the Board of Governors now controls the policies of the supposedly "independent" twelve Federal Reserve Banks.

III. The approximately *6000 Member Banks* are required to purchase stock in their respective regional Federal Reserve banks equal to 3% of the member banks' capital and surplus. This makes the member banks the legal owners of the system. But their power is severely limited. They can elect six of the nine directors of their regional Federal Reserve bank (the remaining three are nominated by the Board of Governors), but these directors have only limited powers. They appoint the President of the Bank, but the appointment has to be approved by the Board of Governors. In fact all important policy decisions are made and have to be approved in Washington, and not by the nine directors of the individual banks, who represent the actual owners.

Open Market Committee The most powerful policy-making body in the Federal Reserve System is the *Open Market Committee,* which developed gradually over the years until it was given official status in 1935. Its members consist of the seven Governors, the President of the New York Federal Reserve Bank, and the Presidents of four other Federal Reserve Banks, with the remaining seven Presidents participating in the discussions. It is this Open Market Committee which determines the monetary policies of the System, whether to increase or to restrict the supply of money and credit.

Functions of the Federal Reserve System

The Federal Reserve was created for two very simple purposes: to hold the reserves of the banking system, and to provide for the necessary supply of money.

Prior to 1913 the currency of the United States consisted of (1) gold and silver certificates, backed dollar for dollar by metal; (2) a small amount of United States Notes, and (3)

National Bank Notes issued by the individual national banks and secured by U.S. Government bonds. The available quantity of gold and silver was clearly limited. The government was prohibited by law to issue more United States Notes. And the amount of government bonds which could serve as a basis for National Bank Notes was likewise limited, since the national debt was small. There was thus no way of creating quickly additional currency, if in times of crisis the bank depositors suddenly demanded currency. Even though the banks might hold perfectly good assets, there was no way of turning these assets into cash in case there was a "run" on the bank. The results were periodic crises in which people lost their savings.

Since the creation of the Federal Reserve System, the banks are able to "shift" most of their assets (chiefly government bonds or certain types of promissory notes and acceptances) to the Federal Reserve, and receive in return Federal Reserve Notes with which to pay their depositors.

Additional Functions

In addition to the two limited functions, provided by the original Act, of holding the reserves of the banking system and of providing the necessary paper currency to take care of seasonal and emergency needs, the system has gradually taken on a variety of other administrative and policy-making chores.

The supervision of member banks is today largely handled by the Federal Deposit Insurance Corporation, although the Federal Reserve retains its supervisory powers.

Federal Reserve Clearing System The Federal Reserve operates the most efficient system in the world of clearing not only checks but any claim payable on demand (such as coupons and matured bonds). In the course of a year the Federal Reserve collects close to 4 billion individual checks and other items with a total value of about $1.3 trillion. On an average business day the collections amount to about $5 billion. For all checks, even if deposited by a bank in Key West and drawn on a bank in Seattle, the Federal Reserve gives credit within two days. Since it often takes longer than 2 days to collect a check, the Federal Reserve actually extends credit to its member banks in the form of the so-called "float," which on an average amounts to about $1–$1.5 billion. It consists of the difference between the checks in the process of collection ("cash items in process of collection") and the amount for which the Federal Reserve has not credited the depositing banks ("deferred availability cash items"). Clearing the member bank's checks and providing them with coin and Federal Reserve Notes are two free services of the System.

Fiscal Agency Functions The System also acts as the "fiscal agent" (the banker) of the United States government, all government agencies, foreign governments, and United Nations agencies. Uncle Sam's checking account, the "United States Treasury General Account," is kept by the Federal Reserve. The "Fed" also issues and retires all government bonds and pays all coupons. For these services, which at times keep 40% of the staff of the Federal Reserve busy, a service charge is collected from the government. However, each year the Federal Reserve pays to the U.S. Treasury as a "voluntary" payment an amount equal to about 80–90% of its earnings, another indication that the System for all practical purposes regards itself as an arm of the government.

Federal Reserve Controls over the Quantity of Money and Credit

Far more complex and controversial than the purely administrative activities are the policy-making functions of the Federal Reserve. Until World War II these largely consisted of the maintenance of the proper supply of money and credit in order to keep prices more or less stable, and the prevention of serious and prolonged balance of payments deficits and troublesome gold losses. The Federal Reserve was reasonably successful in maintaining the international position of the dollar, but it failed to prevent a catastrophic 40% decline in prices during the Great Depression.

After the end of World War II, (without having been told so specifically by Congress) the Federal Reserve took on the difficult and controversial task of trying to manage the supply of credit in such a way as to achieve "full employment"; and, in more recent years, to achieve "maximum economic growth." Since some of these objectives are at times contradictory, the Federal Reserve not infrequently seems to be going in all directions at the same time, while complaining about the "fuzziness of policy directives."

Control Tools of the Federal Reserve

To achieve its various objectives, the Federal Reserve is free to use either direct (specific) or indirect (general) controls. The former are confined at present to the establishment of Margin Requirements, the percentage of the purchase price which the buyer of securities has to pay in cash. If an investor wishes to buy $10,000 worth of stocks or bonds, and the margin requirements, as fixed by the Federal Reserve, are 70%, he has to pay down only $7,000 and can borrow the balance from the broker or a bank. By reducing margin requirements, thus making it easier to buy stocks, the Federal Reserve can stimulate a "bearish" (weak) market, and by raising requirements it can retard a "bullish" (strong) market which threatens to get out of hand.

Consumer Credit Controls During World War II the Federal Reserve also regulated consumer and mortgage loans. It determined the size of the down payment on a car and within how many months the purchaser had to pay off the balance; how large a down payment had to be made on a house and for how long the mortgage could run. At the end of the war the Federal Reserve was only too happy to abandon these controls, which would have brought the System into direct conflict with powerful industrial and real estate interests once the war emergency was over.

Indirect and General Controls

Far more important than the direct controls are the indirect or general controls, which are not directed toward the control of a particular business transaction, such as the sale of a car, but affect, indirectly, the entire economy. The indirect controls consist of (1) changes in reserve requirements (affecting the lending capacity of the banking system); (2) changes in discount rates (affecting the cost of credit); and (3) open market operations (which influence the total supply of credit). These three methods of controlling the supply of credit will be discussed in Chapter 19 as part of the discussion of the monetary and fiscal tools of over-all economic planning.

The Role of Gold in the Modern World

Even though the world has abandoned the gold standard, gold continues to play an important role in international finance and thus affects, at least indirectly, domestic economic policies.

The abandonment of the gold standard by the United States in 1933 symbolized the end of an era and the beginning of a new economic philosophy, even though few people fully understood this fact at the time. During the 19th century and until World War I, economic thought was based on the assumption that mankind lived in an "orderly social universe" governed by inherent laws similar in some respect to the laws which govern the physical universe. The gold standard mechanism was an essential and integral part of this "great machine," which, it was assumed, worked toward an equilibrium at the best possible level. Mankind could thus rely on the "automatic controls" functioning within the system, and it was the gold standard which provided some of the most important of these automatic controls.

Gold as a Regulator of the Money Supply

The Federal Reserve Act of 1913 provided that the Federal Reserve had to maintain a gold reserve equal to at least 40% of the Federal Reserve Notes in circulation and 35% of the Member Bank Reserves (legal and excess reserves). Since the size of the latter was determined by the volume of bank deposits, the size of the Federal Reserve gold holdings provided a ceiling for the nation's money supply. As gold left the country, the monetary base declined.

In January 1934, under the Gold Reserve Act, the Federal Government seized the gold holdings of the Federal Reserve System, and issued in exchange Gold Certificates on a dollar-for-dollar basis which have served as a reserve against Federal Reserve Notes and Member Bank Reserves ever since.

In 1945, the reserve requirements were reduced to a uniform 25% for Federal Reserve Notes and Member Bank Reserves, despite the fact that the country had ample gold reserves at the time. Twenty years later, in 1965, the situation was different. Federal Reserve Notes and Member Bank Reserves amounted to about $52 billion which under existing law, called for a reserve in Gold Cerificates of $13 billion. Actual holdings amounted to $14.3 billion. This was an uncomfortably narrow margin, and Congress decided, therefore, to eliminiate the Gold Certificate reserves behind the Member Bank Reserves. Had Congress not taken this step, and the money supply had continued to expand, while the country had lost additional gold, the free gold reserves would have been exhausted and the Federal Reserve would have been forced to tighten credit in order to reduce the money supply. An effective tightening of credit, in turn, could have reduced business activities and increased unemployment. Congress thus removed the "automatic" safeguard of the gold standard which limited the amount of money by available gold reserves and freed the Federal Reserve to continue the financing of the boom through increased credit. In 1968, Congress removed the remaining 25% gold reserves behind the Federal Reserve Notes.

The Free Flow of Gold Tended to Equilibrate International Price Levels

Prior to World War I, when all major trading nations were on the gold standard, a balance of payments deficit resulted in a loss of gold, and a surplus in an increase in gold holdings. The decline in the gold holdings of the deficit nations, in turn, reduced the supply of money and thus tended to lower prices; while the increase in the gold holdings of the surplus nations had the opposite effect. This tendency was well illustrated by the price-specie flow mechanism, a model first developed by David Hume (1711–76).

Let us take two countries, the USA and Britain, whose respective price levels "P" are determined (according to the quantity theory of money) by the supply of money "M" in relation to the supply of goods and services "G." We then have two equations:

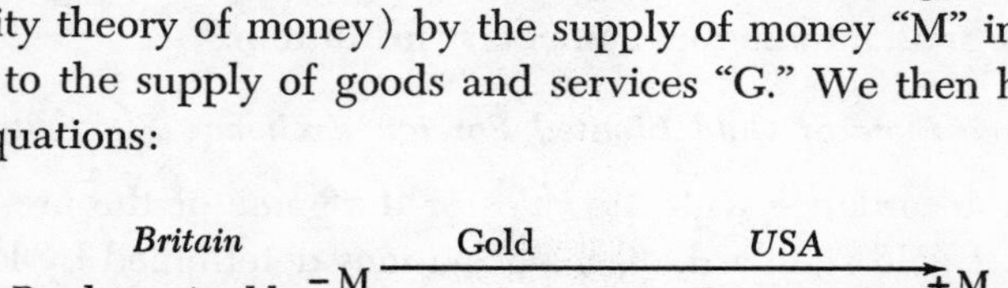

Britain	Gold →	*USA*
P determined by $\frac{-M}{+G}$		P determined by $\frac{+M}{-G}$

Let us assume, prices in Britain increase, and the British are buying more goods in the U.S., "G" would then tend to increase in Britain and decrease in the U.S. and Britain would pay for the excess of imports by shipping gold. This would reduce the supply of "M" in Britain and increase it in the U.S., which, in turn, would make for lower prices in Britain (more goods, less money) and higher prices in America (fewer goods, more money), until the British and American price levels were again in balance thus ending the flow of gold from Britain to the U.S.

As long as the countries of the world adhered to the gold standard, the flow of gold prevented any major differences in the average price levels. No country was able to manipulate prices at home without regard to world market prices.

It was this fact, which induced President Roosevelt in 1933 to abandon the gold standard in the hope of being able to raise domestic prices from their depression lows, irrespective of what happened to world market prices. "We are interested in American commodity prices" he told the world. "What is to be the value of the dollar in terms of foreign currencies is not and cannot be our immediate concern." By manipulating the supply of "M", Roosevelt hoped to create "the kind of dollar which a generation hence will have the same purchasing power and debt-paying power as the dollar value we hope to attain in the near future." The great experiment failed, and within two years the United States returned to a limited gold standard. The Treasury stands ready to buy and sell gold at $35 an ounce provided the seller or buyer is a foreign central bank or an international monetary institution.

Free Flow of Gold Limited Foreign Exchange Fluctuations

In accordance with the rules of the game of the pre-World War I gold standard, all major nations determined by law the amount of gold which their paper currency would buy. At the end of World War II, the International Monetary Fund (I.M.F.) adopted this aspect of the gold standard by requiring all member countries to fix the value of their respective currencies in terms of gold. Some nations have thus far failed to meet this requirement, but with most currencies fixed in terms of gold, the foreign exchange rates (the rate at which one foreign currency can be exchanged for another) are also fixed. In the United States, gold is valued at $35 an ounce. In Britain, an ounce of gold is officially valued at £14.58⅓. By dividing 14.58⅓ into 35, one arrives at the official rate of exchange of £1 = $2.40. As long as the American and the British governments (or the two central banks) stand ready to buy and sell gold at $35 and £14.58⅓ respectively, the $–£ rate cannot deviate much from the official rate of £1 = $2.40.

Gold as the International Medium of Exchange

Even though the gold standard, in its traditional form, no longer exists, and gold no longer regulates the supply of money and the international flow of capital, it remains extremely important as the basic international medium of exchange. Dollars, pounds and other convertible currencies are usually accepted in place of gold, and under the Gold Exchange Standard system (which was in vogue during the 1920's, collapsed during the 1930's, and was again adopted after World War II), so-called "reserve currencies" (chiefly dollars and Sterling) are used by other central banks as part of their reserves in place of gold. But this system functions only as long as the reserve currencies are actually "as good as gold," i.e. are freely convertible into gold. In the end, gold is the only universally acceptable international medium of exchange.

Chapter 12

THE FISCAL SYSTEM

THE BASIC FACTS

The American government has grown extremely rapidly since the 1930's as a result of a changing philosophy of government, changing economic conditions, the impact of the Depression, World War II, and the cold war. Almost 13 million Americans are employed by Federal, state and local agencies. During the 30 years of 1937–1967 the population of the United States grew by 55%, the Federal Budget by 1500%. During the four years of 1960–1964 alone, the Federal debt increased by an amount equal to the total national debt in the early 1930's.

The sheer weight of the tax burden is not the only factor which affects the economy. Probably even more important is the extreme complexity of the American tax system. Even the experts in Washington can no longer predict with any degree of certainty the amount of revenues and expenditures of the Federal Government during the ensuing fiscal year.

Depending upon the methods of accounting used (Administrative, Cash, National Income or Capital Budget), the Federal Government during the 1953–62 decade suffered large deficits or actually showed a surplus.

Government Finance The Federal Government can secure the necessary revenues through taxation, borrowing or the *creation of additional money. There are definite political, social and economic limits to the level of taxation. Assuming near-full employment, an increase in government spending must by necessity result in a corresponding decrease in consumer spending or private investment. It is possible, however, to substitute public investments (e.g., roads and power plants) for private investments; and social consumption (educational facilities, public parks, slum clearance projects, etc.) for private consumption.*

Aims of Fiscal Policies — The objectives of fiscal policy are not confined to purely "fiscal" aspects, the collection of taxes to meet the ordinary expenditures of the government. Taxes and government spending are used to achieve social and political goals (e.g., a greater equality of income), to counteract cyclical fluctuations, and to promote economic growth.

Types of Taxes — While there is no limit to the variety of taxes and levies governments can devise, all forms of taxes can be grouped under five main headings: taxes on property, income, consumption, business activities, and inheritances or estates. The Federal Government relies chiefly on individual and corporate income taxes (more so than any other government in the world). These taxes are based supposedly on the taxpayer's "ability to pay." Actually, however, taxes are shifted, and it is extremely difficult in practice to ascertain the actual "tax incidence."

The Federal Debt — Prior to the 1930's it was assumed that a government should pay off, as soon as possible, the debts which it had contracted during an emergency. Today the public debt is regarded as an essential part of the fiscal and monetary mechanism, and according to modern economic theory, under conditions of unemployment, even a partial repayment of the debt would have adverse effects on the economy.

State and Local Debts — State and local spending increased sharply during the postwar years to finance many needed improvements which had been neglected during the Depression and war years. By the middle 1960's an increasing number of state and local governments were approaching their taxing and borrowing limits, and came to look more and more to the Federal Government for aid in financing a vast variety of social and economic projects.

Public "Bookkeeping"

Like private businessmen, governments have to maintain books in order to keep track of their actual and scheduled revenues and expenditures. There are three sets of accounts which most governments, not only the United States, compile.

The *Federal Budget* deals with fiscal matters. It shows the revenues and expenditures of the Federal Government, and the state of the national debt. It dates back to the days of President Wilson. The second set of accounts, known as the *Balance of Payments,* summarizes all foreign payments, public and private, which were either made or received by Americans in the course of the year. The *National Income Accounts,* finally, show in terms of current dollars the flow of revenues and expenditures throughout the economy. The Balance of Payments and the National Incomes Accounts were developed during the 1930's and 1940's.

In this chapter we shall deal with the fiscal operations of the Federal Government (and to a limited extent with those of the state and local governments) and their impact upon the economy.

The Meaning of the Word "Fiscal"

The word "fiscal" has largely lost its precise meaning in the American language. It is derived from the Latin word "fiscus," meaning "reed basket," and dates back in its present usage to the time before Christ, when the Roman peasant still paid his taxes in the form of produce because the use of money was still limited. A "fiscus," a reed basket, was used to collect and store grain and other produce. Eventually the entire administration of public finance came to be referred to as the "fiscus," just as people now speak of the "White House" in referring to the President.

The Size and Complexity of the American Government

In view of the tremendous growth of the government during the past 30 years, it is impossible to study the American economy without paying a great deal of attention to the public sector. The national debt amounted to $345.2 billion at the end of 1967, compared with $16 billion in 1932, and total federal obligations (including direct, contingent and indirect obligations, such as the commitments of the Social Security and Civil Service Retirements systems) exceed $1.3 trillion, or about $25,000 for every American family of four.

The Government as the Largest Employer Including the 2¾ million men and women in the Armed Forces, Federal, state and local governments employ almost 13 million people or about as many as agriculture, mining, construction, transportation and public utilities combined. And this does not include all the workers (for instance in the airplane industry) who are counted as private employees but who actually work exclusively on government contracts.

The Federal Government is by far the largest employer, the largest consumer and the largest debtor, and, for better or for worse, the more than 25% of the economy which is accounted for by the public sector determines to a large extent the course of the economy as a whole.

Growing Size of Government Operations This has not always been the case. Total Federal spending reached $500 million for the first time in 1900. Peak spending during World War I amounted to about $20 billion. The New Deal raised peacetime spending to $9 billion, and during World War II government expenditures reached what was then regarded as the astronomical figure of $98.4 billion. As the hostilities ended, government spending dropped back to $33 billion. As a result of the Korean War, spending rose rapidly to $74 billion — but dropped back again to $64 billion. Ten years later, however (in 1965), without a special emergency, spending had reached a new all-time high of about $100 billion, and in 1967/68 (partly as a result of the Vietnam war) expenditures exceeded $135 billion. Much of the increase is due to the tremendous growth in defense spending, from $0.9 billion in 1929 to about $80 billion during the 1967/68 fiscal year (including space research). At the same time, however, Federal spending for pensions, subsidies and a large variety of welfare measures rose from $1.2 to almost $30 billion, which reflects the changing character of the American government and American society in general.

Rapid Increase in Public Spending Government expenditures increased particularly rapidly during the early 1960's. During the fiscal year 1959/60 total Federal spending (including trust funds, such as Social Security) amounted to $94.3 billion; by 1964/65 they had risen to $122 billion. Yet these were not years of a national emergency. The sharp rise in defense spending due to the Vietnam war did not occur until 1965/66. By 1968/69 spending had increased to well over $180 billion. In eight years (fiscal 1960 to fiscal 1968) defense spending increased by 68% and non-defense spending by 97%.

Growing Indebtedness To finance this vast amount of spending, the government had to go deeper and deeper into debt. In four years (1960–64), the increase of the Federal debt was larger than the total debt in the early 1930's. Yet at the same time, according to the economic experts of the Kennedy and Johnson Administrations, the tax burden developed increasingly into an obstacle to economic growth. In his State of the Union Message of January 1963, President Kennedy spoke of "our obsolete tax system" which "exerts too heavy a drag on private purchasing power, profits, and employment. Designed to check inflation in earlier years, it now checks growth instead. It discourages extra effort and risk. It distorts the use of resources. It invites recurrent recessions, depresses the Federal revenues, and causes chronic budget deficits."

Complexity of U.S. Taxation

Instead of a thorough reconstruction of the entire tax system which was born, as some people say, out of the emergencies of the Depression years, the war and the post-war inflation (or as others feel, because it was good politics to "soak the rich") Congress for the past 10 years has produced a crazy-quilt of exemptions, to which must be added the multiplicity of state and local taxes. Union Carbide Corporation, in one single year, had to fill out 3,600 forms relating to taxes, and this is not an exception.

Uncertainty of Budget Estimates It is not at all certain that even the experts of the Treasury Department are able to grasp fully the implications of their budget estimates. Admittedly, in some years estimates are on the optimistic side, and in others on the pessimistic, depending upon political expediency; Congress often makes drastic changes on its own; and despite the large number of economic prognosticators in the government, the economy almost invariably develops differently from what the experts in the Treasury Department expected.

State and Local Governments The Federal Government is not alone in demanding taxes and a multitude of forms, even though Washington is by far the most oppressive in terms of taxes and paperwork. In addition to the Federal Government, there are about 90,000 state and local governmental entities which collect a bewildering variety and steadily increasing volume of taxes.

The Federal Budget

There are at least four different ways of calculating the Federal Budget. The *Administrative Budget* does not include such items as the highway building program (which is financed out of a separate highway trust fund), the Social Security and Railroad Retirement Funds, and other items. For the 10 years 1953–1962, the "Administrative Budget" averaged a deficit of almost $3.8 billion a year. The *Cash Budget,* on the other hand, which includes all funds received and paid out by the Federal Government and its many subdivisions, showed an average deficit during the same 10 years of only $2.3 billion. The deficit was even smaller, averaging only $1.4 billion, if we employ the *National Income Budget* procedure, which (1) omits all Federal loans, (2) includes taxes as they accrue (not as they are actually collected) and (3) government orders as they are actually executed by private business and thus affect production and employment (not as they are authorized by Congress [Administrative Budget] or as they are eventually paid for by the Treasury [Cash Budget]).

Finally, there are some economists who feel that the United States should follow the example of some foreign countries and separate current and capital expenditures. As the government builds roads, canals, power dams, buildings, and "invests" in similar "capital improvements," these capital expenditures should be excluded from the current budget. Also omitted should be the receipts and expenditures of the trust funds. If the "Capital Budget" accounting method is used, the Federal Government had an average annual *surplus* of almost $4 billion during the 10-year period between 1953–1962, rather than a deficit of almost $3.8 billion, if the conventional method of accounting were used.

There is no way of saying which one of the four methods of presenting the Federal budget is "correct." Each method has its own advocates and advantages. In this chapter, however we shall use the figures of the traditional Aministrative Budget, which during the 37 years from 1930–67 showed a deficit in 30 years totaling about $325 billion, and a surplus in seven years totaling not quite $18 billion, which caused the national debt to increase from about $17 to over $326 billion, or more than 18-fold. The value of all the goods and services produced annually increased in the same time from $81.9 billion to $652 billion, or about 8-fold.

The Sources of Government Revenue

No government, whether Federal, state or local, whether democratic or totalitarian, has unlimited spending power. Before a government can spend money it must secure the necessary funds. These can come from a variety of sources. The three most important sources of government revenues are (1) taxes, (2) borrowing and (3) (in the case of central governments) the creation of additional money. The ways in which a government obtains the funds it wishes to spend has an important bearing upon the political and economic character of the nation.

Taxation or Borrowing

From an economic point of view there is little difference (at least in the short run) between taxation and borrowing, provided the government does not borrow from the Federal Reserve or commercial banks. As long as the government borrows from individuals, corporations and savings and loan associations, there is no increase in the total money supply. Existing purchasing power is merely shifted from the private sector to the public. Instead of money being spent on consumption goods, or to finance private housing, it goes into defense or welfare spending.

Whether the transfer of purchasing power from the private to the public sector (either through taxation or borrowing) is desirable or not, is a matter of opinion. Some economists (for instance, Professors Hansen and Galbraith) argue that in an affluent society, where the immediate needs of the individual have been met, too much private spending flows into useless gadgets which add little to the national well-being. They therefore advocate a shift — via taxes or government borrowing — from private consumption to public consumption. Other social philosophers disagree violently. They hold, in the spirit of the traditional American individualism, that the individual is better qualified than the government to judge what increases his well-being.

Limits of Taxation

The taxing and borrowing capacity of a government, moreover, is not unlimited. Even John Maynard Keynes, who favored increased public spending during periods of unemployment, warned that if public spending exceeds a certain percentage of the national income, the government will be forced to resort to the proverbial "printing press," the creation of money, in order to obtain the necessary funds. Whether this "critical point," where government spending can no longer be covered through taxation or borrowing, is reached when government spending exceeds 25% of the national income, a figure frequently mentioned during the postwar years, or 30% or 40%, depends to a large extent on two factors: (1) the power of the government to impose its will upon the people through an efficient tax collecting system (the new electronic devices have probably raised the "critical point" by making tax evasion more difficult), and (2) the willingness of the people to make sacrifices for a national cause.

Nobody knows in advance when public spending reaches a level where it becomes a vehicle of inflation because the necessary funds can no longer be obtained through taxation or borrowing. Some economists, e.g., Professor Paul Samuelsen argue that America is operating well below "the economic limits of taxation." Others challenge this point of view. And the "political limits" may actually be lower than the economic. Even the old argument in favor of concealed taxes, to "pluck the goose with a minimum of squawking," has its limits.

"Printing Money"

Modern wars can be financed only through the "printing press." This is true even in totalitarian countries. Modern governments do not actually "print money." Today's "printing press" process is somewhat more involved and less obvious. The governments actually print "bonds" (long-term I.O.U.'s payable out of future tax receipts). These bonds are turned over to the central bank (or commercial banks) which in turn credit the checking accounts of the government (against which the government can draw at any time). The central bank and the commercial banks thus create additional "money" in the form of government demand deposits, and from an economic point of view the end-effect is the same as if the government had "printed money" in the first place.

Since the increase in the supply of money, created by the government to cover its deficits, ultimately leads to higher prices, even the "printing bonds" method of paying for government spending ultimately produces a "tax," even though a concealed one. It is paid (in the form of a reduction in real income) by all those whose nominal income does not increase commensurately with the increase in prices.

No government services can ever be provided "free." Someone has to pay the bill.

Government Spending and the Gross National Product

Nor can any country consume more than it produces — unless it manages to live on international charity, which few nations have been able to do for any length of time. The maximum output of a nation is determined by its resources: the available manpower, the technological know-how, machines and raw materials. The size of the "pie" (Figure 2) can be increased through longer hours of work, an increase in the population, and technological developments. It is also possible to reduce waste due to unemployment, "featherbedding", planned obsolescence, bureaucratic paper-shuffling, and some types of advertising; but the margin of avoidable waste is usually not more than 5-8% of the total amount of goods and services

FIGURE 2 ***The Division of the Potential Gross National Product***

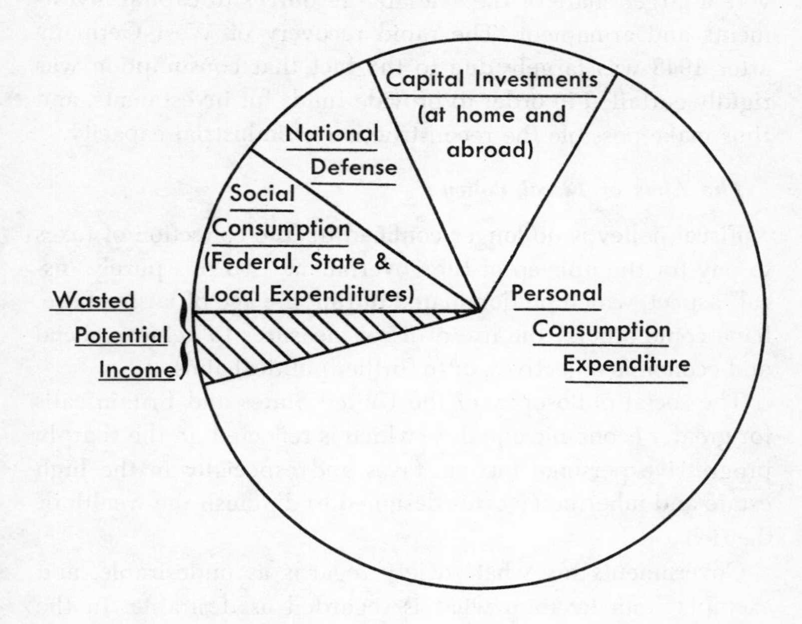

which might be produced. And even this margin may be difficult to eliminate because of institutional factors, such as the lack of training of the unemployed, the power of the unions, the competitive nature of our economy, and the entrenched power of the bureaucracy.

"Guns or Butter"

Since the size of the "pie" is thus fixed during a given tax year, an increase in the size of one slice, let us say national defense spending, will necessitate a reduction in either personal consumption, capital investments, or social consumption. For decades Soviet Russia, and more recently Mainland China, have restricted private consumption in order to be able to devote a larger share of the available resources to capital investments and armament. The rapid recovery of West Germany after 1948 was largely due to the fact that consumption was rigidly curtailed in order to provide funds for investments, and thus make possible the reconstruction of industrial capacity.

The Aims of Fiscal Policy

Fiscal policy is no longer confined to "the collection of taxes to pay for the upkeep of the government." To this purely "fiscal" aspect, which predominated during the age of laissez faire, have come others: the use of fiscal measures to achieve social and economic objectives, or to further political aims.

The social philosophy of the United States and Britain calls for greater economic equality, which is reflected in the sharply progressive personal income taxes and especially in the high estate and inheritance taxes designed to diminish the wealth of the rich.

Governments tax what society regards as undesirable, and exempts from taxation what is regarded as desirable. In the United States, churches pay no taxes; in Russia they are fully taxed. Tobacco and alcohol are taxed heavily in most countries, not only because these "luxuries" are easy to tax, but because at one time, and to some extent even today, the consumption of tobacco and liquor is frowned upon.

Since fiscal policy is not made in a political vacuum, political expediency often outweighs economic and social considerations. The West German turn-over tax, for instance, a small tax levied every time a product passes from the raw material producer to the manufacturer, to the wholesaler, and ultimately to the retailer, had the advantage of producing a large income without the public's being aware of the fact that it is being taxed. The tax was hidden in the increased retail price. The United States corporate income tax has a similar effect — even though this is a much debated issue among economists. From the politicians' point of view it seems easy to levy a 50% tax on corporations. The corporations cannot vote, and only too many people think that the "big, rich corporations" can afford to pay taxes. In reality, the corporate income tax (like the German turn-over tax) is to a large extent passed on to the consumer in the form of higher prices.

The Cost of Tax Collection

A very important aspect of fiscal policy which is often overlooked is a purely practical one: How difficult is it to collect a certain tax? When income taxes were first levied in the United States during the Civil War, the cost of collecting one dollar was about 2½ cents; today the cost is only about ½ cent.

State and local authorities often encounter difficulties in collecting taxes on tangible and especially intangible property. In the end, no system of taxation can be enforced which enough people regard as unreasonable, because the cost of collecting the tax grows out of proportion to the actual revenues.

Taxes and Economic Planning

Of special interest in modern fiscal theory is the use of fiscal measures to achieve certain economic goals. During the 1930's, under the influence of Keynesian theory, fiscal policy was regarded as one of the most important tools to overcome cyclical fluctuations. After the war, fiscal measures were used to assure "full employment," and since the early 1960's, fiscal policies have come to be looked upon as a tool to achieve a more rapid rate of economic growth.

More often than not, the various goals of fiscal policy are in conflict with each other. Steeply progressive income taxes may make for economic equality, but may also hamper capital investments and thus economic growth.

The Various Types of Taxes

There is no limit to the imagination of governments in devising new forms of taxes and levies, from salt to prostitution, and from the numbers of windows facing the street to foreign travel. Well over two dozen different taxes are being levied on an automobile in the process of its production before it is finally driven away by the purchaser. But most of the taxes can be classified under five major headings:

1. *Property taxes,* either on real estate, personal property or intangibles (stocks and bonds and other securities), form the backbone of local taxes.
2. *Income taxes* include personal and corporate income taxes (although the latter could also be regarded as a concealed sales tax). These provide about 80% of the revenues of the Federal Government. More than half the states, and an increasing number of cities, also rely for part of their revenues on income taxes.

The Federal income tax became constitutional in 1913 through the adoption of the 16th Amendment. Table 4 shows the changes in income tax rates during the past 50 years. As late as 1930 only one in 33 Americans paid an income tax; 30 years later the figure was closer to one in four.

More than 85% of the total income tax yield is derived from the base rate. Surtaxes produce less than 15% of the total income tax revenues, and surtaxes above 50% (under the schedule in force until 1964) yielded only about 0.6% of the total.

TABLE 4

The Growth of the Personal Income Tax

	Base Rate	Surtax	Exemption
1913........	1%	1% $20-50,000	$3,000
		6% above $500,000	
1963........	20%	1% beginning at $2000	$ 600
		91% above $200,000	
1965........	14%	1% beginning at $2000	$ 600
		70% above $200,000	

Source: Table compiled on basis of data contained in Shultz and Harris: "American Public Finance" p. 379 and instruction sheets accompanying income tax forms for 1963 and 1965.

3. *Taxes on Consumption* (excise taxes) are levied on a large variety of goods and services. They include state and local sales taxes; the so-called "luxury" taxes levied by the Federal Government; taxes on tobacco and liquor levied by the Federal, state and local governments; the transportation tax; import duties collected by the Federal government and turnover taxes of the type used in Germany and some of the other European countries.
4. *Taxes on Business Activities* include the portion of the Social Security tax paid by the employer, and a multitude of license fees collected from business by the Federal, state, and local governments.
5. *Inheritance and Estate Taxes* are collected by the Federal and state governments.

The division is not clear-cut. Social Security taxes, for instance, can be classified as a business tax, as far as the payments of the employers are concerned, while the portion paid by the employee has the characteristic of an income tax.

While there are minor deviations from year to year, the Federal Government derives its income from the following types of taxes:

TABLE 5

Sources of Federal Tax Revenues (1966/67 Budget)

Individual income taxes	51%	Excise taxes	8%
Corporation income taxes	30%	Other receipts	11%

Basis of Federal Taxation The Constitution gives the Federal government the authority to collect taxes only "to pay the debts and provide for the common defense and general welfare of the United States." The "defense" and "general welfare" clauses, however, have been interpreted as giving the government a virtual *carte blanche* to tax and spend. As part of the "national defense," the government can subsidize graduate work in folklore and church music, and the "general welfare" clause permits the use of taxes collected from a New York clerk to build a ski lift in Idaho.

Sources of State and Local Revenues The states derive the major portion of their income from excise taxes on gasoline (all 50 states tax gasoline), tobacco and liquor (or from the operation of liquor stores). More than 30 states collect a general sales tax, and a growing number of states depend on state income taxes. Property taxes (with some exception, e.g., Illinois) have become relatively unimportant as a source of state revenues. But license fees (hunting, fishing, motoring, business, etc.) are used extensively by all states.

Local governments derive almost 90% of their income from property taxes, the balance from local sales taxes and license fees. A few are collecting in addition a city income tax.

Who Pays the Taxes?

Since the 19th Century a great deal has been written about the social, economic and ethical aspects of taxation. Should a man be taxed commensurate with the *benefits* he receives in return, or on the basis of his *ability to pay?* If a man uses public highways, some people argue, he should pay for their construction and maintenance through the gasoline tax. Bridges should be financed through toll charges. A man who drinks whiskey and smokes cigarettes should pay a special tax for the privilege of being allowed to indulge in what many people regard as "sinful" forms of consumption.

The graduated income tax, on the other hand, is based on the ability-to-pay principle. Under the 1962 income tax schedule a man with a wife and two children (and thus entitled to a deduction of $2400) and an income of $4,800, paid less than $50 in income taxes. Another man, whose income was twice as large ($9600), had to pay 30 times as much in income taxes ($1584). Under the graduated income tax system, taxes rise steeply as nominal income increases (even though this increase could be merely a reflection of widespread inflation) because the nominal (not the real) income is regarded as a measure of the "ability to pay."

Depending on whether a tax is based on the ability-to-pay or the benefit principle, it is termed progressive, regressive, or proportional. A *progressive tax,* such as the graduated personal income tax, increases proportionally faster than the income of the taxpayer. *Regressive taxes,* on the other hand, such as sales taxes and import duties on necessities, weigh relatively more heavily on the lower income groups. A salt tax assures a steady flow of income and is easy to collect, but Ghandi made the salt tax in India one of his major campaign issues because the poorest Untouchable cannot survive without salt. In using about the same amount of salt as the richest maharaja, he had to pay the same amount of tax. A *proportional* tax is levied in direct proportion to the taxpayer's income or wealth. The same percentage is deducted from a worker's wages for Social Security taxes, whether he is paid $2500 or $4000. The same property tax rate applies, whether a property is valued at $15,000 or at $30,000.

Tax Incidence

The problem of progressive taxes, however, with all its political and social overtones, is far more complex than appears on the surface. It is easy to determine who actually pays a tax, but it is often all but impossible to discover who ultimately bears the burden. Corporate income taxes in the United States, and turn-over taxes in Germany, are paid by business, but a large part of the tax burden is actually shifted to the consumer in the form of higher prices. In theory, the tax incidence can usually be calculated very neatly; in reality, it is often all but impossible.

Tax Shifting

A tax on farm land, for instance, is often shifted forward to the consumer in the form of higher food prices. A tax on a apartment house, on the other hand, is capitalized and shifted backward. Assuming that the net rental income of the house is $10,000, and the prevailing rate of return on investments of this type is 10%, the value of the house would be $100,000, 10 times the annual return. If taxes were increased by $1,000, thus reducing the net income to $9,000, the house would be worth only $90,000. The tax would thus be born by the one who owned the house when the tax was imposed, not by any subsequent owner who actually pays the tax but who acquired the house at a lower value based on the increased tax burden.

Income taxes, according to most American textbooks, cannot

be shifted. This is undoubtedly true in the low and medium brackets. Executives, however, in the $25-30,000 bracket and up, whose services are in demand, figure their income in terms of a net income after taxes. New York firms will have to pay a somewhat higher salary than firms in Illinois, because New York has a state income tax while Illinois has none. Personal income taxes (which result in higher salaries) thus become a business expense and are shifted to the consumer.

Shiftability of Excise Taxes

Personal property and inheritance taxes cannot be shifted. Sales taxes on necessities, on the other hand, such as salt, are usually shifted in full to the consumer. In the case of other excise taxes the degree of shiftability is determined by the relative elasticity of demand and supply. The greater the dependence of the buyer upon a certain product or service, the greater the chances that the vendor will be able to shift the tax. If a sales tax were levied on toothpaste but not on toothpowder, and the public could freely substitute toothpowder for toothpaste, the manufacturers of toothpaste probably would have to absorb most of the tax.

Government Spending

While taxes act as a retardent to consumption and investments, government spending acts as a stimulant. The fact that the Federal, state and local governments spend close to 30% of all the dollars which are spent in the United States gives them a tremendous power to influence the course of the economy. Table 6 provides a breakdown of Federal expenditures.

Highways, law enforcement, health and education account for the major share of state expenditures. Schools absorb by far the largest part of local revenues.

TABLE 6

Federal Expenditures (1967 Budget)

National defense	31%	Social Security & other Trust Funds	26%
Vietnam war	13%	Agriculture	2%
Space program	3%	International	2%
Veterans	4%	Others	13%
Fixed interest charges	6%		100%

Concentration of Government Power

Whether the growing concentration of power in Washington is necessary or desirable is one of the chief points of disagreement between the modern liberals (who believe in a strong state to aid and protect the individual) and the conservatives and libertarians (who fear the state and believe that the individual is better able to look after his own needs than the government). The trend of the time seems to be toward greater concentration of power. Both political parties, even though to a somewhat different degree, adhere to the new philosophy. "Modern Republicanism," according to a definition which President Eisenhower gave during the 1952 campaign, is "a philosophy that recognizes the Federal Government's responsibility to lead in making certain that productivity is so distributed that no one suffers privation through any fault of his own." On the Democratic side, the opinions are even more outspoken. Post-World War II America does not share Woodrow Wilson's fear that "a concentration of governmental power . . . always precedes the death of human liberty."

The Federal Debt

The Federal debt increases when Federal expenditures exceed revenues, except in the rare instance where the government has a cash balance on which it can draw. Until the 1930's, fiscal theory and practice called for the repayment of government debts contracted during an emergency. The Civil War debt was repaid in full. For a number of years, in fact, the government was embarrassed by an excess of funds. Tariffs levied to protect industry produced more income than could be spent on "normal" government operations. More than a third of the debts outstanding at the end of World War I (25.5 billion) were repaid during the prosperous 1920's (1930: $16.2 billion).

During the 1930's, however, fiscal practices underwent a radical change; there was never any difficulty in finding additional worthy causes on which to spend. According to the new fiscal theory, moreover, which developed during the 1930's, the repayment of the public debt during periods of unemployment is regarded as actually detrimental to the economy because a reduction of the public debt is assumed to produce a deflationary effect.

Prior to 1917, Congress exercised a close supervision over the national debt. It determined exactly the amounts which were to be borrowed and the interest rates and maturities of the new issues. In 1917, however, these details were turned over to the Treasury, and Congress merely stipulated in the Second Liberty Loan Act that total government borrowing was not to exceed $7,538,945,460.

Debt Ceiling

This was the beginning of the so-called "debt ceiling" idea, which has been part of American fiscal fiction ever since. Very soon the "ceiling" had to be raised, and raised again. In 1941 it was fixed at $65 billion. By the end of the war the ceiling had reached $300 billion. Subsequently the limit was reduced to $275, which sufficed to finance the Korean War. Since 1954, however, Congress has been compelled at regular intervals to increase the ceiling in order to enable the government to borrow enough money to meet the appropriations which Congress had voted without providing the necessary revenues.

Types of Government Securities

In order to appreciate the problems of debt management, which is vital to an understanding of fiscal anti-cyclical and growth policies, it is necessary to be familiar with the various types of government securities, which consist of Marketable, Convertible, Nonmarketable and Special Issues.

Marketable Securities

There are four types of marketable securities which can be freely bought and sold: two types of short term papers, Bills (with a maturity of 90–180 days) and Certificates (maturing in about a year); the medium-term Notes (maturing in 1–5 years), and (3) the long-term bonds (maturing after five years). Certificates, Notes and Bonds pay interest; Bills are sold by the Treasury at a discount. Each week the Treasury sells about $1.5–$2 billion in Bills, and uses the proceeds to pay back the Bills which come due during the same week.

Convertible bonds are held only by financial institutions, and cannot be sold to the general public. However, they can be converted into marketable securities bearing a slightly lower rate of interest.

The nonmarketable bonds consist chiefly of the familiar Savings Bonds, which can be cashed in by the holder but cannot be sold. The Special Issues, finally, are held by U.S. Government agencies and trust funds. The Old Age and Survivor Insurance, for instance, is calculated on the basis of a 3½% return on its investment. Since for a long time no 3½% government bonds were available, the government issued special 3½% bonds to the trust funds, which in effect represented a subsidy of the social security system, since the Treasury could have obtained the funds more cheaply.

"Shortening" of the Debt

Aside from the rapid growth in the national debt, the composition of the debt underwent an important change. The amount of bonds and nonmarketable savings bonds declined by about $14.3 billion during the 20 postwar years. The people wished to use their savings for the purchase of homes and cars and other goods, and the banks found it more advantageous to make loans to business than to hold long-term government issues at a lower interest rate. To secure the necessary funds for the repayment of the bonds, the Federal Government had to rely more and more on Bills.

In 1946 the average maturity of the Federal debt was more than 9 years. By the end of 1965, it had declined to about 5 years. This "shortening" of the debt can have serious effects. If an individual buys a savings bond, or an insurance company buys a long term bond, no additional money is created. Purchase power is merely transferred from the private to the public sector. But if the Federal Reserve and commercial banks buy Treasury Bills there is a very good chance that additional money is created. The shortening of the debt thus tends to have an inflationary effect. Conversely, a lengthening of the debt (the sale of, let us say, savings bonds to pay back Bills) would have a deflationary effect.

State and Local Finance

Between 1946 and 1960, state and local spending increased from 3.8% of the Gross National Product to about 10%. A number of perfectly legitimate reasons explain the sharp increase in state and local spending. For at least 15 years, during the depression and the war, state and local governments fell behind on necessary investments in hospitals, schools, roads, prisons and general improvements. In many instances the population had grown substantially, some of the public facilities had become obsolete, and the total was often inadequate. Beginning in the early 1950's, the postwar baby boom began to put a rapidly increasing strain on educational facilities. The numbers of classrooms and of teachers were inadequate, and after many years of paying substandard salaries, the school boards were suddenly confronted with the necessity of having to raise teachers' salaries and to improve working conditions, in order to fill the growing number of vacancies.

The flight from the city to suburbia deprived many cities of some of their more affluent taxpayers. Lower-middle-class residential areas developed into slums requiring increased expenditures for law enforcement, public health and welfare. To fight the growing slums, state and local authorities, supported by the Federal Government, went into costly urban rehabilitation schemes. The almost 200% increase in the number of automobiles, since the end of the war and the sharp increase in the number of commuters, called for the construction of a new system of speedways in order to connect the suburban residential areas with the urban business centers.

Added to these almost unavoidable demands for large expenditures — and where billions are involved, waste and graft are almost always present — state and local governments, in the spirit of the time, became increasingly liberal with welfare expenditures, thus attracting more destitute migrants from the decaying rural areas to the crowded city slums.

Growing Financial Squeeze

There is no end in sight for the steadily rising state and local expenditures, but the taxing and borrowing capacity of some states and of many municipalities is approaching its limits. Between 1950 and 1962, real estate taxes increased by about 217% from $7.0 to more than $22.2 billion, and home owners are beginning to rebel by voting down new bond issues. At the same time more and more communities, and even large and wealthy states (such as Michigan) have found it difficult, at least temporarily, to meet their obligations.

The Federal Government has, at least in theory, unlimited taxing power, and can always meet its obligations through the creation of more money. The taxing power of the states, and especially local governments, on the other hand, is distinctly limited. Rapidly rising real estate taxes (the backbone of local finance) result in the deterioration of real estate. High local and state taxes drive away industry to localities and states with smaller tax burdens and thus increase unemployment and welfare expenditures. It is thus not surprising that the states, and many large metropolitan areas, turn to Washington for financial aid in one form or another. In less than 10 years, between the early fifties and early sixties, Federal grants-in-aid to the states increased by more than 200%, to account for an average of 20% of total state revenues. At the same time 30% of the states' expenditures go for aid to the hard-pressed local governments.

Regional Allocation of Federal Spending

In addition to the direct financial aid to states and local governments, the Federal Government spends each year, directly or indirectly, well over $100 billion throughout the country. Some of the funds are not subject to Federal discretion, especially Old Age Security and G.I benefits. But in the allocation of some $70–80 billion, the Federal Government has considerable leeway. The largest share involves defense spending, and politicians have long claimed special influence in getting government contracts for their states. Then there are post offices, prisons, Veterans Administration hospitals, power installations and, in recent years, the funds spent by the Urban Renewal and the Area Redevelopment Administrations. The financial difficulties of the states and local entities thus reinforce the trend toward centralization. The power shifts from the elected city council to Washington officials who are largely beyond the control of the electorate.

Chapter 13

CYCLICAL FLUCTUATIONS

THE BASIC FACTS

Modern business cycle theory started with Clement Juglar in the 1860's. Juglar was the first to recognize, and describe in detail, a phenomenon of which man had been aware certainly since the days of Joseph: Over a period of 7–10 years, economic activities tend to rise, reach a peak, decline, and eventually reach a low before rising again.

Economists are, above all, interested in discovering the forces which cause these cyclical fluctuations. Are they outside (exogenous) forces? Or are they forces which work from within the economy (endogenous)? If they are exogenous, such as sunspots, can they be predicted? Or are they unpredictable, such as sudden political events?

The majority of economists have concentrated on the endogenous forces. There are two basically different business cycle philosophies: the overexpansionist and the underconsumptionist theories. The overexpansionists hold that depressions are the normal reaction to a preceding boom. The critics of this notion see in it a reflection of "Puritan ethics": Man is punished with a deflationary hangover for his preceding inflationary excesses. Present-day theory tends toward the underconsumptionist theory. "Full employment" (which, as a rule, is not achieved except during boom periods) is regarded as the "nor-

mal" level of economic activities, rather than a level midway between the peak and the bottom of the cycle.

Economic attitudes and policies differ considerably, depending upon whether a nation thinks in terms of "overproduction" or "underconsumption" as the cause of a depression.

While economists continue to be vitally interested in learning more about the causes *of cyclical fluctuations, some of them, especially those connected with or influenced by the National Bureau of Economic Research, have taken a different approach. They have developed a number of indices which may not reveal the causes of cyclical fluctuations, but which are expected to provide warning signals of impending changes in business activities. Some of these "barometers" have been very helpful. They have not reached a stage of perfection, however, to enable economists to predict business trends with the same (limited) degree of certainity with which meteorologists can predict the weather.*

The 19th Century approach to the problem of cyclical fluctuations was predominantly analytical. Economists tried to discover the forces which produce economic change, so that businessmen could adjust to these forces. The modern approach, on the other hand, is largely operational (at least so far as the government is concerned). Washington wants to know more about cyclical changes in order to take measures to combat depressions and inflation.

The "science" of business cycles is complex. In addition to to the 7–10 year Juglar cycle, there are at least two other cyclical movements: the Kondratieff cycle, which lasts about 30–50 years, and the Kitchin cycle, which lasts about 40 months. The three cyclical movements are overlapping.

Then, too, cyclical developments are not a national phenomenon. Inflationary booms and depressions cross national borders and interfere with national economic planning.

The History of the Business Cycle

The oldest record of a "business cycle" is found in the Bible. Joseph, a keen observer and economic planner, realized that the agricultural production of the Nile valley fluctuated from surplus years to years of inadequate output, and he suggested that the government store the surpluses of the good years and dispose of them during the poor years. Since "seven" was a sacred number, the Bible came to speak of the "seven fat" and the "seven lean" years. Actually the cycles were probably somewhat longer.

Throughout history we can observe cyclical fluctuations, some of them lasting for very long periods. During the 150 years from about 1150 to 1300, for instance, the European economy expanded rapidly. Then followed what would today be called a "prosperity on a high plateau", which lasted some 40–50 years. By the middle of the 14th Century various disasters overtook Europe, followed by about a century of economic decline and stagnation. Even "business forecasters" were not unknown in the late Middle Ages. The famous business trust of the Fuggers, which included banking, manufacturing and international trade, had astrologers whose task it was to read future business trends in the stars.

All this seems "unscientific" to modern business cycle analysts. They do not think in terms of the "seven fat and seven lean years" of the Old Testament, nor the long waves of growth and stagnation during the Middle Ages, but chiefly of a phenomenon which was first clearly recognized and defined during the 1860's — namely the cyclical ups and downs in economic activities, which seem to occur (or at least did occur until World War II) with fair regularity every 7–10 years.

Non-cyclical Fluctuations

There are other types of business fluctuations. Most obvious are the seasonal cycles resulting either from climatic conditions (such as harvest in agricultural areas, and the tourist season in Florida and in the mountains of New Hampshire and Vermont) or from social and cultural factors (fireworks on the Fourth of July, turkeys on Thanksgiving and gifts on Christmas). These seasonal fluctuations have an important effect on business. The department stores in New York City, for example, do about 35–40% of their annual business between Thanksgiving and Christmas.

Juglar Cycles

The first important book devoted entirely to the problem of cyclical fluctuations was written by the French physician-turned economist Clement Juglar (1819–1905). It was published in 1862 under the title *Les Crises Commerciales.* The great merit of the book lies in the fact that the author was the first to conceive the notion of cyclical changes in business activities. Before Juglar, economists had been concerned only with periodic "crises," and had failed to recognize the cyclical nature of business trends. Juglar, moreover, backed his observations with fairly detailed statistical data, although his attempt to find a theoretical explanation for the business cycle remained rudimentary. Since the *Crises Commerciales* was first published a century ago, a great deal has been written on the subject, and our statistical knowledge has increased considerably — especially during the past 40 years.

Two Methods of Cycle Analysis

In trying to discover the causes and the structure of cyclical fluctuations, economists have developed two distinct methods of approach: one is predominantly rational-theoretical, and the other statistical-empirical.

The rational-theoretical approach relies on an analysis of the various factors which "may" cause business to fluctuate. In this way the economist hopes to develop a theory which will indicate a direct cause-and-effect relationship between, let us say, an increase in the supply of credit and rising business activities, or between temporary over-production and declining business. However, since business is affected by a multitude of forces, the business cycle theoriest can never be sure that an upturn or downturn was actually "caused" by changes in the volume of credit, excess production, changes in the rate of investments, rising or falling interest rates, or to whatever "cause" he may ascribe the change in business activities. Any trained logician knows that it is dangerous to rely on post-hoc-ergo-propter-hoc reasoning. (Because "B" happened "after" "A" doesn't mean that "B" was "caused" by "A.")

The second, the statistical-empirical approach, is not primarily concerned with the ultimate causes of the cyclical fluctuations. It concentrates on the collection of statistical data which, it is assumed, "will speak for themselves." They may not reveal the forces which cause the fluctuations, but if they indicate the cyclical turning points they can serve as forecasting tools.

What Causes Business Cycle Fluctuations?

In searching for the causes of business cycle flutuations, economists distinguish between exogenous and endogenous forces—those which impinge upon the economy from the outside, and others which are generated from within the economy.

Exogenous Forces

Some exogenous forces preclude prediction. Business activities can be strongly affected by earthquakes, droughts, floods, epidemics, wars and political developments. President Kennedy's attack on the steel industry in the spring of 1962, which helped to tumble the booming stock market and started (but probably did not "cause") a mild business slow-down, is a typical example of an unpredictable exogenous force. Since such unpredictable events are far from rare in the life of society, all business predictions should really be preceded with the warning "provided nothing unexpected happens."

Sunspot Cycles There may be other exogenous forces which are predictable. The best known of these are the sunspots on which William Stanley Jevons (1835–1882) based his famous business cycle theory. Jevons, a respected economist, had noticed that sunspots appeared in 7–10 year cycles and seemingly coincided with Juglar's business cycles. The explanation did not seem too far-fetched. Sunspots affect the radiation of the sun, which in turn affects the climate on the Earth and thus the crop yields. Good or bad crops in turn determine (at least in an agricultural society) the general level of economic activities. More accurate statistical studies showed subsequently that the sunspot cycles did not coincide as neatly with business cycles as Jevons had assumed. Moreover, since agriculture plays a progressively less important role in an industrial society, changes in agricultural production (whether caused by sunspots or not) are not likely to produce major business fluctuations.

Dewey-Dakin Cycles Shortly after the end of World War II a more sophisticated exogenous theory, backed by a vast amount of statistical data, gained widespread interest.[1] Statis-

[1] See especially Dewey, Edward R. and Dakin, Edwin F.: *Cycles — The Science of Prediction* (H. Holt, 1947) which reached the best-seller list; and the less statistical Huntington, Ellsworth: *Mainsprings of Civilization* (Wiley, 1945).

tics seem to indicate that the whole of nature is subject to regular cyclical changes, which apparently occur at 3½-, 9 (or 9⅔)-, 18⅓-, and 54-year intervals. The Hudson Bay Company, for instance, observed a 9⅔-year cycle in the supply of lynx. Abundance and scarcity of salmon likewise followed a regular 9⅔-year cycle. So did changes in the death rate due to heart disease, pneumonia and influenza in Britain. Wholesale prices seemed to follow a 54-year cycle, and building activities an 18⅓-year cycle. To what extent these periodic changes can be connected with ozone or ultraviolet cycles and their effect on human beings and nature in general, remains an unsolved mystery. But there is at least a chance that some day the explanation for business fluctuations may actually be found "in the stars," where the medieval astrologer-business advisors looked for it.

Endogenous Theories

The endogenous theories start with the implied assumption of the 19th Century economics that the economy functions like a big machine, which the economist, as an unbiased outside observer, can study. Once we know how the mechanism works, we can either adjust the mechanism or adjust our own business to it. We can either take the attitude of 19th Century laissez faire economists, and assume that a wise providence has arranged economic forces in such a fashion that temporary disequilibria will adjust themselves automatically; or we can take the point of view of the modern interventionist, who stands ready to interfere with the economic processes in order to eliminate disequilibria.

The Importance of Cyclical Theories In either case, and especially from the point of view of the interventionist, it is important that we know what causes the ups and downs in business activities. To discover these causes is one of the main tasks of the business cycle economist. Our ability to make scientific business forecasts rests upon the seeming regularity of business phenomena: a wave pattern of (1) an expanding economy leading to (2) a business boom, followed by (3) a business decline, and finally (4) a depression, from which the economy expands anew.

If the fluctuations were predominantly the result of unpredictable outside forces, economists could only guess what the future will hold. They could never hope to be able to make scientific predictions based on past experience and the knowledge of the innate forces of the economy. The United States, or any other nation whose policies involve economic planning on a large scale, could not long endure if economic developments could not be forecast with at least some degree of certainty. In our age of economic planning, business cycle theories, and business forecasts based on these theories, thus assume a fateful importance.

"Overproduction" versus "Underconsumption" There are two basic types of endogenous business cycle theories: those which stress speculative overexpansion, and others which emphasize underconsumption. The two views reflect deep-seated psychological prejudices and basic political philosophies. Today the underconsumption theory is closely linked with the "full employment" philosophy. The overproduction and the underconsumption approach can best be contrasted by the schematic drawing shown in Figure 3.

The "Overproduction" Argument The overproduction theorist believes that the economy fluctuates around a basic trend line, which moves upward from left to right at the rate of about 2½–3½% a year, as a result of the increase in population and tech-

FIGURE 3 ***"Overproduction" versus "Underconsumption"***

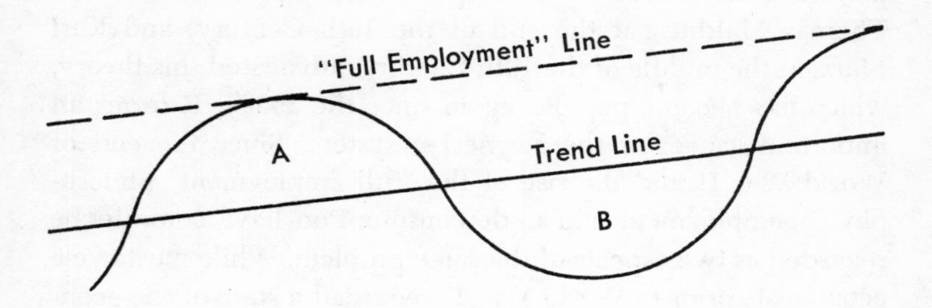

nological developments; the so-called growth rate. At times, people become overoptimistic. The consumer goes deeply into debt to buy new cars and new houses and many other things. The banker provides easy credit. The manufacturer expands his facilities in the hope that business will continue to expand. But gradually the consumer demand begins to fall off, because the consumer has all the goods he needs and he begins to worry about his heavy debts. Bankers become more reluctant to lend because they find their clients over-extended. The manufacturers suddenly find themselves with excess plant capacity and large inventories. Sales, production and employment decline, and the economy slides from a boom into a depression. The excess production and consumption represented by "A" above the trend line are offset by below-normal production and consumption represented by "B." In fact some economists have attempted to show that the depth of the depression ("B") is determined by the height of the preceding boom ("A"). As modern economists like to point out, there is a certain flavor of "Puritan ethics" in this approach: A nation is punished for inflationary excesses by a depression hangover.

The Underconsumption Argument The argument that depressions are caused by inadequate consumption is not new. Thomas Malthus, at the end of the 18th Century, and Karl Marx, at the middle of the 19th Century, advocated this theory, which has become popular again since the 1930's. It forms an important aspect of the Keynesian system. Since the end of World War II and the rise of the "full employment" philosophy, unemployment and underconsumption have come to be regarded as two aspects of the same problem. While most cycle economists prior to World War II regarded a state of the economy as "normal" which was midway between boom and depression (shown as the "Trend Line" in Figure 3), modern economists regard "full employment" as the "normal" goal to be achieved. Anything below "full employment" is subnormal and calls for government intervention. The modern underconsumptionist thus tends to push the "normal" trend line from midway between boom and depression to the "full employment" level, which the overproduction theorists feel cannot be sustained for any length of time.

The difference between the two views can have far-reaching implications for the value of money. If booms and depressions alternate, periods of rising prices will be offset by periods of declining prices (at least this was the assumption prior to the 1930's). If, on the other hand, the economy is permanently held, through government intervention, at the "full employment" or boom level, prices will continuously be pushed up with no intervening periods of price declines. It is for this reason that modern underconsumptionists have come to accept chronic inflation as a necessary evil.

The "Overproduction" Theorists Overexpansion, which in the belief of the overproductionists leads to depressions, can be due to a variety of factors. As a rule more than one is involved, but individual economists have tended to stress specific aspects.

Joseph Schumpeter (1883–1950) argued that technological breakthroughs occur in spurts and produce sudden above-normal capital investments, followed by periods of relatively smaller capital investments associated with periods of relatively slack business. Schumpeter thought that long cycles, lasting 30–40 years, were chiefly due to major technological changes.

A. C. Pigou (1877–1959) blamed the psychological instability of man for the business fluctuations. For a while, man tends to be too optimistic. He cannot imagine that the boom may end some day. Then, after the depression has set in, false optimism gives way to an equally irrational pessimism. During the boom years the consumer buys more than he can afford, thus pushing the boom ever higher. During depression years, he buys less than he can afford, thus deepening the depression. One economist has compared the average consumer with a skater who ventures forth very gingerly upon a frozen pond. Then other skaters arrive, and the more of them that come, the safer all of them feel, even though logic should tell them, while the ice may hold 10, it may not hold 50.

Friedrich A. von Hayek (1899–) *and Arthur Spiethoff* (1873–1957) argued that temporary overexpansion is most pronounced in the field of capital investments. Businessmen are psychologically just as unstable as the consumer. As long as business looks good, they tend to increase their productive capacity beyond the level of existing demand in the belief that demand will catch up. Suddenly they find themselves confronted with unused plant capacity. They reduce their capital investments sharply, and thus trigger a general down-trend in business. This was undoubtedly true 30–40 years ago. Since the end of World War II, however, business planning, at least of the large concerns, has become increasingly long-range, covering 10–20 years, and is seemingly less influenced by cyclical fluctuations.

R. G. Hawtry (1879–) sees business fluctuations caused predominantly by false monetary policies: excessive credit expansion during the boom and equally excessive credit restrictions during the recession. Other economists have blamed the speculative accumulation of inventories.

R. F. Harrod (1900–) distinguished between (1) the "natural rate" of capital investments determined by the rate of population growth and technological changes; (2) the "warranted rate" determined by the amount of investment capital available, which in turn is determined by the rate of savings, and finally (3) the "actual rate," the amount of capital actually invested. If the "actual rate" is smaller than the "natural rate," (as happens quite frequently in underdeveloped countries where the population grows faster than savings) the standard of living is likely to decline. If the "actual rate" is higher than the "warranted rate," (if capital investments exceed current savings and are financed through the creation of credit) the nation is headed for an inflationary boom. If, on the other hand, the "actual rate" is smaller than the "warranted rate," idle savings accumulate, and the economy is headed for a decline.

Composite "Overproduction" Theory

If we combine the various overproduction theories, we arrive at a picture of the causes of economic fluctuations which would look about as follows. Business has been improving slowly but steadily since the last depression or recession two years ago. The momentum is gradually picking up. New inventions call for new machinery, businessmen are expanding their plant capacity, the consumer is buying more on credit. Profits are good, wages are rising, plenty of bank credit is available. People tend to save less and spend more, but the banking system can easily provide the necessary additional investment capital.

After another year or two, excess plant capacity begins to appear. Production cost has risen because of higher wages and rising raw material prices. Profit margins are declining so that businessmen are less interested in making additional investments. The consumer has bought his new house, car and TV set, and is heavily in debt. He decides to drive the "old car" another year rather than trade it in for a new one. The bankers begin to worry about their debtors, about the businessmen whose plants are standing partly idle, and about the consumers who will have a bad time meeting their installment payments if they should lose their jobs. Unemployment is increasing. At this point, a relatively minor exogenous event — a Supreme Court decision which business regards as unfavorable; a major strike; the statement of a powerful politician; an international "crisis" — anything may suffice to start the downward slide.

As business deteriorates, workers are laid off. Consumers curtail their purchases. More plant capacity stands idle and manufacturers reduce their investments. With a large number of unemployed, business is no longer interested in labor saving machinery, and with the consumer demand down, industry is reluctant to promote new consumer goods. Loans are being defaulted and the banks become increasingly reluctant to make new loans. Thus the economy slides downward, and according to some overproductionists the downward slide will be in proportion to the original boom.

Eventually the turning point at the bottom of the cycle has been reached. Weak businesses which had started on a shoestring and false hopes during the boom have gone bankrupt. Plant capacity is beginning to wear out. After 2–3 years of recession or depression, a number of important technological discoveries may have been made. Interest rates have declined sharply, and the banks, loaded with idle cash, are more anxious to lend to strong borrowers. Even wages may be lower (at least they used to be in previous depressions) and workers are willing to work harder when threatened with unemployment than they were during times of "full employment" and shortage of skilled workers. The durable consumer goods (cars, TV sets, washing machines, furniture, even houses) are beginning to wear out, and those consumers who refused to spend money when the depression set in are gradually coming back into the market. Business is picking up slowly. A few years hence it will cross the "natural trend line" and will be headed again into a new inflationary boom.

According to the "overproductionists," booms and depressions are thus self-generating and self-liquidating. There is no reason to fear either chronic inflation or chronic depression — provided the economic mechanism is not disturbed.

The "Underconsumptionists"

The underconsumptionists have a two-fold quarrel with the overproductionists. 1) They hold that depressions are not self-liquidating, but tend to become chronic, and 2) that it is perfectly irrational, and politically and socially unbearable, to permit the economy to swing widely between booms and depressions.

Say and Malthus The ancestry of the underconsumptionists dates back to the 18th and early 19th Centuries. The contrast between the two theories — the overproductionists (who believe that overproduction will be followed by a depression) and the underconsumptionists (who see no danger in maximum production) — was clearly reflected in the conflict between the French economist J. B. Say (1767–1832), the author of what has come to be known as the "Law of Markets," and the English economist Thomas Malthus, a sharp critic of the optimistic beliefs of the Enlightenment.

According to Say's Law, production creates its own market. As a manufacturer produces goods, he has to pay for raw materials and machinery, and he has to pay wages to his workers, so that in producing goods he creates purchasing power which will be used to buy, perhaps not his own goods, but some other goods. While the manufacturer will retain part of the sales price for himself as a profit, he will not, Say argued, let the profits lie idle, but will spend them on consumer goods or capital investments. While there may be unsaleable surpluses of specific goods, there can never be a general overproduction in the long run.

Malthus, on the other hand, and the underconsumptionists ever since, argued that the workers and the suppliers of raw materials and machinery could not consume all the goods produced because they received less than the total retail value of the goods produced. The difference is, of course, the profit of the entrepreneur. But while Say argued that the entrepreneur will spend the profit in one way or another, Malthus held that the entrepreneur is more interested in saving and that he cannot, in the long run, find an outlet for his savings. To prevent overproduction and stagnation, Malthus argued, there had to be "an unproductive class" including landlords, statesmen, servants, ministers, soldiers, judges, teachers and lawyers, who consumed the surpluses not absorbed by the workers and the entrepreneurs. This was bad reasoning from a socio-political, as well as economic, point of view. Malthus just did not understand that his so-called "unproductive classes" provided services, and that from an economic viewpoint, there is no difference between producing and consuming either goods or services.

Karl Marx But the Malthusian underconsumption argument

(just as his overpopulation argument) has remained popular, and thanks to various refinements it has become more convincing. The best-known "underconsumptionist" of the 19th Century was Karl Marx (1818–1883), even though he objected strongly to being classified as such. His business cycle theories are far from clear, and while he seems to argue in the *Communist Manifesto* that periodic economic crises will ultimately lead to the collapse of the capitalistic system, cyclical crises and the long-range decline or capitalism are less closely linked in *Das Kapital,* his main work. Marx regarded the "decennial cycle" as "characteristic of modern industry." It resulted, he thought, from the fact that during boom periods production facilities expanded rapidly, producing excess capacity, a falling rate of profits and, ultimately, the curtailment of new investments. These crises, as Marx saw it, were certain to become increasingly destructive as the capitalistic system approached its unavoidable end.

John Maynard Keynes Largely as a psychological reaction to the impact of the great Depression, the underconsumptionist theory has become the dominant theory of our times. It became extremely popular during the great Depression of the 1930's, partly as a result of the sophisticated Keynesian explanation. That the world suffered from underconsumption during the 1930's was obvious. But there was no way of proving whether this was due (a) to the overexpansion of credit and productive capacity during the 1920's, or (b) to a basic defect in the economic system. Keynes took the latter view. He held that in a "mature economy" such as the United States and Britain, where (a) the population growth had slowed down; (b) a large segment of the people had reached a fairly high standard of living, and (c) there were few fundamental inventions and technological changes which would call for heavy capital investments, capitalists will have difficulties in finding outlets for their savings. Idle savings will thus pile up and produce increasing unemployment and stagnation. One of the ways of increasing consumption and avoiding idle savings, was to distribute income more evenly by taking from those who saved too much and giving to those who could not consume enough.

The Statistical-Empirical Approach

As we have seen in the preceding pages, economists have not yet been able to develop a satisfactory theory to explain cyclical fluctuations. However, they have been fairly successful, at least in the United States, in finding a set of "barometers" which have proved helpful in predicting changes in the economic weather.

Over a period of more than 30 years, Wesley C. Mitchell (1874–1948) (who was joined later by Arthur F. Burns) and the National Bureau of Economic Research studied some 800 statistical series to check the degree to which they reflected business cycle fluctuations. Out of these the Bureau picked 21 key indicators, 8 of which tended to precede turning points in the business cycle; 8 tended to coincide; while the remaining 5 followed. From the point of view of forecasting changes in the cyclical trends, the 8 leading series[2] are of paramount impor-

[2] The eight "leading indicators" are: (1) Liabilities in business failures; (2) Industrial stock prices; (3) New orders for durable goods; (4) Residential building; (5) Commercial and industrial building; (6) Average hours worked; (7) New incorporations, and (8) Wholesale prices of 22 commodities.

Opinions regarding the number of "leading indicators" differ somewhat. The Department of Commerce publishes 30 indicators which have a tendency to lead. The National Bureau of Economic Research occasionally adds four additional indicators to the eight listed above.

tance. The 8 coinciding indicators[3] are helpful in confirming the trend. Unfortunately, the 16 barometers do not always agree. During critical periods some usually point up, others down, and the remainder show no clear trend. A meteorologist would obviously be hard put to predict the weather if his barometers did not agree. In short, while economists have learned a great deal about economic indicators, they have not yet been able to reduce business forecasts to the degree of certainty which meteorologists have achieved during the past 30 years.

Kondratieff and Kitchin Cycles

This is not surprising, because so far as economists know, there is not only one definite cyclical pattern but actually three (and possibly more) overlapping cycles. In addition to the Juglar cycle (with a varying length of 7–10 years), there are the long cycles (30–50 years), first identified by N.D. Kondratieff in 1922; and a short cycle (about 40 months), identified by Joseph Kitchin in 1923.

Much work has been done to synchronize the three cycles, and some economists feel that one of the reasons for the severity of the Depression of the 1930's was the fact that a low of the Juglar cycle apparently coincided with a low of the Kondratieff wave. Generally speaking, Kitchin recessions tend to be more severe if they coincide with a declining Juglar cycle; and Juglar depressions tend to be more serious if they coincide with a downswing of the Kondratieff. All these observations, however, have by no means reached the stage of "natural laws." New observations may find them meaningless.

[3] The eight roughly "coincident indicators" are: (1) Freight car loadings; (2) Employment in non-agricultural establishments; (3) Unemployment; (4) Bank debits outside New York City; (5) Industrial production; (6) Wholesale prices excluding farm and food products; (7) Gross national product, and (8) Corporate profits after taxes.

Cyclical Forecasts Influencing Cyclical Developments

There is another difference between the economist and the meteorologist. The latter is expected merely to forecast the weather. He is not asked to change rain into sunshine. Cyclical studies and business forecasts, on the other hand, are made to counteract impending recessions and depressions. It is very well possible, if these countermeasures prove successful, that a predicted recession may not materialize. The question then remains, was the original forecast wrong, or did the countermeasures actually change the cyclical trends? At the end of World War II virtually all economists predicted, on the basis of past experience, that the inflationary boom of the war years would be followed by a sharp deflation, and throughout the world, governments pledged themselves to prevent such a depression and to maintain "full employment."

As part of the effort to prevent a postwar slump, Congress passed the "Employment Act of 1946." Whatever the cause, instead of the expected postwar depression, the world experienced a prolonged inflationary boom. Were the economists wrong in their forecasts? Or did the forecasts enable the governments to prevent a depression? We shall never know.

International Implications

Cyclical fluctuations are not confined to individual countries. They spread across borders. The efforts of national leaders to isolate their countries have, as a rule, produced more undesirable side-effects than they have actually helped to protect a nation against a world-wide recession. The United States is relatively immune to foreign developments because our foreign trade accounts for only about 5–6% of the Gross National Product, compared with more than 50% in the Netherlands, Belgium, Norway, Japan and Denmark, and about 40% in the case of Britain. There is an old saying in Europe that if the United States sneezes, Europe catches pneumonia. But even American business can be affected by a decline in the foreign demand.

In discussing the balance of payments in Chapter 15 we shall show the more important links which tie the national economies together into a world economy and thus tend to transmit cyclical developments from one country to the rest.

Chapter 14

ECONOMIC GROWTH

THE BASIC FACTS

The widespread interest in the problem of economic growth developed largely during the 1950's for two reasons: (1) the sharp increase in the industrial output of Soviet Russia, resulting in the belief that the USSR might be able to "outproduce" the USA and (2) the recognition that the problem of poverty in the underdeveloped countries could not be solved without rapid economic development.

There is no satisfactory way in which economic growth can be measured. To express "growth" in terms of the per capita value of all the goods and services produced may be misleading.

Prior to the postwar period, economists (with few exceptions) showed little interest in the problem of economic growth. This was due to the fact that the forces which seemed to determine growth (the rate of increase in the labor force and technological improvements) belonged more in the field of sociology than that of the traditional economics. Economists, moreover, were trained to think in mechanistic terms, while the various aspects of economic growth can best be expressed in terms of biological analogies.

The problems of "economic growth" of industrialized nations (such as the United States) are quite different from those of "economic development" of the so-called underdeveloped societies. The former are primarily economic and political in nature; the latter, chiefly cultural.

Economic Growth in the U.S. *At the end of the Civil War the United States was still, by modern standards, an underdeveloped country. However, it possessed certain intangible assets which made possible the tremendous economic development during the subsequent century. The economic growth of the country can be attributed only in part to a large input of labor and capital. Far more important was the increase in "efficiency" in the use of capital and manpower. Government spending and easy credit can produce, at least temporarily, an expansion of production and consumption, but there is no proof that the rate of economic growth can be increased for any length of time through fiscal and monetary policies. On the other hand, inappropriate policies can seriously impede growth.*

An increase in the rate of economic growth is important for the United States for two reasons: (1) to improve human welfare and to provide jobs for the flood of postwar babies who are entering the labor market, and (2) to provide additional revenue for the Federal government. To achieve such an increase, however, may involve drastic changes in fiscal, welfare and educational policies, which in turn call for a basic change in attitude on the part of the electorate.

Economic Development *During the late 1940's it was still generally assumed that if the underdeveloped countries were only given enough aid "to get them started," they would soon be able to carry on without foreign help. This proved a false assumption. During the 1950's the second phase of the foreign aid program developed. It involved the dispatch of large num-*

bers of American and European experts in many fields to the four corners of the earth, to assist the underdeveloped countries in acquiring new skills and attitudes. Again the results were disappointing. By the early sixties it became obvious that economic development is not merely an "economic" issue (such as the development of industries) but part of a gradual social and cultural change. Generally speaking, industrialization is the result, not the cause, of a social and cultural revolution.

Before a modern nation can develop, agriculture has to produce surpluses to feed the non-farm population; the educational system has to train the necessary number of workers and managers; and above all, age-old social attitudes (which hamper social change) have to be overcome.

What Is Economic Growth?

After more than a decade of debating the need for more rapid economic growth, economists must admit that it is not at all easy to define the meaning of the term "economic growth."

Growth in Terms of the GNP As a rule, growth is measured in terms of the Gross National Product, the value, in current dollars, of all the goods and services produced. But the GNP is not a satisfactory measurement of either the national strength or the national well-being. GNP statistics do not distinguish between the construction of an amusement park or a steel mill Yet the latter is obviously far more important in terms of national strength. Should growth be measured in terms of potential productive capacity (which is of vital importance in case of a prolonged war); or in terms of actual production? Or should it be measured in terms of consumer goods, on the assumption that the true wealth of a nation is the income, the standard of living, of the people? In other words, the notion of "growth" involves qualitative as well as quantitative factors.

Economists and Economic Growth Despite the obvious importance of economic growth, few economists 30 or 50 years ago showed any interest in the subject. The topic was hardly mentioned in the textbooks which were most widely used at the end of World War II. Courses were offered in the theory of the business cycle, but not in the theory of economic growth. Economists were obviously aware of the fact that the output of goods and services was increasing, and since the turn of the century the notion of a "secular trend," a long-range rate of expansion, was generally accepted. It was explained, quite simply, by two factors: (1) the increase in population and hence in the size of the labor force, and (2) technological developments made possible by capital investments which increased the productivity of labor. The two factors combined produced an average growth rate of about 2½–3½% a year over the life of the business cycle, depending on the individual country. The rate of growth slowed during the downswing of the cycle (in fact it could be negative) and grew correspondingly more rapidly during boom periods. No efforts were made, however, to analyze more closely the factors which stimulated or retarded growth, and the idea that the United States government should undertake the task of trying to increase the rate of growth would have seemed quite preposterous even during the 1930's.

Nineteenth Century "Growth" Economists Around the middle of the 19th Century the question of economic growth was raised by a few economists, especially in the United States and Germany. Among these, Henry C. Carey (1793–1879) and Friedrich List (1789–1846) were the best-known. Their reason for tackling the subject, however, was quite different from the modern approach. List described a number of distinct stages of economic development, and tried to show that the various stages called for different economic policies. A raw material producing country, for instance, should adhere to free trade in order to sell its surpluses abroad, and import cheaply the industrial products not manufactured at home. During the next stage of development, as domestic industries were being established, protective tariffs were needed to shield the infant industries against foreign competition. A fully industrialized country, finally, which List regarded as the last stage of economic development, should again adhere to free trade in order to secure the needed raw materials cheaply, and to open foreign markets for its surplus of finished products.

Economic Growth in the United States

The forces which affect the rate of economic growth in a highly developed country, such as the United States, are different from the factors involved in the development of the still largely underdeveloped nations. "Growth" and "development" should thus be treated as two quite distinct and separate aspects of the overall problem.

Measured by today's standards, the United States was an "underdeveloped country" at the end of the Civil War. Per capita income was about the same as is the average per capita income in Latin America today (measured in terms of current purchasing power); 60% of the labor force was employed in agriculture; 80% of the people lived in rural areas; the U.S. had fewer railroads than has India today; and child mortality was higher than it is today in Thailand or Zanzibar. The U.S. was certainly no richer in natural resources than Brazil.

Reasons for American Economic Growth

But the U.S. possessed certain intangible assets which made possible the tremendous growth of the country during the subsequent century. During the 125 years from 1838 to 1963 the physical output of goods and services produced in the United States doubled on the average about every 19 years, a growth rate of almost 3.7%. The rate was considerably higher than in Europe, for at least four reasons: (1) The population in the United States increased more rapidly than in Europe, due to heavy immigration; (2) The ratio of natural resources to population was far more favorable; (3) Because of the relative shortage and high cost of labor, mechanization progressed more rapidly, and (4) A very important factor, the United States was not hampered by age-old social traditions which impeded change in Europe.

To these four factors should be added a fifth, and possibly the most important one. The existing political and economic system of personal freedom forced the individual to rely on his own resources and develop his own faculties. At the Frontier it was a question of win or perish. For better or worse, much of this economic and political freedom has been lost since the 1930's. The character and spirit of the American economy have undergone a subtle but important change.

Changes in the Rate of Growth

A minor change in the rate of growth can mean an important difference in the economic strength and the standard of living of a nation. If the growth rate in the U.S. since 1850 had been 3% instead of better than 3½%, the GNP in 1962 would have been only $330 billion instead of $550 billion. Average per capita income would be 40% smaller than it is today. Hence the widespread concern about the fact that the American economy began to lose its "spark" sometime between 1955 and 1957. The growth rate dropped to about 3%, or below, at a time when the war-ravaged economies of Western Europe, Soviet Russia and Japan grew at much faster rates — some as much as 6% and 8% a year.[1]

Growth and Employment The rate of growth will have special significance for the United States during the 1960's because of two reasons: the need for additional jobs and the need for additional Federal revenues. During the 1960's 13½ million additional jobs are needed to provide for the heavy influx into the labor market of young workers who were born during the postwar years. If production increases by only 3% there will not be enough jobs, especially in view of the fact that the high wage level and the lack of skilled workers will encourage automation. Washington experts figure that production will have to increase by 4% or more to keep the unemployment rate down to the "normal" level of 4% of the labor force.

Growth and Government Spending To the unemployment problem must be added urgent fiscal considerations. Just at the time when the economy began to lose its "spark," Federal spending increased rapidly from $69 billion in 1957 to $92.6 billion in 1963 or by about 34%. The result was a budget deficit of more than $30 billion in six years (equal to about twice the total national debt in 1929). Congress and the Administration are not likely to reduce defense and welfare spending to the level of available income. To prevent further large Federal deficits, a substantial growth in government revenues will thus be needed. As early as 1962, however, Washington had come to the conclusion that existing tax rates were already strangling

[1] By the mid-1960's the rate of economic expansion in the United States had increased again to 5–6% annually.

the economy, and early in 1964 Congress approved a tax reduction of almost $12 billion in the hope that a reduction in taxes (which would leave business and the consumer with more money to spend) would stimulate investments and consumption and thus profits and individual income, which in turn would lead to an increase in total taxes (even though the tax rates were actually reduced). In short, given the existing political constellation, the main hope of overcoming the chronic budget deficit, and thus end one of the chief causes of the chronic inflation, will be a vigorous growth of the economy.

The Causes of Growth in the U.S.

The question of economic growth is thus of twofold importance, and economists are attempting to discover what made the American economy grow in the past, and what can be done to stimulate the growth rate. A statistical analysis seems to indicate quite clearly that the increase in the labor force and the increase in capital investments do not explain fully the growth of the American economy during the past 100 years. During the 1930's, 1940's, and 1950's, a third factor — vaguely termed "productivity" or "efficiency"— was actually the most important. The 1930's witnessed a sharp decline in the GNP, while the 1940's and 1950's brought a sensational expansion of production. The total number of manhours worked increased slowly, or by about 16% during the 30 years. New capital investments apparently accounted for only about 15% of the overall growth. The remaining 69% of the total increase in output were due to the greater efficiency of capital and labor. A million dollars invested in 1960 added far more to the total output than a million dollars (calculated at the same purchase power as in 1960) invested in 1930. Ten thousand additional workers added more to the GNP in 1960 than 10,000 workers in 1930. This increase in productivity was due to a better general educational background of labor; more effective on-the-job training; the economies derived from large scale production; a more efficient use of raw materials and a better allocation of resources; increased research and more effective management techniques, and finally, a higher quality of capital goods. The same amount of capital invested buys more productive machinery and longer-lasting tools and general equipment.[2]

Policies to Promote Economic Growth The ever-changing quantitative and qualitative factors which combine to produce economic growth are difficult to measure statistically. Economists have a fair idea which factors were most important in the past, but they can only guess as to their relative importance in the future. The United States has enough capital and labor to permit a substantial increase in production. But the "quantity" of labor and capital in the past 30 years apparently accounted for less than one third of the growth rate. Was the reduction in the rate of growth since the late 1950's due to "qualitative" factors (e.g., the lack of skills or a wide-spread "Let's-take-it-easy" spirit)? Or was it due to an oppressive tax structure, or top-heavy minimum wages? Economists don't know the answer. And without a proper diagnosis it is difficult for a doctor to prescribe a cure.

Growth and Economies of Scale Nor is the government able to do much to increase the economies which are derived from large-scale production. In fact some anti-trust measures, such as the opposition to railroad mergers, clearly hamper greater efficiency, and thus a more rapid rate of growth.

[2] For further details see a resume of two books (John Kendrick: *Productivity Trends in the United States* and Edward Denison: *The Sources of Economic Growth in the United States and the Alternatives before Us*) which appeared in "Business in Brief" No. 51 July/August 1963, published by the Chase Manhattan Bank, New York.

In short, while America desires and needs a more rapid rate of growth, some of the steps which might help to increase productivity are in conflict with deeply rooted political and social ideas.

The "Output Gap"

This explains the search for other — and politically easier — ways of stimulating economic growth. In order "to sell" the American people and the members of Congress on the need for a more rapid economic growth, the Kennedy Administration presented the issue by calculating the so-called "output gap," the difference between what the economy actually produced and the potential output if unemployment were reduced to 4%. According to government calculations the "gap" amounted to $50 billion annually in early 1961, although the government statisticians added that "calculations like these are at best hazardous and uncertain, and ours do not pretend to be definitive."

As happens so often, if extremely complex issues are dramatized and popularized, they tend to lose touch with reality. Business leaders and many economists immediately challenged the basic assumptions as well as the statistical calculations. Professor Arthur F. Burns, the Chairman of President Eisenhower's Council of Economic Advisors, and one of the nation's most highly respected economists, characterized the "gap" calculated by President Kennedy's Council of Economic Advisors as largely due to unrealistic assumptions and a false interpretation of figures. The "gap" debate, which had been intended to dramatize an important issue, quickly deteriorated into political partisanship.

Economic Growth and Deficit Spending

After illustrating, by means of the "gap" theory, the need for a more rapid rate of economic growth, Washington planners decided that the rate could be increased and the "gap" closed through a massive injection of additional purchasing power. Between 1960 and 1965 Federal spending increased by 25%, while the Federal Reserve Bank credit grew by more than 40% between the end of 1960 and the middle of 1965. The result was a sharp increase in the output of goods and services. In five years the GNP grew by well over 30% without a serious rise in the cost of living. The policy thus seemed to disprove the old notion that a large increase in spending power must automatically lead to substantially higher prices.

Actually the American experience of the early 1960's is in conflict with the experience of the past. As a rule, boom conditions fed by a steady stream of additional credit make for administrative inefficiency and reduced productivity of labor, the two factors which during the 1940's and 1950's accounted for about two thirds of the growth of the American economy.

Government Policies and Economic Growth

While economists disagree whether a government can, in the long run, effectively stimulate economic growth in a free society, a fairly good case can be made to show that some government policies tend to retard the economy. Fiscal measures can stimulate economic activities, and they can hamper them; government policies can create and destroy "confidence," this most elusive and yet perhaps most important factor determining the level of economic activities.

Fiscal Measures

The American fiscal system, with its irrational complexities and its "soak-the-rich" spirit, is probably hampering economic growth. Compared with Western Europe the total tax burden may not seem excessive (and even in Europe the slowing of the rate of growth since the early 1960's is widely blamed on the impact of heavy taxation), but the structure of the tax system is probably a retarding force in the economy.

The 50% corporate income tax (reduced from the 1963 level of 52%) induces corporations to operate with borrowed capital (since interest charges can be deducted as an expense). But small and new firms have difficulties in obtaining loans, and for companies which venture into new fields it is dangerous to operate with borrowed capital. New investments financed through stock issues are impeded, because a company would have to earn well over 16% before taxes in order to pay a 50% income tax and still be able to pay the stockholders an 8% return. With an 8% return needed to finance a risky venture, and a rate of profits between 16% and 20% doubtful, the venture will not be undertaken. Large diversified companies can compensate losses in one sector by correspondingly larger profits in another. They can take the risk of research and new developments. Small companies can do neither. Under the existing tax system it is often more profitable to rebuild old machines and charge the cost of rebuilding against maintenance, than to buy new and more efficient machines if these have to be financed through new equity capital.

Personal Income Taxes

The personal income tax rates above 50% produce only a fraction of 1% of the total income tax revenues, but they drive wealthy men, who should take the risk of providing venture capital, into tax-exempt state and municipal bonds, where they finance large social consumption rather than economic growth.

But economic rationality, which calls for a drastic downward revision of the corporate income and the graduated personal income taxes, clashes with political expediency and deep-rooted social ideas. To reduce the tax on corporations (which cannot vote) and the tax on the relatively small number of the very rich (whose voting strength is negligible) is likely to offend large numbers of voters, whose taxes are not reduced correspondingly. For more than half a century progressives have advocated the ability-to-pay principle of taxation. The "rich" should pay a far greater portion of their income in taxes because "they can afford it." The difficulty with the policy is that it may hamper economic development and thus hurt the poor, those who are unable to get a job, far more than the very rich.

Tax Incentives

Attempts have been made in various countries to develop tax features which will speed economic growth. After 1948 West Germany permitted taxpayers to deduct from their taxable income the amounts invested in projects which speeded Germany's recovery. If a taxpayer earned 20,000 Marks, and invested 5,000 Marks in bonds of, let us say, the Hamburg harbor (which was being reconstructed), in railroad bonds or in similar projects, he had to pay taxes on an income of only 15,000 Marks. Various Latin American countries have attempted to tax idle farm land more heavily than land under production. Tax refunds are granted for the production of new crops which involve an additional investment, but which can be sold abroad or used by domestic industries. More recently the suggestion was made by a group of Princeton economists to grant tax rebates to businesses which show a better-than-average rate of growth.

Impediments to Economic Growth

The system of taxation, however, is not the only way in which governments affect economic growth. The emphasis upon "economic security" (which has characterized political and social thought in the United States for 30 years) has tended to produce economic rigidity and prevent the best possible use of economic resources. This does not mean that the welfare state policies should, or can be abandoned, but policy changes may be necessary to the extent that welfare policies are in direct conflict with the need for more rapid economic growth. Subsidies to ailing segments of the economy, and to areas of the country faced with special economic problems, tend to retard the shift of productive resources — both capital and manpower — from activities and areas where their output is below average (otherwise they would not be in need of subsidies) to activities where the same manpower and capital can produce a greater return, and hence increase the overall rate of economic growth.

Economic Development

The forces affecting economic growth of developed countries, as we have seen, are far from simple. The multitude of social, cultural, political and economic factors which determine whether an underdeveloped country will continue at a low level of underdevelopment, or whether it reaches the "take-off point," are even more complex. The basic problems are similar in most underdeveloped countries: a rapid population growth; a high rate of illiteracy; an inadequate food supply; low productivity; lack of savings, hence lack of investment capital; inadequate communication and transportation facilities and a wide variety of social taboos which hamper social and economic change. Yet the solution is likely to vary from one country to the next.

Industrialization and Economic Development

There is no single factor which will turn an underdeveloped country into a modern industrialized nation. The construction of modern factories will not produce an industrialized nation, as the leaders of many underdeveloped countries assume, unless other social and economic changes occur at the same time. Under favorable conditions industrialization can speed constructive changes in the social structure. As a rule, however, industrialization is the result, not the cause, of social change. The United States is the most powerful and wealthiest nation because of its vast productive capacity. This ability to produce, however, is not merely the result of huge factories, but of a complex institutional and social framework. It is not primarily a question of "investment capital."

Agriculture and Economic Development

In order to support a growing urban population and an increasing number of industrial workers, a country must produce enough food. For every peasant who becomes a factory worker, those who remain on the soil must produce more food and fibers if the process of industrialization is not to result in more people going hungry. This perfectly logical sequence of economic development was obviated since World War II by the American policy of giving vast amounts of surplus farm products to the underdeveloped countries, thus making it possible for them to allocate a disproportionately large share of their limited resources to the development of industries (some of which were of questionable economic value) while neglecting the necessary agricultural improvements.

Education and Economic Development

Nor is it possible to operate a modern industry with large numbers of operationally or completely illiterate former peasants and farm workers. There can be no economic development without improved education. Experience has shown that 4–6 years of schooling are needed to produce a minimum degree of literacy. Children who have gone to school for only 2 years generally have forgotten all they have learned by the time they are 20. A 4–6 year universal basic education, however, is far too costly for most underdeveloped countries. Yet, like industrialization, "universal education" seems to most underdeveloped countries the key to economic progress. As a result vast numbers of children are given some education, even though many will sink back into illiteracy. At the same time many underdeveloped countries produce more university graduates than are needed, especially in the humanities and law, while there is an acute shortage of skilled workers and technicians.

Social Attitudes

Even more fundamental than the educational system, as far as economic development is concerned, are the basic social attitudes and the prevailing ethical system. Tens of millions of Indians accept poverty as a matter of fate against which they are powerless. As long as the people believe in Karma, they will do little to improve their material existence, and economic progress will be slow. But the destruction of the belief in Karma among the masses (as it has been destroyed among the intellectuals) can have serious consequences. There is no way of abolishing poverty in India within a generation, and if the Indian masses should suddenly come to the conclusion that their poverty is not the result of an unchangeable fate, but that it can be lifted from them by the government fiat — and enough American aid — an extremely explosive situation could result.

Economic Development and Foreign Aid

The extreme difficulty of achieving economic development through foreign aid was not clearly recognized during the late 1940's. Barely $16 billion in loans and aid had made it possible for a war-torn and hungry Western Europe to recover within a few years and enjoy a rapidly rising standard of living. From this it was concluded that if the underdeveloped countries of Asia, Africa and Latin America only had enough investment capital "to get them started," they would be able within a decade or two to carry on without foreign aid. This assumption disregarded completely the fact that while Europe's factories and transportation systems were destroyed, its store of raw materials depleted and its millions hungry, the people of Europe were highly educated and skilled, and their social and institutional system was adapted to the needs of a modern economy.

The Need of Experts Most of these prerequisites are absent in underdeveloped countries, and the funds spent on modern factories are often wasted because the infra-structure — the social, political and educational system — is lacking. Early in the 1950's Washington recognized that in addition to financial aid, the underdeveloped countries needed technical aid, the help of educators, agricultural experts, political scientists and public health officials. Thousands of American experts went to the four corners of the earth, prepared reports, or devoted years of conscientious work to assist the underdeveloped countries in improving their methods in that particular field in which the American representative was an expert.

The Need for Basic Cultural Change

Again, the results were negligible, considering the vast amounts of money and efforts involved. It gradually became apparent that economic development is not a question of industrialization, of improved agriculture, of a better educational and public health system, or of a more stable political structure. All these are prerequisites. But more is needed. Economic development is part of a slow process of cultural change, which in Western Europe required centuries.

Chapter 15

THE BALANCE OF PAYMENTS

THE BASIC FACTS

A balance of payments is a statistical compilation of the international payments which a nation (its individuals, corporations and government agencies) has made or received in the course of a year. A surplus or a deficit in the balance of payments, just as above or below normal barometric pressure, points to disturbances of the economic equilibrium at home or abroad.

Even the richest nation cannot sustain indefinitely a deficit in its balance of payments without injury to its international credit standing.

The type of balance of payments statistics which are compiled today by more than a hundred countries evolved slowly during the 1920's and 1930's. Prior to World War I there was little need for such data, since temporary surpluses and deficits were assumed to adjust themselves automatically with the help of the gold standard mechanism.

The Decline of the Gold Standard *As a result of the increasing rigidity in prices and wages, the growing economic nationalism and the emphasis on national economic planning, the gold standard no longer functions today as an effective means of achieving an international balance of payments equilibrium. The United States has suffered a deficit in the balance of payments since 1950, which resulted in a sharp decline in the country's international liquidity. At the same time, however, American long term claims against the rest of the world increased much faster than her short-term obligations.*

Five Ways of Offsetting the Deficit *There are five ways of coping with a balance of payments deficit. A nation can sell part of its gold reserves; it can contract short- and long-term obligations; domestic prices can be reduced (thus facilitating exports and reducing imports); the currency can be devalued (thus making it cheaper for foreign countries to buy the nation's goods); and, finally, foreign exchange restrictions can be imposed in order to adjust foreign payments to the available income.*

The United States has rejected the idea of artificially lowering domestic prices, of devaluing the dollar, and of instituting foreign exchange restrictions. Instead the American government is expecting foreign prices to rise faster than American prices, a trend which in due course is expected to restore the equilibrium in international payments.

The American Balance of Payments *Contrary to a widespread belief, foreign aid cannot be blamed for the deficit in the balance of payments. Repayments of loans by foreign nations in some years actually exceeded new loans and aid. The United States enjoys a substantial surplus of exports over imports. This surplus, however, is not large enough to cover American military expenditures abroad. The United States is thus confronted with the choice of reducing military expend-*

itures, of curtailing other expenditures, or of increasing the surplus of exports over imports. Suggestions have been made to curb American tourist expenditures abroad, or to reduce the outflow of short-term and long-term capital. All of these remedies, however, involve serious political, social and economic problems.

The Balance of Payments as an Economic Barometer

One can look upon the balance of payments in two ways: either in terms of the actual flow of goods, services and capital between one country and the rest of the world or as a statistical compilation showing the international payments which a nation — its individuals, corporations and government agencies — has made and received in the course of a year. While all economic forces — prices, wages, cyclical fluctuations, the rate of investment, employment and growth — are interrelated and interdependent, the dependence on other factors is particularly pronounced in the case of the balance of payments. It is helpful in fact, to think of the balance of payments primarily as a barometer which indicates the state of the nation's economy in relation to the rest of the world. A surplus or a deficit, just as above or below normal barometric pressure, points to disturbances of the economic equilibrium at home or abroad.

The basic principle which underlies the balance of payments is quite simple, but economists disagree regarding the causes which determine the international flow of funds, and the mechanics of the balance of payments accounting can become extremely involved. We are concerned here primarily with the basic principles and the conflicting theories, and only to a limited extent with the accounting details.

Balance of Payments Deficits

Just as an individual cannot continue indefinitely to spend more than he takes in, a nation cannot afford a chronic deficit in its balance of payments. A wealthy man can afford to live above his income for a number of years, because he can draw on his reserves. Similarly, the United States could afford a balance of payments deficit since 1950, because of the vast gold reserves accumulated during the war, and because of the basic strength of the American economy. But even the United States, despite her great wealth, cannot go indefinitely spending more than she takes in.

Changing Balance of Payments Theories and Policies

The type of balance of payments statistics which are compiled today by more than 100 countries (some of them admittedly in a very rudimentary form) were developed slowly during the 1920's and 1930's. This does not mean that the 19th Century was not aware of the problems involved in the flow of international payments, but in the laissez faire spirit of the time it was generally assumed that surpluses and deficits would adjust themselves automatically with the help of the gold standard mechanism, so that there was no need for the compilation of elaborate statistics.

The Role of the Gold Standard

To understand the forces which determine the flow of goods and gold, it is helpful to refer to Hume's Price-Specie-Flow model which we discussed in Chapter 11. While Hume's balance-of-payments model represented an over-simplification even in the 18th Century, and is even less realistic today, the basic forces which the author tried to illustrate are still at work today: people still tend to buy goods in those countries where they are cheapest and invest their money where the return is highest. But the free flow of goods and money (determined by the difference in prices and the rate of profit) assumed a number of prerequisites: (1) that all major trading nations stood ready to purchase and sell gold at a fixed price in terms of their currencies; (2) that paper money could be freely converted into gold, and gold could be exported and imported without restrictions (neither of which is the case today in the U.S.), and (3) and possibly most important, that domestic prices were flexible and fluctuated with the changing supply of money. A deficit in the balance of payments, resulting in an outflow of gold (and thus a decline in the supply of money) could thus be relied upon to lead, in due course, to a decline in the domestic price level. The cure for "inflation" (a domestic price level which was higher than the international price level), according to 19th Century theory, was "deflation" (a decline in domestic prices), just as the 19th Century business cycle theorists believed (as we saw in Chapter 14) that a depression was the result of previous inflationary excesses.

The Decline of the Gold Standard For better or for worse, the ideas of the 19th Century have lost much of their appeal in our world of economic planning and nationalism.

Rigidity of Domestic Wage and Price Structure In most countries, including the United States, wages and prices are no longer responsive to changes in supply and demand as they were 50 years ago. The growth of powerful labor unions, and the general opposition of the union leadership to a reduction of wages, have made it increasingly difficult to reduce labor cost. Both labor and the general public have come to accept as natural and unavoidable that wages and fringe benefits will increase almost every year, irrespective of market conditions. Despite chronic and fairly widespread unemployment since the late 1950's, wages of production workers in manufacturing industries (excluding overtime) rose from $2.05 an hour in 1958 to $2.66 by the end of 1965, or by almost 30% not including fringe benefits.

There is a similar tendency in many key industries to raise prices whenever market conditions permit, but to avoid price reductions when the demand declines. The tremendous growth of fixed investments on which a return must be earned, and the relatively small number of large firms in many key industries, have tended to reduce price competition.

Economic Nationalism There is a tendency throughout the world for economic planners to concentrate on the solution of domestic problems and to disregard the international consequences.

This is not a new development. Since the days of Plato, i.e., for well over 2000 years, economic planners have rebelled against the fact that international forces which they cannot control interfered with their domestic plans. Rather than abandon the latter, they advocated the closing of the frontiers.

Modern Opposition to Price Declines The tendency of modern economic planning to concentrate on domestic issues coincides with a widespread belief that a decline in prices (even if the decline merely cancels previous price increases) will produce unemployment and reduce the rate of growth. The belief probably derives from the traumatic experience of the Great Depression, when widespread unemployment coincided with a collapse of the price structure. Historical evidence, however, does not support the popular belief that declining prices must impede growth and reduce employment opportunities. The United States experienced a very rapid rate of economic growth and a rapid expansion of job opportunities between the 1870's and 1890's, despite the fact that commodity prices declined by almost 50%.

The modern tendency of economic planners to rely on inflationary measures to combat unemployment and to stimulate economic growth, (irrespective of international consequences) is well illustrated by the 1963 report of the Brookings Institution, *The United States Balance of Payments in 1968*. It was prepared for the Council of Economic Advisers, and the Joint Economic Committee of Congress called it "a major document for policy-makers and the public." The report deplored that the prolonged deficit in the American balance of payments had prevented the government from pursuing more inflationary policies.

There are three major forces which militate against an adjustment of the domestic price, wage and interest rate levels to the levels prevailing abroad: (1) the growing rigidity of the domestic wage, price and interest rate structure; (2) the tendency of economic planners to concentrate on domestic problems and to disregard international consequences, and (3) the widespread fear of "deflation" combined with the popular belief that "a little inflation" acts as an economic stimulant.

The Gold Standard versus Economic Planning

As long as the major trading nations of the world adhered to the gold standard, a country could not pursue a policy of chronic creeping inflation, because it would have resulted in the loss of gold and thus a shrinkage in the stock of money. And with less money in circulation, prices would have tended to decline. It was for this reason that President Roosevelt, who wanted to raise domestic price levels irrespective of world market prices, abandoned the gold standard in 1933. To this day, all those economists who believe in national economic planning and in the possibility of maintaining full employment and a rising rate of economic activities through chronic inflation, are strongly opposed to the gold standard. And those who advocate the gold standard as a useful check on inflationary policies are suspected of being enemies of economic planning.

Dollar Depreciation and the Balance of Payments Deficit During the war years (1940 to 1945) the dollar lost about 25% of its domestic purchasing power; during the 20 years following the end of World War II the purchasing power declined by another 46%. The goal which President Roosevelt tried to achieve when he abandoned the gold standard in 1933, namely, to create "the kind of dollar which a generation hence will have the same purchasing power and debt-paying power as the dollar value we hope to attain in the near future," has not been achieved.

For about two decades (during the 1930's and 1940's) the United States was able to pursue domestic economic policies with little regard for their effect upon the position of the dollar in world markets, because the political uncertainties in Europe during the 1930's, World War II and the postwar chaos resulted in a heavy influx of foreign flight capital. Even though the domestic purchasing power of the dollar depreciated rapidly during the 1940's (caused in part by the policies of the government), it provided better protection than most foreign currencies.

The Turning Point The situation changed rather suddenly with the outbreak of the Korean War and the economic recovery of Western Europe. By the middle 1950's it had become quite obvious that the international position of the United States was undergoing a basic change. At about the same time, or shortly afterwards, certainly by 1957, the "spark" seemed to have gone out of the American economy, just at a time when the economies of Western Europe and Japan expanded particularly rapidly. The result was a progressive deterioration of the American balance of payments. The world, including millions of American entrepreneurs and consumers, found foreign investments and foreign goods and services more advantageous than American, which led to a heavy outflow of American gold. Between 1949 and 1966 American gold holdings declined from $24.5 to $13.2 billion, while short-term obligations increased from $7.6 to about $29.8 billion. By the end of 1967, gold holdings had declined to $12 billion, while liquid liabilities had risen to $34 billion.

Short Term Debtor; Long Term Creditor This does not mean that the United States became $35 billion "poorer" during the 17 years. The opposite was actually the case. While the gold reserves dropped by more than $12 billion, and the short-term obligations increased more than $27 billion, American private and government long-term investments abroad rose from $16 to over $85 billion, and American short-term assets likewise increased substantially.

The United States thus finds herself in the position of a bank which is basically sound and has large amounts invested in long-term mortgages, but which lacks liquid assets with which to pay the depositors should they wish to withdraw their demand deposits. From a highly liquid position at the end of the war, the United States slipped within a decade and a half into a position of international illiquidity, and became dependent upon the cooperation of foreign central banks to prevent a devaluation of the dollar.

The Balance of Payments Deficit: Causes and Cures

The prolonged American balance of payments deficit can be

due to either of two basic causes: The United States may have overtaxed her resources in fighting the cold war, and should hence aim for more limited objectives; or the social and economic policies pursued by the United States since the end of the war may have prevented the fullest development and use of the nation's potential resources. The balance of payments does not tell us which of the two possible causes produced the prolonged deficit, but like a barometer it points to the existence of an impending storm which cannot be averted by "fixing" the barometer. There are five ways in which a government can cope with a balance of payments deficit.

Sale of Surplus Gold If a country possesses enough gold, and the deficit is regarded as temporary, it can be made up by selling gold. This is what the United States has done since 1950. In fact during the early 1950's the transfer of gold from the United States to Western Europe was regarded as a desirable development, since it resulted in a "redistribution" of the world's monetary gold reserves.

Credits to Offset Temporary Deficits Provided the credit of the country is good, i.e., the country's currency is regarded as being "as good as gold"— (the dollar was officially thus defined in the Bretton Woods Agreement) — the deficit country may not be called on to transfer gold. The surplus nations may be satisfied to increase their holdings of the deficit country's currency — always assuming, of course, that these balances are convertible into gold on demand. This was the second method by which the United States has "paid" for her chronic balance of payments deficit.

Devaluation of the Currency

But even the richest nation cannot indefinitely lose its gold reserves and increase its international short-term obligations. The United States thus has to choose between three possible ways of coping with the balance of payments deficit. The U.S. can strive for lower domestic prices to stimulate exports and discourage imports; she can devalue the dollar (i.e. raise the price of gold in terms of dollars) thus making it cheaper for foreigners to buy American goods; or she could cut the nation's economy off from the rest of the world by instituting foreign exchange restrictions.

A devaluation of the dollar in terms of other currencies, however, would probably provide only temporary relief, because other nations would take the same "easy way out" and devalue their currencies, which would result in a progressive world-wide depreciation of currencies and chronic world-wide inflation.

The Role of the "Fund"

To prevent such a development was one of the main objectives of the International Monetary Fund, which was set up at Bretton Woods at the end of World War II. The members of the Fund (with a few exceptions) pledged themselves not to change the value of their currency in terms of either gold or the dollar (except within a very narrow margin) without permission from the Fund. The Fund, in turn, is granting short-term credits to nations which are confronted with temporary balance of payments deficits. The Fund thus provides an additional "cushion" which gives deficit nations more time to achieve the necessary domestic adjustments, or — as critics of the Fund argue — which makes it possible for them to postpone unpleasant adjustments, and renders the final solution that much more difficult and drastic. In the end the Fund almost invariably gives its formal approval to the devaluation of an overvalued currency, such as the British pound in 1949 and 1967.

In fact, between 1945 and 1967 more than half the currencies of the world were devalued, some of them a number of times, despite the efforts of the Fund to achieve international currency stability.

Foreign Exchange Restrictions

Foreign exchange restrictions represent in effect an attempt of "fixing the barometer" by blocking the international flow of goods, services and capital. This may take many forms. The flow of goods has always been affected by tariffs. By raising customs duties, a country can hamper imports and may, if other factors remain unchanged, improve its balance of trade which is the difference between exports and imports. During the 1930's a host of other methods were introduced. While the United States, more than most countries, favors freer trade, Washington has been using the same tools of trade restrictions as other countries: Quotas have been established for certain imports (e.g., sugar and oil); certain exports (especially farm products) are subsidized; foreign aid is "tied" as much as possible, i.e., the beneficiary countries must use U.S. grants and loans to buy American goods; aid shipments have to be made on American ships; and in 1964, Congress adopted a 15% "equalization" tax payable by American citizens who buy foreign securities, in order to retard the outflow of long-term capital from the United States. Other nations have gone much further. In many of them, all foreign exchange transactions are handled through the Central Bank, which determines what may be imported and whether residents may travel abroad. The Central Bank also fixes the exchange rates at which exporters have to turn over the foreign exchange which they receive for their exports, and the rates which importers have to pay to get foreign exchange.

Balance of Payments Statistics

Balance of payments data can be presented in many ways. The methods differ widely from one country to the next and there is no "correct" or "generally accepted" form. The United States balance of payments for the preceding year is published annually in the March issue of the "Survey of Current Business" published by the U.S. Department of Commerce.

Chapter 16

INTERNATIONAL TRADE AND FINANCE

THE BASIC FACTS

Exports and imports represent the most important accounts in the balance of payments of the United States, and while foreign trade plays a less important role in the American economy than in that of other countries, America is dependent upon many imports, and American agriculture and individual industries rely on exports for a substantial portion of their sales.

Like economic theories and policies in general, foreign trade theories have undergone a basic change since the 1930's. The traditional theory of the comparative advantage which dates back to the early 19th Century and which was designed to explain the composition of international trade, has been supplemented and partly replaced by the modern income approach which relates the balance of payments (reflecting the external equilibrium) and the trends of domestic employment and income (the internal equilibrium). While the 19th Century theory relied heavily on the flow of gold to regulate price levels and bring about a balance of payments equilibrium, modern theory assumes that gold serves merely as a medium of exchange to offset temporary disequilibria, and that the true equilibrating mechanism is to be found in the changes of employment and income in the individual countries and their effect on the volume of imports.

International trade theories and policies are closely interwoven with the old conflict between free traders and protectionists, which has formed an important aspect of American politics since the days of Jefferson and Hamilton. While economic theorists can prove logically that free trade increases general well-being throughout the world, the advocates of protection can present numerous seemingly convincing arguments, such as national security, the safeguarding of infant industries, the need for balanced economic growth (Paul Prebisch's "Theory of the Periphery") and others.

Foreign trade can be regulated in many ways: through a variety of tariffs, through quotas, foreign exchange restrictions, embargoes and a multitude of administrative regulations. Generally speaking, the United States, since the 1930's has pursued, at least in principle, a policy of promoting greater freedom of trade, and has been a strong supporter of the General Agreement of Tariffs and Trade (GATT).

The Importance of Foreign Trade

Even though America's foreign trade (exports and imports) accounts for only about 5–7% of the total amount of goods and services produced (abt. 10–12% of the movable goods), and the United States is far less dependent upon exports and imports than most countries (in Britain and Germany e.g., foreign trade is equal to about 30% of the Gross National Product, and in Denmark to more than 50%), some 4–5 million American jobs depend directly or indirectly on exports, and the normal functioning of the American economy is closely linked with the orderly flow of international trade.

American industry imports almost its entire requirements of natural rubber, burlap, manila fiber, quebracho, industrial diamonds, tin, nickel, asbestos, mica, tantalum and chromite. Many of America's most widely used consumer goods such as coffee, tea, cacao, bananas, spices, chicle and silk come from abroad. And the country is dependent on imports for 75–90% of its needs of manganese, cobalt, mercury, platinum, newsprint, tung oil and flaxseed.

Exports have grown rapidly since the war. On a per capita basis, exports amounted to an average of $38.50 in 1926–30. They declined to $15.55 during depression years of 1931–35, rose to $78.16 during the postwar period of 1946–50, and reached almost $140 in 1966.

Agricultural exports fluctuate widely depending upon the size of the American crop and world market conditions. About 20–40% of the cotton crop is usually exported, 20–30% of the cash grains and usually more than 30% of the tobacco crop. Well over 20% of the coal produced has been exported in recent years, 25–35% of the carbon black, 30–45% of the copper smelter and refining products, 30% of the construction and mining machinery and equipment, 25–30% of the oil field equipment, more than 20% of the machine tools, textile and metal working machinery, 15–20% of airplanes and airplane parts and an average of 35% of small arms.[1] Moreover, exports and imports represent by far the most important accounts in the American balance of payments (and the same holds true in the case of most countries). America depends upon a sufficiently large export surplus to pay for foreign aid and international military commitments which are necessary to maintain the country's position as the leader of the free world.

[1] United States Department of Commerce: *Statistical Abstract of the United States 1966*, p. 864.

International Trade Theories and Policies

The international flow of goods and capital is not governed only (and possibly not even primarily) by economic forces. Equally important are political considerations. As the political framework and the general socio-political philosophy changes, so do the international trade theories and policies.

The traditional 19th Century theory assumed (1) that foreign trade was carried on among individuals who happened to live in different countries, (2) that exchange rates were more or less stable, (3) that finished goods, capital and factors of production moved freely from one country to another (including unimpeded emigration and immigration), and (4) that the resources of the individual countries were fully employed. Modern theory, as it has developed since the 1930's, starts with a different set of premises. It assumes (at least by implication) (1) that international trade is carried on between nations (rather than individuals), either through government trade monopolies or (if the trade is actually carried on by individuals) on basis of government regulations and directives, (2) that foreign exchange rates need not be stable, but can be flexible or depreciating at varying rates, (3) that the movement of finished goods, capital and factors of production (including the migration of labor) is subject to government control and directions, and (4) that some if not all nations suffer from periodic or chronic productive overcapacity and underemployment.

While traditional theory assumed that the individual exporters and importers were guided by the desire to maximize personal gains, modern theories and policies are primarily concerned with the macro-economic goals of full employment and a maximum rate of economic growth, as well as with a variety of political goals such as the strengthening of the country in the cold war or "economic independence" in the case of newly emerging nations.

According to traditional theory the flow of trade was the result of international price differentials (an importer was expected to buy goods where they were cheapest). Modern theory, on the other hand, stresses the changes in income and employment in the different countries as the basis of foreign trade (as we shall show in detail in the subsequent pages).

Traditional theory, (assuming full employment of the factors of production in each country) postulated that an increase in exports of one product would lead to a shift of productive resources in order to increase the supply of the goods in demand, while reducing the output of goods which were less in demand and, hence, generated a smaller rate of profit. Foreign trade was thus thought of as producing changes in the composition of output (resulting in increased total profits), but no changes in the total volume of employment. Modern theory, on the other hand, (to the extent that it assumes overcapacity and underemployment) looks upon an export surplus as an injection of additional purchasing power which will lead to increased production and employment.

International Division of Labor

International trade is based on the international division of labor. In theory, each country should concentrate on the production of those goods and services for which it is best qualified. Switzerland can provide tourist facilities and dairy products; Norway, herrings and cheap water power (and hence cheap aluminum); Ghana, cocoa; the United States, intricate machinery calling for large capital investments, skilled workers, and research. Other countries have natural resources. Chile has nitrate and copper; Venezuela has oil; Australia has vast areas of cheap land suitable for wool raising. This does not mean that densely populated Belgium and Holland could not also raise wool, but only at a much higher cost.

Theory of Absolute and Comparative Advantage

In trying to develop a rationale for free trade, 19th Century (chiefly British) economists developed a theory of absolute and comparative advantage. If a country can produce a certain product more cheaply than another, it has an absolute advantage. Most countries enjoy an absolute advantage with regard to one product or another. But even if country X were able to produce everything more cheaply (that means with a smaller outlay of labor and capital) than country Y, foreign trade might still be to the advantage of both countries, if each had a comparative advantage over the other in certain products. Let us assume that the combination of an annual cost of $500 in capital (5% interest on a $10,000 investment) plus the labor of one worker produces

In Country X	*In Country Y*
90 tons of steel	30 tons of steel
or	or
2000 bu. of wheat	1500 bu. of wheat
(1 ton of steel = 22.2 bu. of wheat)	(1 ton of steel = 50 bu. of wheat)

In this case, it would be more advantageous for country X to concentrate on the production of steel (because it can produce three times as much steel as country Y) and import all the wheat it needs from country Y (because it can produce only 33% more wheat than the latter).

The theory was developed by David Ricardo at the beginning of the 19th Century and was elaborated later on by John

Stuart Mill and Alfred Marshall. Both preserved the Ricardian framework despite the fact that in order to present a logical and simple justification for free trade, Ricardo had omitted important variables which complicated the model.

Ricardo, for instance, assumed that an hour of labor constituted a uniform measure of input. Yet an hour's labor of an unskilled Indian worker is obviously less productive than an hour's labor of a highly skilled American worker. Ricardo further implied that the production cost is constant irrespective of the volume of output. Actually, unit cost varies as a rule with the volume of production. The average cost of producing wheat is likely to increase as expanding demand necessitates the use of inferior land. On the other hand the cost of steel making is likely to go down as demand increases and existing plant capacity can be used more fully.

Completely omitted was the factor of mobility of capital, despite the fact that international finance played an important role throughout the 19th Century. The steel manufacturing companies in country X, for instance, could decide to use their technological know-how and capital resources to build a more efficient plant in country Y rather than increase production in their own country in order to pay for the increase in wheat shipments. This is exactly what happened during the 1950's. Rather than increase the domestic output, (produced with the help of high-cost labor and under often adverse conditions of taxation), American companies exported their know-how and capital (instead of the finished product) and produced abroad usually on basis of a lower production cost.

Keynes and the Foreign Trade Theory

While Keynes himself failed to spell out clearly the implications of his *General Theory,* Keynesian notions have had a profound effect on international trade theories and policies. As the emphasis shifted from the international equilibrium (a balance in the country's international payments and receipts) to the internal equilibrium (full employment on basis of stable prices), a new approach developed to foreign trade policy and theory.

The Keynesian approach does not deal (in a microeconomic sense) with price differentials, but relates two macroeconomic phenomena: (1) the propagation of income (i.e., cyclical) fluctuations from one country to another, and (2) the process of adjusting balance of payments disequilibria.

Where the traditional theory relied on the price-specie-flow model to show how price differentials among countries resulted in the flow of goods and gold until the international price equilibrium was reestablished, the Keynesian approach shows how surpluses and deficits in the balance of payments are the result of fluctuations in domestic business conditions, i.e., changes in income and employment.

An increase in income in one country (whether it is the result of a cyclical upswing or of an artificial expansion of credit) is likely to result in an increase in imports, which in turn may produce a deficit in the balance of payments. As the domestic purchase power increases, the immediate result will be an increase in the demand for domestic goods and services, which in turn will lead to an increase in capital investments. Part of the expanding purchasing power, however, will be used to import goods from abroad. As the boom progresses, imports usually increase faster than the domestic output of goods and services. Between 1960 and 1965, for example, the total production of goods and services in the United States increased by 34%, while imports rose by 47%. In 1966 alone, domestic production rose by another 8½%, while imports jumped by almost 20%. The boom which develops in one country is thus "exported" to other countries as the prosperous country demands more imports from abroad. The resulting expansion of exports in other countries may lead either to an increase in employment and income (if the productive resources were previously not fully employed) or to rising prices (if the resources were already fully used). Thus, European economists and government officials complained that the Kennedy-Johnson boom of the 1960's aggravated the inflationary pressure in Europe.

"Exporting" Booms and Depressions

As prosperity, let us say in the United States, leads to increased imports (and has thus an adverse effect on the balance of payments) the resulting increase in exports from, let us say Germany, leads to a larger surplus in the German balance of payments. But it also leads to an increase in income within Germany which, due to the "multiplier effect," will be substantially larger than the actual increase in exports. As the German exporter spends the proceeds of the sales either for consumer goods or to expand his business, the money he originally received passes from hand to hand, each time resulting in an addition to the total demand for goods. A million Mark increase in German exports (due to the boom-created demand for German goods in America) can add 3–5 million Marks to the total demand in Germany.

Part of the additional income, moreover, will be spent on imports. The increase of American purchases from Germany will thus result in increased German purchases from Ecuador, Nigeria and other countries, which, in turn, will increase their imports. The increase of American purchases from Germany States. In due course, the increase in imports by the United States will lead to an increase in demand for American goods (because the American imports have created a world-wide increase in income which is reflected in increased imports). The original balance of payments deficit of the United States, and the balance of payments surplus of Germany will thus eventually disappear, and world trade will again be in equilibrium, but at a higher level.

The New Role of Gold The role of gold (which served as balancing force and was thus of paramount importance in the price-specie-flow mechanism of the traditional theory) plays a rather subordinate role in the Keynesian type of approach. It serves merely as a means of paying for the temporary balance of payments deficit, while the equilibrating forces work through changes in the income and employment in the individual countries which produce changes in the demand for imports.

Full Employment and the Balance of Payments The "automatic" aspects of the modern theory are supplemented by direct policy measures. The (automatic) expansive effects of an export surplus are supposed to be taken into consideration by the economic policy makers who are expected to pursue a correspondingly more restrictive fiscal and monetary policy. The theory ran into difficulties during the 1960's in some of the European countries, especially Germany. To compensate for a large export surplus (resulting in a substantial injection of additional purchasing power) the German government should have pursued a restrictive fiscal policy. But this proved impossible for political reasons and the growing demand for welfare expenditures. The resulting excess of foreign and domestic demand led to a sharp increase in prices.

Since a decline in employment and income in one country (commonly known as a recession) leads to a reduction of imports, the recession will be "exported" to other countries whose exports decline. To offset the declining income from exports, government policy should call for expanding demand at home (by means of deficit spending and an easy credit policy) in order to maintain full employment. The ultimate goal of economic policy must always be the maintenance of the internal equilibrium (full employment on basis of stable prices), if necessary at the cost of a temporary deficit in the balance of payments. This has been the policy of the United States since 1950, and especially since 1960. Washington has continued its expansionist fiscal and/or monetary policies despite the fact that the American balance of payments has shown a deficit since 1950.

How to Overcome the Deficit As long as a country has ample liquid resources (gold, the right to draw on the International Monetary Fund, and the ability to obtain other foreign credits), it can continue to pursue an expansionist policy at home, despite the adverse effect on its balance of payments. If, on the other hand, a country, such as Britain, is at the end of its liquid resources it has to choose between three policies: (1) Curb the domestic boom in order to reduce the demand for imports, (2) impose import restrictions and (3) devalue the currency. Since a deflationary policy at home would undermine the "internal equilibrium," the advocates of full employment reject this solution (although Italy in 1964 and Britain in 1966 were forced to adopt it). They advocate instead either import restrictions (to reduce the boom-inflated imports to their "normal" level) or a devaluation of the currency (to reestablish the purchase power parity betweeen the boom-inflated domestic and the international price level).

Import restrictions obviously interfere with the free flow of goods and the optimum international division of labor, and modern foreign trade theorists are careful to emphasize that import restrictions and currency devaluations must not be used for an aggressive "beggar-thy-neighbor" policy, but only as a limited protective measure to safeguard the internal full employment equilibrium.

In practical politics, however, it is often not easy to make this fine distinction, and policy makers are often inclined to pursue expansive domestic policies (large welfare expenditures, public work programs and easy credit policies are usually expedient from a political point of view) with little regard for the effects on the balance of payments. The result has been a world-wide inflation since the end of World War II.

International Monetary System

To finance the new international trade policies and make it possible for individual countries to pursue a continued expansive full employment policy at home, Lord Keynes and other postwar planners attempted to create a suitable international monetary and credit system. Their aim was to provide adequate international credit facilities to finance economic expansion (thus assuring full employment) and to bridge temporary balance of payments difficulties of individual countries. The Bretton Woods (New Hampshire) conference in 1944 created the International Bank for Reconstruction and Development (World Bank) (IBRD) (to provide long-term credits for the reconstruction of war-devastated countries and for the development of the emerging underdeveloped countries) and the International Monetary Fund (to provide short-term credits to assist countries which suffer from temporary balance of payments deficits). The Fund agreement called for international currency stability. All members were required to fix the price of gold in terms of their own currency (thus establishing a system of fixed gold-related foreign exchange rates) and to pledge themselves not to change the gold price without approval from the Fund. Actually, some countries (including Canada and France) never legally linked their currencies to gold.

Yet even though the Fund failed to achieve stability of foreign exchange rates. The goals of the Bretton Woods system were quite clear: (1) The industrialized countries were to maintain a policy of full employment through appropriate domestic fiscal and monetary policies; (2) the underdeveloped countries were to speed economic development with the help of foreign financial aid; (3) if these expansive policies throughout the world resulted in balance of payments deficits (which were expected to be "temporary" because of the anticipated "automatic" increase in imports on the part of the surplus countries) the International Monetary Fund was to provide temporary aid so as to make it unnecessary for the individual countries to abandon their expansive policies at home.

"Soft Credits" The scheme was successful in expanding world trade and in generating a high level of prosperity in the industrialized nations. Total exports rose from $55 billion in 1950 to $180 billion in 1964, and per capita income in the developed countries reached record levels.

The high prosperity, however, did not extend to the majority of the underdeveloped countries which account for about 65% of the world's population, because the increase in production was largely off-set by a rapid population increase. By the late 1950's it became apparent that neither the long-term credits of the World Bank nor the short-term accommodations of the Fund could solve the problems of the underdeveloped countries and a new institution, the International Development Association (IDA), was created in 1960 to provide "soft" credits. The interest-free loans run for 50 years. Amortization begins after a 10 year period of grace. During the subsequent 10 years 1% of the principal is repayable annually, and during the final 30 years 3%. Aside from the deferred repayments, the borrowing countries merely pay an annual service charge of ¾% of the amount outstanding.

Yet even the "soft" IDA loans apparently cannot solve the

problems of underdevelopment. Moreover, the vast expansion of international trade during the postwar period and the prosperity in the developed countries was financed through a tremendous expansion of credit at the domestic and international level, and in 1967 the members of the IMF accepted plans for a major revision of the international monetary system. In addition to gold and dollars a new international medium of exchange is to be created by the IMF in the form of "supplementary drawing rights" which are to be made available to deficit countries in order to prevent "international illiquidity" from restraining the further growth of the world economy.

Arguments in Favor of Protection

While foreign trade theories and policies underwent far-reaching changes during the postwar years, there were few changes in the arguments presented by the advocates of protection and in the methods used to prevent an unwanted influx of foreign goods.

Even Adam Smith, one of the strongest advocates of free trade, agreed in 1776 that "defence is much more important than opulence," and, ever since, industries have demanded special protection in the name of national security, including the American merchant marine and shipbuilding industries.

Another popular argument calls for the protection of infant industries until they become able to compete with the established and hence more efficient industries in other countries. German and American writers (including Friedrich List and Henry C. Carey) put forth this argument during the mid-19th Century against the then popular British free trade theories. And the same policies are advocated today by many of the underdeveloped countries which claim that free trade will perpetuate the "industrial domination" by the developed countries.

While the defence and infant arguments are probably valid

within certain limits, only too often so-called infant industries turn out to be costly hot-house developments which consume large amounts of scarce capital and offer only limited prospects of ever becoming competitive.

Prior to World War 1, Britain was the "factory of the world." She exported coal and finished products and relied on other countries for low-cost imports of raw materials and food. When World War I broke out, British agriculture could produce only enough food to feed the British people for 10 weeks. Food equal to 42 weeks' consumption had to be imported, which left Britain extremely vulnerable to the German submarine blockade. In relying heavily on low-priced food imports, Britain had emphasized "opulence" at the expense of national security, and by the time World War II broke out the output of British agriculture had been increased sufficiently to provide for 20 weeks' consumption. But since domestic wheat and meat were more costly than imports, the increased reliance on domestic foods had (in theory at least) an adverse effect on the general standard of living.

Far less plausible as a rule than the national security and infant industry arguments are the claims for increased protection which are put forth by American and European manufacturers. The Americans claim that they cannot compete with foreign firms which pay materially lower wages, while the Europeans argue that they cannot compete with the automated and high capital intensive American plants. Neither wages nor capital investments alone determine production cost, but the combined cost of all factors of production. An American textile worker earning $2 an hour and using modern machinery may well be able to compete with an Indian worker who receives only $1 a day.

The situation changes, however, as the productive efficiency abroad increases. Japanese and West-European workers are, as a rule, less productive than their American counterparts, but the difference in productivity is often less than the difference in wage levels, which has made it possible in recent years for Japanese and West-European manufacturers to flood the American market.

"Theory of the Periphery"

The traditional principle of the international division of labor provided the rationale for the formation of the European Common Market which proved highly successful. The same principle, however, is often rejected in underdeveloped countries for psychological-political as well as economic-social reasons. The production of raw materials has come to be associated with "colonialism," and "industrialization" (especially the development of heavy industries) has become the symbol of economic independence, even though improved methods of agriculture are usually far more urgently needed for the welfare of the people than a high-cost steel mill.

To this psychological element must be added the arguments of a well-known international economist, Raul Prebisch, who has become the spokesman not only of his native Latin America but of underdeveloped countries in general. His "theory of the peripheral economy" is designed to show that the economic position of raw material-producing countries will continue to deteriorate and that their only hope lies in the development of industries and a "balanced economy."

Most underdeveloped countries depend on one, two or at best four commodities. Virtually all exports from Latin America, for example, consist of primary products. Oil, sugar, coffee and cotton ordinarily account for about 65% of total Latin American exports. Meat, hides, wool, grains, copper and other minerals, cocoa, and bananas account for another 25%. The prices of most of these products fluctuate widely in world markets. Copper prices dropped more than 30% between 1956 and 1958. Coffee prices fluctuated wildly from a post-war low of 26¢ to a peak of 79¢ in 1953, and back to 34¢ in 1959. About two-thirds of Brazil's exports consist of coffee, 70% of Haiti's and Guatemala's, more than 80% of Colombia's and El Salvador's. The wide fluctuations of coffee prices thus make economic planning in these countries extremely difficult. A 1¢ decline in the price of coffee means a $19 million drop in Brazil's national income and a $7 million drop in Colombia's.

Terms of Trade

Moreover, as Prebisch and other economists from raw material-producing countries point out, raw material prices, since the end of World War II, have shown a general tendency to decline, while the prices of manufactured products of industrialized countries have had a tendency to increase. The result has been a deterioration of what is known as the terms of trade of the raw material-producing countries, namely the relationship between the prices these countries receive for their exports and those which they have to pay for needed imports.

The decline in raw material prices is due to improved production methods and the tremendous increase in production in Africa. The rise in prices of manufactured products is largely the result of the steady upward pressure of wages in the industrialized countries. The underdeveloped raw material producing countries thus receive less for their exports and have to pay more for their imports. It has been estimated that a 5% decline in export prices and a 5% increase in import prices, would cost Latin America about $1 billion a year on basis of the 1960 foreign trade volume, an amount which happens to be identical with the annual aid promised Latin America under the Alliance for Progress.

The trend of declining raw material prices and rising prices for manufactured products may be only temporary. During the decades preceding World War I the prices of both raw materials and manufactured products declined. But the prices of manufactured products declined much faster. The terms of trade thus favored the raw material producers and worked against the exporters of manufactured products. But this did not prevent Britain, the most important exporter of finished products, from enjoying a high degree of prosperity.

Tariffs

In order to protect domestic industries against foreign competition a large arsenal of weapons has been developed. The traditional and most widely used method is the imposition of tariffs (or import duties), a tax collected as the goods enter the country. Tariffs differ depending upon how they are collected, their applicability and the general rate structure. One distinguishes between *revenue* and *protective tariffs.* The former (which do not concern us here) are designed to produce revenue for the government, the latter to provide protection for domestic industries. Britain has long relied on tariffs (e.g., on wine and tea) for part of its government revenues. In the United States, on the other hand, tariffs produce less than 4% of Federal revenues and are almost entirely protective in design. The more effective a tariff as a protective measure, the smaller the revenue it produces. A 100% effective protective tariff will produce no revenue.

Types of Protective Tariffs Depending upon the ways in which the duties are collected one distinguishes between ad valorem, specific and mixed duties.

Ad valorem duties are levied on basis of the value of the goods imported. It is easy for Congress to construct an ad valorem tariff, and since the duties rise as prices increase, ad valorem tariffs provide the same relative protection in times of inflation. The chief disadvantage of ad valorem tariffs lies in the difficulty of establishing a fair import value. The value (for customs purposes) may be fixed by Congress (in which case the customs value may differ considerably from the real value); it can be based on the prices prevailing in the country of origin, the actual price which the importer paid (or claimed he paid, because invoices can be falsified), on the prevailing American wholesale or retail price, or on the production cost (which is often difficult to ascertain).

Specific duties are based on the quantity of goods imported measured in terms of pounds, dozens, etc. The weight (for customs purposes) may be based on the weight of the goods themselves, the "legal weight" (which includes the weight of the goods and the container, e.g., a can of sardines) or the "gross weight" (which includes the weight of the goods, the container and the wrappings). Specific duties eliminate the problem of determining the proper valuation of an import, but it is difficult to draft a law which covers the multitude of different products, and articles of different values may pay the same duty. (A duty of $20 per dozen dresses, e.g., would apply equally to $10 apiece and $100 apiece dresses.) Specific duties, moreover, do not change with changing prices. In times of rapid inflation specific duties thus provide little protection.

American Tariff System

Roughly 45% of the customs collected by the United States are in the form of ad valorem duties and a similar percentage in the form of specific duties. The balance is accounted for by *mixed, compound or compensating duties* which represent a combination of ad valorem and specific rates. The 1930 tariff law, e.g., fixed for woolen goods a specific tariff of 50¢ per pound (which was equal to the duty levied on raw wool and designed to protect the American wool raisers) and a 60% ad valorem duty (designed to protect the American manufacturer of woolen goods).

The same goods are often subject to different duties depending upon the country of origin. One thus distinguishes between single and multiple tariff systems. Under a *single tariff system* (also known as unilinear tariff) a uniform rate applies to the same article irrespective of the country of origin. The United States is traditionally a single tariff country, while most European countries favor multiple tariffs. All reciprocal trade agreements negotiated by the United States contain a *most-favored-nation clause,* which provides that American goods will be admitted to the foreign country at the most favorable tariff rate applying to any other countries (although there are some exceptions), and the same arrangements apply to foreign goods entering the United States. Under a *multiple tariff system* the duties for the same article differ depending upon the country of origin. The legislature as a rule fixes maximum and minimum rates leaving it to the executive to apply different rates to different countries under the so-called *general and conventional tariff system.* While a general rate applies to all countries, the government can reach tariff conventions with specific countries which provide for lower (conventional) rates. Canada, for example, provides a minimum tariff for members of the British Commonwealth, a conventional rate for the most-favored-nation countries, and a maximum rate for the rest.

One further distinguishes between simple and complex tariff systems and surtaxes. Simple tariffs provide for the same ad valorem rate to be applied to all goods irrespective of their country of origin. This system was widely used in the past by countries which lacked an experienced staff of customs officials. China for many years levied a flat 5% (later an 8%) duty on all imports, whether badly needed medical supplies or frowned-upon luxuries, such as whisky. Most countries now rely on *complex tariffs* which provide for different rates for different products, as a rule including both ad valorem and specific duties. Occasionally, some countries levy *surtaxes* (special duties) to meet specific situations. Some of the Latin American countries, during the 1920's pledged part of their special customs revenues as security for foreign loans. France levied a surtax on British goods in the 1930's after the devaluation of the pound.

There are many other tariff complications, including the so-called *countervailing duties* to off-set real or imaginary advantages which the foreign manufacturer possesses over the domestic manufacturer. During the 1930's, the United States levied a 25% countervailing duty on all imports from Germany, supposedly because Germany used a variety of blocked Marks to finance her exports.

In view of the fantastic complexity of the tariff laws it is not surprising that foreign exporters, American importers and even the customs authorities are not always certain as to which rate applies, and it is not uncommon for the appeals of rate decisions to take 6 years or more to be finally decided by the courts.

Reciprocal Trade Agreements Tariffs are fixed by Congress, although under the *Reciprocal Trade Agreements Act* (a 1934 Amendment to the Hawley-Smoot Act), the Administration was given the power to negotiate reciprocal tariff reductions with other nations up to 50% of the original rate. A supplementary authorization in 1945 enabled the Administration to negotiate additional 50% reductions, so that, in theory, American tariffs could have been reduced to 25% of their 1930 level. Before tariffs are changed (either upward or downward) the probable effect of the changes has to be studied by the *United States Tariff Commission,* a bi-partisan body which consists of

6 members, each appointed for a 12-year term. The function of the Commission is advisory. It has no power to change rates.

Other Means of Regulating Imports

In addition to tariffs, governments have developed a large arsenal of other means of restricting imports.

Import Quotas Governments can fix the actual quantity of a certain product which may be imported and then allocate fixed percentages of the total to various countries. This system has been used for years to regulate the importation of sugar into the United States. There can also be "voluntary quotas." Threatened with more severe import restrictions by the American authorities, Japanese exporters "voluntarily" agreed to establish quotas for the exportation of Japanese textiles to the United States.

Foreign Exchange Restrictions By controlling the right of individuals to convert their money into foreign exchange (e.g., Indian rupees into dollars), the authorities can control the flow imports. This system developed and was widely used during the 1930's and is still being used today by many countries. Before a prospective importer can buy foreign goods, he must obtain the necessary allocation of foreign exchange which is granted (or refused) by the foreign exchange authorities, usually the central bank. An Indian manufacturer cannot order a needed spare part (even if the lack of the spare part forces him to shut down part of his factory). He must first obtain permission to spend the required amount of sterling, and to obtain this permission may take weeks and months. If the authorities feel a specific import is not needed from the point of view of the national economy, they can refuse the necessary foreign exchange and thus prevent the importation. In some countries, the foreign exchange authorities have established different rates for different products. A South American importer may have to pay twice as many pesos for a dollar if he wishes to import an American car as if he plans to buy medical supplies.

Embargoes Under certain circumstances, the authorities have the right to exclude certain products completely. If the American Secretary of Agriculture decides that foot-and-mouth disease exists in a certain country, he can prohibit the importation not only of animals and meat, but also of meat products. This provision was used for many years to exclude Argentine corned beef from the United States, even though it was purchased at the same time by the U.S. Navy. Under the Defense Production Act of 1950 the Department of Agriculture placed a complete embargo on peanuts, peanut oil, butter and non-fat dried milk solids.

"Buy American" Act of 1933 Many governments have passed laws excluding foreign goods from public consumption, or have tried to make it appear a patriotic duty to buy local products rather than those of foreign countries. The "Buy American" Act of 1933 requires the Federal government to buy American in preference to foreign goods. Similar laws have been passed by individual states. The 1950 Appropriations Act for the National Military Establishment limits the purchase of "any article of food or clothing not grown or produced in the United States." During the 1930's American exports to Argentina suffered because of the Argentine "buy from those who buy from us" campaign which favored the importation of British goods because the British bought more Argentine goods than the United States.

U.S. Foreign Trade Policy

Despite the multitude of import restrictions and administrative red tape which continues to hamper the flow of international trade, the United States, since the 1930's, has pursued, at least in principle, a policy of reducing trade barriers. The same is true of many other countries since the end of World War II. In 1947 some 20 countries including the United States agreed in Geneva on a number of mutual trade concessions. The arrangement came to be known as the *General Agreement on Tariffs and Trade* (GATT). It was subsequently joined by other countries and developed into a regular international organization which promotes through international agreements the progressive removal of trade barriers.

Chapter 17

NATIONAL INCOME ACCOUNTS

THE BASIC FACTS

National Income accounts were developed gradually during the 1930's and 1940's to provide the necessary factual information for economic planning.

While the data are the best available and extremely helpful, they must not be regarded as a "photograph" of reality. They are based on assumptions which differ somewhat from country to country, so that international comparisons are often misleading.

The National Income is calculated in two ways: on the basis of the total income paid to the factors of production, and on the basis of the value of the goods and services produced. The two methods produce more or less the same results.

There are five major National Income Accounts: Gross National Product, Net National Product, National Income, Personal Income and Disposable Income. Each of these provides a special type of information which is valuable for economic planning. The GNP, for instance (on the basis of full employment) reflects the maximum productive capacity of a nation for a short period of time (since it makes no allowance for depreciation and depletion). The Disposable Income shows how much the consumer can spend (or save).

National Income Accounting an Instrument of National Planning

The national income accounts were developed gradually during the 1930's and 1940's as a logical concomitant of modern economic planning. Under the impact of the Depression, World War II and the postwar "full employment" policy, the traditional laissez faire policy gradually gave way to government intervention and planning, and this, in turn, made it necessary for the government to have more accurate and detailed data regarding the economic performance of the nation.

During the Depression years, government economists and policy makers were primarily interested in the problem of inadequate purchasing power, which led to the development of the concept of National Income. During the war the productive capacity of the nation became all-important, resulting in the further development of the Gross National Product data. To these two basic "aggregates" (meaning: totals) three others were added: Net National Product, Personal Income, and Disposable Income. Each of the five aggregates tells something important about the economy of the nation as a whole.

Differences in Assumptions and Statistical Methods

Today all major countries compile national income data. Most of them appear quite similar at first sight. Actually, however, the basic assumptions and the statistical methods employed are far from uniform, so that the national income data of different countries (and the rate of economic growth indicated by these statistics) are not necessarily comparable. Besides, great technical difficulties are involved in gathering and processing the statistical material. Highly skilled statisticians, intimately familiar with the economy of the nation, are needed, and many countries do not have the facilities to compile reasonably accurate national income data. Economic planning in these countries thus starts from a rather unreliable basis. American foreign aid officials have found it necessary at times to make their own estimates of a nation's National Income and Gross National Product, and these American estimates have differed as much as 15–20% from the official data compiled and published by the nation's own agencies.

Statistics not a Photograph of Reality It is extremely important to realize that national income accounts do not constitute a photograph of reality. They are a statistical construction based on many assumptions. If these assumptions are changed, the statistical picture changes. Like Alice in Wonderland, we can never fully rely on the picture which we see in the "mirror," we have to step "through the looking glass" to see reality. But whatever defects the national income aggregates may have — and they are serious — , the available data are the best which we have and probably the best which our present statistical knowledge permits.

National Income

There are two ways of looking at the National Income: (1) One can regard National Income as the total income earned by all factors of production, i.e., total wages, rent, interest payments and profits. This is the method employed by the Department of Commerce. Or (2) one can look on the National Income as the market value of all the goods and services produced. This method is used by the National Bureau of Economic Research. The two approaches look on the same process from different sides (as shown in Figure 4), but produce more or less the same results.

FIGURE 4 Two Ways of Defining National Income

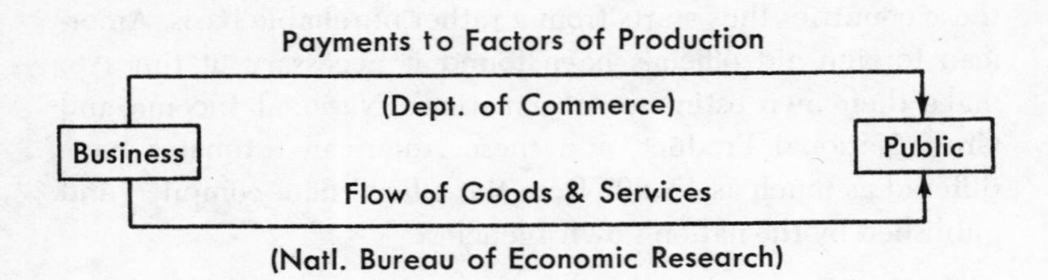

Department of Commerce Approach Both approaches involve complications. The Commerce Department, which attempts to measure the income of the factors of production, must by definition exclude "unearned income." An inheritance may provide a substantial income for the lucky heir, but it is not figured as part of the national income; neither are veterans' bonuses or unemployment insurance payments.

Since national income data are expressed in current dollars, the National Income may show an apparent increase of 5% from one year to the next, but if prices have risen by 5% during the same year, the real national income has remained the same.

National Bureau Approach The National Bureau of Economic Research's method runs into other difficulties. How can one measure the value of goods and services received; for instance, the value of the food which the farmer produces for himself? Economists like to measure income in terms of the satisfaction which the purchaser of goods and services derives from them. But there is no way of measuring satisfaction. This makes it necessary to assume that the price which the purchaser is willing to pay for goods and services reflects the value which he places on them, and the satisfaction which he expects to derive from them. Once "satisfaction" is expressed in current dollars, however, the National Bureau of Research approach is confronted with the same problem as the Department of Commerce, namely, that the value of the dollar changes from year to year.

Exclusion of Intermediate Steps Only the value of the final product is included in the National Income data: the amount which the consumer pays for the bread, not the money the miller pays for the grain or the baker pays for the flour. Oil used by the baker to heat his oven is not part of National Income, but the oil used to heat his home is. A salesman invites a client to dinner: Is the dinner a final product (based on the satisfaction which it gives to the client) or is it merely a business expense which has to be added to the value of the final product? These are some of the statistical and conceptional difficulties involved in calculating national income aggregates, and they indicate how dangerous it is to accept the national income data as a photograph of reality.

The Five National Income Accounts

Whether national income accounting is an art or a science, or both, is a moot question, but there is little doubt that it is highly technical and complex. We shall confine ourselves to the five major accounts — Gross National Product, Net National Product, National Income, Personal Income and Disposable Income — and the relationship of the five accounts to each other.

The Gross National Product (GNP) represents the value, in terms of current market prices, of all the goods and services produced during a year, including (1) those produced for the final consumer; (2) investment goods; (3) net exports; and (4) goods produced for the government. Table 7 presents the composition of the GNP in recent years.

TABLE 7

Composition of Gross National Product

	(in billion dollars)		
	1964	1965	1966
Gross National Product	632.4	683.8	743.2
Personal consumption expenditures	401.2	433.1	465.9
Durable goods	59.2	66.0	70.3
Nondurable goods	178.7	191.2	207.5
Services	163.3	175.9	188.1
Gross private domestic investment	94.0	107.4	117.9
Nonresidential construction	61.1	71.0	80.2
Residential construction	27.1	27.0	24.3
Changes in inventories	5.8	9.4	13.4
Net exports	8.5	6.9	5.1
Government purchases	128.7	136.4	154.2
National defense	50.0	50.1	60.5
Other Federal	15.2	16.7	16.5
State and local	63.5	69.6	77.2

Source: U.S. Department of Commerce "Survey of Current Business" July 1967, p. 13.

Cyclical fluctuations as a rule affect above all (1) the purchase of durable consumer goods by the public, (2) new construction and (3) the purchase of machinery by industry. If people defer the purchase of a new car or do not build a new home, and industry fails to build a new plant and reduces its purchase of new machinery, the economy as a whole is likely to decline — unless government purchases are increased to take up the slack.

Under conditions of full employment, as they existed during World War II, the GNP measures the maximum productive capacity of the nation on basis of the existing social and technological order. If the work-week were stepped up from 40 to 50 hours, the GNP could be expanded. It could also be expanded (although not immediately) through the installation of more efficient machinery. Since the GNP makes no allowance, however, for the depletion of resources and the wear and tear of machinery, it is not a sound measure for the productive capacity of a nation over the long run.

The Net National Product (NNP), namely, the GNP less depreciation, is more realistic in this respect. Just as a company must make allowance for the depreciation of its machinery before calculating its net income, a nation must allow for the depletion of its natural resources and the depreciation of its man-made capital in calculating its "net" production of goods and services for the year.

The GNP and NNP are based on the market price of the goods and services sold, while the National Income measures either the "value received" by the consumer (National Bureau of Economic Research approach), or the income earned by the factors of production in producing the goods (Department of Commerce approach). If the consumer buys a pack of cigarettes for 32¢ (the basis for calculating the GNP and NNP), he gets only 15¢ worth of cigarettes, and the producers get only 15¢. The remaining 17¢ go to the government in the form of excise and sales taxes.

The *National Income* (NI) can thus be defined as being equal to the NNP less excise taxes (and some other minor adjustments). It is a rather abstract concept, and some economists regard its practical value as limited. It does not represent a satisfactory measure of consumer purchasing power, because it does not equal the total payments received by the factors of production. It includes total corporate earnings, which are divided into three parts: about half the earnings go to the government in the form of corporate income taxes, another portion is retained by the corporations and added to the surplus, and only about 35% are actually paid out to the stockholders in the form of dividends and thus form a part of the personal income. The NI also includes the amounts which the corporations pay to the government in the form of social security taxes. On the other hand, individuals receive from the government and from corporations so-called "transfer payments," i.e., payments for which they have not rendered services, at least not during the given year. These so-called transfer payments include unemployment insurance and old age security payments, GI and veterans' benefits, payments under private and public pension systems, etc.

Personal Income (PI) represents all the payments actually received by the individual, whether they represent rewards for services rendered (wages, interest, rent and profits) or transfer payments. But even PI does not constitute a reliable measure of the actual spending capacity of the individual. To arrive at Disposable Income, one must deduct from the PI the amounts paid to the Federal, state and local governments in the form of direct (i.e., chiefly personal income) taxes.

Disposable Income (DI) measures the actual spending power of the people, which can be used to defray consumption expenditures or to increase personal savings. The rate of savings varies. Since the early 1950's, when the American public saved about 7% of its Disposal Income, the rate declined until it reached about 5% in 1965. Instead of spending about 93¢ out of every dollar earned, the people spent about 95¢.

Table 8 shows in some detail the National Income Accounts for 1950 and 1965, and 1966.

TABLE 8

National Income Accounts, 1950, 1965, 1966

	1950	1965	1966	Percent Increase 1950–1966
Gross National Product	$284.6	$683.8	$743.3	+161%
less depreciation	—19.1	—59.9	—63.5	+232%
Net National Income	265.5	623.9	679.8	+156%
less excise taxes and var. adjustm. plus gov't subsidies (less profits of gov't enterprises)	—23.7	—61.5	—63.1	
National Income	241.9	562.4	616.7	+141%
less corp. profits and inventory adjustments	—35.6	—74.9	—82.2	+130%
social security taxes	— 6.9	—29.7	—38.2	+454%
plus gov't transfer payments	+14.3	+37.2	+41.2	+188%
interest on gov't bonds	+ 4.8	+20.4	+22.2	+363%
corp. dividends	+ 9.2	+19.8	+21.4	+133%
business transfer payments	+ 0.8	+ 2.5	+ 2.7	+238%
Personal Income	228.4	537.7	584.0	+155%
less personal income taxes	—20.8	—65.5	—75.2	+262%
Disposable Income	207.6	472.2	508.8	+145%
Consumption expenditures	195.0	445.0	479.0	+146%
Individual savings	12.6	27.2	29.8	+137%

Source: U.S. Department of Commerce, *Survey of Current Business*, July, 1967, pp. 15 and 20.

A study of Table 8 reveals a number of interesting facts: while the GNP grew by 161% personal income taxes increased even faster than the GNP, (despite a reduction in tax rates in 1964), so that the Disposable Income of the people increased by only 145%.

The Disposable Income seemingly would have increased

even less if it had not been for the 149% increase in government transfer payments. This impression, however, is misleading, because the sharp increase in transfer payments is offset by a 316% increase in Social Security taxes. In other words, while more people received unemployment, old age security and veterans benefits from the government, other Americans had to provide the funds through higher taxes.

Basic Assumptions

In compiling the data shown in Table 7 and 8, the statistician must make certain basic assumptions. Thus he assumes, in the spirit of American capitalism, that anything for which anybody is willing to pay is worth the price for which it sells. No qualitative distinctions are made either from a social or individual point of view. In other words, national income statistics are purely quantitative and make no allowance for the often extremely important qualitative elements. In theory, it would be possible for the GNP to grow while at the same time the standard of living of the people declined and the economy stagnated. Such a situation may have existed in France prior to the Revolution of 1789, although we have no statistics to prove it. An elaborate government questionnaire which keeps thousands of people busy throughout the country (who could otherwise be employed productively) adds to the GNP, but it may very well not add a corresponding amount to either the national strength or the well-being of the people.

Comparison between American and Russian Statistics

A comparison between the American and the Russian national income statistics illustrates the importance of the underlying philosophic assumptions. The Russian data are based on the Marxian dictum that only the worker but not the "capitalist" "produces." The salaries of some highly paid managers are thus excluded from the Russian GNP. In theory, the wages of a soldier standing guard should be excluded, while the wages of the same soldier while he assists in building a road should be included. The Russians argue, therefore, that the American GNP is inflated through the inclusion of salaries paid to "non-productive" workers, namely, the key leaders of business. In turn there is evidence that the Russians are not as careful in distinguishing between intermediate and final products. While in the U.S. only the final product is included, there is some evidence that the Russians at times include some intermediate products.

A special case is the housewife, who works hard from morning to night to keep the house in order, raise the children and feed the family. In Russia the work of a housewife is regarded as "productive" and its monetary equivalent is included in the GNP total. In the United States, "for technical reasons," the labor of a housewife is disregarded. American housewives may not think so, but so far as national income statistics are concerned they are regarded as "non-productive." Mr. Jones has a housekeeper whom he pays a monthly salary of $300. These $300 form a part of the GNP. Eventually Mr. Jones marries his housekeeper and now gives her a monthly allowance of $400. So far as the national income accounts are concerned, however, the $400 do not count, and Mr. Jones' marriage to his housekeeper has resulted in a decrease of the GNP by $3600 annually!

Price Indexes and Changes in the Cost of Living

In speaking of "rising prices" or the "cost of living" economists do not think in terms of the prices of hundreds of different goods and services—a pack of cigarettes, a bus ride, a pound of meat, an appendectomy, a refrigerator—but in terms of a price index which reflects the average price of a large number of goods and services. The two most widely used price indexes in the United States are the Index of Consumer Prices (popularly referred to as the "cost-of-living" index) and the Wholesale Price Index. Both are compiled monthly by the Bureau of Labor Statistics of the U.S. Department of Commerce.

Since finished products (which form the basis of the Consumer Price Index) involve a larger amount of labor than raw materials and semi-finished products (which are used for the Wholesale Price Index), the Consumer Price Index will advance more rapidly than the Wholesale Price Index if wages increase faster than raw material prices. During the seven years from 1959 to 1966 the Consumer Price Index advanced from 101.5 to 114 (1957–59 = 100) or by about 13%, while the Wholesale Price Index rose from 100.6 to 107 or by only 6.3%.

As prices advance, the purchase power of the dollar (its "value") declines. How much the "value" of the dollar declined between 1959 and 1966 thus depends upon whether one measures its purchase power in terms of the Consumer Price or the Wholesale Price Index.

The "cost of living" and the changing "value of money" are usually measured in terms of the Consumer Price Index which is calculated on basis of a so-called "market basket" reflecting the prices of some 400 goods and services in 50 areas throughout the United States, including New York, Chicago, 31 other metropolitan and 17 non-metropolitan areas. The "market basket" is composed of items which the average-size families of typical wage earners and clerical workers buy. The index thus does not reflect changes in the cost of living of either an unemployed West Virginia coal miner or a Palm Beach millionaire, and it would be impossible to construct a price index which reflects changes in the cost of living of all income classes in all parts of the country. In order to show regional differences in the cost of living, the Bureau of Labor Statistics publishes 17 regional consumer price indexes, as well as separate indexes for "city workers families" in 20 cities and for "retired couples" in the same 20 cities.

The techniques of developing reasonably reliable price indexes have much improved during the past 35 years in the United States and other advanced countries. In most underdeveloped countries, on the other hand, and even in some advanced countries, the officially published price indexes often do not provide a reliable measure of the changing cost of living.

While the compiling of the actual Consumer Price Index involves many complexities, the basic principle is simple as the hypothetical indexes of a very small "market basket" in Table 9 and 10 indicate.

TABLE 9

Consumer Price Index for 1966 (1960 Base Year)

	1960			1966		
	Price		Percent	Price		Percent of 1960 Price
Rent	$50	=	100%	$53	=	106%
Steak (lb.)	80¢	=	100%	88¢	=	110%
Bus ride	20¢	=	100%	25¢	=	125%
Oranges (each)	15¢	=	100%	12¢	=	80%
			400%			421%
1960 (Base year) price level: 100				1966 price level: 105.2		

But this simple method of just averaging all prices is misleading. A 6% increase in the rent affects the average consumer more than a 20% decline in the price of oranges. In order to provide a more realistic picture of the actual changes in the cost of living, the prices have to be "weighted" according to the relative importance of the respective goods and service, which in turn is measured by the amount of money which the typical family spends on each item.

TABLE 10

Weighted Consumer Index for 1966 (1960 Base Year)

	1960	1966			
	Price	Price	as % of 1960	Weight	Percent x Weight
Rent	$50	$53	106%	50	5300
Steak (lb)	80¢	88¢	110%	30	3300
Bus ride	20¢	25¢	125%	15	1875
Oranges (each)	15¢	12¢	80%	5	400
				100	10,875

Weighted index for 1966: 108.75

The Effect of Price Level Changes

As prices (reflected in the price index) advance, the purchasing power of the dollar (its "value") declines. Between 1945 and 1966 the Consumer Price Index rose from 62.7 to 114, indicating an increase in the cost of living of about 82%, which corresponds to a decrease in the purchasing power of the dollar by 45%, and people, therefore, speak of a "55 cents dollar."

The declining purchasing power of the dollar has had a different effect on various economic classes. Labor as a whole did not suffer from the increase in prices between 1945 and 1966 because wages rose much faster than prices. Home owners and farmers who had mortgages outstanding benefited, since they are able to repay their debts in depreciated dollars. On the other hand, those people who invested their money in U.S. Savings Bonds or deposited it with savings and loan associations and savings banks are being repaid in dollars which buy materially less than the dollars which they originally invested or deposited. And all people who depend upon fixed income such as pensions and Old Age Security payments, have been severely hurt, unless payments were adjusted to the rising cost of living.

Chapter 18

THE THEORY OF MACROECONOMIC PLANNING

THE BASIC FACTS

The theory of macroeconomic planning rests upon three basic premises. (1) The innate self-equilibrating forces of the economy (upon which 19th Century economists relied) are no longer able to assure full employment because of institutional obstacles. (2) For social and political reasons, these institutional obstacles cannot be removed. It is thus necessary to replace the automatic self-equilibrating forces of yesteryear by government planning and controls. (3) These controls can best be exercised through the regulation of the supply of money and credit.

The Theory of National Equilibrium *The theory can be presented in three different forms: through a flow chart; a set of equations, and a graph. All three tell the same story. In order to maintain the Net National Product at the full employment level (avoiding both unemployment and inflation), total demand (consisting of consumer spending, private investments and government spending) must be equal to the total value of goods and services which the economy can produce by using all its resources. To achieve this optimum level of total demand, government fiscal policy must "compensate" for the failure of the private sector to absorb total savings.*

The chief cause of inadequate demand, according to modern theorists, is the accumulation of "idle savings," for which there is no investment demand. The more affluent a society, it is argued, the larger the amount of savings, and the more limited the possible investment outlets. The theory appears perfectly logical, but actual experience does not generally support it. Despite the fact that the Disposable Income of the American consumer more than doubled between 1950 and 1963, the rate of savings actually declined.

Socio-political Appeal *The economic theory of oversaving, however, has a strong socio-political appeal. (1) If the private sector is unable to absorb the accumulating savings, government spending has to be increased to absorb idle savings and thus prevent unemployment. This notion appeals to all who wish to expand the public sector. (2) Since the low income groups spend more, and the high income groups save more, income should be shifted from the high to the low income groups in order to prevent excessive saving. This idea obviously meets with the approval of all those who consider themselves as belonging to the low income groups.*

The basic elements of the theory of macroeconomic planning are fairly simple. In practice, however, a multitude of complicating factors enter the picture, including, for instance, the multiplier and accelerator effects. It is thus not surprising that economic planning has thus far not succeeded in achieving its goals of full employment, stable purchasing power, maximum economic growth, and a balance of payment equilibrium.

The Premises of Economic Intervention

The theory of macroeconomic intervention and planning is based on three implied premises.

The Breakdown of the Self-equilibrating Forces

Nineteenth Century economic theory assumed that the economy is governed by inherent, self-equilibrating forces. If not interfered with, these forces will work not only toward an equilibrium between the supply of and demand for goods, services, labor and money, but toward the best possible equilibrium which will assure the fullest and most effective use of all productive resources. The 20th Century rejects this optimistic assumption. It admits that economic forces may, in theory, tend toward an equilibrium between supply and demand, revenues and expenditures. But this equilibrium may occur at any level, and more likely than not at a level below that of full employment. Institutional factors have apparently developed which impede the equilibrating forces of the economy to such an extent that they have ceased to function smoothly.

Institutional Obstacles and Government Intervention

Given the choice between (a) attempting to remove the institutional obstacles to a free flow of the economic forces, and (b) government intervention designed to bring about full employment and maximum economic growth, modern economists advocate government intervention, because they regard it as either impossible or undesirable to eliminate the oligopolistic structure of the modern economy which makes for price rigidity; the power of unions which prevents a downward adjustment of the labor cost; or the unemployment insurance system which enables workers to "sit out" a recession rather than accept lower wages.

Reliance on Indirect Controls

Given the need of government intervention and the desire to avoid direct controls because of their effect on individual freedom, modern economists hold that the level of economic activities should, and can, be determined through monetary and fiscal policies.

Three Methods of Presentation

There are three ways in which the basic arguments for government intervention can be presented: (1) through a flow chart, (2) through a set of equations and (3) through a diagram. Each method presents the story from a slightly different angle and in a different form, but all three are designed to show how government intervention can prevent unemployment and inflation through the proper control of the supply of money and credit and government fiscal policies.

FIGURE 5 Flow of Income and Expenditures

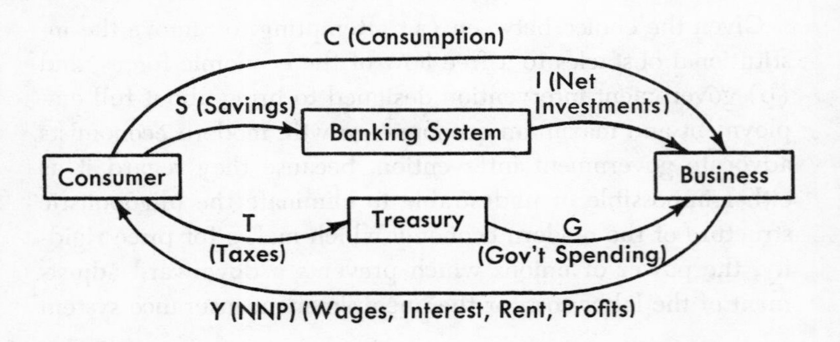

Flow Chart The flow of income and expenditures is in equilibrium if business expenditures (Y) are equal to business income (C + I + G); ($550 bill. = $370 bill. + $30 bill. + $150 bill.) Or to express the same idea slightly differently, if the total production, valued at $550 billion, is absorbed by the consumer ($370 billion), through new capital investments ($30 billion), and government spending ($150 billion).

Two Viewpoints One can look upon the flow of income and expenditures either from the point of view of the "Public" (the consumer) or "Business" (the producer). As seen from the Consumer viewpoint, total income (Y) consists of wages, interest, rent and profits. Out of this income the Consumer first of all must pay taxes (T). Of the remainder, the major portion (approx. 95%) is used to pay for non-durable and durable consumer goods and for services (C), and the balance goes into savings (S). Hence, Y = C + S + T.

As seen from the viewpoint of "Business," wages, interest, rent and profits (Y) represent total expenditures, Y being equal to total production cost plus net profits (equal to the Net National Product). These total expenditures (Y) cannot exceed for any length of time the total income of "Business" which consists of consumer spending (C), the demand for investment goods (I), and government spending (G). Hence, Y = C + I + G.

The economy will be in balance if the expenditures incurred by "Business" (Y) are equal to "Business" revenues (C + I + G), and this in turn presupposes that the savings of the "Consumer" are returned to "Business" in the form of investment spending (S = I), and that the taxes collected by the government are equal to government spending (T = G). Or at least that S + T = I + G.

If total "Business" expenditures (Y) are larger than total

"Business" receipts (C + I + G), production will be curtailed. On the other hand, if "Business" receipts (C + I + G) are larger than "Business" expenditures, i.e., if the demand for goods and services on the part of the consumers (C), investors (I) and the government (G) is larger than the output (Y), production will increase—provided additional productive capacity is available. If, on the other hand, the economy is already operating at or near full capacity, an increase in demand (of either "C", "I", or "G" will result in an increase in prices, popularly known as inflation.

Below Full Employment Equilibrium According to modern economic theory it is possible for the flow of "Business" expenditures to be equal to the flow of "Business" income (Y = C + I + G), even though the economy operates at less than full capacity. The 19th Century economists denied this possibility. They assumed that if the demand for goods and hence labor declined (because of a decline in consumption, investments or government expenditures), prices and wages would go down, so that full employment would be maintained even though the size of the Net National Product (Y) measured in dollars would be smaller. Modern economists assume that wages and prices do not adjust downward to match a decline in demand. In order to maintain full employment, it is thus necessary to maintain total expenditures (C + I + G) at the full employment level on the basis of prevailing wage and price levels.

Declining Demand Let us assume that the flow of income (Y) received by the "Public" is equal to $550 billion. Out of this total, taxes (T) absorb $150 billion and $370 are spent on consumption (C), leaving $30 billion as savings (S). Let us assume further that the government budgets are balanced

(G = T). Businessmen, however, are worried about the future and reluctant to invest money. Investments (I) therefore amount to only $25 billion, and $5 billion of the $30 billion saved by the "Consumer" remain as "idle savings" in the Banking System. This would mean the "Business" expenditures would amount to $550 billion (Y) and revenues to only $545 billion. ($370 billion for consumption goods, $25 billion for investment goods, and $150 billion in the form of government spending.) To put it differently, "Business" has produced $550 billion worth of goods and services, and finds that the demand amounts to only $545 billion. To cope with this overproduction, "Business" will have to reduce its output until "Y" (the payments made to the factors of production) has been reduced to $545 billion. Such a reduction in output would produce unemployment.

Compensatory Spending

Under the Employment Act of 1946, however, the government is required to maintain economic activities at the level of maximum employment. The $5 billion decline in investment spending would thus have to be off-set by a $5 billion increase in government spending. In order to obtain the necessary funds, the government could borrow the $5 billion of "idle savings" which have accumulated in the Banking System (because savings amount to $30 billion and investments to only $25 billion). This form of government spending, designed to compensate for the failure of the private sector to make use of all the savings which have accumulated, is called "compensatory spending." It implies, of course, that during boom periods, when private investments exceed savings, the government must have a surplus (i.e., the amount of taxes collected must be larger than total government spending). This surplus would be used to pay back government obligations, thus making available to the economy (via the Banking System) additional funds to be used to finance the investment demand in excess of current savings.

The Balancing Mechanism The balancing mechanism postulated by the theory of "compensatory spending" thus lies in the proper flow of funds between the private sector (represented by the "Banking System"), and the public sector (represented by the "Treasury"). This flow is expected to prevent (a) the accumulation of idle savings (if savings exceed investments), and (b) excessive total demand. Demand would be excessive if total government spending and private investments (G + I) were to exceed total savings and tax revenues (S + T).

"Compensatory spending" designed to offset inadequate private investments can be achieved either by increasing government spending (G) or by reducing taxes (T), thus giving the public more disposable income, most of which would flow into consumption. This increased consumption in turn is assumed to stimulate investments. The deficit in the government budget, in turn (resulting from a reduction in taxes while expenditures remain unchanged) would be financed either by drawing on the "idle savings" (as we indicated above) or by creating additional money by borrowing from the Federal Reserve System and/or commercial banks.

In real life the flow of income and expenditures is, of course, infinitely more complex than shown in Figure 5, and some flow charts have been designed with a bewildering mass of lines. The major portion of government expenditures (G), for instance, does not flow directly to "Business," as Figure 5 indicates. It is paid in the form of salaries to government employees who then use this income to pay taxes, purchase consumer goods, and save. Government expenditures, to a large extent, thus influence "Business" income only indirectly. But this and many other complications, while adding "friction" which may somewhat distort the overall effect, do not alter the basic principle illustrated by the flow chart.

Equations

Let us now tell the same story in the form of equations. A look at the flow chart will show that:

Seen from the point of view of the "Consumer"

$$Y = C + S + T$$

Seen from the point of view of the "Business"

$$Y = C + I + G$$

The "Y" and "C" in the two formulas are obviously identical, so that we can combine the two equations into

$$S + T = I + G$$

The government has little or no control over the rate of savings. If people fear the future, they will consume less and save more. If they are full of confidence, spending will increase and savings will decrease. Nor does the government have much control over the rate of investments. If business is optimistic, investments will increase. If business is pessimistic, investments will decrease. It is possible, of course, for the government to increase or decrease taxes, but this is usually a slow process, and since taxes, at whatever level, are absorbed into the business calculations, any changes in the tax structure can have unpredictable reactions on the part of business and individuals. A reduction in taxes is likely to produce an increase in business (the 1965–1966 boom was probably in part at least due to a reduction in personal and corporate income taxes), but lower taxes need not necessarily lead to a corresponding increase in investments. If business has ample unused plant capacity and is fearful of the future, it will not add to its investments.

In our equation $S + T = I + G$, the government thus has little influence over two variables, Savings and Investments (S and I), while the third variable, Taxes (T), cannot readily be manipulated. This leaves "G," government spending, as the logical "lever" through which the government, as a rule, will attempt to influence total spending and thus the rate of production and employment. To illustrate this point, we rewrite the equation $S + T = I + G$, as follows $G = T + (S - I)$.

Government spending should be equal to taxes, plus or minus the difference between savings and investments. Let us assume first that the economy is in balance ($S = 30$; $I = 30$). In this case, the government budget should be balanced ($G = T$), and our equation would read:

$$150\,(G) = 150\,(T) + (30\,(S) - 30\,(I))$$

If investments are smaller than savings, government spending has to be correspondingly larger: $155\,(G) = 150\,(T) + (50\,(S) - 45\,(I))$.

If, on the other hand, investments are larger than savings, government spending, in accordance with the theory of "compensatory spending," should be correspondingly smaller than taxes: $145\,(G) = 150\,(T) + (50\,(S) - 55\,(I))$

Diagrammatic Presentation

We shall now tell the same story in diagrammatic form, employed a great deal in aggregate analysis.

Figure 6 illustrates the relationship between the flow of income and expenditures with the economy in equilibrium. "Y", the total expenditures of "Business" (which is the same as the total goods and services produced), is measured on the horizontal axis OM (known as the "X" axis or abscissa). On the vertical axis OK (known as the "Y" axis or ordinate) are measured consumption (C), investments (I), and government ex-

FIGURE 6 National Income Diagram

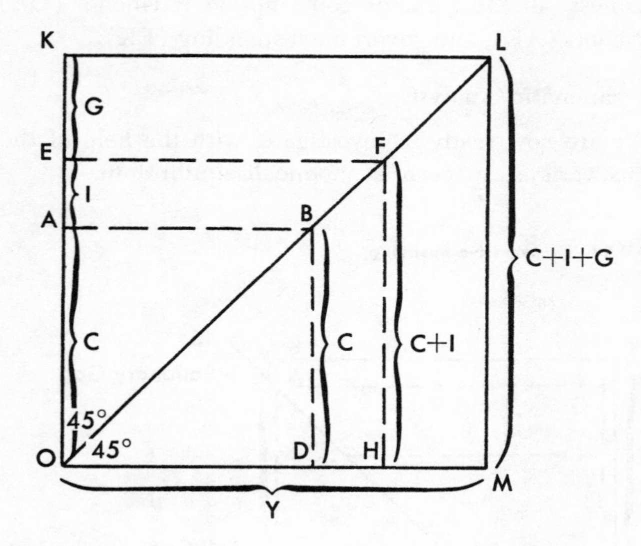

penditures (G). In other words, the demand for the goods and services measured on the "Y" axis, the supply on the "X" axis.

In order for the economy to be in equilibrium, total payments made by "Business" to the factors of production (Y or OM) must be equal to total receipts received by "Business" in the form of consumption, investments and government spending (C + I + G or OK). The line which connects O and L divides the square into two equal halves; and it also divides the 90° angle at "O" into two 45° angles. The line OL is thus referred to as the 45° line. Any point on this line is equi-distant from the horizontal and the vertical lines (AB = BD; EF = FH; KL = LM).

This representation tells the same story we have previously told with the help of the flow chart and the equation. In order to be in equilibrium, payments by "Business" to the factors of production (OM) must be equal to the funds received by "Business" in the form of consumption payments (OA), investments (AE), and government spending (EK).

Diagrammatic Analysis

We are now ready to investigate, with the help of the diagrams, various aspects of economic disequilibrium.

FIGURE 7 **Excessive Spending**

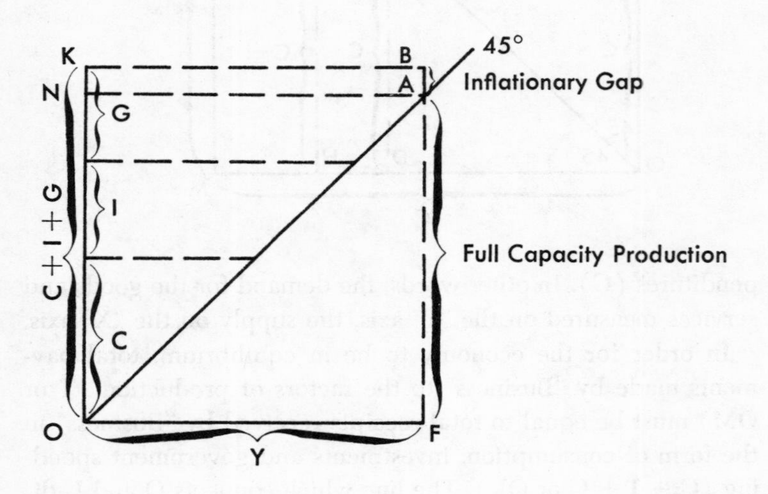

An Inflationary Situation

Figure 7 indicates an inflationary situation, such as the United States experienced during most of the postwar years. The total goods and services which the economy can produce is equal to OF (which in turn is equal to ON and FA). Consumption (C), investments (I) and government spending

(G), however, total OK, or more than the economy can produce at the full employment level. Total demand exceeds total capacity by NK (which is equal to AB). We thus have an "inflationary gap," i.e., demand (C + I + G) is in excess of supply FA (determined by the productive capacity of the economy.) And if demand exceeds supply, prices rise, and we have inflation.

Where did the additional spending power come from? The answer is quite simple, so far as the postwar years are concerned. The American people had accumulated vast savings during the war years in the form of savings bonds and savings accounts, and once the war ended they began to convert their savings into homes, cars and home furnishings. In other words, they spent not only what they earned but some of their previous savings. In addition, many of them borrowed money. Consumer credit increased from $5.6 billion at the end of 1945 to $44.9 billion at the end of 1957. With the tremendous demand for consumer goods, business investments increased rapidly and the corporate debt grew from $99.5 billion in 1945 to $293.4 billion in 1957. Since, during the Depression and the war years, state and local governments had not been able to make many needed improvements, they also tried to catch up during the postwar years, and in order to finance the rapidly rising expenditures, they increased their debts from $16.6 to $52.5 billion in 1957.

With demand (the flow of expenditures) thus exceeding current income and the productive capacity of the economy, prices rose to make up for the gap. The consumer price index (1947–49 = 100) which stood at 76.9 in 1945 had risen by 1957 to 120.2 or by 56%.

The "Causes" of the Inflation What "caused" the inflation? There was no single cause. Consumer (C), business (I) and government (G) expenditures increased at the same time and their total exceeded the productive capacity of the economy. According to the theory of "compensatory spending," the Federal Government should have curtailed its expenditures (or increased taxes) sufficiently to produce a surplus equal to the excess spending of the private sector. But quite aside from the fact that the Korean War and the cold war called for steadily rising defense expenditures, it is difficult to imagine many politicians voting for increased taxes or reduced government spending at a time when the government revenues increased rapidly. Thus, instead of having a large surplus (to offset the excessive spending of the state and local governments and in the private sector), the Federal Government actually ran up a deficit of more than $30 billion during the 11-year period July 1946 to June 1957.

As a result of this experience many economists have come to doubt whether the principle of "compensatory spending" can actually be used to counteract inflationary pressure in a democracy whose government is extremely sensitive to the spending demands of pressure groups.

Deflationary Situation

From a political point of view, the Federal Government is in a better position to combat inadequate demand, because this involves more rather than less public spending. Figure 8 illustrates a "spending gap."

As Figure 8 indicates, the economy could, if fully employed, turn out goods and services valued at OF. But the actual output (Y) is only OM, because total demand (C + I + G) is only ON (while it should be OK). The result is an "underconsumption" (NK) resulting in "underproduction" (MF). This is the "spending gap" or "production gap" which the government policy makers are trying to close by increasing government ex-

FIGURE 8 Spending Gap

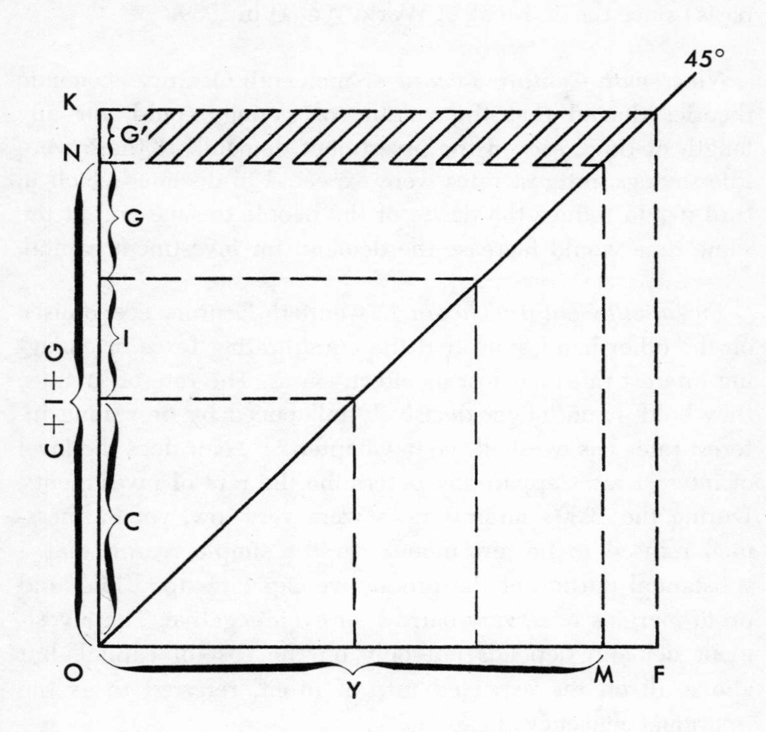

penditures from "G" to "G + G′," thus raising total "Business" revenues from ON to OK.

The Theory of Excess Saving

According to Lord Keynes and his followers, the chief cause of inadequate spending is excessive saving, i.e., the "Consumer" saves more than "Business" can absorb in the form of investments (S is larger than I). This was undoubtedly the situation during the 1930's in Britain and the United States. It has not been the situation, however, (certainly not on a worldwide basis) since the outbreak of World War II in 1939.

Nineteenth Century Theory Nineteenth Century economic theories denied that the volume of savings could, for any length of time, exceed the investment demand. If there were idle savings, interest rates were expected to decline, which in turn would reduce the desire of the people to save and at the same time would increase the demand for investment capital.

Twentieth Century Theory Twentieth Century economists, on the other hand, hold that the equilibrating force of changing interest rates has lost its effectiveness. The rate of savings, they hold, is no longer decisively influenced by prevailing interest rates (as we shall see in Chapter 24). Nor does the level of interest rates apparently determine the rate of investments. During the 1930's interest rates were very low, yet businessmen refused to borrow money for the simple reason that a substantial portion of the productive capacity stood idle, and profit margins were very narrow, or even negative. The investment demand depends not only on the cost of capital, but above all on the expected rate of profit, referred to as the "marginal efficiency of capital."

Foreign Outlets During the 19th Century and down to World War I excessive savings in one country (e.g., in Britain and France) could find an outlet in developing countries (e.g., the United States which was a capital-importing country until the beginning of the 20th Century). While the French economy did not use all French savings, Russian and American railroads were only too glad to absorb the surplus. Since World War I, and especially since World War II, investments in developing countries have become increasingly risky because of the growing xenophobia (hatred of foreigners), socialism and communism. While there could be idle savings in the United States and an acute shortage of investment capital in Latin America, this does not necessarily mean that American capital will be invested south of the Rio Grande. In view of the experiences which American investors have had in Bolivia, Cuba and Brazil, the rate of return would have to be very high to offset the obvious political risk. In fact the rate would probably be too high to be acceptable to the Latin American entrepreneurs.

Different Economic Theories

Economic policies differ, depending upon what economists regard as the cause of the prevailing unemployment. During the 19th Century economists believed that unemployment was due to the fact that wages were higher than the value of the goods which the worker produced. Unemployment could thus be overcome by a reduction of the wage level. From a microeconomic point of view, this is a perfectly logical explanation.

In underdeveloped countries, unemployment (or underemployment) is usually due to the lack of investment capital. The country does not have enough factories and machines to provide jobs for the partially employed rural workers. The solution would thus call for an increase in savings and investments, or in attracting investment capital from abroad.

According to modern economic theory, finally, unemployment in "mature" or fully developed industrial countries is likely to be the result of excessive savings and inadequate investment outlets. Assuming this to be the case (and economists disagree in this respect), it would be logical to curb savings and to stimulate investments. This is exactly what modern economists suggest.

A New Terminology The widespread concern with this

problem during the past 30 years has resulted in the development of a number of technical terms. The tendency to consume is referred to by modern economists as the "average propensity to consume" (APC) and the tendency to save as the "average propensity to save" (APS). Economists also speak of the "marginal propensity to consume" and the "marginal propensity to save." Let us assume that a man has a Disposable Income of $4000 a year. He spends $3600 for various goods and services, and saves $400. In this case his "propensity to consume" would be 0.9 (or 90%) and his "propensity to save" would be 0.1 or (10%). PC + PS must always be equal to DI (Disposable Income); or, in arithmetic terms, equal to one $(0.9 + 0.1 = 1)$.

Let us assume further that the man's income is raised to $4400: he thus has an additional (a marginal) income of $400. Much of the additional income will be spent on consumption, but the man is likely to save a larger share of his additional income than he did of his smaller original income. Assuming that out of the $400 additional income he spends $320 and saves $80, his "marginal propensity to consume" would thus be 0.8 and his "marginal propensity to save," 0.2 (compared with his "average" propensity to save of 0.1).

Increasing Rate of Savings Spending patterns change from time to time. An increase in income may lead to a more than proportional increase in consumption. But the opposite is seemingly more likely. According to the National Income theory, the rate of savings can be expected to increase faster than the rate of income. This is important because as savings increase, idle savings may accumulate (leading to unemployment) unless investment opportunities increase as fast as savings. In other words, investment opportunities have to increase proportionally faster than income in order to prevent unemployment. Many economists fear that in "mature economies" with fully developed industries, the demand for investment capital is not likely to increase rapidly enough to keep pace with the increasing rate of savings.

Theory Questioned

The theory that savings are likely to increase at a faster rate than Disposable Income sounds perfectly plausible. Empirical evidence, however, does not support the theory; at least not in the simple form as it is usually presented. An increase in Disposable Income does not necessarily lead to a proportionately larger increase in the rate of savings (which would necessitate a corresponding increase in the rate of investments). Between 1950 and 1965, for instance, the Disposable Income of the American people increased by almost 110%. Yet the rate of personal net saving actually declined. After fluctuating between 6% and 7% during the 1950's — with the changes in the rate of savings seemingly influenced by cyclical fluctuations — the rate of savings dropped below 5% in the middle 1960's despite a record increase in Disposable Income.

Theory as Basis for Socio-political Program

The economic theory of over-saving, which seems "self-evident" on first sight, serves as a basis for two important socio-political theories. If, as the nation grows richer and the per capita income increases, it becomes more and more difficult to find an outlet for the ever-increasing savings in the private sector, the expenditures of the public sector will have to be increased in order to prevent the accumulation of idle savings. This argument is advanced (a) by such Keynesian economists as Professor Hansen and especially Professor Galbraith; (b) by government officials who find their power increasing in proportion to the amount of money which they spend, and (c) by Congressmen who use the argument to justify public spending demanded by pressure groups. The economic notion of "over-saving" thus serves as a theoretical underpinning for a policy designed to expand the public sector at the expense of the private. Whether we call this "socialism" (as some opponents do) or not is beside the point. The fact remains that the advocates of steadily increasing government spending present a seemingly logical (but in reality far from proved) economic argument in favor of their policies.

Emphasis on Low Income Groups It seems also "self-evident" that the average propensity to save is small in the low, and large in the high income brackets. Thus if we wish to avoid "excess savings" we could reduce the income of the high income groups. This is the basic economic argument in favor of steeply progressive income taxes. (In Chapter 12 we discussed the "ethical" or "ability to pay" argument.) Since we also have to increase consumption in order to stimulate investments, and the marginal propensity-to-consume of the lower income groups is much greater than that of the higher, the flow of income should be shifted as much as possible from those having a high income to those having a low income. This is the argument used by Walter Reuther and other labor leaders who demand higher wages to stimulate consumption, if necessary at the expense of profits, because, as union leaders often argue, profits (the income of the "rich") merely increase idle savings.

"Paradox of Thrift" Some economists present a third argument, which Paul A. Samuelson calls the "paradox of thrift." If an individual saves, he accumulates assets and hence tends to become richer. On the other hand, if an entire nation increases its savings (and thus reduces its consumption) and there are not enough investment outlets for the increased amount of savings, idle savings will accumulate, which will lead to unem-

ployment, less production, and a shrinkage in the national income. The key to the argument lies, of course, in the assumption that there will be no investment outlet for the additional saving. And this in turn rests ultimately on the Keynesian "mature economy" doctrine. Actually, for more than a quarter of a century capital formation (savings) has been inadequate on a world-wide basis (and probably also in the United States). The lack of savings has been made up through the creation of credit, which led to the depreciation of the dollar and the worldwide inflation.

FIGURE 9 "Paradox of Thrift"

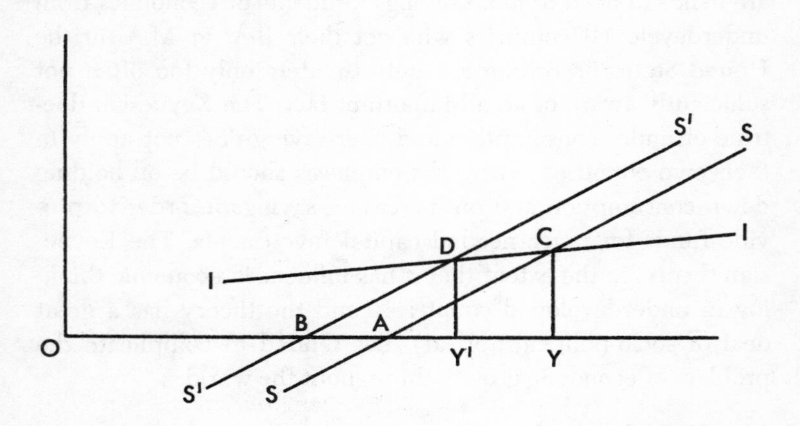

Assuming that public spending is in balance (T = G), the size of the Net National Income (Y) will be determined by the relationship of savings and investments. In Figure 9, if savings are equal to SS and investments equal to II, savings and investments will be equal at C, producing a Net National Product of "Y." On the other hand, if savings increase (and the line which represents the "savings schedule" is moved upward to S′S′), savings and investments will be equal at D (rather than C) and the Net National Product will shrink from Y to Y′. This presupposes, of course, that we accept the basic argument that increased savings (resulting in decreased consumption) will not be matched by an increase in investments, despite the fact that an increase in investment funds (larger savings) will tend to make for lower interest rates.

Theory Applied to Underdeveloped Countries

Obviously the theory does not hold true in developing countries, which suffer from a shortage of investment capital and are hence in need of more savings. Students of economics from underdeveloped countries who get their B.A. or M.A. in the United States or Britain are unfortunately only too often not sufficiently aware of an all-important fact. The Keynesian doctrine of under-consumption and over-saving does not apply to their own countries, where the emphasis should be on holding down consumption and on increasing savings in order to provide funds for much-needed capital investments. The Keynesian theory, to the extent that it has influenced economic thinking in underdeveloped countries (and the theory has a great deal of socio-political appeal), has tended to complicate the problem of economic growth throughout the world.

The Multiplier and Accelerator

Thus far we have studiously avoided all complications in order to simplify the model as much as possible. We shall now introduce two complicating factors, the multiplier and the accelerator.

Multiplier If the government economists decide that the flow of income and expenditures is $10 billion below the full employment level, they will not advocate a deficit of $10 billion for the Federal Government. They will calculate instead the necessary deficit (necessary to achieve full employment) on the basis of the nation's expected marginal propensity to consume. If the MPC is 0.8 (and the MPS 0.2), the additional government spending needed to achieve an increase of $10 billion in the Net National Product will be only $2 billion. The reasoning behind this argument is that the first $2 billion of additional government spending will have a chain reaction. The first recipients will save 20% ($400 million) and spend $1,600 million; the recipients of the $1,600 million will again save 20% ($320 million) and spend the balance of $1,280, etc., etc.

How much of an increase in the Net National Product will the injection of $2 billion in additional spending produce? The following equation (derived from the algebraic formula for an infinite geometric progression) provides the answer. The multiplier (K) will be equal to "One" divided by the marginal propensity to save. If MPS is equal to 0.2, K will be equal to $\frac{1}{0.2}$ or 5. An injection of an additional $2 billion in the spending stream can thus be expected — over a period of two or three years — to produce an increase in the flow of income and expenditures five times $2 billion, or of $10 million.

If the MPS is small (i.e., the portion of the additional income which may turn into "idle savings" is small) the multiplier will be large. The larger the MPC (the more of the additional income is spent) the greater the multiplier effect.

The multiplier effect has an important bearing on the overall expansion and contraction of the economy. An increase in idle savings or a deficit in the balance of payments (provided the deficit results in an outflow of gold and a corresponding shrinkage in the supply of money and credit) will have a multiple contractive effect on business activities. An expansion of credit, on the other hand, whether in the form of consumer credit or investment credit, or the mobilization of idle savings, should in theory result ultimately in an expansion of the flow of income and expenditures several times the original additional investment.

Accelerator Table 11 shows the operation of a hypothetical firm which requires 100 machines to turn out 100,000 units of a given product, i.e., each machine can produce 1000 units per year. The machines have an expected useful life of 10 years, so that on basis of 100 machines in operation 10 of them (those installed 10 year previously) will have to be replaced each year. If the demand for the final product increases (as, for instance in 1963) the company has to purchase more than 10 machines (needed to replace those which can no longer be used because of age). If, on the other hand, (as in 1965) the demand for the final product declines, the company need not replace some of the worn-out machines. Relatively minor changes in the demand for the final product result, as Table 11 indicates, in wide swings in the demand for machinery.

TABLE 11

Illustration of the Accelerator Effect

Year	Number of Units Produced	Change in Output	Machines Needed	Replacement Demand	New Machines Needed	Total Machines Needed	Change in Number of Machines Needed
1962	100,000	—	100	10	—	10	—
1963	110,000	+10%	110	10	10	20	+100%
1964	110,000	—	110	10	—	10	− 50%
1965	100,000	−10%	100	—	—	0	−100%

While the demand for the final product has fluctuated within a relatively narrow margin (it increased by 10% in 1963 and decreased by less than 10% in 1965) the demand for machinery doubled from 1962 to 1963 and dropped to zero in 1965. The accelerator principle thus illustrates the problem which confronts those industries which used to be known as "feast and famine" industries. While a 5% increase or decrease in the Net National Product has little effect on the sale of Coca Cola or cigarettes, it may result in a 25% increase or decrease in the demand for steel, and in a 50% fluctuation in the demand for machine tools and railway cars.

If we now combine the accelerator effect (which affects the employment in various segments of the economy in different ways) with the multiplier effect (which translates the specialized accelerator into an overall effect on the flow of income and expenditures throughout the economy), we can get a vague idea of the extremely complex calculations — or "intelligent guesses" — which underlie macroeconomic forecasts. It is not surprising, therefore, that many of the "intelligent guesses," forecasts and policies dictated by purely economic reasoning (rather than political expediency) have proved wrong.

Chapter 19

THE TOOLS OF ECONOMIC INTERVENTION

THE BASIC FACTS

Monetary and fiscal policies are based on the assumption that it is possible for the Federal Reserve System and the U.S. Treasury to regulate the flow of credit in such a way as to achieve full employment and a rapid rate of economic growth without inflation and without a deficit in the balance of payments.

The task involves the difficult problem of coordinating the policies of two agencies, the central bank and the treasury. According to 19th Century monetary theory the central bank should be free from political control to assure the integrity of the currency. Modern theory leans toward greater coordination of central bank and Treasury policies. This coordination, however, involves the danger that the government will force the central bank to finance an ever larger government deficit through the issuance of more money.

Federal Reserve Policies *The Federal Reserve can rely on direct (specific) controls (of which only Margin Requirements are now being used), or on indirect (general) controls. The latter consist in (1) changes in the discount rate, (2) changes in reserve requirements, and (most important) (3) open market operations. The effectiveness of these tools, however, is not unlimited.*

Fiscal Policies *The U.S. Treasury can rely on (1) automatic built-in stabilizers (such as the Unemployment Insurance System, which tend to counteract cyclical fluctuations), and (2) on direct measures which require specific decisions on the part of Congress or the Treasury. These measures can be grouped under three general headings: (1) a "flexible budget," (2) long-range tax policies, and (3) debt management.*

Basic Premises of Economic Planning *The policies of government economic intervention rest on a number of premises. (1) According to the socio-economic philosophy which developed during the past 30 years, it is the function of the government to assure every willing worker of a suitable job, and if this is not possible, to see to it that the worker and his family do not suffer privation. (2) To achieve the goal of "full employment," production and the rate of economic growth must be maximized. (3) The government can achieve these goals through the proper monetary and fiscal controls. A slack in employment can be overcome by increasing the available purchase power through an expansion of credit. Conversely, inflationary pressure can be removed through a reduction in the supply of credit. The key to the modern policy of full employment and maximum economic growth (both to be achieved through government planning) thus consists of monetary and fiscal controls.*

Central Bank-Treasury Relationship

Two agencies are involved in the conduct of monetary and fiscal policies: the central bank and the treasury. Because of institutional differences, monetary and fiscal techniques vary somewhat from country to country, but the basic principles and problems are the same.

The conduct of monetary policies rests with the central bank; the conduct of fiscal policies with the treasury. With two agencies responsible for the achievement of four different goals, the problem of coordination is of primary importance. The treasury is part of the government, and thus politically controlled. The status of a modern central bank is less clearly defined.

Independent Central Bank According to traditional economic and monetary theory, the central bank should be free from political control because of the potential danger that the government might use its power over the central bank to overexpand the supply of money.

The experience of many centuries seems to indicate that virtually all governments in the end succumb to the temptation of financing an ever larger portion of their expenditures through the creation of more and more money. Printing money has always seemed politically more expedient than increasing taxes or reducing public spending. The danger is particularly great in the case of governments which depend for their very existence on the support of economic pressure groups. For this reason almost all central banks were originally organized as private banking institutions with the dual objective of protecting the stability of the currency and of providing the economy with an adequate supply of credit.

Changing Economic Philosophy The attitude changed as the philosophy of free enterprise gave way to a growing reliance on state intervention. Today about 90% of the world's central banks are government-owned, and even those central banks which are not owned by the government, such as the

Federal Reserve System, have become, for all practical purposes, an arm of their governments.

This does not mean, however, that treasury and central bank always see eye to eye on monetary and fiscal matters. In 1951, for instance, the Federal Reserve System openly defied the U.S. Treasury by refusing to purchase more government bonds at a fixed price, since these purchases were adding to the already dangerous inflationary pressure. The dispute led to the so-called "Accord," which gave the Federal Reserve a freer hand in determining its policies.

Since then the relationship between the Federal Reserve and the U.S. Treasury has been on a day-to-day personal basis. No attempt has been made to achieve a formal and official coordination. In the eyes of those who fear political control over the supply of money, this may be the best possible solution, because if the Federal Reserve were placed directly under the direction of the President (as some members of Congress have suggested) all monetary and economic measures would be subject to direct political control, without checks and balances.

Federal Reserve Monetary and Credit Policies

The history and structure of the Federal Reserve System was discussed in detail in Chapter 11. We also mentioned briefly that the Federal Reserve exercises both direct (specific) and indirect (general) controls in manipulating the supply of credit. We shall now discuss these control tools in detail.

Specific Credit Controls

Direct (or specific) credit controls were fairly important during World War II, when the Federal Reserve determined the maximum terms of consumer and real estate credit. Such direct controls, if exercised in peacetime, would give the Federal Reserve System far-reaching powers over some of the major industries of the country. By determining the minimum down payments on cars, TV sets, washing machines, refrigerators and homes, the Federal Reserve could influence effectively the rate of sales and employment in these industries.

This would involve the System in direct conflicts with some of the most powerful industrial groups and unions in the country. The Federal Reserve was, therefore, most anxious to abandon these controls at the end of the war. The implementation of direct controls, moreover, would involve the Federal Reserve System in serious administrative difficulties.

The only remaining direct controls still in force are the so-called Regulations "T" and "U," through which the rate of credit advanced by brokers (Regulation "T") and banks (Regulation "U") for the purchase of securities is regulated. Through changes in the Margin Requirements, (the "margin"-or down-payment which must be made by the purchaser of securities) the Federal Reserve can affect the demand for stocks, which in turn has a bearing on stock prices. If the market seems to rise too fast, margin requirements are increased (which tends to reduce the demand for stocks bought partially on credit); if it drops, margin requirements are lowered. (During the 12 years 1955–1966, Margin Requirements fluctuated between 60% and 90%.)

General Controls

Far more important and, from the point of view of the economist, far more interesting than direct and specific controls are the indirect and general methods of control which consist of: (1) changes in the discount rate, (2) changes in reserve requirements and (3) open market operations.

Changes in the Discount Rate If member banks wish to borrow from their regional Federal Reserve banks, they are charged interest at a fixed rate, known as the discount rate. The rates may vary from one Federal Reserve Bank to another, but nowadays the rate tends to be uniform throughout the country. While still legally fixed by the individual Federal Reserve banks, the discount rates are largely dictated by the Board of Governors in Washington.

An increase in the discount rate tends to raise the cost of borrowing throughout the economy, and thus tends to discourage borrowing. Less borrowing in turn means fewer derived bank deposits, hence less purchasing power and probably a decline in business activities and prices. An increase in the discount rate thus represents an effort on the part of the Federal Reserve to prevent prices from rising. A lowering of the rate reflects an effort to stimulate borrowing and thus increase general business activities.

Declining Importance of Discount Rate Changes In recent years the Federal Reserve has relied less and less on changes in the discount rate as a means of controlling the supply of credit — and this for two reasons.

Periodic campaigns against "high interest rates" have been an important aspect of American politics for almost 200 years. The issue is still popular with some Congressmen, who claim to protect the "public" against the "usurious" practices of "the bankers." To this traditional political argument must be added the belief of many modern economists that the level of interest rates has an important bearing on capital investments, and thus on the rate of employment and economic growth. An attempt on the part of the Federal Reserve to raise the discount rate in order to combat inflationary tendencies is thus likely to meet with strong opposition on the part of some Congressmen and economic theorists. In order to avoid criticism, the Federal Reserve has therefore largely abandoned the idea of controlling the demand for credit through changes in the discount rate.

Most of the changes in the official discount rate usually take place only after the market has more or less established a new interest rate level.

The second reason for not relying on changes in the discount rate is very simply that such changes as a rule are not a very effective tool in the United States. European commercial banks are usually indebted to the central banks, so that an increase in the discount rate has an immediate effect on the entire banking system. In the United States, on the other hand, according to a well established tradition, commercial banks are expected to rely on their own resources, and to use Federal Reserve credit only temporarily. An increase in the discount rate thus does not, as a rule, affect the member banks directly and immediately. It merely *warns* them that they will have to pay higher rates, should they need Federal Reserve credit in the future.

Changes in Reserve Requirements Far more effective than changes in the discount rate are changes in reserve requirements because the latter affect the actual lending capacity of the banking system rather than the potential cost of credit. As we have seen in Chapter 11, member banks are required to maintain a legal reserve with their Federal Reserve Bank equal to a certain percentage of their demand and time deposits. The Board of Governors can change the level of these reserves within the limits fixed by Congress, as shown in Table 12:

TABLE 12

Reserve Requirements for Member Banks

Type of Banks	Number of Banks as of June, 1967	Range of Reserve Requirements: Demand Deposits	Range of Reserve Requirements: Time Deposits
Reserve City banks	188	10% — 22%	3% — 6%
Country banks	5919	7% — 14%	3% — 6%

Source: Federal Reserve Bulletin, Sept. 1967.

Assume that the Reserve City banks hold about $75 billion in demand deposits, subject to a 16 ½% legal reserve requirement (equal to $12.4 billion), and the Federal Reserve decides to pursue an "easy credit" policy by reducing reserve requirements to 15 ½%. The member banks will thus gain $750 million in excess reserves, which they can use, in theory, to increase their loans by $4.8 billion. (For the mechanics of the calculation of the fractional reserve, see Chapter 11). A reduction of the reserve requirements thus increases the ability of the banking system to expand credit (and thus stimulate business), while an increase in the reserve requirements has the opposite effect.

Open Market Operations By far the most widely used and most important tool of controlling the supply of credit consists of the open market operations, i.e., the purchase and sale of government securities by the New York Federal Reserve Bank, acting on behalf of the Federal Reserve System as a whole. The trading is done (behind carefully locked doors) by the "Trading Desk," which operates in close contact with the Board of Governors in Washington and the U.S. Treasury. Table 13 illustrates how the open market operations function:

TABLE 13

Open Market Operations of the Federal Reserve System

Federal Reserve System		*Commercial Banking System*	
Assets	*Liabilities*	*Assets*	*Liabilities*
Gold Certificates	Federal Reserve Notes	Cash	Deposits
		Reserves with F.R.	Capital Accts.
+U.S.Gov't Securities	Member Bank Reserves	Required	
		+Excess	
	Required	—U.S. Gov't Securities	
	+Excess		
		Loans	

In order to increase the lending capacity of the commercial banking system, the Federal Reserve purchases in the open market U.S. Government securities. As a result the amount of these securities held by the Federal Reserve increases (+) and the amount held by the banking system decreases (−). The Federal Reserve pays for the securities by crediting the account of the member bank from which it has purchased the government securities, thus increasing total Member Bank Excess Reserves. The latter thus exchanges an investment (namely Government securities) for a cash balance with the Federal Reserve, which can be used to make additional loans and thus help to stimulate the economy.

In order to simplify the explanation, we are assuming here that the Federal Reserve System purchases the securities from commercial banks, thus increasing the free reserves of the banking system. In practice, the Federal Reserve System can purchase government securities also from non-bank holders, such as insurance companies, trust funds and large corporations. These non-bank sellers would then receive from the Federal Reserve funds which would be deposited with the commercial banks, thus enabling the banks to make more loans.

If the Federal Reserve wishes to add to the lending capacity of the banking system, it buys government securities, and pays for these securities by crediting the Member Banks' Reserves, thus enabling them to make more loans to business and the general public. Conversely, if the Federal Reserve sells U.S. Government securities, excess reserves (and thus the lending capacity of the banking system) will be reduced, whether the securities are purchased by the banks directly or by the general public.

Treasury Bills One of the most effective ways in which the

Federal Reserve can change the credit volume is through the weekly "auction" sale of Treasury Bills. Every week the Treasury sells to the highest bidders $1–$2 billion of Treasury Bills (most of them with a three-months maturity) in order to obtain funds to pay off the Bills sold three months earlier and now falling due. All bids are turned in to the Federal Reserve, which thus knows how high a price the System has to pay in order to buy whatever quantity it wishes to acquire.

Limitations of Federal Reserve Controls

In theory, the Federal Reserve seems to have powerful tools to regulate the supply of credit and thus the rate of business activities. In reality this is not fully the case. The Federal Reserve can supply the banking system with additional lending power, but it cannot induce business and the public to borrow, even though interest rates may be very low. During the Depression of the 1930's, for instance, excess reserves amounted to $5 billion, which would have permitted the banking system to make additional loans equal to the total national debt then outstanding. But even though interest rates were at a record low, people just did not care to borrow.

Effects on Balance of Payments

Nor can the Federal Reserve reduce interest rates too far, because short term investors would then transfer their funds to Europe, where they can earn a higher rate of return. This transfer of funds would add to the deficit in the balance of payments. An easy credit policy, designed to stimulate the economy, is thus faced with two serious limitations.

Velocity of Money and Bank Balances

On the other hand, if the Federal Reserve tightens the credit to dampen an inflationary boom, business and the public may reduce their average idle bank balances and turn over the available funds more rapidly. This turnover of bank balances (and of currency) is called "velocity." Let us say a man spends one dollar for his breakfast, the restaurant uses the same dollar to pay the milkman, and the milkman uses it to buy lunch. The lunch counter in turn pays his dishwasher with the dollar, who spends it on a movie ticket. In other words, the one dollar bill in the course of the day bought \$5 worth of goods and services. It did the work of \$5, because its rate of turnover (its velocity) per day was 5. Our original formula $P = \frac{M}{G}$ (in Chapter 10) should thus more correctly read $P = \frac{MV}{G}$ (where "V" stands for Velocity). Prices are determined by the supply of goods and services in relation to the quantity of money and credit available — multiplied by the number of times currency and bank deposits change hands. The Federal Reserve (within limits) can control the supply of money and credit (M), but it has little or no control over the velocity (V).

In short, monetary policy cannot achieve all the objectives to the extent that modern economic planners desire, and it is therefore necessary to supplement monetary with fiscal measures.

Fiscal Measures

In Chapter 12 we discussed the structure of the fiscal system of the United States. At this point we are interested in the various ways in which the fiscal system can be used to influence the level of economic activities. To an economist of 30 or 40 years ago, such an approach would have seemed almost incomprehensible. Fiscal operations in those days consisted of the collection of enough taxes to meet government expenditures and to pay off gradually the debts accumulated in the past.

Today fiscal operations are judged no longer from a strictly fiscal point of view, but primarily with an eye upon their effect on the economy in general. The reason for the change in attitude is partly the result of the tremendous increase in public spending. Total Federal expenditures during the five-year period 1926–30 averaged less than $3.2 billion a year, while the National Income in 1929 reached $87 billion. Federal spending thus amounted to about 4% of the National Income. During the fiscal year ended 1967, Federal spending reached $125.7 billion, while the National Income for the 1966–67 fiscal period had risen to $763.1 billion, raising the percentage of Federal spending to more than 16%. The impact of fiscal operations upon the economy is thus at least four times as great as it was 35 years ago. In the meantime, also, public policy has changed from a reliance on the self-equilibrating forces of the market to government intervention, and the fiscal operations offer an effective tool to influence the level of economic activities.

Direct Government Controls

While the Federal Reserve System can employ direct monetary controls (although, as we have seen, they are used very sparingly), there are no direct fiscal controls. Other government agencies, however, exercise an increasing number of such direct and specific controls, such as the establishment of minimum wages, maximum hours and overtime rates; protective tariffs and import quotas; the fixing of farm prices; the regulation of railroad and air fares and of utility rates; and, more recently, the "guideline," "guidepost" and "voluntary cooperation" techniques developed by the White House under the Kennedy and Johnson Administrations, through which the President in effect tries to regulate wages, prices and the international flow of capital. All these and many other direct interventions in the economy affect both cyclical fluctuations and the rate of economic growth.

General Controls

In addition to the direct and specific controls, the government uses a variety of fiscal operations as indirect and general controls.

According to modern macroeconomic theory, depressions and unemployment are, as we have seen, due to inadequate consumer demand and an inadequate volume of investments. The deficiency can be overcome by increasing the overall (or "aggregate") purchasing power. If the Federal Government incurs a deficit, government securities are likely to be sold to the Federal Reserve (or to the commercial banking system), which in turn credits the government's accounts. As the government draws on these accounts to pay for goods and services not covered by regular tax revenues, additional purchasing power is put into circulation. By incurring a deficit and by off-setting the deficit through loans from the Federal Reserve or commercial banks, the Treasury thus pumps additional purchasing power into the economy. Conversely, a surplus in the Federal budget is likely to result in the destruction of purchasing power (through the repayment of bank credits) and will thus have a dampening effect on the economy.

Built-in Automatic Stabilizers

Among the fiscal controls used to regulate the flow of credit, one must distinguish between (1) built-in automatic stabilizers and (2) fiscal measures which require direct action by Congress or the Treasury.

About half the corporate income is paid to the government in the form of corporate income taxes. A decline in economic activities, resulting (as is usually the case) in a more than proportional decline in corporate earnings, leads to a correspondingly sharp drop in government revenues. Since government expenditures are likely to remain constant the decline in tax revenues will lead to a deficit in the Federal budget. The government in turn is likely to borrow from the banking system or the Federal Reserve in order to meet its deficit, so that the overall supply of credit will be increased.

The same holds true of the progressive personal income taxes. As business flourishes and personal incomes increase, income taxes increase more than proportionally, since with higher earnings, individual taxpayers fall into higher income-tax brackets. Consumer purchasing power, which could add to the inflationary pressure, is thus absorbed by rising taxes. On the other hand, if business and personal incomes decline, personal income taxes decline proportionally faster, so that the consumer's disposable income, which represents his purchasing power, declines less rapidly than his gross income before taxes. This provides a cushion for consumer spending. At the same time the government deficit increases, which leads to an expansion of credit.

The unemployment insurance program provides another automatic stabilizer. During periods of high employment, social security taxes withheld from the workers' paychecks exceed the disbursements of the unemployment insurance system, thus reducing the overall consumer purchasing power. During periods of relatively high unemployment, on the other hand, the payments to the unemployed tend to exceed the taxes collected from the employed workers, thus adding to the aggregate consumer spending power.

Whether these automatic stabilizers actually suffice, as some economists have argued hopefully, to prevent the recurrence of a serious and prolonged depression, such as the country experienced during the 1930's, is doubtful. More drastic measures would probably be needed. While the automatic stabilizers may help to flatten minor cyclical fluctuations, periodic "recessions" are still with us, just as they had been prior to the 1930's when the country relied on the self-equilibrating forces of the market.

Far more interesting from an economic point of view are the direct fiscal measures designed to control cyclical fluctuations and stimulate economic growth. The measures involve (1) the methods of taxations, (2) the volume and types of government spending and (3) the administration of the public debt.

The Flexible Budget

In order to achieve maximum effectiveness of government intervention, the system of taxation and government spending should be as flexible as possible, so that the government can promptly "compensate" for fluctuations in consumer and investment spending.

Various suggestions have been made to achieve this goal. If Congress, instead of fixing definite tax rates, were to provide for a sliding scale (let us say for a rate of 14% to 20% for the personal income tax, or for 46% to 52% in the case of the corporate income tax), the administration would be free to adjust tax rates promptly whenever private spending declined or increased too fast. Similarly, Congress could approve a "public works backlog," leaving it to the Administration to decide the most opportune moment, from an economic point of view, to start the actual work and thus create jobs and provide additional purchasing power.

So far Congress has shown no inclination for abandoning to the Executive the immediate control over the nation's finance — and this is probably wise. Time and again, public works projects and relief measures have apparently been undertaken for reasons of political expediency rather than of economic rationality or social needs. Irrespective of which party may be in control of the government, the temptation would be extremely great for the Administration to manipulate taxes and public spending in order to gain votes — and given enough leeway, any Administration could in this way perpetuate itself in power.

Compensatory Spending

Compensatory spending is thus likely to follow the established path, with Congress voting changes in taxes and providing for changes in government spending, including public works. The process is admittedly slow and cumbersome. The $11 billion tax reduction bill, finally adopted in 1964 to stimulate the rate of growth of the economy, was first drafted in 1962. Some controversial public works programs have been debated by Congress for years. The method is thus far too slow to counteract effectively minor cyclical fluctuations. Even after Congress has approved major public works programs, a year or more usually elapses before construction can actually begin. By this time the recession, which the public works program was designed to cure, may be nearing its end, and the "anti-deflation" measure may actually be undertaken when price increases rather than large-scale unemployment may be the chief concern.

Long Range Fiscal Policies

From a long-range point of view, on the other hand, Congress has considerable power to affect the character and the operation of the economy through fiscal measures. A system of taxation and public expenditure can promote consumption (either public or private) or capital formation and investments. The decision can be vital. Postwar Britain promoted public consumption through the development of an elaborate welfare state, and there are indications that she neglected capital formation, which was probably one of the reasons for her relatively slow postwar recovery. Western Germany, on the other hand, pursued a policy of curtailing consumption, even though the standard of living of the masses was low, and of promoting capital formation and investments. It was this fiscal policy, advocated by the then Minister of Economic Affairs Ludwig Erhard, which formed the basis of the "German Miracle."

Fiscal Policies to Stimulate Consumption

United States fiscal policy has been affected since the 1930's by the Keynesian doctrine that the American economy does not provide adequate investment opportunities for the vast amount of savings which accumulate in an "affluent society." At the same time, it is argued, there is not enough demand for all the goods and services which modern technology can produce. Keynes recommended, therefore, a curtailment of savings (to prevent the accumulation of "idle savings") and monetary and fiscal measures to increase consumer spending power.

Supplementing this Keynesian theory was a widespread feeling during World War II that social justice demanded that war profits be held at a minimum. The result was a steeply progressive system of taxation, which was continued even after the war had ended. In fact the progression was so steep that it could have paralyzed the economy, had it not been for a maze of "loopholes" which enabled taxpayers in the upper income brackets to pay substantially lower rates than indicated in the tax tables. Not until 1962 was the strangling effect of the wartime rates fully recognized, and it was not until 1964 that Congress reduced the tax rates.

Fiscal Policies to Stimulate Investments

In order to curb savings a government will place the tax burden mainly on middle and higher incomes, while relieving the lower income groups in order to stimulate mass consumption. On the other hand, to curb consumption and stimulate investments, the government will levy consumer taxes (such as the Federal luxury tax and state and local sales taxes.). At the same time the income tax progression will be flattened, so that the lower income groups (which account for the bulk of consumption) pay a relatively larger share of the government's expenditures, while the middle and upper income brackets (which account for the major portion of savings and investment) pay relatively less.

Underdeveloped Countries

In an underdeveloped country which is not in a position to satisfy the demands of the masses for consumer goods, progressive taxation — even though politically and socially expedient — is likely to be detrimental from an economic point of view, because it will tend to increase the inflationary pressure and will reduce the supply of available investment capital.

Psychological Aspects

In discussing fiscal policies from an economic, political or social point of view another aspect, the psychological one, is often overlooked. There is no way of proving that steeply progressive personal income taxes generally hamper private initiative, and that heavy corporate taxes affect adversely the development of new enterprises. Yet there are enough individual instances where such results can be shown. Even if the tendency is not universal, there can be little doubt that the American tax structure of the 1950's (which was the result of the equalitarian social philosophy of the "New Deal" and of the Keynesian theory that the American economy suffered from oversaving) was not conducive to stimulating risk-taking and economic growth. The system of taxation also contributed, as many economists assume, to the outflow of investment capital, which aggravated the balance of payments difficulties and may have reduced employment opportunities.

Disagreement as to Policy

The type of long-range fiscal policy which a country should pursue depends to a large extent upon its long-range economic needs. One reason for the conflicting fiscal policies pursued by many countries (including the United States) is the fact that even men of good will, who think themselves free from preconceived political, economic and social prejudices, are often in disagreement regarding the needs of an economy. Experts, for instance, hold different views whether improvements in agriculture or the development of industry is more important in an underdeveloped country; or, in the case of the United States, whether greater emphasis should be placed on monetary stability or the rate of economic growth, whether chronic unemployment can be cured through fiscal and monetary measures, or whether changes in the institutional framework are needed.

Long-range fiscal policies thus presuppose aggreement (1) regarding the goals to be achieved and (2) regarding the methods best suited to attain these goals — and such agreement is generally lacking. Even long-range fiscal policy is thus usually the result of political compromises rather than of pure economic rationality.

Debt Management

At least as effective as either a "flexible budget" policy, or long-range changes in the fiscal structure, can be a suitable policy of debt management. As we pointed out in Chapter 12 (page 204), the Federal Government has outstanding various types of securities, including Bills and Certificates (short term issues), Notes (medium term issues) and Bonds (which run for more than 5 years). The potential buyers of these issues are the Federal Reserve System, commercial banks, savings banks and insurance companies, corporations, and private individuals.

Creation of Additional Purchase Power

If the securities are purchased by either the Federal Reserve System or the commercial banks, the supply of money is likely to be increased because "payment" for the government securities is apt to be in the form of a credit entry on the books of the buying bank. If the Federal Reserve buys $100 million of government bonds it will merely credit the "U.S. Government General Account" with $100 million. The government can then draw on the balance to meet its expenditures, and the credit on the books of the Federal Reserve enters the economy in the form of additional money and credit. If the government securities are sold to a commercial bank the effect is likely to be the same, namely, an increase in the supply of money.

Shift of Savings from Private to Public Sector

On the other hand, if savings banks and life insurance companies buy goverment securities their ability to buy mortgages or corporate bonds will be reduced correspondingly, the results will thus be a shift of savings from the private to the public sector.

Reduce Consumer and Investment Spending

Finally, if corporations and private individuals buy government securities, they are tying up funds which they would have used otherwise either for capital investments or for the purchase of consumer goods. The sale of government bonds to individuals or corporations is thus likely to lead to a reduction in consumer and investment spending. This was the purpose of the sale of billions of war bonds during World War II. It was a costly and cumbersome method of financing the war, but it helped to soak up surplus purchasing power, which would otherwise have increased the inflationary pressure.

It makes a great deal of difference, therefore, how a government finances its deficit. It can add to the total purchasing power; it can shift savings from the private to the public sector; or it can hamper private investments and consumer spending. Which one of the three goals is most desirable depends on the economic situation.

Different Buyers of Long Term and Short Term Securities While it is possible, of course, that commercial banks will buy medium-term Notes and long-term Bonds, and a large corporation may acquire 90–Day Treasury Bills as a convenient short-term investment, the Federal Reserve and commercial banks, as a rule, purchase short-term issues, and savings banks, insurance companies and private individuals buy long-term bonds.

The Treasury can thus influence the economy by issuing short-term securities, which are likely to increase the supply of money and will have an inflationary effect; or long-term issues, which will result in a shift of funds from the private to the public sector, and may have a deflationary effect (at least temporarily) by reducing consumer spending and the supply of funds for private investments.

Limitations of Debt Management Policies

But again, the government is not a completely free agent. During the postwar years, when consumer prices increased by almost 80% (between 1945 and 1965) the government was reluctant to push the sale of long-term and especially savings bonds (which would have reduced the inflationary pressure) because it was feared that a marked reduction in the purchase power might result in a "postwar depression."

During the early 1960's, in turn, when the country was confronted with chronic unemployment, the Treasury was not free to sell large quantities of short-term obligations. Large sales of Treasury Bills to the Federal Reserve would have added to the general purchase power, but they would also have depressed short-term interest rates by adding to the money supply. This in turn would have stimulated the transfer of funds to Europe (where short-term rates were substantially higher) and would thus have complicated further the balance of payments problem.

Limitation of Fiscal and Monetary Policies

In short, while monetary and fiscal policies can and do influence the economy, no system has yet been discovered which enables economic planners to foresee future economic developments and to direct them toward the desired goals. This does not mean that macroeconomics is a failure because it has not been able thus far to achieve the four great goals of full employment, monetary stability, maximum economic growth and a balance of payments equilibrium. Medicine is not a failure because it has not yet found a way of curing cancer. But just as it is important for people to realize the limitations of medical knowledge, it is vital for them to be aware of man's limitation in shaping the economy to his liking.

PART IV
Microeconomics: Price, Value and Distribution

Chapter 20

PRICE, THE BASIC ISSUE OF MICROECONOMICS

THE BASIC FACTS

Macroeconomics deals with the problems affecting the economy as a whole; microeconomics, with the problems which concern (directly) the individual firm and the individual wage-earner and consumer. Macroeconomics is based on aggregates (statistical averages and totals) which reflect the happenings in the economy as a whole. Microeconomics deals with concrete prices, actual wages and the volume of output of a specific plant. Both approaches are necessary to an understanding of the complexities of the modern "mixed" economy.

Price Theories *The economic decisions of the individual entrepreneur and of the individual consumer revolve around the price. A price increase will tend to reduce total sales. It may or may not increase profits.*

Price theories are affected by the prevailing general intellectual and cultural climate. During the Middle Ages prices and wages were determined in part by ethical considerations based on the existing hierarchical social order. During the Age of Mercantilism wages and prices of necessities were kept low in order to boost exports and thus make possible the ac-

cumulation of gold and silver. In our own age "general welfare" considerations and political expediency (rather than the unimpeded "forces of the market") determine many prices.

Microeconomic Price Theory *Microeconomic price theory is based on the assumption that prices should be (and are) determined by the forces of the market (supply and demand). The classical school thought that prices were determined by the cost of production; the marginalist school stressed demand as the basis of price; Alfred Marshall, finally, showed that the time element had to be taken into consideration in determining the price.*

In the short run, prices are determined by demand; in the intermediate run (long enough to produce more goods, but not long enough to build new factories), by the variable cost; and in the long run, by the total cost.

Imperfect Competition *More recently writers have shown that only under conditions of perfect competition and monopoly can economists rationally calculate the best possible price-output combination. Under the far more frequent conditions of oligopoly the individual entrepreneur cannot predict with certainty what the best output and price will be. The Theory of Games (based on the theory of probability) can provide the answer so long as there are not more than three competing firms. If there are more than three, the complexities are beyond our present mathematical knowledge.*

Macro- and Microeconomics

The distinction between macro- and microeconomics is not as simple as most textbooks seem to imply. The terms are to some extent misleading. It is not a question of the "big" (macro) against the "little" (micro). Both macro- and microeconomics study the same economy, but they look on economic developments from different points of view. Macroeconomics deals with the economy as a whole. It is concerned with price averages rather than with the specific price of a ton of steel or a pair of shoes; with total exports and imports rather than the sale of 100 bales of cotton to a British mill; with consumer spending power in general rather than with the $125 which Bill Jones finds in his pay envelope. Microeconomics studies the economy from the viewpoint of the individual producer, merchant and consumer. It tries to find out why a ton of steel and a pair of shoes are sold at certain prices; why the American exporter sells 100 bales of cotton to a British importer and at what price; why Bill Jones earns $125 a week rather than $100 or $150; and why he uses his earnings to purchase food, shelter, clothing, amusements, etc., in the way he does. Whether the giant General Motors decides to raise the price on next year's model by $50, or whether the corner grocery store decides on Saturday afternoon to have a special sale of fresh strawberries, both are microeconomic decisions, even though the former may involve hundreds of millions of dollars, and the latter less than $50.

Statistical Abstractions The microeconomist deals with everyday realities, even though he tends to study these realities more from a rational and theoretical than from an empirical point of view. The macroeconomist, on the other hand, deals almost exclusively with aggregates, statistical averages. The "median income of American males 35–44 years old" was $6233 in 1961. This is a statistical average, arrived at through complicated statistical methods. It is a macroeconomic concept. Actually there were probably very few male Americans who just happened to earn exactly $6233 in 1961. While modern statistical methods try to come as close to representing the essential aspects of reality as possible, the statistics on which macroeconomics has to rely represent an abstraction of reality, and thus involves the danger that economists and the general public subconsciously mistake the statistical aggregates for reality.

Microeconomic Aspects The microeconomist, on the other hand, tends to pay inadequate attention to the national economy as a whole, which is not merely a sum total of the individual decisions of many millions of producers and consumers, as the 19th Century assumed. It involves some additional factors which are difficult to explain in microeconomic terms. The higher the rate of savings of an individual, for instance, the greater will be the wealth he eventually accumulates. On a national scale, however, large savings may spell economic stagnation. An increase in savings means a decrease in consumer demand, and unless there is an investment outlet for the savings, the latter will lie idle as they did during the 1930's, thus causing a corresponding decrease in employment.

Emotional Overtones Possibly most important, and most difficult to appreciate, is the fact that the difference between macro- and microeconomics involves emotional, philosophical and political overtones. The microeconomic approach reflects the individualism of the 19th Century with its stress on private enterprise. Macroeconomics, on the other hand, developed as a part of economic planning, with increased emphasis on collective action by society or the state rather than the individual.

Various Price Theories

Macroeconomic goals change as the objectives of public policy change. During the Age of Mercantilism, in the 16th–

18th Centuries, the public policy was directed toward the accumulation of gold and silver which were regarded as the basis of national wealth; during the 1940's and 1950's the emphasis was on "full employment," and during the early 1960's the goal shifted somewhat, with "economic growth" becoming at least temporarily the chief objective.

The microeconomic objective, on the other hand, remains more or less the same: How can the individual maximize his income in relation to his efforts? Microeconomics is thus, above all, concerned with the all important concepts of value, and price. What is the "proper" price of a product, of labor, of capital or land? These are the questions which microeconomics tries to answer.

Price Theory Determined by Cultural and Political Framework

The answers differ according to the cultural framework within which the economy functions and in which the economists develop their theories. During the Christian Middle Ages, the emphasis was on a "fair" price and a "just" wage, and in a stratified and fairly static society it was possible, within limits, to define "fair" and "just" in terms of the established tradition. If "for times immemorial" — a phrase which may have stood for 30, 50, or 100 years — a worker had been given a certain quantity of grain, flax and wool for his labor, and what he received was adequate to sustain him and his family, the wage was regarded as "just." Income was determined by the social status of the worker (which God had determined at the individual's birth), not by his productivity. A "fair" price provided the craftsman and the merchant with an income "commensurate with their social status." These notions were admittedly vague, and scholastic writers tried for centuries to arrive at a logical and practical way of determining what prices and wages should be, to satisfy the often conflicting demands of established ethics and the market place.

Age of Mercantilism

During the Age of Mercantilism authorities tried, as much as possible, to fix prices and wages with one objective in mind; namely, to increase the wealth of the nation through the accumulation of precious metals. Wages were kept close to the subsistence level, in order to hold production cost down and thus make it easier to export goods in exchange for gold and silver. Farm prices were held down so that workers could buy their food cheaply and could subsist on lower wages. The prices of most other goods, on the other hand, were raised to curtail consumption and thus make available a greater supply for export. A particularly heavy tax was placed on imported goods to restrain imports.

Modern Price Policies

In our own age, "general welfare" considerations and political expediency determine many prices. Railroad freight rates are kept high to protect truck lines; farm prices are inflated for the benefit of the farmer; and under the Fair Trade Act, merchants are prevented from selling goods below what the manufacturers regard as a proper price. In all three instances the government seems to act against the welfare of the consumer. On the other hand, private business concerns are hailed into court if the Department of Justice suspects that they have agreed, even in the most tenuous way, to fix prices and output. In short, a substantial portion of the prices in our modern mixed economy is determined by government fiat, and is not, or only partly, allowed to respond to the forces of the market.

Microeconomic Price Theory

Microeconomic price theory has nothing to do with the "ethical" approach of the Middle Ages, or the political and "general welfare" price theories of Mercantilism and the modern regulated economy. Microeconomics is based on the assumption that prices are the result of natural forces which work within the economy — provided these forces are not interfered with through government intervention. To discover the structure of these forces is the task of the economist, and during the 180 years between the first struggling efforts around the middle of the 18th Century and the 1930's, economists have learned a great deal about how prices come about.

The Evolution of the Price Theory

We can distinguish three steps in the evolution of the price theory. At first, prices were explained, chiefly by the classical economists in Britain, as the result of the cost of production. A pair of shoes is "worth" $10, because it costs $10 to make them. But this explanation was only partly satisfactory. It did not explain why an Easter hat, which the store tried to sell for $20 before Palm Sunday, should suddenly be worth only $12.95 a week after Easter. Around 1870, therefore, some economists, especially the so-called Marginalist School in Austria, argued that prices are determined by demand, rather than the cost of production. Finally, in the 1890's, the English economist Alfred Marshall showed that both supply (which reflects the cost of production) and demand (based on the satisfaction which the buyer expects from the product) have a bearing on the price. Supply and demand act like the blades of a pair of scissors.

Time Element Marshall introduced one very important factor, the time element. If the goods are on the shelves of the merchant, their "value" is determined by the price which the public is willing to pay, and this price may be well below the cost of production. Under such circumstances — when the selling price is below production cost — the manufacturer, however, would not be willing to continue making the goods, and once all the goods on the shelves and in the warehouses have been sold, the public will have to pay a higher price — high enough to cover "production cost" — in order to get more goods.

Production Cost Production cost is divided into "fixed cost" and "variable cost." The "fixed costs" include all those expenditures which have to be met whether the plant is in operation or not, such as real estate taxes, interest on the mortgage, insurance premiums, reserves for obsolescence and general administrative overhead. "Variable costs," on the other hand, vary with the volume of output. They include wages, raw materials, electric power, heat and other utilities, repairs, reserves for depreciation, selling cost, etc. Let us assume that the fixed cost of a company is $1,000,000, and the variable cost $5 per unit. (Actually the variable cost per unit is likely to change with the volume of output.) If the manufacturer sells 200,000 units the unit cost will be as follows:

Fixed cost of $1,000,000 allocated to 200,000 units	$ 5. — per unit
Variable cost	5. —
Total average cost:	$10. — per unit

Operating at a Loss Would the manufacturer continue production — at least for the time being — if the best price he could get were $6 per unit? He would! Because in doing so he would lose on 200,000 units only $800,000 ($4 per unit), while he would stand to lose $1,000,000 (i.e., the total fixed cost) if he did not operate at all. On the other hand, if the price dropped to $4.90, 10 cents less than the variable cost, production would be discontinued. In other words, once the production facilities have been built, the price at which goods will be produced must be at least slightly higher than the variable cost.

Once the machines wear out, however, and the mortgage has been paid off, the manufacturer will not buy new machinery or build a new factory unless he can be quite certain that the selling price will cover his total cost, both variable and fixed.

Short-run and Long-run Price

What then determines prices:

1. In the short run, when goods have been produced and are ready for sale, the price is determined by demand;
2. In the intermediate term — long enough to produce more goods but not long enough to build a new factory — the price must be somewhat higher than the variable cost to pay for at least a portion of the fixed cost.
3. In the long run — long enough for a new plant to be built to satisfy the demand — the price must equal total cost.

All this seems perfectly obvious once somebody has pointed it out. But it took some of the most brilliant minds of Europe more than a century to arrive at this explanation.

Imperfect Competition

The price theories discussed thus far are based on the assumption that prices and the volume of output fluctuate freely; in other words, they assume "perfect (or pure) competition." But this ideal market situation exists rarely, if ever. "Perfect competition," as the concept is used in price theory, is a theoretical construct not the picture of a real life market structure. It assumes: (1) A large number of buyers and sellers so that no single buyer or seller can affect the market price. The individual seller (e.g., a small farmer) can sell his entire output at the existing market price, and the individual buyer (a housewife buying canned vegetables in a supermarket) can buy all he (or she) wishes at the existing price. (2) A homogeneous product such as 1 inch middling cotton or No. 4 Santos coffee, (as against a "differentiated" product such as various types of toothpaste), so that it makes no difference to the buyer from whom he purchases the product. (3) Free entry and exit, in order that potential producers are not prevented (through the need for huge capital investments [as in the auto industry], through patents or a shortage of necessary factors of production) from turning out the product, and existing producers are free to stop production at any time (and are not compelled to continue operations at little or no return because their investment is "frozen" in a large plant.) (4) Buyers and sellers know the cost of production at various levels of output as well as the market price at which supply and demand will be equal.

Alfred Marshall, writing in the 1890's, was fully aware of the fact that "perfect competition" did not exist, but he also realized that it was impossible to construct a model which at the same time retained the necessary simplicity to be readily understood and yet included the multitude of variables to be found in real life. He thought that the theoretical conditions of "perfect competition" were close enough to reality, so that the concept could be used as basis for a sufficiently realistic price theory.

Other economists did not fully share this view. As early as 1908 the "perfect competition" premise was challenged and important articles appeared during the 1920's dealing with various market situations other than perfect competition. However, it was not until the 1930's that the climate was right for economists to develop independently a number of new theories. The best-known writers in the field are Joan Robinson (1903–) (*Economics of Imperfect Competition*) and Edward H. Chamberlin (1899–1967) (*The Theory of Monopolistic Competition*). Both authors deal with specific aspects which arise in the "grey" area between monopoly and competition. What happens (1) if instead of many sellers and buyers (none of whom can influence the market price) there are only two sellers (duopoly), a few sellers (oligopoly) or a few buyers (oligopsony); (2) if the product is not uniform but differentiated due to the use of trade names, differences in packaging, different "images" created through advertising; (3) if the individual producer cannot predict how his competitors will react if he increases his advertising, raises or lowers his price, or introduces special services?

To all but the professional economist, the largely technical differences between Mrs. Robinson's "imperfect" and Chamberlin's "monopolistic" competition seem rather insignificant, but there are differences which can lead to different policy recommendations. Chamberlin, looking upon the market from the point of view of competing firms, found elements of both monopoly and competition. (Due to "product differentiation" Ford has a "monopoly" in Ford cars, General Motors in Chevrolets. Yet the two compete sharply.) Joan Robinson looked upon the problem from the point of view of an industry as a whole, and stressed the absence of price competition and its social and economic implications.

Nine Possible Market Situations Less well-known in the United States than Joan Robinson and Chamberlin is the German economist H. von Stackelberg (1905–46) who worked in the same general area. According to Stackelberg there are nine possible market situations as shown in Table 14.

TABLE 14

Nine Possible Market Situations

	Many Sellers	A Few Sellers	One Seller
Many Buyers	Perfect Competition	Oligopoly	Monopoly
A Few Buyers	Oligopsony	Oligopoly-Oligopsony	Limited Monopoly
One Buyer	Monopsony	Limited Monoposony	Monopoly-Monopsony

The Impossibility of Determining Output and Price

Of these nine typical market forms, only four (perfect competition, monopoly, monopsony, and monopoly/monopsony) permit rational predictions regarding the price and volume of output, as we shall show in Chapter 21. On the other hand, whenever either an oligopolistic or an oligopsonistic situation exists, it is not possible, on the basis of the traditional analytical apparatus, to determine what the price and output will be.

Unfortunately, oligopolistic and oligopsonistic market situations are most prevalent in a modern economy. In most major industries there are 3, 4, 5 and rarely more than 10, large firms which account for 90% of the output. Each firm tries to maximize its income by producing just the right quantity of goods which will result in the greatest profit. If production is increased, prices may decline. On the other hand, if one of the oligopolists should attempt to raise prices by curtailing output, his competitor would immediately try to take over a larger share of the market. Under an oligopolistic market structure, price competition is thus extremely risky — and hence rare. Fords and Chevrolets sell more or less at the same price for comparable models. If Ford were to cut its price by $200, General Motors most likely would make a similar price reduction. On the other hand, if Ford were to raise its price $200, enough people might switch to a Chevrolet, so that the decline in sales of Ford cars might more than off-set the gain resulting from the higher price. Oligopolistic prices are thus based on "intelligent guesses" as to what the competitor might do.

Oligopolistic Price Determination

In practice, an automobile producer bases his price (a) on the variable cost and (b) on the fixed cost allocated on the basis of anticipated volume of sales. Let us assume that the variable cost per car is $1500, the fixed cost is $500 million, and the anticipated volume of sales is 1 million cars. The total cost (including a "normal" rate of profit), based on an output of 1 million cars, would thus be $1500 plus $500, or $2000. If actual sales were to total only 900,000 cars, the per unit fixed cost would increase to $555 and the profit per car would be reduced by $55. On the other hand, if sales were to rise to 1.1 million cars, the per unit fixed cost would decline to $454, and profits per car would increase by $46. Since both fixed and variable costs are more or less the same for General Motors and Ford, and they must sell at about the same price in order to avoid a suicidal price war, the rate of profit is determined by the number of cars sold. Hence the frequent style changes and tremendous amount of advertising to attract buyers.

But while the chances of a price war or of major price changes are unlikely once an oligopolistic market situation has developed, there is no way of rationally predicting what the price will be. In theory at least Ford and General Motors could decide individually — acting on the basis of a similar market analysis, telepathy, or a "criminal conspiracy" — to raise prices by $500. The demand would probably fall off, some buyers would switch to foreign cars, and even if Ford and General Motors were to stick to their higher prices, we do not know whether their profits would increase or decrease in the long run. There is no way of determining in advance in an oligopolistic market what price will yield the highest return, as can be predicted (at least in theory) under conditions of free competition, monopoly and monopsony.

The Theory of Games

Shortly before World War II a well-known economist, Oskar Morgenstern, and a brilliant mathematician, John von Neumann, attempted to develop a theory of probability to predict the action of an oligopolist. This is the well-known Theory of Games. But, as the authors warned at the outset, their work represented merely the beginning of a major effort which may require generations of mathematicians to complete.

The Theory of Games starts with the assumption that all "players" (entrepreneurs) are attempting to maximize their profits through the best possible combination of output and price. (If the output is too large, the price is likely to decline; if the price is too high, sales will decline.) On the basis of microeconomic theory it is possible to calculate the best possible output-price combination — but only under conditions of perfect competition and monopoly. Under perfect competition the individual entrepreneur "knows" what all his competitors will do as long as they act as rational beings, (as we shall discuss in detail in Chapter 21.) Under monopoly, the entrepreneur does not have to worry about competitors because there are none. In each case the individual entrepreneur can thus calculate "with certainty" what will be his best policy.

In an oligopolistic market situation, however, the individual entrepreneur cannot predict with certainty which one of a substantial number of possible moves his competitors will make. Yet each of these moves affects the market situation, and thus the best possible output-price combination of each "player." "Planning" thus involves guessing the probable actions of the competitors and the consequences of these actions. The best action of each "player" is based on the probability as to the possible action and counter-action of all "players." So long as the number of "players" is limited (not more than three) and the number of strategy choices (possible policies) is not too large, probability mathematics and modern computors can provide the logical answers as to the best strategy which each "player" should adopt. On the other hand, if there are more than three "players" (three competing firms in a given market) and there are many possible strategies (as is the case in real life), the complexity of possible combinations exceeds the grasp of the human mind, the capacity of electronic computers and, most important, the present state of mathematical knowledge.

A typical oligopolistic market situation with a half-dozen or more competitors and a large number of possible policies (as to price, volume of output, quality and type of product, advertising programs, etc.) thus cannot be solved at present through the Theory of Games.

No "Scientific" Theory of Price

In other words, if it is the chief objective of microeconomics to develop a theory which under all circumstances and with certainty will tell the businessman which volume of output and which price will produce the greatest profit, we must admit that we have not yet accomplished this goal so far as the most important modern market structures — oligopoly and oligopsony — are concerned. We have made progress toward the goal, and we know a great deal more about the forces which determine prices than people did 100 years ago, but microeconomics has not yet come up with a final answer, and as Morgenstern and Neumann warned, we may not achieve the goal in our lifetime.

Chapter 21

SUPPLY, DEMAND, AND PRICE

THE BASIC FACTS

Price is determined by many factors. The two most important of them are (1) the cost of production; (2) the utility and relative scarcity of the product.

Supply *"Supply," in the language of the economist, refers to a "supply schedule," each price corresponding to a given volume of production. As prices rise the output increases; as prices decline the output declines. "Changes in supply" (involving a shift of the supply curve) may be due to many causes, but not to changes in price. Rising production costs and stable prices make for declining output, and hence unemployment. Conversely, stable production costs and rising prices make for rising profits, and thus for increased production and employment.*

Demand *"Demand" is based on the utility of a product or service. Utility, however, is a relative concept. It involves the usefulness of an article in relation to its own price, as well as in relation to the usefulness of a great many other goods and services and their respective prices. Moreover, utility usually diminishes when the buyer acquires another unit of the same product.*

Total demand is assumed to be the addition of the demand schedules of hundreds of individual consumers, each determined by the rational choice of the individual.

Modern economists question the logic of this explanation of demand. The emphasis has shifted from the individual deciding to buy or not to buy, to the government providing the consuming public as a whole with enough purchasing power to consume all the goods and services which the economy can produce.

Price and Scarcity *If something is "free for the taking," it is known as a "free good." Nobody will pay for it. Anything which demands a price (because the demand is greater than the supply) is an "economic good" ("scarce good"). The value of an article is determined (aside from its usefulness) by its relative scarcity.*

Marginalist Demand Theory *The traditional theory of demand was based on three assumptions: (1) that the consumer will select those goods and services which (in relation to their price) will give him the greatest satisfaction; (2) that the market price of an article reflects its average utility to the multitude of consumers; and (3) that all buyers and sellers know the market price, the price at which supply and demand will be equal. The three assumptions are "unrealistic." Yet they are helpful in explaining basic tendencies.*

Supply and Demand *While it is a gross oversimplification to assume that the price formation can be explained purely in terms of "supply and demand," simple supply and demand graphs can be very helpful in showing the effects of so-called "over-production" and "inadequate supply" brought about by the raising or lowering of prices above or below their equilibrium level.*

Elasticity of Supply and Demand *The notion of elasticity indicates the degree of change in the quantity of goods supplied or demanded as a result of price changes. The elasticity of supply is usually determined by time: the longer the time period, the greater the elasticity.*

In speaking of elasticity of demand, the economist distinguishes between elastic demand (an increase in price results in a decline in total sales receipts), inelastic demand (an increase in price results in an increase in total sales receipts) and unitary demand (total sales receipts increase and decrease in proportion to price changes). If the demand for his product is elastic a businessman will want to reduce prices (to the extent that the production cost permits). If the demand is inelastic he will try to increase prices (if his competitors permit).

General Equilibrium *From a philosophic point of view, and in order to get a better understanding of the multitude of interlocking forces which determine the economy, it is more helpful to think in terms of a "general equilibrium" rather than in terms of the better-known "partial equilibrium."*

The Basic Aspects of Price Theory

In the preceding chapter we discussed price theories in general. In this chapter we shall consider some of the factors which determine prices: the cost of production which governs supply; and utility and scarcity which determine demand. We shall also discuss the extremely important notion of marginal utility, and the concept of elasticity of demand and supply.

In discussing these topics we shall make two basic assumptions: (1) that there are no monopolistic or oligopolistic restraints, and no government intervention and (2) that the institutional and cultural framework remains unchanged. Both assumptions are "unrealistic"—just as it is "unrealistic" for a physicist to assume a perfect vacuum which obviously does not exist on this earth. As we saw in the preceding chapter, perfect competition constitutes only one out of nine typical market situations, and it is virtually non-existing in everyday modern life. Likewise, as we showed in Chapters 2 to 8, the institutional and cultural framework is constantly changing.

Nevertheless, our "unrealistic" assumptions are not without justification. They make it possible to gain a better understanding of some of the most basic economic processes which would be far too complex to grasp, or even to express in words, if we were to introduce all the variables at the same time.

Cost of Production, Price, and Supply

The terms *supply, demand, scarcity* and *utility* have a somewhat different meaning in the language of the economist from the way in which they are used in everyday language. This is unfortunate, because it has led to many misunderstandings. It is therefore extremely important that a student of economics be always aware of the different meanings of these terms.

To the man in the street the word "supply" refers to the goods available at a certain place, possibly including those which can be obtained on short notice. To the economist the term implies a "supply schedule," which shows the quantities of a given product which are available at *different* prices in a given market. "Supply," in the language of the economist, thus does not refer only to the availability of a certain product, but to the changing quantities which will be available for sale as prices rise or fall.

Rising Production Cost and Stable Prices Supply is determined (a) by the cost of production and (b) by the prevailing price. If the cost of production increases and the price of the product remains unchanged, fewer goods will be produced, because the less efficient plants and the less fertile fields can no longer be operated profitably and will hence be taken out of operation. Rising production costs and stable prices thus make for unemployment. On the other hand, if prices rise faster than the production costs, the total output will increase, because (a) less efficient plants can now be operated profitably, and less productive workers can be employed, and (b) the promise of greater profits will induce additional entrepreneurs to enter the field.

Rising Prices and Increased Production Supply thus involves three variables: the cost of production, the prevailing market price and the quantity supplied. If the demand for wheat increases, as it did during World War I and II, prices will rise. This in turn will make it possible for farmers to use more fertilizer and to work less fertile land, and farmers who never thought of raising wheat before will turn grazing land into wheat fields. In short, rising prices, as a rule, are associated with increased production, and declining prices with lower production.

TABLE 15

Supply of Eggs (hypothetical figures)

Billions produced	Average market price
40	15 cents (per dozen)
45	20
50	25
55	30
60	35
65	40

In charting the type of data shown in Table 15, economists have adopted the practice of measuring prices ("P") on the vertical axis (ordinate) and quantities ("Q") on the horizontal (abscissa). A typical supply curve will thus slope upward from left to right.

FIGURE 10 ***Supply Curve***

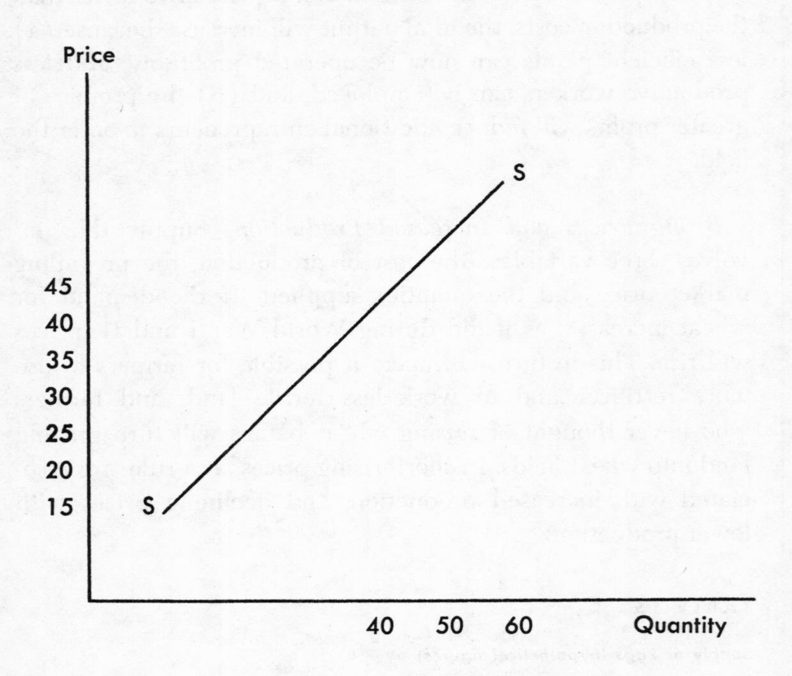

The entire supply schedule (Table 15) and the entire supply curve (Figure 10) represent what the economist calls "supply," whether it be 40 billion eggs at 15¢ or 65 billion at 45¢. *Price changes* result in *movements on the supply curve.* They do not, in the language of the economist, produce *changes in supply.*

Fixed Relationship Between Price and Output

The economist assumes that, given a certain supply schedule, a fixed relationship exists between the price and the volume of goods produced and sold. Changes in price will result in corresponding changes in the quantities supplied. Changes in quantities demanded will call for corresponding price changes.

Changes in Supply "Changes in supply," i.e., changes in the supply schedule, can be the result of many factors, but never, in the language of the economist, of price changes. Improved technology may result in a lowering of the production cost. Increased wages or taxes, or the exhaustion of the supply of cheap raw materials, may lead to rising cost. These and many other factors would result in a "change in supply," or a *shift* of the supply curve from SS to S′S′ or S″S″. S′S′ represents a decrease, and S″S″ an increase, in supply.

Let us repeat: *Changes in the quantity supplied* (within a supply schedule) are due to price changes. *Changes in supply* (resulting in a shift of the supply curve) are due to factors other than price changes.

Demand — The Result of Utility and Scarcity

While "supply" involves the ability and willingness of the producer to provide certain quantities of goods at different prices, "demand" involves the desire of the buyer to acquire certain goods or services, and the willingness and ability to pay for them.

Analogous to the economist's use of the word "supply," "demand," in the language of the economist, is a schedule of certain quantities of goods which the public is willing to acquire at various prices in a given market. Generally speaking, the quantity of goods demanded will increase as the price declines,

FIGURE 11 ***Changes in Supply***

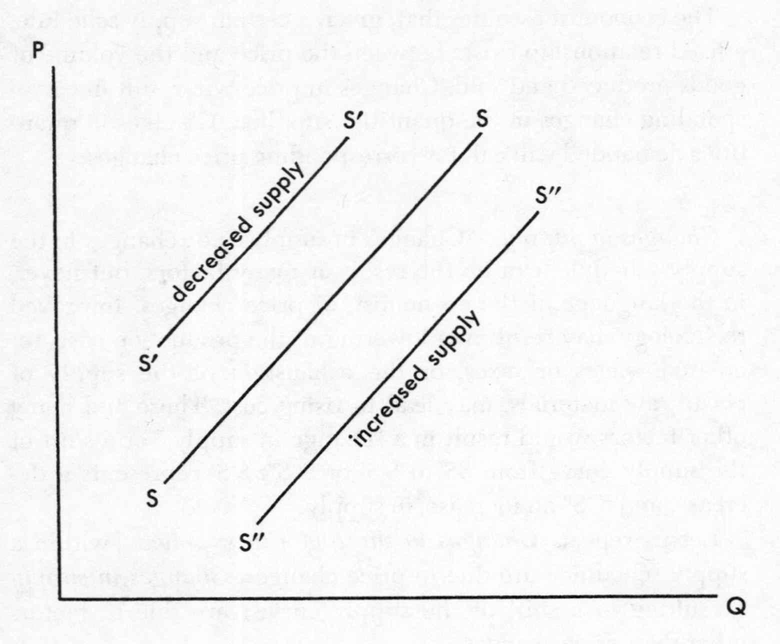

and decrease as the price rises. Demand thus varies inversely with the price, and a demand curve will ordinarily slope downward from the left to right. Changes in price will result in *movements on the demand curve;* changes in demand will produce *shifts of the demand curve* to D′D′ (decreased demand) or D″D″ (increased demand), as shown in Figure 12.

Utility and Scarcity

The price that people are willing to pay for an article or service depends (1) on its usefulness, its "utility" and (2) on

FIGURE 12 ***Changes in Demand***

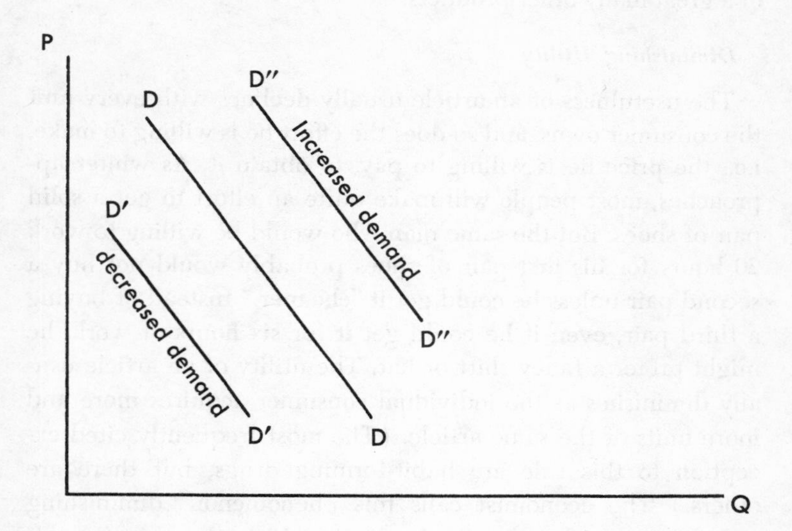

the quantity available, its "scarcity." Aside from a good deal of semantic confusion, the two terms involve some conceptual difficulties.

Utility, a Relative Concept

Utility is not an absolute but a relative concept. A Cadillac is no doubt useful, but its "utility" to the prospective buyer depends on the price at which the car can be purchased, and the prices and relative usefulness of a great variety of other goods and services. A prospective car buyer may reason that a $10,000 down payment on a house, a trip around the world with his family, a motor boat, or a $10,000 deposit in the bank, may give him more "satisfaction" than a $10,000 Cadillac. The "utility" of an article or service thus varies according to its own price and usefulness in relation to the prices and the usefulness of a great many other products.

Diminishing Utility

The usefulness of an article usually declines with every unit the consumer owns, and so does the effort he is willing to make, i.e., the price he is willing to pay, to obtain it. As winter approaches, most people will make quite an effort to get a solid pair of shoes. But the same man who would be willing to work 20 hours for his first pair of shoes probably would not buy a second pair unless he could get it "cheaper." Instead of buying a third pair, even if he could get it for six hours of work, he might prefer a fancy shirt or hat. The utility of an article usually diminishes as the individual consumer acquires more and more units of the same article. (The most frequently cited exception to this rule are habit-forming drugs, but there are others.) The economist calls this phenomenon "diminishing utility," and refers to the last unit which the consumer is willing to buy on the basis of the existing price as the "marginal unit." The price at which the last unit changes hands is known as the "marginal price."

The Individualistic Basis of the Demand Schedule

If we combine the individual demand schedules (each based on the diminishing utility which the article offers to the individual consumer) we arrive at the market demand schedule for the product.

This notion of millions of rational individuals determining what quantities of a given product they are willing to buy at various prices is typical of the 19th Century individualistic approach to the problem of demand.

Modern Approach

Modern economists are more likely to disregard the individual and to think in terms of "aggregate purchasing power." In order to be able to sell all the goods and services which the economy can produce at the full employment level, enough consumer income must be generated to equal the retail value of all the goods and services produced. The emphasis thus shifts from the individual deciding to buy or not to buy, to the government providing the consuming public as a whole with enough purchasing power which, it is assumed, will induce the public to buy all the goods which have to be produced to maintain full employment. It is no longer a question of satisfying the wants of the individual, but of providing an outlet for the productive capacity of the nation.

Price and Scarcity Whether we take the 19th Century approach (assuming that demand is based on the utility of a product to the individual consumer) or the 20th Century approach (holding that demand is the result of a carefully manipulated volume of consumer purchasing power), the price of an article (in relation to the price of other articles) continues to be determined by its relative utility and scarcity. If the supply is unlimited for all practical purposes (such as the supply of air) there is no reason for people to pay anything for it, even though it might be extremely useful. On the other hand, an article may be quite scarce, yet virtually useless at the same time, because man has discovered no use for it. This was the case with uranium ore in the early 1940's, before the development of atomic power.

"Scarce goods" "Scarce goods," also called "economic goods" in the language of the economist, are the opposite of

"free goods." So long as a good is not free for the taking, such as air, it is a "scarce" or "economic good." Salt, even though it may cost only 10¢ a pound, is a "scarce good."

"Paradox of Value"

The fact that there seems to be no direct relationship between the "usefulness" of an article and the price people are willing to pay for it, produced a great deal of confusion during the 18th Century, and led economic theorists astray for almost a century. Adam Smith tried in vain to solve this "paradox of value." "Nothing is more useful than water," he wrote, "but . . . scarce any thing can be had in exchange for it. A diamond, on the contrary, has scarce any value in use; but a very great quantity of other goods may frequently be had in exchange for it." The seeming paradox disappears if we combine the notions of "utility" and "scarcity" into one concept; namely, the idea of "marginal utility." If diamonds were as plentiful as gravel, their price would not be much higher; where water is scarce, as it is in the desert, it can fetch a fairly high price.

The Basic Assumption of the Marginalist Demand Theory

In order to construct a logical price theory out of the notions of diminishing utility and scarcity, the Marginalist School had to make three assumptions: (1) that the consumer was essentially rational; (2) that the actual demand reflected the relative utility of the goods sold, and (3) that the markets are "transparent." All three assumptions have been challenged as "unrealistic," although one can hardly deny their usefulness as analytical tools.

Rationality of the Consumer

In real life few people calculate exactly whether another pair of shoes at $20 or a sports jacket at the same price will provide greater satisfaction. Consumer buying, including the purchase even of large objects such as cars and homes, is often determined emotionally rather than by rationally calculating the "marginal utility" of each article. Yet, the marginal utility theory assumes that the consumer carefully allocates his spending in such a way that the marginal utility of each and every article and service purchased will be equal to the marginal utility provided by all other goods and services. If one rejects this premise, that man is inherently a rational being (and many modern writers reject the premise), the whole concept of "consumer rationality" and the marginal utility approach in general, to the extent that it is based on the notion of human rationality, become "unrealistic." However, if we take this position and assume that the average consumer cannot be expected to act rationally most of the time when buying goods and services, we must also question the likelihood of his acting rationally when he goes to the polls to make political decisions. This, in turn, would challenge the very foundation of democracy.

Can "Utility" be Measured Much more questionable is the second premise of the demand theory; namely that we can measure utility by the price which the public is willing to pay for an article. This chain of reasoning — demand is determined by utility, and utility in turn is measured by the demand (as expressed by the price the buyer is willing to pay) — is purely formal and tells us nothing about the actual forces in the market place. What the businessman really wants to know is *why* a man prefers a $20 pair of shoes to a $20 sports jacket. The multitude of rational and often irrational forces which determine the consumption pattern are reduced in the traditional demand theory to the dual forces of scarcity (which we can measure within certain limits) and utility (which we cannot measure, except by saying that utility is reflected by demand). To analyze the notion of utility and its component psychological and social aspects is the objective of the modern studies of consumer behavior.

"Transparency" of the Market The third assumption of the marginalists, the "transparency of the market," seems likewise unrealistic on the basis of everyday experience. It assumes that all buyers and sellers of a given product know the quantities which will be available for sale at varying prices and the quantities which will be purchased. In other words, the theory assumes that everybody connected with the purchase and sale of an article knows exactly the price at which supply and demand will be equal.

If taken literally, this assumption is clearly unrealistic. If taken as an ideal toward which we all strive, it is a helpful premise. How many people have refused to buy an article, which they wanted and needed, before Christmas because they figured that the merchant will not be able to sell his entire supply at the pre-Christmas price, so that they can get a bargain in the January sale? This is a type of "market transparency" which any reasonable person will accept, even though he may reject as unrealistic the assumption of perfect "transparency of the market." Yet even this imperfect knowledge of the market has an important bearing on the determination of prices.

Grain dealers have a fairly good idea of how much wheat can be sold and exported at various prices, and government statistics provide them with details regarding the probable supply. If the crop is large, some of the wheat will have to be sold to potential buyers who ordinarily cannot afford wheat or prefer, let us say, rice. In order to open this additional market, the price will have to be lowered. In case of a small crop, on the other hand, wheat dealers do not have to worry about the marginal markets, and can pay a higher price for future deliveries, knowing fully well that the smaller supply can be sold at a higher price. Having a fair idea of the supply and demand schedules, the grain trader also knows approximately how low the price will have to go (disregarding government price support schemes) to sell the last bushel of wheat (the marginal unit), and he will obviously not pay more than this price. This line of reasoning is basic to the demand theory of the Marginalist School. Given the "transparency of the market" the average price at which the goods are sold will tend to be equal to the marginal price at which the last unit can — and will have to be — cleared, because (1) nobody will want to pay more than the marginal price (knowing full well that ultimately the price will have to be reduced to the marginal price in order to dispose of the last, or marginal unit) and (2) the seller obviously will not offer the goods for a lower price than the one he knows he can get from the "marginal" buyer, the buyer who is willing to purchase the last unit. The market price will thus be equal to the marginal price.

FIGURE 13 ***Forces Determining Price***

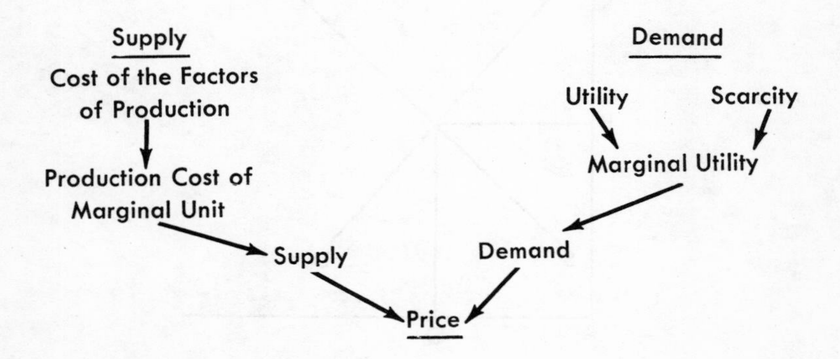

Supply and Demand

As shown in Figure 13, the price of a product is the result of an interplay of numerous forces culminating in the supply of and demand for the product. These forces, as we shall see shortly, are actually more complex than Figure 13 would seem to indicate. The realization that the price is neither the result of the cost of production as the classical economists assumed during the first half of the 19th Century, nor of demand, as the marginalists thought after the 1870's, is largely due to the work of Alfred Marshall.

With the supply curve sloping upward from left to right and the demand curve sloping downward, there must be a point where the two curves meet, indicating that supply and demand at this particular point are identical. At the "P" price (in Figure 14) the same quantity of goods "Q" is supplied and demanded, and the market is in equilibrium.

FIGURE 14 ***Supply and Demand***

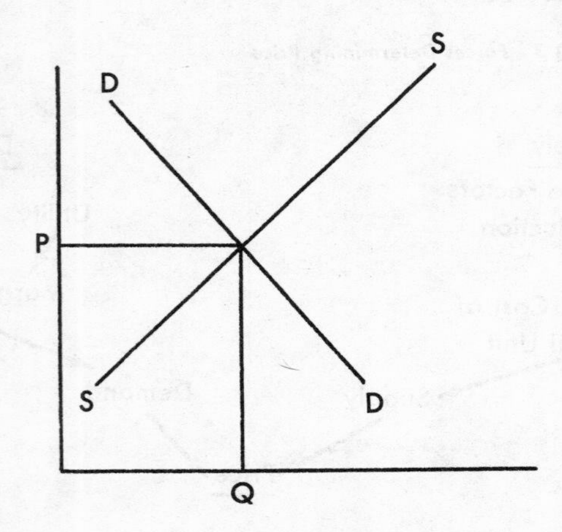

Elasticity of Supply and Demand

The concept of elasticity is more easily explained than defined. It indicates the degree of change in the quantity of goods demanded and supplied in response to price changes.

Elasticity of Supply

The degree of elasticity of supply depends to a large extent upon the time factor. The immediate supply is determined by the quantity of goods which the seller has on hand. It does not change even if the buyer were willing to pay twice as much. In other words, the supply is totally inelastic. Given a few days or weeks, the merchant could order more goods from the manufacturer; and the manufacturer, using his existing facilities, could produce more goods in response to increased demand and rising prices. Finally, given enough time to increase production facilities, the producer could increase the output still further by building a new plant.

An increase in the price from $5 to $10 (in Figure 15) has no effect on the immediate supply, which remains 100 units. Given enough time to order more goods and use the existing production facilities to produce more goods (i.e., during the intermediate period), an increase in the price from $5 to $10 will result, let us say, in an increase in supply from 100 to 200 units; and in the long run, with enough time to build additional plants, a doubling of the price might result in an increase in supply to 450 units. In other words, the longer the period, the greater is, as a rule, the elasticity of supply. The length of the period needed to increase the supply is determined by a variety of factors including communication and transportation facilities and technological aspects. As the G.I.'s returned from World War II the demand for fancy sports jackets and automobiles increased sharply — and so did the prices. But the

FIGURE 15 *Elasticity of Supply*

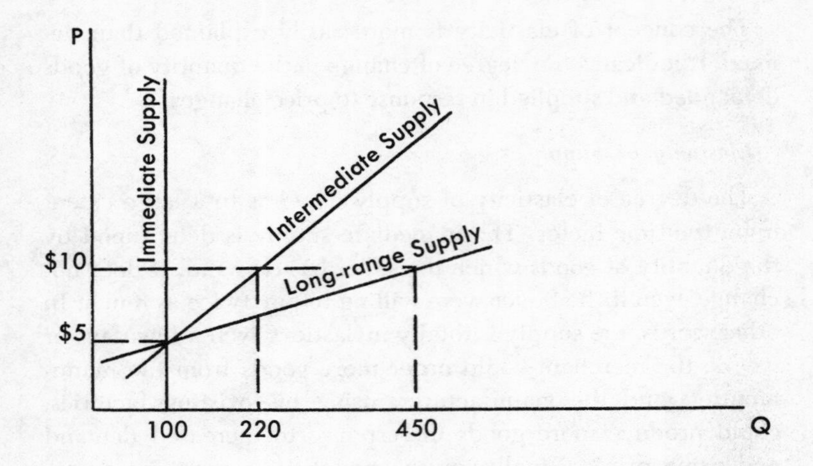

price advances for the jackets was relatively short-lived, since the elasticity of supply was relatively great. It was quite simple to increase the supply in line with the demand. In the case of automobiles, however, the elasticity was much more limited. It took two years or more to increase the supply of new cars. The price of cars thus remained high.

Elasticity of Demand

When economists speak of the elasticity of demand, they refer to the responsiveness of the demand for a given product to changes in its price. A price increase is likely to lead to a decrease in the quantity demanded, but how much will the demand decrease in response to a price increase? Will the total sales receipts increase, decrease or remain the same? Economists distinguish between elastic, inelastic and unitary demand. If the total quantity demanded shows percentagewise a smaller decrease than the percentage increase in the price, the demand is inelastic. If, on the other hand, the percentage decrease in the quantity demanded is greater than the percentage price increase, the demand for the product is said to be elastic.

A manufacturer sells 100,000 units at $1. His sales thus total $100,000. He decides to raise his price to $1.10; this leads to a sharp reduction in sales to, let us say, 85,000 units. His total sales receipts now amount to only $93,500. The demand for the product was elastic. The quantity of goods sold decreased relatively more than the price increased.

Another manufacturer is in a more fortunate position. He also raises his price from $1 to $1.10, but his sales decline only from 100,000 to 95,000 units, so that his gross income, as a result of price increase, increases from $100,000 to $104,500. The demand for the product was inelastic.

Conversely, if the price is lowered and total sales receipts go up, the demand is elastic. If the price is lowered and total sales receipts go down, the demand is inelastic.

In theory, finally, it would be possible for total sales receipts to remain the same whether the price is raised or lowered, because the volume of sales fluctuates proportionately with the changes in price. This would be called unitary elasticity, a notion which is helpful in theory, although the situation is rarely to be found in reality.

Factors Determining the Elasticity of Demand

There are a variety of factors which affect the elasticity of demand.

If the product is a necessity, the demand tends to be inelastic. People will buy the same amount of salt, whether the price is 10¢ or 20¢ a pound.

If the article involves only a minor percentage of the total spending of the consumer, the demand tends to be inelastic.

People will go on smoking nearly the same number of cigarettes, even if a 3¢ tax is added.

If the article represents only a small part of the finished product, the demand will tend to be inelastic. An increase in the price of chromium is not likely to affect materially the demand for chromium by the auto industry.

The demand for consumer durable goods tends to be more elastic than the demand for food. An increase in prices may have only a small effect on the demand for steaks and milk, but people may defer for a year or two the purchase of a new car or a new refrigerator.

Elastic and Inelastic Demand If demand is *perfectly* (infinitely) *elastic* it is pictured by a straight horizontal line. This is the situation which confronts the individual small farmer. He can sell all the wheat he has at the current market price, but he could not sell one bushel more if he reduced his price (because he already sells all he has) and he could not sell anything if he raised his price. If the demand is *perfectly inelastic* the demand curve is a straight vertical line. The individual demand for a minimum of drinking water or salt, for instance, is almost perfectly inelastic.

The elasticity of demand for most products lies between the two extremes, and varies with changes in the price. For most people in a typical American community the demand for water to be used for cooking and drinking purposes is perfectly inelastic. But if the price of water is increased sharply, less water will be used to water the lawn. And if the price rises still further, some of the poorer people will use less water for bathing.

General versus Partial Equilibrium

In this and in the preceding chapter we have thus far considered the notion of the equilibrium price, at which supply and demand are equal, only with regard to a single product. We did mention that the price of a given product or service may be influenced by extraneous forces (forces other than supply and demand) which result in a change in supply and demand (i.e., a shift of the supply and demand curves). But we considered these outside forces only in relation to their effect upon the price of one single product or service, i.e., a minute "part" of the entire economic process. This "partial equilibrium" approach is used widely by many economists. It is most closely associated with Alfred Marshall, and is therefore referred to as the Marshallian equilibrium.

General Equilibrium

The approach is helpful as a first step toward an understanding of the notion of equilibrium, but it has its great weaknesses. Actually one cannot think of the economy as a whole as being composed of millions of partial equilibria, each functioning within its own frame of reference. In real life these millions of partial equilibria are all interconnected and should hence be thought of in terms of a "general equilibrium." The man who developed this notion was the French-Swiss economist, Leon Walras (1834–1910), one of the most brilliant economists of all time. We are therefore speaking of the Walrasian Equilibrium. The notion is simple, but to present the theory, as Walras did, involves a good deal of mathematics and a number of fairly complex notions.

Implications of the Walrasian Equilibrium

Walras approached the problem from a microeconomic point of view, in the way we have discussed the formation of price in this and the preceding chapter, but he ended with a macroeconomic overall picture. Every single economic event — whether it be Mrs. Miller's purchase of a dozen eggs at the corner grocery store, or the construction of a $100 million steel plant — has an endless chain of ramifications. The fact that Mrs. Miller buys eggs rather than meat affects, in an ever so minute way, the supply of and demand for eggs and meat, and hence their prices. It affects indirectly the demand for chicken feed, and thus the employment in feed mills, as well as the supply of leather, and hence the price of shoes and the rate of employment in shoe stores. Everything in this world affects everything else. The basic idea of the general equilibrium is not only a highly important economic notion, but also a profound philosophic one. It has intrigued thinkers since the days of the French mechanistic school of the 18th Century. Every action, however seemingly unimportant, has an endless chain of consequences, most of which we do not and cannot know. A stone thrown down a steep hill may come to rest at a tree, it may crush a flower, or it may start a small avalanche. But the fact that we cannot foresee the chain of consequences also places on the individual — and much more so on the law maker and the economic planner — a tremendous moral responsibility. What may seem expedient at the moment might well appear irresponsible if viewed in the long chain of national and international consequences.

The Input-Output Model

During the 1930's and 1940's Wassily W. Leontieff applied the theory of the general equilibrium — or, as he preferred to call it, general interdependence — to "an empirical study of the interrelations among the different parts of a national economy as revealed through covariations of prices, outputs, investments, and incomes."

It was the purpose of the study to develop a technique which would enable the economic planner to estimate the interconnection "between even the remotest parts of a national economy."

This is the theory which has come to be known as the "input-output" model — the "input" of one firm or industry corresponds to the "output" of another. It involves an extensive use of mathematical equations, and usually the use of electronic computers, to process the vast amount of data. The system is used extensively by private business firms in managerial planning ("decision making") and by developed and underdeveloped nations whose planning experts are setting up "development models" which provide a blueprint for the most efficient use of the available resources.

Chapter 22

THE THEORIES OF PRODUCTION AND DISTRIBUTION

THE BASIC FACTS

The theories of production, supply and demand, and income distribution are all based on the notions of marginal utility and scarcity.

Theory of Production *The theory of production assumes (1) that the economy is based on a division of labor and roundabout production methods, (2) that the entrepreneur strives to maximize profits and (3) that the factors of production are rewarded according to their relative contribution to the final product. The theory thus does not apply to primitive economies with limited division of labor and limited production for profit. Nor does it apply to the socialist systems, under which the cost of the factors of production is determined by the government.*

Production methods may be determined by technological considerations (to maximize the output irrespective of cost) or by economic (to achieve the optimum relationship between the cost of the input and the market value of the output). To achieve this economic goal the entrepreneur will continue to employ additional factors of production until the marginal-revenue-product is equal to the marginal-factor-cost. He will also try to substitute one factor of production for another until the ratios between the marginal-physical-product of all factors of production in relation to the respective marginal-factor-cost are equal.

Theories of Distribution *The distribution of income may be based (1) on the notion of "to each according to his needs," (2) on the relative political power of the various factors, or (3) on the principle "to each according to his productivity." The latter forms the basis of the marginalist theory of distribution.*

The demand for factors of production is a "derived demand." Their remuneration will be determined ultimately by the price which the consumer is willing to pay for the final product. It is also a joint demand. The income of one factor of production may decline if another (joint) factor succeeds in raising its own share. Finally, the "wages" of the individual factor of production are influenced by the relative elasticity of supply and demand.

The Theory of Production

The theory of production was developed by Eugen von Boehm-Bawerk (1851–1914) and John Bates Clark (1847–1938) toward the end of the 19th Century. It is concerned with two problems, which are closely interconnected, namely: (1) How are the factors of production (raw materials, machinery, manpower, and entrepreneurial and managerial skills) to be combined to produce the greatest possible output at the lowest possible cost, and (2) how is the price of these various factors of production to be determined?

Applicability of the Theory

The theory deals with the mode of production which prevails in a developed economy in which the factors of production are largely privately owned. It assumes (1) that the production involves division of labor and round-about production methods (a portion of the factors of production is employed to produce capital goods [factories and machinery] which later on will make possible a correspondingly larger output of consumer goods); (2) that the entrepreneur strives to maximize his profits; and (3) that the factors of production are rewarded according to their respective contributions to the final product.

The theory does not apply, or only to a limited extent, to a predominantly self-sufficient household economy, with a limited division of labor and with the primary aim of satisfying the needs of the economic unit rather than earning a profit — a situation which is still widespread in many parts of the world. Nor does it apply to a socialist system, where the prices of the factors of production — and hence the cost of the final product — are determined largely by government fiat. The lack of an effective theory of production is one of the important weaknesses of the Soviet economic system as the Russians themselves have come to admit. The disregard of the notions of maximizing "profits" and of pricing the factors of production according to their relative scarcity and marginal utility, leads to an often fantastic waste.

Technological and Economic Aspects

Production planning involves both technological and economic aspects. Given a certain state of technological development, it is possible to calculate a production function, namely, the relationship between every possible combination of factors of production (the input) and the corresponding output.

An agronomist, for instance, can fairly well calculate how many bushels of wheat can be raised on a piece of land through various combinations of fertilizer, machinery and labor. An engineer can calculate even more exactly how labor, machinery and raw materials must be combined to achieve various levels of output. But while they can tell us, from a technological point of view, how to maximize the output, neither the agronomist nor the engineer are primarily concerned with production costs and profits. Yet all economic systems, whether capitalistic or socialistic, must try to achieve the optimum relationship between the *cost* of the input and the *market value* of the output.

Basic Notions of the Theory of Production

The theory of production involves two basic notions, for which the economist has developed a rather involved terminology: (1) the marginal-revenue-product versus marginal-factor-cost principle, and (2) the least-cost-substitution principle.

Let us assume that a landowner uses the same amount of land, the same quantity of seed and fertilizer, but he decides to use one additional worker. Due to the more intensive working of the land, made possible by the addition of one more man to the labor force, the output is likely to increase. This increase is known as the marginal-physical-product, and it's value in terms of dollars as the marginal-revenue-product. As long as the marginal-revenue-product is just a little larger than the cost of the additional factor of production employed to produce the marginal product (in this case the wages of the additional worker), it will pay the entrepreneur to employ the additional factor of production. We thus have the basic rule: additional factors of production will be employed until the cost of the last factor employed (the marginal factor of production) equals the marginal-revenue-product. If wages rise faster than productivity, while prices remain constant, the cost of the marginal worker will eventually rise above the marginal-revenue-product, resulting in the discharge of the worker.

Least-cost Substitution Principle The second principle of the theory of production involves the substitution of one factor of production for another, e.g., machines for labor. There are obvious technological limitations to the substitution principle. Labor may be very cheap in India and machinery may be very expensive, yet it is not possible to produce steel by substituting labor for a rolling mill. Still there are wide possibilities of substitution, and long before the principle was formulated by economists, people acted upon it. In the United States, for example, land was plentiful and cheap during the 19th Century, while manpower was scarce and expensive. American agriculture developed, therefore, along extensive lines, with a large input of relatively cheap land and capital (in the form of machines and fertilizer) and a small input of the relatively expensive farm labor. The situation is quite different in Japan, where farm labor is relatively plentiful and cheap, while good farm land is limited. Japanese agriculture is thus based on an intensive use of the land with a high input of manpower.

In order to minimize the cost of the input in relation to the value of the output, the entrepreneur must employ those factors of production which cost the least in relation to their output. It will pay him to substitute one factor of production for another until the ratios of the marginal-physical-products of all factors of production, in relation to their marginal-factor-cost, are equal, as shown in the following equation:

$$\frac{\text{Marg.-Phys.-Product of raw materials}}{\text{Marginal-factor-cost of raw materials}} = \frac{\text{Marg.-Phys.-Product of manpower}}{\text{Marginal-factor-cost of manpower}} = \frac{\text{Marg.-Phys.-Product of machinery}}{\text{Marginal-factor-cost of machinery}}$$

Translated from the lingo of the economist into the less precise everyday language, this means that it will pay the entrepreneur to substitute, let us say, machinery for labor if the output per machine (in relation to the cost of the machine) is greater than the output of labor (in relation to the cost of labor).

The Law of Diminishing Returns

A century and a half ago the famous English economist David Ricardo (1772–1823) pointed out a basic tendency which can frequently be observed in economics as well as technology and which has come to be known as the "Law of Diminishing Returns." If additional units of a factor of production (i.e., labor) are added, while the other factors of production (land, machinery, etc.) are kept constant, the total output will grow for a while at an increasing rate, but in due course the rate of increase will diminish and as still more units of the variable factor of production are added a point will eventually be reached where further additions of the variable factor will not result in a further increase in the total product. If more and more workers are employed on a given piece of land, the additional crop harvested per additional worker will eventually decline. The input of labor will rise faster than the output of wheat. A 10% increase in the labor force may result in a 12% growth of the crop, but a 20% increase in the number of workers may add only 15% to the total harvest. The same principle applies not only to agriculture, but to industry as well. It is important from a micro- as well as macroeconomic point of view.

Theories of Distribution

While the theory of production explains how the entrepreneur combines the factors of production to maximize profits, the theory of income distribution (or briefly: distribution) indicates the relative income derived by the various factors of production. Distribution, in the language of the economists, does not mean retailing, but the division of the total revenue among the factors of production. If a car brings $3000, how much of this amount will go to labor, to the suppliers of the various raw materials, to the owners of the machinery and factories, to the entrepreneur who runs the operation, etc.

During the Middle Ages the theory of distribution was based on the notion of social justice: each factor of production was supposed to be paid a "fair wage" to enable him to live according to his status in society. The approach barely met the needs of the static medieval society. It is obviously unsatisfactory in times of socio-economic upheavals, when the social status of whole classes changes within a generation and individuals are not satisfied to remain in the class, and income bracket, into which they were born.

During the past 200 years a number of attempts have been made to find a better theory. Looking at the economy from the viewpoint of labor, Karl Marx proclaimed that all value is ultimately created by labor, and hence the whole value of the final product should go to labor. This would mean, of course, the expropriation of the propertied classes, and hence the end of the supply of private investment capital. The means of production would have to be taken over by the government, which would then provide the necessary investment capital out of its general revenue.

Distribution Based on Relative Productivity

Against the expropriatory theory of Marxism, and against a system of income distribution based on political intervention, the 19th Century marginalist theory presented a solution based on the automatic forces of the market. It assumes that each factor will be paid on the basis of his relative contribution to the final product.

The demand for the factors of production is a "derived demand." As people switched from horse and buggy to the automobile, the demand for the blacksmith to shoe the horses all but disappeared. It is thus not the manufacturer who ultimately determines the demand for the factors of production, but the consumer. And it is also the consumer who ultimately fixes the reward paid to the productive factors. If the consumer does not want the final product, there is no demand for the factors of production and they will eventually become unemployed. If the consumer demand is slack in relation to the potential supply (as has been the case in the textile industry for many years) the price of the finished product will decline and the "wages" of the factors of production will be relatively low.

Joint Demand

In most instances the demand for the factors of production is a "joint demand." The factors are used in combination with each other. In order to build a house we need labor, building material and land, and the final price has to be in line with what the prospective homeowner is willing and able to pay. If the price of labor increases sharply, thus raising the total price, the demand for houses is likely to fall off, and even though the price of building materials has not changed, the demand for building materials will decline. Similarly, a sharp increase in the wages of, let us say, plumbers and bricklayers may reduce the job opportunities for carpenters, whose total income may thus decline.

According to the least-cost substitution principle, moreover, a factor of production will not be paid more than another factor which performs the same service. The income of each factor of production is thus determined by its marginal productivity in relation to the marginal productivity of all other competing factors. A dollar spent on wages must produce the same return as a dollar invested in machinery.

On the basis of this reasoning, some economists hold that even powerful unions cannot raise the workers' income beyond their marginal productivity. As the workers' income rises above their marginal productivity, they will be laid off, or replaced by machines. Actually, however, many unions, with the direct or indirect support of the government, have been able to prevent the replacement of labor by cheaper means of production. They have thus been able to raise wages above the level of the marginal productivity of labor, and of that of competing factors. The result has been an increase in the cost of the final product.

Elasticity of Demand and Supply Another element which influences the distribution of income is the relative scarcity of a given factor of production. If there are not enough bricklayers and plumbers to meet the demands of a building boom, the builders, in bidding against each other, will raise the wages of the scarce skills. If possible, they will try to shift the increased cost to the ultimate homebuyer. But if this is not possible they will try to reduce the cost of other factors of production by using cheaper building materials or calling upon the government for lower interest rates. The ultimate "wage" paid to the various factors of production will thus be affected by the relative elasticity of supply of the various factors of production and the elasticity of demand for the final product.

Chapter 23

WAGE THEORIES

THE BASIC FACTS

While there are numerous wage theories, there is none which has been generally accepted as a valid basis for determining the "proper" level of wages. Each theory reflects the prevailing socio-economic and political philosophy.

The scholastic writers of the Middle Ages held that wages should provide the worker with an adequate income to support himself and his family according to his social status. Wages were not thought to be based on either productivity or the relative scarcity of the worker's skills. The Mercantilists advocated subsistence wages in order to keep down consumption and increase exports. An export surplus made possible the acquisition of gold and silver, and thus strengthened the power of the state. The classical wage theory, while not advocating subsistence wages, assumed that wages would always tend toward the subsistence level.

According to Marxian theory the workers are entitled to a wage equal to the selling price of the final product (after allowance for maintenance and depreciation of the machinery). The theory has been extremely effective as a political weapon. It has not been useful from an economic and managerial point of view.

Two Conflicting Modern Wage Theories *At the present time, in the Western World there are two conflicting wage theories: the marginalist and the macroeconomic (or "purchase power") theory. The marginalist theory, which was developed during the last quarter of the 19th Century, is based on the two notions of productivity and scarcity. A worker's wages will not (and cannot) for any length of time exceed his productivity. An increase in wages (without a corresponding increase in productivity) will make for fewer jobs. Increased productivity and stable wages will make for more employment. The approach is essentially microeconomic and individualistic.*

The macroeconomic approach starts with the notion that full employment requires a corresponding level of consumer demand. Since the majority of the consumers are workers, wages must be adjusted so as to create enough aggregate demand to maintain full employment.

The marginalist and the macroeconomic approach to the problem of wages are often in conflict. No theory has yet been developed to reconcile the two views.

Six Different Wage Theories

There is no single, generally accepted wage theory. We shall discuss six different theories — the scholastic, mercantilistic, classical, Marxist, marginal productivity and aggregate demand theories. Each reflects the socio-economic and political philosophy of the period during which it was developed. Each has been regarded at one time or another as a valid explanation of the wage system, yet all of them are in direct conflict with each other.

The Scholastic Wage Theory

Scholasticism, the predominant philosophy of the Middle

Ages, assumed that everything in this world reflected a divine plan. Man's worldly existence was merely a transitory stage on the way to eternal life or death. His purpose in this world was to play the role assigned to him by God. A man born a serf should strive to be a loyal serf. A man born a bootmaker should try to make the best possible shoes at a reasonable price. A man born the lord of the manor should carefully fulfill his duties toward his serfs and peasants on the one hand, and to his liege lord on the other. Wages were largely determined by tradition. They were expected to provide each man with an adequate income to support himself and his family according to their social status. Individual wages (in theory at least) were not based on the productivity of the worker or the relative scarcity of his skills but on the worker's needs, which in turn were determined by the hierarchical structure of society. When there were not enough jobs, the employers — the guild masters — were bound to look after their journeymen and apprentices. They were also expected to take care of their workers when they were sick, and of the worker's descendents if the former died. Journeymen arriving in a strange city reported to the master of their guild. If there was no work, the guild would house and feed the wandering journeyman. On the other hand, if there was a scarcity of labor, workers could not use the opportunity to demand higher wages or abandon their master for a better-paying job. Each man, whether employer or employee, performed the task assigned to him by providence. This at least was the theory. In reality, employers at times exploited their workers, as they have done at all times. And during periods of labor shortage, such as after the Black Death of the 14th Century, during which millions perished, workers tried to obtain higher wages and abandoned their masters for better jobs. As early as the 12th Century, pitched battles were fought in the textile centers of Flanders between the workers and the forces of the employers.

The Mercantilist Wage Theory

The snug little world of the Middle Ages gave way, in the 16th and 17th Centuries to the modern nation state (with its large empires, and its increasingly impersonal employer-employee relationship). A new theory of wages developed which formed an integral part of the new political order.

It was a time of great social, economic and intellectual unrest, and without a strong state to protect him, man's life was likely to be "solitary, poor, nasty, brutish and short." It was thus in the interest of the individual to strengthen the state, and in order to perform its many functions, the state in turn needed military might and a powerful navy, as well as many government and court officials. This required money in the form of gold and silver (because specie was in those days the only generally accepted form of money). Those nations whose colonies produced few precious metals, including England, France and the Netherlands, had to export more than they imported, in order to be able to collect the difference in the form of specie. In order to achieve an export surplus, domestic prices and domestic consumption had to be kept low to make more goods at a low price available for exports, and since the cost of production consisted chiefly of wages, these had to be kept as low as possible. While the scholastic wage theory demanded a "fair wage," in accordance with the prevailing social order, the mercantilist theory called for "subsistence wages" for the masses in order to strengthen the state.

The Classical Wage Theory

As the overall political philosophy changed toward the end of the 18th Century, mercantilist ideas gave way to the theories of the classical English school. The two key figures in the development of the classical wage theory were Thomas Malthus

(1766–1834) and David Ricardo (1772–1823). We mentioned Malthus' population theory in Chapter 3. It was based on a belief (widespread at the time, and probably true in some areas, as it is true in some areas today) that the population was increasing more rapidly than the food supply, so that some of the people would always subsist at the fringe of starvation. It was on this population theory that the classical economists built their wage theory. Wages, it was assumed, could never rise for any length of time above the subsistence level. If the income of a worker increased he was able to provide better for his family. More children survived infancy and grew to become workers. And as more and more workers clamored for a limited number of jobs, wages would decline again to their "natural," i.e., subsistence level. As Ricardo put it: "The natural price of labour is that price (wage) which is necessary to enable the labourers, one with another, to subsist and to perpetuate their race, without either increase or diminution."

The Marxian Theory of Wages

While the classical wage theory provided arguments for the entrepreneurial bourgeoisie, the Marxian doctrine furnished ammunition for the wage earners. Karl Marx (1818–1883), a keen but biased intellectual, seized on one of the weakest notions of the classical theory and proceeded to build upon it a towering superstructure of political and economic ideas.

Marx attempted to show that the political, economic and social system of his time was based on the exploitation of the workers by the employers, of the many by the few. He used the writings of the classical economists as the starting point for his arguments. Adam Smith had spoken of labor as "the real measure of the exchangeable value of all commodities." "Labour," he wrote, "was the first price, the original purchase-money, that was paid for all things." And David Ricardo had concluded that "the value of a commodity, or the quantity of any other commodity for which it will exchange, depends on the relative quantity of labour which is necessary for its production." Seizing on quotations of this type, Marx tried to show that even the classical economists, who were generally accepted as the spokesmen of the entrepreneurial and propertied classes, agreed that labor was the source of all value. Since the wages paid to labor were admittedly less than the final sales price of a product, Marx argued that the workers were being robbed of part of the income due to them. His aim was the "expropriation of the expropriators."

Public Ownership of the Means of Production Marx realized, of course, that the owners of the raw material and machinery used in the production of goods had somehow contributed to the final product, and might thus be entitled to a part of the proceeds. He eliminated this potential argument against his theory by demanding that all land and capital goods be taken over by society. If these means of production belonged to "the people," and the people in turn were the workers, it seemed perfectly reasonable that the entire proceeds (after the necessary depreciation and other reserves had been set aside) be turned over to the workers in the form of wages.

The Marginalist Theory of Wages

The marginalist theory of wages was the first "scientific" wage theory. It tried to explain why a skilled worker may receive $5 an hour and an unskilled farm hand only $1; why the head of a large concern is paid $100,000 and a clerk in his office only $8000; why wages are higher in the United States than in Europe, and 10 times as high as in parts of Asia.

The demand for labor is a derived demand. It depends on the demand for the finished product. The quantity of goods demanded by the consumer, in turn, is largely determined by their price. Since the price of the finished goods depends, in the long run, on the cost of production (including wages) the volume of goods sold (and hence the number of available jobs) depends, at least in part, on the wage cost. (This presupposed, of course, that the demand schedule is not changed through changes in the volume of purchasing power.)

FIGURE 16 ***Supply of and Demand for Labor***

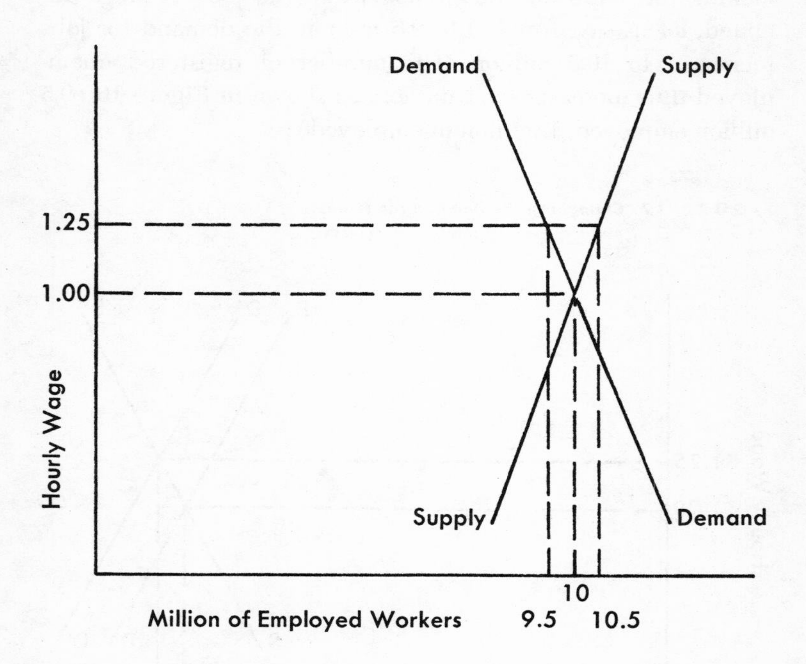

Let us assume that there are job-openings for 10 million unskilled workers at $1 an hour, because a corresponding amount of goods (which the workers produce) can be sold on the basis of existing prices. If the government raises the minimum wage from $1 to $1.25, the production costs will go up (even allowing for the fact that the productivity of the workers might increase somewhat). The chances are that the prices will go up also. With an increase in prices, according to traditional theory, demand will decline. With fewer goods demanded, the production of goods will decline, and fewer workers will be needed. Yet at the same time marginal workers, such as housewives, who were not interested in working for $1 an hour, are now looking for a job at $1.25. Thus while the job openings declined, let us say, from 10 to 9.5 million, the demand for jobs increased to 10.5 million. The number of registered unemployed thus increases by 1 million, as shown in Figure 16 (9.5 million employed, 1 million unemployed):

FIGURE 17 *Changes in the Demand for Workers*

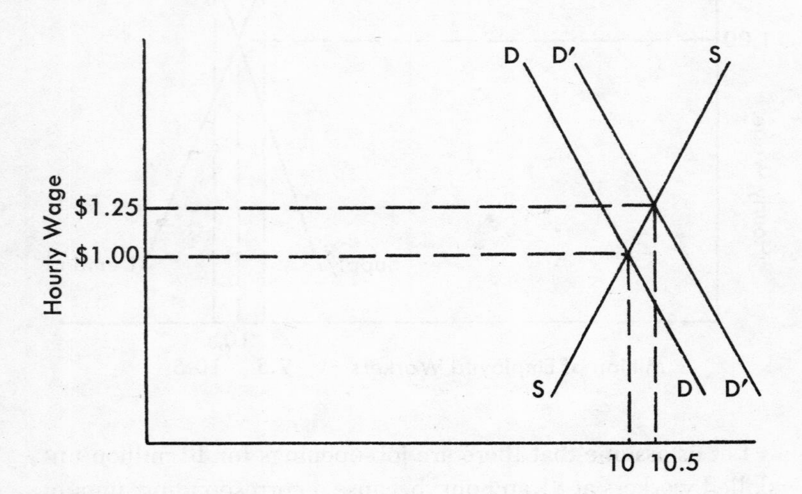

Wage Cost and the Rate of Employment

In order to restore the equilibrium in the labor market, i.e., to create jobs for the one million unemployed, we can either increase the demand for labor (see Figure 17) through public works or subsidized exports (shift the demand curve from DD to D′D′), or we can in effect reduce the supply of labor by shortening the work week from, let us say, 40 to 35 hours. Either method will do away with the unemployment — at least for the moment. But if a nation chooses to increase the demand for labor by employing workers on government projects, either taxes will have to be increased, or the government has to increase the supply of money. Such an artificial expansion of demand would result in a general advance in prices, and thus the partial expropriation of fixed income groups. A reduction in the supply of labor through a shortening of the work week can produce two results: (1) if the *hourly* wages remain the same, the regularly employed workers, whose work week has been reduced from 40 to 35 hours, will suffer a corresponding reduction in total income. The equivalent of this loss suffered by one group of workers would be shifted to the formerly unemployed who are now given jobs. Or (2), (and this is what the unions demand) if the *weekly* take-home pay remains the same (even though the work-week has been reduced from 40 to 35 hours), the "spreading the work" scheme would mean, in effect, a 12½% wage increase, which would be reflected in higher prices for the finished product. Higher prices, in turn, would result in a decrease in demand, leading to more unemployment. Even if government intervention and public pressure should prevent an increase in prices, this might not prevent the decrease in employment opportunities. As wages rise (without a corresponding increase in productivity) profits will decline, marginal plants will be closed, new investments reduced, and investment funds will be transferred abroad in search of greener pastures.

In short, just as there is an equilibrium price for coal and cabbage — namely, a price level at which all the coal and cabbage produced is purchased by the consumer — there is an equilibrium wage for labor. If wages rise above this level, demand for labor will decline and workers will become unemployed. Conversely, if labor cost declines in relation to output, more workers will be employed and unemployment will decline.

Wage Rates, the Result of Supply and Demand

The wide differences in income between, let us say, the president of a corporation and a worker at the assembly line, is due to the scarcity of certain skills. Even top corporate officials, however, are subject to the laws of supply and demand. Their value to a corporation is determined by their ability to increase corporate profits. A man is worth $100,000 to the stockholders if his ideas result in a more than $100,000 increase in net profits. On the other hand, an executive who fails to show profits may not be worth $25,000.

Wage Levels Determined by the Availability of Machinery

The large wage differentials between countries is due to the relative scarcity or abundance of labor — in relation to the supply of other factors of production.

Raw materials, machinery and labor are needed to produce a final product. In the United States more than 95% of all the power produced is inanimate power. A man driving a truck, or operating a steam shovel or a huge crane, controls productive power equal to hundreds of human beings. As mechanization and the use of inanimate power (electricity, gas, combustion engines, etc.) increase in other countries, foreign wage levels are likely to rise. The important question from the American point of view is whether they will rise faster or more slowly than productivity. If foreign wages rise more slowly than productivity, the competitive position of the United States will suffer in world markets. Whether this has been the case in recent years, and whether this is one of the reasons for the American balance of payments difficulties are much debated questions.

Institutional Obstacles

The marginalist theory of wages, which we have just discussed and which assumes that wages are determined by the relative scarcity and productivity of labor is still extremely helpful in explaining present-day developments, even though some of the basic assumptions on which the theory rests are admittedly unrealistic. The theory assumes perfect competition in the labor market, i.e. no interference by the government, unions or employers with the supply of and demand for labor, with wages and working conditions. It also assumes that workers can move freely from one job to another, and from one city to another, to take advantage of better job opportunities; and that the employer is free to discharge workers who are no longer needed. None of these assumptions holds true today. The government interferes with wages and working conditions by fixing minimum wages and working hours; unions insist on uniform wages and work norms, even though some workers may deserve higher and others lower pay; and employers tried at least in the past to control working conditions by controlling the demand for labor through close cooperation with other employers. Company pension systems and seniority rules make it difficult for a worker to move from one company to another, and the fact that he owns his home and has established social ties within the community militates against his moving to another part of the country; otherwise all the workers in Mississippi and North Carolina, where the average hourly wages were $1.64 in 1962, would be migrating to the State of Washington, where average hourly wages were $2.81. Nor is the employer always free to discharge workers who are no longer needed.

Purchase Power Theory of Wages

The theory which assumes that wages are determined — and should be determined — by the relative scarcity and productivity of labor is rejected today by many moralists, sociologists, politicians and economists for a variety of reasons. We are interested here only in the economic arguments.

The marginalist wage theory accepted, in the spirit of the 19th Century, a wide difference in income as a natural reflection of the basic inequality of man, his productive capacity, and the relative scarcity of his skills. Since then, the socio-political philosophy has undergone far-reaching changes, and the United States as well as Europe have come to favor a much greater degree of economic equality for social, political and economic reasons. In the eyes of the sociologist, crime, juvenile delinquency, disease, ignorance, and hence chronic unemployment are largely the result of poverty. The politician has discovered that the households classified by the government as "poverty-stricken," i.e. families with an income of less than $3000, comprise some 9 million voters. The modern economist, finally, believes that full employment cannot be maintained without steadily rising wages.

Given a certain state of technological development, a certain number of workers, and the prevailing cost of the factors of production, it is possible to calculate the value of the total output of goods and services on basis of the full employment of the factors of production. Let us assume that the value of the total output is $600 billion. In order to maintain full employment, the agregate demand must also be $600 billion.

The 19th Century assumed that the prices of the factors of production, including wages, were the result of a derived demand, determined by the ultimate demand for the finished product, so that a decline in the demand for finished goods led to a decline in the payments made to the factors of production. Modern economic theory, on the other hand, assumes the total value of the aggregate output at the full employment level as given, and it sees the key to full employment in the maintenance of what might be called a full employment level of aggregate demands; i.e. in our example of $600 billion.

This demand will come primarily from the great mass of consumers who are wage earners. Seventy percent of the national income consists of wages and salaries. Hence, in order to maintain mass consumption, the income of the worker/consumer must be maintained at a level high enough to assure the necessary demand for all the goods which can be produced at the full employment level. Wage rates must thus be determined by macroeconomic considerations (the maintenance of an adequate aggregate purchasing power) rather than by microeconomic (the relative scarcity and productivity of the individual worker).

The new aggregate approach to the theory of wages has led to the establishment of minimum wages and maximum hours, and the arguments of union leaders that wages must be steadily raised to provide additional aggregate purchasing power; that workers, even though no longer needed, must not be laid off, because of the effect which the decrease in their purchasing power will have on the aggregate demand; that the unemployed must be given enough purchasing power in the form of unemployment and supplementary unemployment benefits, so that they can continue to maintain their rate of consumption.

The modern aggregate income theory of wages with its emphasis on the maintenance of aggregate purchasing power is thus radically different from the traditional marginalist approach with its emphasis on the marginal productivity of the individual worker.

Chapter 24

THE CHANGING ROLE OF INTEREST

THE BASIC FACTS

For 4000 years the taking of interest was condemned as asocial, unethical and unnatural. This opposition to interest taking was due to a failure to understand the nature of capital (as a factor of production) and of interest (as its price). Interest taking did not become generally accepted until the early 19th Century, and ancient prejudices still affect subconscious ideas even in the United States.

Justification of Interest *Various arguments were developed to justify the taking of interest. As early as the 14th Century it was pointed out that capital (like any other factor of production) is entitled to its "wage" (a fact which the Romans had recognized in ancient times).*

Equilibrium Theory of Interest *The 19th Century theorists looked upon interest as an equilibrating mechanism which (1) regulated the rate of consumption and savings and (2) brought savings and investments into balance. There are many institutional factors which interfere with this equilibrating mechanism, but the basic forces continue to operate.*

Interest Rates as a Tool of Monetary Policy *Modern economic theory sees in interest rates a tool which can be used by the economic planner to regulate investments and consumption (and thus indirectly employment). Past experiences at home and abroad, however, do not justify the belief that business activities are primarily affected by interest rates. Monetary management, moreover, is hampered by the fact that it is difficult to predict the impact of a multitude of other variables (other than interest rates) and that changes in interest rates can have adverse effects on the balance of payments.*

The Sins of Usury

"Usury," the taking of interest at whatever rate, has been condemned since the days of the Sumerian king Ur-Nammu, who lived more than 2000 years before Christ. His code of law, which formed part of his social and economic "New Deal," is the oldest written expression of economic thought which has come down to us. It had a profound influence on the better known code of the Babylonian king Hammurabi, which was copied in part, at times almost literally, by the writers of the Old Testament. The latter in turn influenced the writers of the New Testament, and thus Christian thought, for almost 2000 years. The medieval opposition to usury, which still affected American business practices at the time of Washington and Jefferson, thus had a very long ancestry. Yet, even though lawgivers and moralists, businessmen and jurists discussed and condemned usury for about 4000 years, none of them seem to have been able to explain why a practice persisted which had been denounced as immoral and unnatural, and often had been subject to severe penalties. The reason was undoubtedly that man never fully understood the economic nature of interest payments.

Usury Theories throughout History

In the Old Testament (Deuteronomy XXIII, 19/20) the Jews were told that they should "not lend upon usury to thy brother . . . ," although "unto a stranger you mayest lend upon usury." The distinction between "brother" and "stranger," which marks the laws as a social measure rather than an ethical commandment, had far-reaching effects during the Middle Ages. While Christians were not permitted to collect interest from fellow Christians, their brothers, Jews could collect interest from Christians because they were "strangers" to them, which is one of the reasons that Jews played such an important role as money lenders and bankers.

In his "Politics," which was used as a textbook in the social sciences throughout Europe for almost 2000 years, the Greek philosopher Aristotle pointed out that the Greek word "tokos" has a double meaning: off-spring and interest; and he thought that it was obviously "unnatural" (and hence immoral) to expect a piece of "barren metal" to breed young.

The Roman Law added to the confusion of the medieval Christian theory of interest. The Romans accepted the taking of "usuria" (interest) as a normal business practice, even though the government from time to time fixed maximum interest rates. But Roman Law often referred to interest as "fructus" (fruit) and it classified money as a consumable (as against a nonconsumable) good. If a farmer borrows 10 bushels of seed grain, he is expected to return another (not the same) 10 bushels of the same grade, because grain is a "consumable good." On the other hand, if a man rents a house he is expected to return the same house to the owner, because a house is not a consumable good. The Roman legal classification of money as a "consumable good" was thus perfectly logical. It is still followed in modern law. The medieval writers, however, argued as follows: if money is "consumed" as it is spent by the borrower, it does no longer exist. How then can this money produce "fruit" (interest). Hence interest was obviously "unnatural" and thus against the laws of God.

It was this type of theorizing which limited interest payments and thus indirectly the use of borrowed capital for more than a thousand years and hampered economic development. While the anti-usury laws were increasingly widely circumvented, certainly after the 13th Century, and ever new loopholes were found which enabled businessmen to collect and pay interest without formally violating existing laws, "usury" remained an important issue throughout the 17th Century, in Catholic Spain as well as Protestant England. Interest-taking did not become legal in France until the French Revolution. During the Napoleonic Wars changes in the discount rate of the Bank of England were still governed by usury laws. To this day subconscious attitudes, acquired over thousands of years, continue to color people's outlook. This is true not only in Moslem and in some of the predominantly Catholic countries, but one can readily discover traces of the ancient attitude even in the United States.

Arguments to Justify Interest

The economist is thus confronted with a dual task: (1) He must produce reasons why interest charges (which had been condemned for thousands of years as asocial, unethical and unnatural) are actually justified, and (2) as an analytical scientist, he must discover the forces which determine the level of interest rates. A number of arguments have been presented to justify interest charges.

Capital a Factor of Production

The most logical explanation of interest, which the Scholastic writers of the 14th Century already fully understood, is based on the realization that capital, just as other factors of production, is "productive." If a manufacturer borrows $100,000 to build an addition to his plant, he does so in the anticipation of increasing his profits by, let us say, $10,000. It would thus be only fair that he should share his additional income with the man who made it possible by lending him the $100,000.

Reward for Abstinence

An argument which is not highly regarded today, but seemed particularly logical during the 19th Century, was the so-called "reward for abstinence" theory. In order to be able to lend money, an individual must first of all save part of his income by "abstaining" from consumption. As the 19th Century economists saw it, here was a man standing before a shop window wrestling with himself whether or not to buy a pair of shoes. If he bought the shoes he would not have the $10 to lend to his neighbor, who wanted to enlarge his shop. The expectation of interest would obviously make it easier for the potential buyer to "abstain," and thus provide the needed working capital for the neighbor.

"Time Preference" Theory

A somewhat more sophisticated version of the "abstinence" argument is the "time preference" theory, which became popular toward the latter part of the 19th Century, when psychology began to play an increasingly important role in economic thought. Most human beings, according to this explanation, prefer present over future consumption. In order to induce a man to defer consumption by saving part of his income, he must be paid for the difference between the satisfaction which he derives from present consumption and the smaller value he places on future consumption.

"Liquidity Preference" Theory

Keynes himself added another explanation of interest. All people, he argued, prefer to hold their assets in more rather than less liquid form: in cash and demand deposits, which they know they can use whenever they wish, rather than in bonds which may have to be sold at a loss. Hence, in order to induce people to give up their liquidity, and to invest their money, they will have to be paid a compensation in the form of interest.

The Equilibrium Theory of Interest

All these explanations of interest tell us *why* some people feel that they are entitled to interest payments and others are willing to make such payments. The various explanations, however, tell us nothing about the forces which determine interest rates. This second step was not reached until the end of the 19th Century, when economists developed a theory of interest which made interest an integral part of the general theory of equilibrium. Interest rates are affected by a large variety of factors and in turn affect virtually all other aspects of the economy. In particular, interest rates perform an automatic dual balancing function: (1) They regulate consumption and savings, and (2) they balance savings and investments. Whether we employ the "abstinence" or the "time preference" argument, people demand a premium for non-consumption, namely, interest on their savings. If interest rates rise there is a greater inducement to save more and consume less; conversely, if interest rates decline, savings are likely to be smaller and consumption can be expected to increase. The entrepreneur, on the other hand, is likely to borrow more money if interest rates are low, and he will borrow less if they are high. Interest rates thus determine both the supply of and the demand for savings. They will tend toward an equilibrium level, where all available savings will be absorbed by investments.

Equilibrium Involving Many Factors

The level of interest rates is the result of many factors which influence the supply of and demand for capital.

In order for interest rates to be low, the supply of capital must be ample in relation to the demand. This requires that savings will have to be high (unless investment capital is created artifically by the government through fiscal and monetary policies). A high rate of savings, however, implies a relatively low rate of consumption, hence less demand for goods and services. While low interest rates should stimulate investments, the likely concomitant of low interest rates, a relatively low rate of consumption, discourages investments.

Consumption can be stimulated by increasing mass purchasing power. Since more than 70% of the disposable income consists of wages, a logical way to stimulate consumption (and hence investments) would be to increase wages while holding down interest rates. But investments depend not only upon the level of interest rates. They depend on total production cost, and even a minor increase in wages (designed to stimulate demand) can more than off-set a substantial reduction in interest rates.

The 19th Century, with its faith in the self-equilibrating forces of the market, relied upon the automatic forces of supply and demand to achieve that level of interest rates which would result in the most effective use of all factors of production. The 20th Century, which has lost much of this faith, attempts to achieve the same results, at least in part, by manipulating interest rates. The role of interest has thus changed from being considered as an automatic self-equilibrating mechanism, into being regarded as a tool to achieve certain goals, such as full employment and maximum economic growth.

Interest Rates as a Tool of Economic Planning

The modern theory rests upon the assumption that low interest rates stimulate (1) capital investments and (2) consumer spending for durable goods and home construction. Low interest rates are thus regarded as an important tool to achieve and maintain "full employment." Actually, the theory is valid only on basis of certain assumptions. The cost of production is determined by many factors of which interest charges, as a rule, is a relatively minor one. And home construction and consumer purchases of durables are likewise determined by numerous other factors in addition to interest rates. The sensational recoveries of postwar Germany and Japan were not seriously hampered by the fact that interest rates ranged from 7% to 10%, while the postwar recovery of Britain, where interest rates were much lower, was materially slower. The sharp decline of interest rates in the United States during the 1930's did not end the great Depression, nor did the substantial increase in interest rates during the 1950's and 1960's end the postwar boom.

Yet, even though changes in interest rates do not necessarily result in changes in economic activities, low interest rates tend to stimulate and high interest rates to retard business, and these tendencies are used by economic planners by increasing or decreasing the supply of money.

Interest Rates and Capital Formation

Whether the level of interest rates has a decisive effect on capital formation is another point of disagreement between 19th and 20th Century economists. The former held that the rate of savings is influenced by the prevailing rate of interest. Modern economists, on the other hand, believe that the volume of savings is controlled primarily by institutional rather than monetary factors. The rate of individual savings has declined slowly since the late 1940's from about 8% to less than 5% of the Disposable Income in 1966, despite the fact that interest rates in 1966 reached the highest level since 1930. People save by paying their life insurance premiums, by buying government savings bonds under a payroll deduction plan, by making monthly payments on their mortgage, and so forth. The prevailing level of interest rates seems to have little effect. And the very wealthy, who cannot possibly consume their entire income, will save whether interest rates are high or low.

Interest rates, however, continue to affect the flow of capital. The Savings and Loan Associations, which for years have rivaled with each other in paying higher and higher interest rates (substantially higher than what commercial banks were allowed to pay on their time deposits) were able to increase their total assets by 450% between 1950 and 1962, while the time deposits in commercial banks increased by only 170%. After the commercial banks were finally permitted to increase their interest payments on time deposits, the latter increased rapidly from $97 billion in 1962 to almost $150 billion in 1965. There are also indications that at least some people refuse to buy 3% goverment securities (on which, until 1964, they had to pay a minimum tax of 20%, thus reducing the net return to 2.4%) when the cost of living increases by 2½% a year. Chronic creeping inflation calls for correspondingly higher interest rates. The attempt to hold down interest rates through an easy credit policy, which leads to a slow but chronic depreciation of the currency, is thus in the end self-defeating. Creeping inflation makes for higher interest rates.

Chapter 25

THE THEORY OF RENT

THE BASIC FACTS

Rent (also referred to as "economic rent") is the price which is paid for the use of land and other natural resources. It must not be confused with the "contractual rent" which a tenant pays to his landlord.

From the point of view of the individual businessman, rent is "price-determining." It represents part of the overall cost. From a general economic point of view, on the other hand, rent (according to the Ricardian theory) is "price-determined." Rent is the difference between the income obtained from a superior piece of land and the income derived from the least productive land which is still being used.

The marginalist school rejected this notion of "differential rent." Instead, it treated land like the other factors of production, capital and labor. The use (and the price) of land was determined by its relative productivity in relation to the productivity of the other factors of production.

The marginalist rent theory has not diminished the appeal of the so-called "rent socialists," who base their arguments largely on the Ricardian notion of "unearned monopoly profits."

A practical application of the theory of the "rent socialists" (the name is largely a misnomer) to the system of real estate taxes is the use of different tax rates for land and for improve-

ments. There is some evidence that such a tax system stimulates real estate improvements, and at the same time captures for society part of the "unearned profits" resulting from increased land values.

Definition of Terms

Economists use the term "rent" somewhat differently from the way in which it is used in everyday language. We pay a rental fee when we hire a car, and we pay rent to the landlord for an apartment. Both rental payments are made in accordance with a (written or verbal) contract. We therefore speak of "contractual rent."

Economists are interested in a different type of rent which may be called "economic rent," namely, the income which is derived from land and other forms of natural resources.

Classical Theory of Rent

The theory of rent played a far more important role in economic theory during the 19th Century than it does today. This was due to the fact that the classical economists saw a fundamental difference between land on the one hand, and the other factors of production on the other. While additional land may be gained through irrigation, drainage and land reclamation, and some land is lost through erosion, for all practical purposes the supply of land appeared constant. The supply of labor and capital, on the other hand, increased steadily. Higher interest rates produced an increase in the rate of savings. Higher wages attracted more workers. An increase in rent, however, did not result in a greater overall supply of land. It was on this basic distinction that the classical school built its theory of rent and, indirectly, its entire theory of distribution.

The cost of labor and capital is determined by supply and

demand. Changes in the cost of land, on the other hand (certainly in the case of settled countries without "free land") is determined only by demand. And changes in demand for land, in turn, are largely the result of an increase or decrease in population. Had the classical economists lived at the westward-moving Frontier instead of in England (where virtually all the land was publicly or privately owned) they would probably have been more impressed with the seemingly unlimited supply of "free" land, rather than the fact that the supply of land was apparently constant, and they might have developed a different theory of rent.

The Philosophic Justification of Rent

There are two schools of thought regarding the basis of rent. One looks on rent as the result of the bountifulness of nature; and the other, as the result of its niggardliness. Which of the two ideas predominates at a given time depends largely upon the prevailing intellectual climate.

In the 18th Century, under the impact of the Enlightenment, when man looked upon his surroundings as potentially "the best of all worlds," a group of French philosopher-economists, the Physiocrats, argued that God had arranged the world in such a way that nature provided a surplus. The farmer produced more food and fiber than he needed for his own sustenance, thus making it possible for some members of society to devote themselves to industrial and cultural pursuits and the general advancement of mankind. In fact as the Physiocrats saw it, nature (i.e., agriculture) alone produces a "net product," a surplus, while industry and commerce merely convert or transfer existing wealth. Rent in the eyes of the Physiocrats, was thus the result of the bountifulness of nature. This God-given bounty, they reasoned, should be used, in part, to support the institutions of society, through a single tax to be paid by the owner of the land.

Half a century later, with the French Revolution and the long Napoleonic Wars still a vivid memory, the people were less convinced that man lived in "the best of all worlds." And in the spirit of the time, the classical economists, most important among them David Ricardo (1772–1823), developed a theory of rent based on the notion of the niggardliness of nature. If there were enough good land available, they argued correctly, nobody would pay rent. The classical-Ricardian philosophy of scarcity, rather than the Physiocratic notion of plenty, became the basis of the 19th Century theory of rent.

Price-determined or Price-determining

From the point of view of the individual farmer or businessman, rent represents part of their operating expenses, just as wages and interest. It is recognized as such by the Bureau of Internal Revenue. Rent is thus "price-determining."

From the point of view of the economy as a whole, however, rent is "price-determined." No farmer or businessman will pay a higher rent than the land will produce in ultimate revenue. While the same principle applies to wages and interest, there is one significant difference. If wages increase, the supply of labor will increase also, and the same holds true of interest and capital. While largely determined by the demand for the final product, wages and interest rates are, in addition, also affected by the changing supply. With the supply of land constant, on the other hand, rent is completely "price-determined," namely, by the price which the public is willing to pay for the final product.

Differential Rent Starting with the basic assumption that the supply of land is constant, while the demand increases as the population grows, the classical economists developed the notion of "differential rent." Given a population with a more or less fixed demand for food and fiber, a certain amount of land will be needed. It may be assumed that the farmer will use that portion of the available land which will enable him to produce the required food and fiber most cheaply. The land may be either the most fertile, the most conveniently located so far as the markets are concerned, or it may represent the best possible combination of fertility and location. As the population grows, or the existing population demands more food, additional land will have to be employed and the cost of production on this additional land will be higher, since the best land was used first.

For theoretical purposes, economists assume that the rental value of the poorest land will be zero. It will certainly be very small in relation to the investment in labor, fertilizer and machinery.

Let us assume that a farmer spends $200 per acre on labor, fertilizer and machinery. His best land produces crops worth $300 per acre; his poorest, $201. The best land then yields an economic rent of $100 ($300 minus $200) and the poorest, of $1. Rent is thus exactly equal to the difference in productivity between a given piece of superior land and the poorest land still being used. Rent only appears, to quote Ricardo, "when the progress of population calls into cultivation land of an inferior quality and less advantageously situated." It does not enter in the calculation of the cost of production, either in the case of good land, which yields a high rent, or in the case of marginal land, which yields virtually no rent.

Marginilist Rent Theory

The marginalist writers, chiefly the Austrian school of the 1870's and 1880's, and Leon Walras (1834–1910), rejected the classical theory of a differential rent. Instead, they treated land and natural resources in the same way as labor and capital. In other words, they chose to disregard the aspect (that the total supply of land is "price-inelastic") which formed the basis of the Ricardian rent theory. Rent was determined by the "marginal utility" of the land. If land was relatively cheap, it was used extensively (e.g., by constructing only one-story buildings). If land was dear, tall buildings would be erected. The relative marginal cost of land (rent) and of capital (interest) thus determined the use of the land.

The new theory, however, failed to replace the Ricardian ideas. Joseph A. Schumpeter blamed "irrational sentiments" for this fact: "An emotional resistance to a theory that seemed to treat the landlords 'unearned incomes' on the same plane with the workman's compensation for the sweat of his brow." Pure theorists, such as Alfred Marshall, continued to defend the Ricardian ideas.

Changes in Real Estate Taxes

For well over a hundred years a minority of economists in this country and Europe, including the highly respected English economist John Stuart Mill and the American social reformer Henry George (1839–1897), have argued that the "unearned increment" of rising land values should be captured for society, which has earned them the name of "Rent Socialists."

In most parts of the world, urban real estate taxes are levied at a flat rate on both land and improvements. Some economists argue that this is unsound. Different rates should apply to land and to improvements, with the land being taxed considerably more heavily than the improvements. Let us assume that a house is assessed at $18,000 and the lot at $7,000, and that the tax rate is 2%. The total annual tax would thus be $500. Any improvements which the owner of the house makes would be taxed at the same 2% rate. An additional room assessed at $2000 would add $40 to the tax bill. Now let us assume that the house and all future improvements were taxed at only 1%; the land, on the other hand, at 4½%. The total payable by the homeowner would thus be about the same ($180 for the house plus $315 for the land). But if he now added the additional room to the house, the tax would increase by only $20 rather than $40.

A lower tax rate on improvements could be expected to stimulate improvements, particularly in slum areas, where the present tax system places an added burden on the property owner who improves his buildings.

On the other hand, if the land value should increase by, let us say, 50% (from $7,000 to $10,500), which is not unusual in rapidly growing suburban areas, the tax on the land would increase to $472.50. This would raise the total tax from $570 (on the basis of a flat rate of 2%) to $652.50 (on the basis of differentiated tax rates). The increase in taxes would be particularly heavy in the case of unimproved land held off the market to be developed as the community grows. In most instances a differentiated tax would not only tend to encourage improvements and thus combat the growth of slums, but would also discourage the speculative withholding of land, and would thus tend to hold down land prices.

The system has been used with considerable success in Pittsburgh and other cities in Pennsylvania, as well as in Sydney, Australia.

Chapter 26

PROFIT AS A DYNAMIC FORCE

THE BASIC FACTS

There is no satisfactory way of defining profits or to express the "proper rate" of profits in quantitative terms. A rate which may be adequate or even exorbitant under some circumstances may be quite inadequate if the risk is great and the supply of investment capital limited.

For thousands of years people have failed to recognize the nature and role of profits as the reward of the entrepreneur for his efforts (just as a worker is paid his wages) and as an incentive for risk-taking.

Profits in Economic Theory *Classical economists looked upon profits as the residue after the payment of all operating expenses. An increase in wages or rent thus tended to diminish profits. This implied an inherent conflict between the interest of the wage-earner and the entrepreneur.*

The marginalist school rejected this notion of conflict. It suggested, instead, that in a free economy the forces of supply and demand would determine wages as well as profits. It was not the entrepreneur who determined either, but the impersonal forces of the market.

There exists at present no satisfactory theory of profits ap-

plicable to the modern mixed economy. The private sector continues to be governed largely by the forces of supply and demand and the "profit motive," while the public sector is governed predominantly by other considerations.

Profits as a Basis for Economic Planning *The mixed economy has a great advantage over a completely socialistic economy, as in Russia, in that the public sector can build upon the price structure which has developed in the private sector through the interplay of supply and demand. In Russia, where virtually no free market exists for either factors of production or finished products, the price structure has to be determined by government fiat, which hampers (or makes impossible, as some believe) the most efficient allocation of resources.*

Profits as a Dynamic Force *In a predominantly free enterprise economy, the profit motive serves as the dynamic force which induces risk-taking and thus promotes employment and economic growth. Past experience has not shown that this striving of the individual to better himself can be replaced successfully by centralized social and economic planning.*

What are Profits?

The profit motive, the desire for personal gain, is one of the most important forces in a free enterprise economy — and one of the least understood. The notion involves the usual semantic difficulties: the lack of a precise definition, and strong emotional overtones. The implications of the concept are quite different, depending upon whether the term is used (1) from an ethical or pseudo-ethical point of view; (2) as part of the traditional 19th Century economic theory; (3) as the basis of rational business calculations, or (4) to describe the dynamic force which makes for progress in a free society.

It is very simple to say that profits represent the excess of income over expenditures in a business transaction. If a merchant pays $1 for a pair of stockings and sells them for $1.50, his "gross profit" is 50%. But from this gross profit must be deducted the cost of selling the stockings: rent, wages, light and administrative overhead, which, let us say, total 44¢. The "net profit" would thus be only 6%. On this net profit the merchant has to pay income taxes. If the business is a corporation and corporate income taxes amount to 50%, the "net after taxes" would be 3%. What then is the merchant's actual "profit": 50%, 6%, or 3%? Now let us say the merchant turns over his inventory three times a year, each time earning a "net after taxes" of 3%. The annual return on his invested capital would thus be 9%, which is the usual way in which a business expresses its profits and losses.

"Profits" and the Rate of Depreciation There are other complications. Let us assume (to return to our first example) that the 44¢ in general expenditures per pair of stockings sold include 7 cents set aside as an allowance for the depreciation of the building and fixtures. In order to show a bigger "profit," the company could reduce the depreciation allowance to 6 cents. The "net profit" would then increase to 7%, and the "net after taxes" to 3½% — a substantial gain in the rate of "profit" through a change in the depreciation allowance. For tax purposes, the rates of depreciation and depletion are fixed by law. These legal rates, however, may be either too high or too low, so that the rate of profit may be artificially depressed or raised. During a period of chronic inflation (even if prices increase by only 2% a year) a businessman will have to pay materially

more in 1975 for the same machinery for which he paid $10,000 in 1965. A depreciation allowance based on $10,000, or $1,000 a year, thus will not suffice to replace the worn out machinery after 10 years. To the extent that the depreciation was inadequate to replace the machines, the profits during the 10-year period were overstated. If they were paid out in full in the form of dividends, the net worth of the company in 1975 would be less than it was in 1965.

Profits and the Degree of Risk In short, it is misleading to speak of "profits," even in a strict accounting sense, without specifying whether we refer to gross or net profits, or to "net after taxes." From the point of view of the economist, the level of profits has to be related to the general economic environment. A 5% "net after taxes" may be a generous return for a well-established company in a period of declining prices, while a 10% profit might be inadequate under conditions of rapidly rising prices and in a country subject to a great deal of political unrest. Assuming price stability, and a return of 5% on government bonds, the rate of profit on a business investment (net after taxes) with an average rate of risk, would have to be about 10%, according to a long accepted rule of thumb. It is thus not surprising that in underdeveloped countries, where the government has to pay 8% or more, and business ventures are subject to many unpredictable risks, the rate of return must be in the neighborhood of 16–20% to attract capital. This is not a sign of usury or of the exploitation of the people by rapacious capitalists, but the result of the relative scarcity of investment funds and the considerable danger of loss involved.

"Opportunity Cost" and Rate of Profits Another factor, which is often overlooked, involves what economists call "opportunity cost." A man with the necessary training and ability

who can get a $15,000 teaching job with little or no risk involved, has an "opportunity" to earn $15,000. But he decides to go into business instead. This requires a capital investment of $100,000, on which the investor could earn 5% ($5,000), if he made a first mortgage loan. A "profit" of $20,000 would thus about equal the $15,000 income of a professor.

Even more important than the proper definition of the term "profit," and the conditions under which it is used, is the recognition of the fact that the notion of profit can be viewed from at least four different viewpoints.

Public Attitude toward Profits

For thousands of years, profits have been associated with the role of the middleman, the peddler, who bought cheaply and sold dearly. That the same concept applied also to the farmer and the craftsman, both of whom derive their livelihood from selling the goods they produce at a price which must be higher than the cost of production, was not fully recognized until the 19th Century. As far back as written records exist, to the days of the Sumerians, the "peddler" has been regarded with suspicion. In the Old Testament we find the 8th Century prophet Hosea referring to Ephraim, apparently a wealthy businessman, as a "trafficker" — "the balance of deceit are in his hand; he loveth to oppress." To this, Ephraim replies: "Surely, I have become rich, but in all my labors they shall find in me no inequity that were sin." But Hosea is not satisfied. Even if Ephraim has broken no laws, his wealth can only be the result of sharp dealings.

The Greek philosopher Aristotle distinguished between *Oeconomia* (production for use within the household) of which he approved as "natural," and *Chrematistike* (production for profit) which he regarded as "unnatural." His teacher, Plato, one of the first great social and economic philosophers, wanted to pass a law that no gentleman may conduct a retail business. It was to be carried on exclusively by foreigners. The rate of profits and expenses was to be fixed by the government after "consultation with experts in every branch of the retail trade" to provide a "moderate gain for the trader." "No good Christian," proclaimed St. Augustine in the early 5th Century, "should be a merchant."

Reasons for Distrust This deep-seated distrust of the "peddler," and of the businessman in general, was — and to some extent is — often not without justification. Throughout the centuries, merchants have used false measures, have adulterated their merchandise and have misled their customers. Even if they did not directly defraud the public, their wealth was often the result of sharp dealings.

These bad experiences over thousands of years make it difficult for the general public to recognize the fact that the merchant provides a service for which he deserves a reward; that a businessman is as much entitled to a reasonable profit as a government official is entitled to his salary, and a physician to his fee. The late Scholastics, after the 13th Century, gradually recognized that a merchant must earn a profit for carrying merchandise from one place to another (thus adding "place utility" to the goods, to use the language of the modern economist) or for storing goods for future use ("time utility").

Modern Popular Misconceptions

Even today profits are viewed with suspicion by the general public, and are often blamed for rising prices and unemployment. The average citizen tends to have a greatly exaggerated idea of the level of profits earned by business. According to a Gallup poll, for instance, the average American thinks that the profit of a typical manufacturing company amounts to about

20% of its sales. Actually the rate has been less than 5% most of the time since 1929, and has never exceeded 7%.

A "Fair" Profit Everyone will agree that cheating and gouging the public is morally and socially reprehensible. The danger, however, lies in the fact that only too many people have a vague feeling that profits must somehow be the result of improper activities, that a businessman is more likely to cheat the public than a politician, lawyer, physician, teacher or preacher. And if prices rise and unemployment increases, politicians and labor leaders promise to cure the economic ills by reducing profits to "a reasonable level." Yet for thousands of years moralists and politicians have tried in vain to determine what constitutes a "reasonable level," a "fair" and "economically sound" rate of profit. At least in our own times, more unemployment is probably caused by inadequate rather than excessive profits. As we shall see shortly in more detail, investments lag as profits decline, and without the necessary capital investments there are not enough jobs for the growing labor force.

Profits in Economic Theory

To have established objective standards for wages and profits is one of the great achievements of 19th Century economic theory, even though some moralists and politicians reject the "objective" standards of the economist. As far back as the 14th Century, scholastic writers agreed that a profit should be accepted as "fair" and "natural" if it resulted from the free interplay of the forces of supply and demand. Yet it was not until the latter part of the 19th Century, 500 years later, that the theory of profit was fully developed.

Classical Theory

It is important that we realize the fundamental difference

between the theory of profit of the early 19th Century writers, chiefly the British classical school, and that of the writers of the late 19th Century. Ricardo, the great exponent of the classical school, adopted a "slicing-off" process in explaining profits. He started with the total proceeds obtained from the sale of goods. From this he deducted, first of all, the wages paid to the workers (which he thought were determined by the cost of subsistence of the worker's family), and then rent (which he felt was increasing steadily as the population grew while the supply of land was limited). The remainder was profit. Since the cost of wages was fixed, and that of rent was increasing, the rate of profits was likely to decline.

The Marginalist Theory

The marginalist school, 60 years later, saw the picture differently. It was no longer a question of deducting the cost of the various factors of production from the value of the final product, leaving the profit as the final residue. Instead, each factor (including the services of the entrepreneur) was now assumed to be paid according to its relative scarcity and the contribution it had made to the production of the final product. The rate of profits, as the rate of interest, rent and wages, thus became the result of a great many variables. It fluctuated with the relative supply of capital, and the ability of the entrepreneur to produce salable goods and services.

Profits Regulating the Volume of Production

If the profits in a given line of business are above average, entrepreneurs enter the more lucrative line. Very soon production increases faster than demand, and profits begin to decline. This has been the experience with many new products; e.g., electronics during the postwar years. On the other hand, if profits in a certain line of business continue below the average level, entrepreneurs will switch to other more promising activities. This reduces the total output in relation to demand until profits begin to rise again. The relative shrinkages of the coal and textile industries are two well-known examples.

Profits as a Basis for Economic Planning

Socialists and modern liberals often argue that production should be for "use," not for "profit" and that it should serve the "needs" of the consumer rather than provide for the enrichment of the producer. But who is to determine what these "needs" are? For about 200 years, western social and political philosophy has been based on two assumptions: (1) that the individual is the best judge of his personal needs, and (2) that, as a rational being, the individual will do his share to maintain society for his own and for the common good. It is on this second assumption that the notion of universal suffrage, and of democracy, rests. If we accept these assumptions, we must accept the profit system as the regulatory machinery of the economy. Millions of individuals, being the best judges of their own and of society's needs, will demand the goods and services which satisfy these needs. And the businessman, in turn, responding to the popular demand, will provide the goods and services demanded, and in doing so will derive a profit for himself. If a businessman were to try to sell merchandise for which there is no demand, or if he were to charge higher prices than the public is willing to pay, he would soon find his warehouses bulging with unsold goods, and incur losses instead of earning profits.

The Profit Motive in an Affluent Society

Modern economic planners challenge this "simple 19th Century picture" as no longer reflective of 20th Century reality. They argue that the basic needs — food, clothing and shelter — of the great majority of the American people have been satisfied. Additional needs have to be created artificially through advertising. In Professor Galbraith's words: "The modern corporation must manufacture not only goods, but the desire for the goods it manufactures." This implies, of course, that the individual is not smart enough to recognize the benefits he may or may not derive from new goods. Instead, he is hypnotized by modern advertising into buying the goods which the manufacturer wishes him to buy, even though they fill no real needs. At the same time, real needs — or what economic planners regard as real needs — remain unfilled, because the individual, duped by the advertisers, does not recognize what is really good for him.

The Basic Philosophic Conflict

The conflict between the traditional argument of "consumer sovereignty" and the modern argument of the "irrationality of consumer demand" cannot be decided in economic terms. It rests on basic philosophic attitudes. The traditional view assumes that the individual is inherently rational and knows how best to satisfy his own and society's needs. It reflects the traditional individualistic view of society. The modern approach, on the other hand, questions the rationality of the consumer (although modern liberals do not question the rationality of the individual as a voter). Instead, it assumes that the "experts" know better what is good for the individual and society.

The two conflicting views can be reconciled within certain limits by postulating that the individual (as a rational being) recognizes that "society" can fill certain needs more efficiently than the individual. He therefore uses his power at the polls to direct the government to provide the collective needs which the individual cannot provide for himself, or at least not as efficiently. The profit motive is thus replaced by political decisions.

Profit as the Basis of Price Calculations

Whether individual consumption patterns are rational or irrational, the fact remains that the major portion of the nation's output of goods and services — about 80% of the total (the balance being purchased by Federal, state and local agencies) — is still determined by the needs (or whims) of millions of individual consumers. They determine what prices they are willing to pay and in doing so, they determine the margin of profit of the manufacturer, the wholesaler and the retailer. The prices paid by the government are determined by the prices paid by the general public. Generally speaking, the government cannot pay less than the general public, and as a rule will not pay more. The cost calculations of the public sector are thus based on the price structure in the private sector. And the latter, in turn, rests upon the profit system: Prices must provide for a normal rate of profit in the long run, or production will decline. (The major exception to this principle is the farm price support program. And, as we have seen, its difficulties are due largely to the fact that it violates the basic principles of price formation and substitutes for them social and political expediency.)

Profits as a Dynamic Force

Possibly the most important, and the least understood, aspect of profits is their role as the dynamic force in a free economy. The scholastic writers of the late Middle Ages did not recognize this role, because they were too preoccupied with ethical aspects. Nor did the economists of the late 19th Century, because they were fascinated with the idea that the rewards of all factors of production (including profits) could be treated alike and fitted neatly into the equilibrium system. This is no doubt true from a theoretical point of view. But the fact that profits (like rent, interest and wages) tend toward an equilibrium does not make adequate allowance for the peculiar role which profits play in the economic system. Adam Smith recognized this fact very clearly when he wrote that "it is not from the benevolence of the butcher, the brewer, or the baker, that we expect our dinner, but from their regard for their own interest."

Many people disapprove of this emphasis on the "selfishness" of businessmen, and as Adam Smith realized, society will disintegrate unless the desire for gain on the part of the individual is balanced by a sense of social responsibility.

Self-interest versus Social Planning

"Regard for their own interest" is not confined to businessmen. It impels lawyers and physicians, university professors and politicians, and even clergymen. And without man's desire to better his own lot, progress would be very slow. Socialists and 20th Century liberals recognize clearly that if they do away with the individual striving for personal advantage, they must find some other force to take its place to avoid economic stagnation. This they believe to have found in government planning. Instead of millions of individuals each trying to improve himself in his limited sphere, the government plans for the improvement of society as a whole and assigns to each individual an appropriate role in working toward the social goal. It is one of the necessary assumptions of socialism that man will exert himself as much in achieving the goals set by the government as he will in furthering his own personal interest. Yet even in "ideal societies," such as religious orders, the complete subordination of individual desires to the common goal does not, as a rule, survive the original enthusiasm. Unless "discipline" enforced by leaders assures continued progress, stagnation will set in. The carrot of profits is replaced by the whip of the government planner. Even the totalitarian socialism of Soviet Russian found it necessary to make concession to the individuals' "regard for their own interest."

Profits and "Full Employment" The emphasis on profits as a dynamic force in economic growth appears to be in conflict with the modern economic theory that economic growth, a high rate of employment, and general prosperity are possible only if wages are sufficiently high to provide the necessary mass purchasing power. High profits, it is argued, are likely to increase savings (for which there may be no outlet); while high wages are likely to increase consumption (which in turn will stimulate production and employment). Profits should thus be kept to a minimum in order to boost mass purchasing power through higher wages.

What are "Minimum" Profits? This brings us back to the vexing problem which plagued the scholastics 500 years ago, when they searched for a "fair" rate of profit; and to the theory of the 19th Century economists that the "normal" rate of profit would automatically be achieved through the unimpeded forces of the market. It doesn't make sense to say that a 4% rate of profit is inadequate, 6% is adequate and 10% is excessive. The rate of profit is determined by many factors, including the amount of risk involved, the availability of capital and the opportunity of making profits in other fields or other parts of the world. If an American auto manufacturer can earn 6% in the United States and 10% in Europe, he is likely to push the output of his European subsidiaries. The fact that the American rate of profits was lower than the prevailing rate in Europe thus reduced the job opportunities for the American worker. If average profits are low, the rate of investments is low. As long as one can get 4½% interest on savings deposits, why should anyone wish to run the risk of building an addition to his factory, if he can expect a return of only about 5½% on the new investment?

As Keynes himself warned: "Short of going over to Communism, there is no possible means of curing unemployment (and, we may add, of increasing the rate of growth) except by restoring to employers a proper margin of profit." It was for this reason that Keynes at one time argued for wage stability and increasing profits as a means of stimulating the economy.

How to Measure Profits From the point of view of microeconomic theory, we can say that the level of profits is "normal" (in equilibrium) if all savings find a productive outlet. Unfortunately it is not possible to reduce this general theoretical statement to concrete percentages.

Nor is it possible to express the "proper rate" of profit in macroeconomic terms. We can express total profits (1) as a percent of the national income (2) as a percent of the volume of business, or (3) as a rate of return on the invested capital. None of the three methods is fully satisfactory. But they indicate certain trends. While profits rose sharply during the early years of World War II (although high corporate and excess profit taxes held down the net income), the rate of increase in net corporate profits during the postwar years generally lagged behind the rate of growth of the national income. Net profits dropped to 3.3% of total sales in 1944 due to heavy taxation. By 1950 it had recovered to 7.7%, only to decline again and remain below 6% during the early 1960's. Between 1950 and 1965 corporate profits increased by 80% from $24.9 to $44.5 billion, while the Gross National Product rose by 138% from $241 to $554 billion.

Tables 16, 17, and 18 show the trend of corporate earnings as percent of the Gross National Product, total assets and total sales.

TABLE 16

Net Corporate Profits as Percent of GNP

	Gross National Product (in Billion dollars)	Corp. Profits and Inventory Adjustm. (in Billion dollars)	Percent
1940	$99.7	$9.8	9.8%
1950	284.8	37.7	13.2%
1955	398.0	46.9	11.8%
1960	503.8	49.9	9.9%
1965	676.3	73.1	10.8%

Source: U.S. Department of Commerce: *Statistical Abstract of the United States, 1966,* p. 320.

TABLE 17

Net Corporate Profits as Percent of Total Corporate Assets

	Total Assets (in Billion)	Net after Taxes (in Billion)	Percent
1940	$ 320	$ 6.37	2.0%
1950	598	25.29	4.2%
1955	888	25.74	2.9%
1960	1,206	21.64	1.8%
1963	1,479	28.97	1.9%

Source: U.S. Department of Commerce: *Statistical Abstract of the United States, 1966,* p. 494.

Declining Profits in the American Economy As Tables 16–18 indicate, corporate profits, however measured, failed to expand during the great boom of the first half of the 1960's at the same rate as the national income. After reaching their peak in the early 1950's, profits began to stagnate during the second half of the decade, and despite general boom conditions and a substantial increase in sales during the 1960's, profits (meas-

TABLE 18

Net Profits as Percent of Sales of 500 Largest Industrial Corporations

	Sales (in Billion)	Net Profits (in Billion)	Percent
1955	$161.39	$11.2	6.9%
1960	204.72	11.6	5.7%
1963	245.09	14.04	6.0%
1965	298.06	20.01	6.7%

Source: "The Fortune Directory of the 500 Largest U.S. Industrial Corporations," published annually in the July issue of "Fortune."

ured as percent of either the Gross National Product, total assets or total sales) failed to reach the level of the early 1950's.

Economists cite at least three reasons for this development. (1) Labor cost apparently rose faster than productivity during the second half of the 1950's. (2) As a result of the reconstruction of the European industries and the industrial development in some of the underdeveloped countries, American manufacturers lost their dominant position in world markets. This was particularly true with regard to steel. And (3) due to the sharp expansion of industrial capacity (total corporate assets more than doubled from $598 to $1,206 billion between 1950 and 1960) industry was operating well below capacity during the late 1950's. As the use of plant facilities increased from 72% in 1959 to 92% in 1966 the rate of return recovered gradually.

There is obviously no single explanation for the "profit squeeze." Nor is it possible to prove that the relatively high rate of unemployment and the low rate of economic growth during the late 1950's, as well as the heavy outflow of American capital into foreign markets were the results of inadequate profits; — inadequate by international standards and in comparison with the return on other investments, such as real estate.

Groping for a Theory of Profits In short, as in so many areas of economics, we are still groping for a well-defined theory of profits. All we can say is that, generally speaking, employment opportunities increase as capital investments increase, and capital investments grow as the rate of profit grows. If profits remain at a low level (be it because of foreign competition, rising labor cost, heavy taxes, or the general uncertainty created by zealous government regulators) the rate of investments will decline. While this need not affect the general level of prosperity, it is likely to affect the rate of growth and employment. To provide the millions of new jobs which are needed during the 1960's to cope with the problem of chronic unemployment requires capital investments of about $75 billion a year, or an increase of about 80% over the level of the prosperous year 1963. Without an adequate rate of profits these investments are not likely to be made, despite the popular modern argument that the 19th Century entrepreneur has been replaced by the 20th Century professional manager, whose investment decisions are based on long-range forecasts of demand rather than on short-range profit trends.

Actually, even the corporate bureaucrat who has no personal investment in the company which he manages will avoid unprofitable investments, if only for the reason that he may lose his job if he does not earn an adequate profit for the stockholders.

Despite the development of the modern mixed economy, it is still safe to assume that the rate of profits has a fundamental bearing on the rate of economic growth and the number of job opportunities.

Glossary

The glossary is intended to be used as a supplement to the text. Many economic terms, such as Federal Reserve System, central bank, gold standard, etc. which have been explained in the text, have been omitted from the Glossary. On the other hand, non-economic terms which have been used in the text without full explanation, such as Enlightenment, positivism, epistemology, scholasticism, etc. are included and briefly explained in the Glossary.

"Ability-to-pay" Principle A tax theory according to which taxes should be levied according to the taxpayer's capacity to pay. A man with a $20,000 income should pay more than twice as much in taxes as a man with a $10,000 income, even though both may derive the same benefit from government services. Progressive income taxes are based on the "ability to pay" principle. See also "benefit principle."

Absolutism The political philosophy which predominated in Europe from the 16th to the 18th Century. It is based on the notion that the people made a "social contract" with their ruler giving him absolute powers. The contract cannot be abrogated. (Medieval political philosophy assumed a balance of power between Church and State, with the power of the rulers further restricted through the feudal rights of their subjects.) The philosophy of government which developed during the 18th Century in opposition to the Absolutism of the time, also assumes that the people have made a contract with their rulers (namely the Constitution), but this contract can be abrogated whenever the people so desire. Besides, the contract sets definite limits to the power of the rulers. The economic system which predominated during the time of Absolutism is known as Mercantilism.

Abstinence Theory A theory developed to justify the taking of interest. Immediate consumption provides greater enjoyment than consumption at some future (and hence uncertain) date. People must thus be rewarded for "abstaining" from immediate consumption; namely, in the form of interest which they receive on their savings.

Acceleration Principle Indicates how changes in the demand for consumer goods result in much larger changes in the demand for machinery and other production goods.

"Accord of 1951" Agreement between the Treasury and the Federal Reserve System which settled a bitter disagreement regarding the purchase of government securities by the Federal Reserve. The agreement provided that the Federal Reserve would provide for an "orderly market" for government securities, but would no longer be expected to "peg" government security prices at above market levels.

Administrative Budget Customary form in which the accounts of the Federal Government were approved by Congress until 1968. The Administrative Budget does not include such items as the highway building program (which is financed out of a separate trust fund) or the Social Security and Railroad Retirement Funds. Other forms of presenting the government accounts are the "Cash Budget," National Income Budget," and "Capital Budget." Depending upon which method of accounting is used, the federal government has a larger or smaller deficit. President Kennedy referred to the "Administrative Budget" as "simply irrelevant" and "actively misleading."

Agency Shop While the "closed shop" agreement between employers and unions (which was outlawed by the Taft-Hartley Act) provided that the employers could hire only union members; and the "union shop" requires all workers to join the union as a condition of employment; under the "agency shop" agreements individual workers need not actually join the union, but must pay the union the equivalent of union dues as an agency fee. If they refuse to make these payments (which are usually deducted directly from their wages by the employer), the employer is required to fire them.

American Federation of Labor (AFL) Founded in 1881 by Samuel Gompers as a loose association of independent craft unions. Local unions are united into national and international unions (with branches in Canada) which combine to form the AFL. — Samuel Gompers was followed in 1924 by William Green, who in turn was succeeded in 1952 by George Meany. — In 1935 the industrial unions, under the leadership of John L. Lewis of the United Mine Workers, broke away from the AFL to form the Congress of Industrial Organizations (CIO). The two great labor organizations reunited in 1955 as the AFL-CIO, with George Meany as president.

Analytical Discipline A branch of knowledge (such as economics) which attempts to gain an understanding of the inherent forces which shape reality by "dissolving" their complex manifestations. Science relies on the analytical approach. Analytical economics is based on the assumption that man can discover, behind the seeming chaos of daily life, a system of orderly forces, the "economic laws," which govern economic life, just as the laws of gravitation govern the physical universe. One can also regard economics as a normative or as a pragmatic-operational discipline.

Anarchy A political philosophy which regards all forms of government as oppressive, and hence strives to do away with governments.

Atomistic Society There are two basic concepts of society: the atomistic and the organic. Under the atomistic concept of society, the human beings are compared with self-contained grains of sand, each a unit in itself, all more or less alike, and all subject to the impersonal forces of nature. If one grain of sand is lost, it will have no effect on the sand dune. Under the organic concept of society, man is compared with the cell of a body. The cell can survive only as long as the body as a whole (society) is healthy. A sick cell can poison the whole body. The ultimate entity is not the individual (the grain of sand) but society (the organism in its entirety). During the 19th Century the atomistic (individualistic) view of sciety predominated; during the Middle Ages, the organic; the trend in modern times is again toward an organic concept. Whether a society thinks of itself in atomistic (individualistic) or in organic (statist-social) terms has a great deal to do with the type of socio-economic theories it develops.

Automatic Stabilizers An important concept in modern fiscal theory. Certain taxes and certain forms of government expenditures fluctuate automatically with business activities, and in such a way as to compensate for changes in personal and business spending. Corporation income taxes, for example, fluctuate much more sharply than business activities, so that a relatively minor recession results in a substantial decline in government revenues, which is likely to lead to a deficit (which in turn will result in additional purchase power being pumped into the economy), even though Congress has made no changes in tax rates and in government spending. Similarly, unemployment insurance payments tend to be smaller than Social Security taxes when most people are employed (thus reducing aggregate purchasing power); they tend to be larger during times of heavy unemployment (thus adding to the purchasing power).

Balance of Payments A statistical compilation showing all the international payments which a nation — its individuals, corporations and government agencies — has made and received in the course of a year.

"Benefit Principle" Tax theory which assumes that taxes should be levied according to the "benefits" which the taxpayer derives from government expenditures. E.g., highways should be constructed and maintained through tolls and gasoline taxes paid by those who use the highways. The opposite of the "benefit principle" is the "ability to pay" principle.

Bonds Secured, long-term obligations of a corporation. The security may consist of real estate (mortgage bonds), chattel (such as railroad cars) or intangibles (securities). Each bondholder holds the company's promise to pay a fixed amount of interest annually (interest is usually paid every six months), as well as the principle at the time the bond matures according to the original loan agreement. The lien on the assets (pledged as security for the bonds) is held by a trustee, usually a bank or trust company. If the debtor company fails to pay interest as provided by the loan agreement, the trustee will move to foreclose on the pledged property, which involves throwing the company into receivership. The usual par value of a bond is $1000. Bonds are quoted as percent of par. Thus, if a bond is quoted at 96 the purchaser will have to pay $960 (plus the interest which has accrued since the last interest date) for a $1000 bond. Government bonds are direct unsecured obligations.

Branch Banking System A system of commercial banking in which a few large banks (such as the Bank of America in California) have many local branch offices. Branch banking is prohibited or restricted in most states, the chief exception being California. Most foreign countries have branch (rather than unit) banking systems.

Business Cycle Fluctuations in business activities. Economists distinguish four phases: boom, downswing, depression (or recession) and recovery. The U.S. Department of Commerce publishes, under the title "Business Cycle Development," a monthly compilation of statistics which have a bearing on the cyclical fluctuations of the American economy.

"Capital Budget" A form of presenting government accounts which is used by several foreign countries, but not by the U.S. government. Under the "Capital Budget" procedure, the government has two sets of accounts: one which covers all current operations, and the other (the "capital account") which includes all "capital investments" such as roads, canals, power dams, buildings, etc., which are financed out of loans rather than current taxes. — The U.S. highway building program, which is financed out of a separate trust fund, is a reflection of the

"Capital Budget" notion. — Other forms in which government accounts can be presented are: the "Administrative Budget," the "Cash Budget" and the "National Income Budget."

Capital Goods Also referred to as "production goods," or merely as "capital," consist of factories, machinery, transportation facilities, etc.; in short, all those goods which are intended not for consumption but to produce consumption goods. A hammer in a factory is a production good, just as is a steel mill.

Capitalism Term coined and popularized by Karl Marx in a derogatory sense as the opposite of socialism. It describes an economic system based on private ownership of the means of production, and implies freedom of private enterprise. Werner Sombart (see his article on "Capitalism" in the *Encyclopedia for the Social Sciences*) stressed the fact that capitalism involved a socio-ethical philosophy and general cultural aspects, because of the emphasis of capitalism on profit rather than the satisfaction of obvious needs — (a distinction which overlooks the fact that there can be no profits without the satisfaction of real or imagined needs). Sombart distinguished between commercial capitalism of the 17th and 18th Centuries (chiefly Mercantilism), the industrial capitalism of the 19th Century, and modern finance capitalism (since World War I) characterized by the shift of control from the individual entrepreneur to the large-scale financial institutions. In his quasi-historical, quasi-economic writings Sombart predicted further changes in the character of capitalism through increased government controls, a system which is currently called "mixed capitalism," or "mixed enterprise."

Cash Budget A method by which the accounts of the Federal Government can be presented to include all funds received and paid out by the Federal Government and its many agencies. Economists regard the "Cash Budget" (officially adopted in 1968) as more significant than the old "Administrative Budget" in showing the actual role of the government in the economy. Two other methods of presenting the Federal accounts are the "National Income Budget" and the "Capital Budget."

Check-off System The agreement between management and unions under which the employer deducts the union dues from the wages of the workers and remits the dues directly to the union. This relieves the union of the often difficult task of collecting the dues.

Chrematistike Term used by Aristotle, corresponding to the modern concept of "production for profit," of which Aristotle disapproved. (See also *Oeconomia*)

Clayton Anti-Trust Act of 1914 An amendment to the Sherman Anti-Trust Act of 1890. It prohibits interlocking directorates, exclusive selling contracts, local price cutting to destroy competition, etc. One of the most important provisions was the exemption of agricultural cooperatives and labor unions from the prohibition of "combinations in restraint of trade," since "the labor of a human being is not a commodity or article of commerce." This makes it possible for labor unions to restrain trade through concerted action, such as strikes and boycotts, while similar concerted action on the part of the employers would be illegal.

Closed Shop Agreement Contracts between employers and a labor union according to which the employer can hire only members of the union. If a worker is rejected by or expelled from the union he cannot be employed. The Taft-Hartley Act (Labor-Management Relations Act) made all closed shop agreements illegal. At the time closed shops were banned, about 3.3 million workers were covered by such agreements.

Common Stock Certificates of ownership indicating a proportional share in the ownership of a corporation. The aggregate par value of all shares is equal to the capital stock of the corporation. E.g., if a company has a million shares of $10 each outstanding, the total capital stock of the company is $10 million. If the company shows a net profit of $1 million, the earnings per share are equal to $1. The common stock holders are the "residual owners" of the company. They are entitled to all earnings (and, in the case of dissolution, to all assets) after all prior claims, including those of the creditors and preferred stockholders, have been satisfied. Instead of having a par value (e.g., $10) a stock may have "no par" value. To ascertain the book value of a no par stock, one divides the number of shares (e.g., one million) into the amount of the total capital as shown in the balance sheet of the company (e.g., $10 million). — Stocks are quoted in the quotation sheets in dollars per share. Thus if a stock is quoted at 47, a hundred shares will cost $4700.

Co-determination The demand of organized labor to have a voice in business decisions, including those which may affect labor only indirectly, such as dividend and investment policies.

Compensatory Spending Basic concept in modern fiscal theory. The theory assumes that savings may at times exceed investments, thus leading to the accumulation of "idle savings" and a corresponding decline in the rate of production and employment. If such a situation arises, the government is to "compensate" for the "inadequate" spending in the private sector through a corresponding increase in public spending, with the deficit in the government sector equal to the idle savings accumulating in the private sector.

Congress of Industrial Organizations (CIO) In 1935 a group of industrial unions broke away from the AFL, which was dominated by the traditional craft unions, and formed the CIO under the leadership of John L. Lewis of the United Mine Workers Union. The AFL and the CIO reunited in 1955 to form the AFL-CIO.

Contract Rent Payments made by the lessor to the lessee in accordance with a contract, e.g., the rent paid by the tenant to the landlord. The term "rent" (or "economic rent") as used by the economist has a different meaning than contract rent. It refers to the income derived from land (not from buildings) and other items of natural capital.

Convertibility The term, referring the quality of being able to be modified or changed into something else, is used in various ways in economics. A currency is convertible if it can be exchanged freely into the currency of another country. Inconvertibility, on the other hand, means that it requires a special authorization of the government or central bank to buy a foreign currency, i.e., convert, let us say, Argentine pesos into dollars. If a currency is not freely convertible, a free market (also called "black market") usually develops in which the non-convertible currency is sold at a discount in terms of convertible currencies. Convertible preferred stock is preferred stock which can be exchanged for common stock. Convertible bonds can be exchanged for other bonds or stock.

Corporation An association of individuals (shareholders) which enjoys all the privileges and obligations of a single natural person. A corporation can enter into contracts, hire workers, own assets, borrow money, sue and be sued. Since it is a creation of the state, a corporation as a rule is subject to special taxes (corporate income tax). The liability of the owners of the corporation (shareholders) is limited to the amount invested. As a rule a corporation has a perpetual life (while a partnership automatically comes to an end if one of the partners dies). A corporation can attract vast funds, and the owners of the corporation, as a rule, can freely dispose of their participation by selling their shares in the stock market.

Corporation Income Tax Tax paid by corporations on their net income figured after payment of interest and depreciation. The corporate income tax was reduced from 52% to 50% in 1964, and to 48% in 1965. Small private corporations pay a lower rate.

Craft Unions Associations of skilled workers of a particular occupation (or craft), somewhat similar to the medieval guilds (such as building trades workers, typesetters, photoengravers, etc.). Craft unions, as a rule, provide for an apprenticeship system designed both to teach the necessary skills and to limit the number of qualified workers. Some of them provide extensive welfare and recreational facilities for their members. The Craft Unions are united in the AFL. Craft Unions (which confine their membership to special occupations) often clash with "industrial unions," which try to organize all workers in a given plant or industry, irrespective of their specific skills and occupations.

Danbury Hatters Case A famous Supreme Court decision of 1908 which held every member of a union as well as its officers personally liable for the damages caused by a boycott. The court held that the organized action of labor in restraint of trade was in violation of the Sherman Anti-trust Act of 1890. Six years later, and partly in response to the Danbury Hatters Case, Congress passed the Clayton Anti-trust Act of 1914, which specifically exempted labor unions from prosecution under the anti-trust laws unless the union acted in concert with employers.

Debentures According to American terminology (which differs from the terminology used in England) are long-term obligations of a corporation which are not secured through the pledge of specific assets.

Deficit Spending Modern fiscal theory, largely based on Keynesian ideas, according to which the government should run a deficit (expenditures exceeding tax revenues) whenever the spending of the private sector fails to produce full employment, which, it is assumed, is due to the accumulation of "idle savings." The government is expected to off-set the inadequate investments in the private sector through "compensatory spending" — the "deficit" in the public sector to be equal to the accumulation of "idle savings" in the private sector.

Depletion The using up of natural resources. Depletion reserves are set aside before the calculation of net income in order to compensate for the gradual exhaustion of mines, oil wells, etc.

Depreciation Reserves set aside for the wear and tear of "man-made capital," such as buildings, machinery, transportation facilities, etc. Since "capital goods" have to be replaced when worn out, the net income of a business (and of the economy as a whole) must be calculated after due allowance for depreciation.

Derived Demand The notion that the demand for the factors of production (land, labor, capital) is the result of the demand for the finished product. There is no demand for "labor" per se, only for the goods and services which labor provides. Wages paid to labor — or to any other factor of production — thus depend upon the price which the consumer is willing to pay for the final product.

Discount Rate (formerly known as the rediscount rate). The interest rate at which the Federal Reserve banks stand ready to extend credit to their member banks. The discount rate is (in theory) fixed independently by the 12 Federal Reserve banks, and in decades past the rate differed at times from one Federal Reserve district to the next because of differences in the supply of and demand for credit. In recent years the discount rate has tended to be uniform throughout the country, even though it is still fixed by the individual Federal Reserve banks. An increase in the discount rate increases the cost of credit throughout the economy, and is thus expected to have a dampening effect on economic activities.

Disposable Income (DI) Statistical estimate of the aggregate income remaining to the individuals after payment of personal income taxes. The Disposable Income may be used either for consumption expenditures or for savings.

Due Process of Law Provisions in the 5th and 14th Amendments which are among the most important of the Constitution as far as the protection of the rights of the individual is concerned. "Due process of law" originally meant simply that the legal procedure had to be observed according to common law, especially regarding the accusation and trial of the accused. Today "due process of law" stresses the "reasonableness" of the law itself as passed by Congress, and of the procedural application. What is to be regarded as "reasonable" is determined by the Supreme Court. The term is thus a very elastic one, and its interpretation, especially regarding private property rights and the freedom of contract, has changed considerably during the past 35 years, thus altering the character of two of the most important economic institutions: private property and contractional rights.

Economic Goods (also known as "scarce goods"). Products and services which are not free for the taking. The opposite are so-called "free goods" including air, and in the old days timber and water at a time when the land was not yet publicly or privately owned. Even though the government may drown in wheat surpluses, wheat is a "scarce" or "economic good." The same is true of water which comes from the faucet. Some goods which were free goods in the past, because man had not yet discovered a use for them, such as uranium ore in the 1930's, became economic goods as man learned to use them. The economist is interested only in economic or scarce goods. In fact economics is often defined as dealing with the allocation of scarce goods.

"Economic Man" A theoretical construct which pictures man as being entirely — or certainly predominantly — guided by "economic" motivations, i.e., the desire to maximize material gains and minimize his efforts to achieve these gains. As against the "economic man," which 19th Century economists postulated, the medieval man was pictured as the "religious man," and some modern political scientists look upon man as predominantly a "political man." By assuming that human beings will always act as "economic men," the economist can logically predict how man will act in a given situation. The trouble with this approach is that man's reactions are either completely unpredictable, or certainly not with the certainty which the "economic man" premise implies.

Economic Rent Income derived from land and other forms of natural capital. (The rent which a tenant pays to the landlord is known as contract rent.)

Elasticity of Money The ability of the money supply to increase and decrease according to the demands of the economy. Prior to the 1930's, the elasticity was largely automatic. If commercial banks needed additional cash they "rediscounted" (i.e., they "sold") to their Federal Reserve bank the promisory notes and acceptances which they had taken in from their clients.

Elasticity of Supply and Demand Degree of responsiveness in the quantity of goods supplied and demanded as a result of changes in the price. Economists speak of "elastic demand" if a reduction in price results in a more than proportional increase in sales, so that total revenue increases; or if an increase in price results in a decline in total revenue. If the demand is "inelastic" (as in the case of necessities) an increase in price results in an increase in total revenue. The "elasticity of supply" is largely determined by the time element.

Empiricism The pursuit of knowledge through sense perception (observation) and experiments, and the philosphic assumption that all knowledge is based on sense perception. Economics is based only to a very limited degree upon purely empirical knowledge. Statistical data (the so-called empirical raw material of the economist) do not constitute actual economic reality, but an abstraction. In making this abstraction (i.e., in compiling the statistics) the economist may, knowingly or unknowingly, change essential features of reality.

Encyclicals Literally: circular letters. Official pronouncements by the Pope setting forth doctrinal views of the Catholic Church. The encyclicals are written in Latin and known by their first words. Economists are particularly interested in the so-called social encyclicals, which set forth the socio-economic ethics of the Church by which the day-to-day activities of all Catholics should be guided. The social encyclicals are modern expressions of normative economics. The best known are (1) "Rerum Novarum" (Revolutionary change), (1891) also known as "The Condition of Labor"; (2) "Quadrogesimo Anno" (Forty Years) (1931), "Reconstructing the Social Order," (3) "Mater et Magistra" (The Church as mother and teacher) (1962), (4) "Progressio Populorum" (The Development of Nations") (1967).

Endogenous Business Cycle Theories Theories which are based on the assumption that business cycle fluctuations are due to forces which operate within the economy, such as the overexpansion of credit. Other theories postulate exogenous (i.e., outside) forces which may be either predictable or unpredictable.

Enlightenment Philosophic movement of the 18th Century which constituted a strong reaction against the philosophic assumptions of the Age of Absolutism. The Enlightenment assumed that man was inherently a moral, social and rational being, able to govern himself and to understand the innermost forces of the world in which he lived. It was an optimistic age. While there was a great deal of poverty and misery, the leaders thought that all the defects in this "best of all worlds" were due to human interference with the divinely designed "perfect machine." It was for that reason that the Physiocrats (a group of 18th Century French philosopher-economists) demanded "Laissez faire! Laissez passer! Le monde và de lui même" (Freedom of production! Freedom of trade! The world runs by itself). The philosophy of the Enlightenment provides the philosophic rationale for both democracy and the economic theory of free enterprise. Jefferson was one of the outstanding representatives of the Enlightenment in the U.S.

Epistemology The study of the methods of acquiring knowledge, and of the limits and validity of various forms of knowledge. There are two basic ways in which man can acquire knowledge: through reasoning from "self-evident truth" (rationalism), and through sense perception and experimentation (empiricism). In practice, the two approaches cannot be separated neatly from each other. Some people believe that there is a third source of knowledge: revelation. If we say "I 'know' that my redeemer liveth," this "knowledge" rests on more than either rational or empirical evidence.

Equilibrium Price The price at which the supply of and the demand for goods are in balance. Similarly, equilibrium wage: the wage rate at which the supply of and demand for workers in a labor market are equal.

Excess Reserves All member banks of the Federal Reserve System must maintain with their Federal Reserve bank a "legal reserve" equal to a certain percentage (fixed from time to time by the Board of Governors of the Federal Reserve System) of their demand and time deposits. Many of the banks (especially smaller ones) maintain reserves slightly in excess of the required legal reserves. This excess is referred to as "excess reserves" and reflects the potential lending capacity of the individual bank. If the excess reserves of all banks are added together, and from this total the amounts are deducted which some banks (usually the larger ones) owe to the Federal Reserve System, we arrive at the "free reserves," which indicate the lending capacity of the system as a whole.

Excise Taxes The origin of the word "excise" is uncertain. It may derive from the Latin "ad census" which, freely translated, would mean "as evaluated for tax purposes." It is a tax levied on the production, sale and/or consumption of goods and services, such as sales taxes and luxury taxes. The type of taxation was first used in modern times in 17th Century Holland and England. When excise taxes were introduced in the U.S. in 1791 they aroused great indignation and were repealed by Jefferson in 1801. They were used again as "war emergencies" during the War of 1812, the Civil War and the Spanish-American War, but were always repealed after the war was over, except for the tobacco and liquor taxes. The vast number of excise taxes now collected by Federal, state and local governments are the result of the 1930's and of World War II. Especially important (besides tobacco and liquor taxes) are the taxes on gasoline.

Exogenous Business Cycle Theories Theories which assume that business cycle fluctuations are the result of forces operating outside the economy proper, such as Jevon's famous sunspot theory. (Sunspots affect the climate and hence agricultural production, which in turn affects general business activities.) Other theories postulate endogenous forces operating within the economy.

Fabians (also known as Fabian Socialists). A group of middle-class English intellectuals founded about 1883, who preached a typically English type of socialism with the emphasis on gradual reform rather than violent revolution. The group included George Bernard Shaw,

Sidney and Beatrice Webb, H. G. Wells, Graham Wallas, Annie Besant and others. The group derived its name from Fabious Cunctator, the Roman general who fought Hannibal by carefully avoiding a head-on battle, concentrating instead on winning small and by themselves unimportant skirmishes. The group became well-known through the *Fabian Essays* (1889). Their philosophy is characterized by the statement: "The economic side of the democratic ideal is, in fact, socialism itself." The group advocated the nationalization of essential industries as well as of the rent of land, and the distribution of wealth (since it is of social origin). The Fabians rejected the Marxist doctrine that all wealth belonged to labor. They are the intellectual forebears of the British Labour Party, and some people feel that their philosophy had a considerable influence on the "New Deal" liberalism in the U.S. The Fabian attitude toward "cold socialization" is characterized by the following passages from the *Fabian Essays:* "Slice after slice has gradually been cut from the profits of capital . . . by socially beneficial restrictions . . . Slice after slice has been cut off the incomes from rent and interest by the gradual shifting of taxation from consumers to persons enjoying incomes above the averages . . . On every side the individual capitalist is being registered, inspected, controlled, and eventually superseded by the community . . . The economic history of the century is an almost continuous record of the progress of socialism."

Factors of Production The creation of goods and services requires the employment of a number of agents: (1) labor, (2) raw materials, (3) machinery and (4) managerial and technological skills. The French economist Jean Baptiste Say (1767–1832) was the first to point to this fact. For many years economists spoke of "Land, Labor and Capital" as the three Factors of Production, to which were later on added Managerial and Technological Skills. By "Land" the economist means all forms of natural resources, whether urban real estate (soil), farm land, mines, oil wells, forests, etc.; by "Capital" he means all man-made factors of production, such as factories, machinery, mining installations, transportation equipments, highways — in short, everything built by man for the purpose of ultimately producing consumer goods.

"Featherbedding" An attempt of labor to pad the payrolls with unnecessary workers. While the employers complain about "featherbedding," workers complain about "speed-ups." It is not easy to establish work norms which are fair both to the employer and the worker, yet there are obvious cases of "featherbedding" in many union contracts, as when theaters have to pay for an orchestra even though no music is needed or provided, or if the railroads have to pay for work which is neither needed nor performed. "Featherbedding" raises the cost of production and thus prices, and tends to lower the average standard of living.

Federal Deposit Insurance Corporation (FDIC) A government insurance system to protect bank depositors. The creation of the FDIC was one of the major features of the Banking Act of 1933, designed to prevent a repetition of the epidemic of bank failures which had shaken the country in 1932–33. The law was amended through the Banking Act of 1935, at which time all deposits in insured banks were protected up to $5000. The amount was raised to $10,000 and more recently to $15,000. All member banks of the Federal Reserve System must be members of the FDIC, and most non-member banks are. At the end of 1966 more than 13,000 banks were insured, compared with fewer than 300 non-insured banks. Some of the latter had failed to meet the minimum standards of safety. Mutual Savings Banks and Trust Companies may also apply for insurance. Building and Loan Associations and Savings and Loan Associations, on the other hand, are not insured by the FDIC, but by the Federal Savings and Loan Insurance Corporation. The FDIC is managed by a Board of three directors, consisting of the Comptroller of the Currency and two other directors appointed by the President for six years. The insurance premium payable by the insured banks amounts to 1/12% of the average total (not only of the insured) deposits, but the actual semi-annual assessments are reduced through a system of rebates.

Federal Reserve Notes The chief form of paper money used in the United States. The Notes, which come in denominations from $1 to $10,000, bear a green seal. They are the joint obligation of the Federal Reserve System as a whole, the issuing Federal Reserve bank (whose seal and number (1–12) appears on the note) and the Federal government. As security behind the notes, the issuing Federal Reserve bank maintained holdings of "gold certificates" (which were backed dollar-for-dollar by gold held by the U.S. Government at Fort Knox) equal to at least 25% of the face amount of the notes outstanding, with the balance secured by U.S. Government bonds.

Fiscal From the Latin word "fiscus," the reed basket in which the Roman tax collectors collected the grain and other produce which the peasants used to pay their taxes. Even before the time of Christ, "fiscus" referred generally to the administration of government finance. Fiscal policy (as against monetary policy) involves measures adopted by the Treasury, such as changes in tax rates or shifts in the public debt, and changes in government expenditures.

Fixed Cost That portion of the cost of production which remains constant irrespective of the volume of output, including real estate taxes, interest on bonds and mortgages, insurance, depreciation, obsolescence, etc. (See also Variable Cost.)

Flexible Budget A plan of government income and expenditures which can be adjusted freely to compensate for changes in the spending of the private sector. From a practical point of view, government budgets are rarely "flexible."

"Flight Capital" Highly volatile funds, whose owners are primarily interested in security rather than in big returns. Flight capital moves from one country to another whenever the owners fear that a currency (which they try to sell) may be devalued, or foreign exchange restrictions (which prevent the free movement of funds) may be instituted. During the 1930's and 1940's "flight capital" moved from Europe to the United States, and during the 1950's and 1960's large amounts of Latin American "flight capital" continued to come to the United States. However, by the middle 1950's capital (both American and foreign) began to move from the United States to Europe, having an adverse effect on the American balance of payments and resulting in substantial gold losses.

Free Reserves All member banks of the Federal Reserve System are required to maintain a certain percentage of their demand and time deposits (the pecentage is fixed from time to time by the Board of Governors of the Federal Reserve System) with their respective Federal Reserve banks in the form of "legal reserves." Some banks maintain more than the required reserves, the excess being known as "excess reserves." Other banks borrow temporarily from the Federal Reserve System to maintain their minimum "legal reserves." By deducting the amounts borrowed by some banks from the excess reserves of the other banks, one arrives at the "free reserves" of the banking system as a whole, which indicates the potential lending capacity of the banking system; e.g., if free reserves total $1 billion, and the legal reserve requirements average 14%, the total lending capacity of the banking system would be about $7.1 billion. ($1 billion free reserves = 14% of $7.1 billion lending capacity.)

Fringe Benefits Benefits received by workers in addition to their regular and overtime wages, such as paid vacations, old age pensions, medical care, supplementary unemployment insurance, etc.

"Full Employment" A notion developed during and immediately after World War II. With the large-scale unemployment of the 1930's a fresh memory, there was a widespread feeling in the U.S. and Western Europe that it was the duty of government to prevent a postwar depression. The notion implies that "the Federal Government is ultimately responsible for full employment" (Henry Wallace). This goal could be accomplished only "by planning in advance to synchronize all government programs with the programs of private enterprise so that the whole national income will be maintained at the full employment level" (Wallace). President Roosevelt first adopted the notion in the 1944 Presidential campaign. The intellectual father of the Full Employment notion was Lord Beveridge (*Full Employment in a Free Society,* 1945) who argued that there should always be more jobs than workers to fill them. "Jobs, rather than men, would wait." He recognized the danger of inflation and proposed to solve it by giving the government the power to fix wages and prices, and if necessary allocate labor to specific tasks. Full Employment, according to Beveridge, may (or must) in the end entail a complete regimentation of the economy. Even American advocates of the Full Employment policy admit that "Full Employment policies are loaded with inflationary dangers" (Alvin Hansen). The notion crystallized in the "Employment Act of 1946," which calls for "maximum employment." This has variously been interpreted as meaning that enough jobs are to be created, if necessary through government intervention, for at least 96% to 97½% (unemployment of 4% to 2½%) of the labor force. The Full Employment policy represents one of the cornerstones of modern government planning. The goal is to be achieved through monetary and fiscal policies (and if necessary through direct intervention, such as public works programs and youth corps). Skeptics question whether the government can achieve full employment without inflation and regimentation of the economy.

Functional Illiteracy A modern notion describing a level of education which may be adequate for a simple quasi-rural existence and for unskilled jobs, but which is inadequate to meet the needs of a more advanced job in a modern technologically advanced economy.

General Equilibrium (also known as the Walrasian Equilibrium after Léon Walras who developed it). The notion that all prices tend toward a level at which the demand for and supply of all goods will be in balance. While the "partial equilibrium" theory of Alfred Marshall dealt with the equilibrium of supply and demand of one product, assuming all other factors to be constant, Walras stressed the fact that the millions of partial equilibria must be conceived as being interconnected, so that one cannot assume "other things being equal." A change in the price of wheat affects not only the income of farmers and the price of bread, but may also affect the demand for tractors and hence the employment in steel mills, the demand for rye, and for shipping space, etc.

Greenbacks Paper money first issued during the Civil War, officially known as "United States Notes," of which $323 million were still outstanding in 1967. The "greenbacks" are unsecured I.O.U.'s of the Federal government. They come in $2 and $5 denominations and bear a red seal (green seal for Federal Reserve Notes and blue seal for Silver Certificates which are being withdrawn).

Gross National Product (GNP) Statistical compilation representing the aggregate value (usually expressed in current dollars) of all the goods and services produced during a given year, with no allowance made for depreciation. If all the resources of a nation are fully employed, the GNP indicates the maximum productive capacity of a nation, assuming existing technological and social conditions.

"Guide-line" Policy A theory presented by President Kennedy's economic advisors, based on the notion that if wages on an average do not increase more than the average productivity of the workers, there is no reason for prices to increase, and since over a period of years the average productivity of American labor has increased by about 3.2% a year (other estimates range from 2.8% to 3.4%), average wages can be increased safely by 3.2% a year without causing a rise in prices. The theory was first presented in West Germany during the 1950's and rejected as impractical. The difficulty lies in the fact that productivity increases vary from year to year, and certainly from occupation to occupation. While the productivity of a worker in a newly automated plant will increase sharply, the "productivity" of a physician or college professor increases only very slowly. Uniform wage increases based on the "average" increase in productivity will thus lead to cost and price increases in some industries and occupations, while in mechanized industries, where the productivity rises faster than the "average," the workers feel that they do not get what is due them. During 1964 and 1965 a wage increase of 3.2% was declared to be "non-inflationary." By 1966 the government-established guidelines came to be widely disregarded with the unions demanding and obtaining wage increase of 6% or more. At the same time the productivity increase declined sharply to about 1%–2%.

Holding Companies Corporations which own the stock of other companies. Holding companies can serve a dual purpose: (1) They make it possible to control a large complex of companies through a relatively small investment, and (2) if a holding company holds the controlling interest in competing companies, it can as a rule reduce the competition among its subsidiaries. The pyramiding of holding companies, which was popular during the 1920's in the public utilities field, is no longer legal. Nor can the holding company device be used as a means of limiting competition.

Idle Savings An important concept in modern macroeconomic thought and one of the basic arguments for government intervention. If total savings exceed investments, the difference accumulates in the form of "idle savings," which will result in a corresponding decline in production and employment. According to 19th Century economic theory, "idle savings" could not persist for any length of time, because they would lead to a decline in interest rates, which in turn would result in lower savings and greater investments, thus eliminating idle savings. Modern economists argue that because of institutional obstacles, the "interest rate mechanism" has lost its effectiveness in preventing the accumulation of "idle savings," thus necessitating government intervention. Under the theory of "compensatory spending," the government is expected to absorb the "idle savings" accumulating in the private sector by increasing government spending (resulting in "deficit spending"), thus assuring full employment.

Imperfect Competition (also referred to as monopolistic competition). A market situation which combines monopolistic and competitive aspects. (1) There are more than one producer of the same or comparable products, but the number of competitors is relatively small (oligopoly), so that each competitor can significantly affect the total supply and hence the market price. (2) The individual producer attempts through "product differentiation" to create a quasi-monopoly for his own product. There is little difference between the competing brands of breakfast foods, cigarets, chewing gum, or toothpastes, but the producers stress in their advertising fancied or minor differences in order to distinguish their product from that of their competitors, and thus gain the advantage of offering a "unique" product.

Income Taxes Government levies either on individuals (personal income taxes) or on corporations (corporation income tax). Personal income taxes provide about 55% of Federal tax revenues, and corporation income taxes, another 25%. The Constitution specifically prohibited a Federal income tax in its present form. Article I, Section II, Paragraph 3 requires that "direct taxes shall be apportioned among the several States . . . according to their respective numbers," and Article I, Section IX, Paragraph 4 provides that "no . . . direct taxes shall be laid, unless in proportion to the census or enumeration herein before directed to be taken." The Constitutional prohibitions were removed in 1913 through the Sixteenth Amendment, which gives Congress the power "to lay and collect taxes on incomes, from whatever source derived, without apportionment among the several States . . ." Despite the phrase "from whatever source derived," the Supreme Court still holds to the decision made shortly after the Civil War (Collector vs. Day, 11 Wall 113) that the Federal Government cannot tax the instrumentalities of the states (i.e., interest from state bonds). The doctrine was subsequently extended to municipal bonds (Pollock vs. Farmers Loan & Trust Co. 157 U.S. 429 and 158 U.S. 601). Since the interest on their bonds is exempt from Federal income taxes, state and local governments can borrow at lower interest rates (in some instances considerably lower than the Federal government). Congress could probably override these Supreme Court decisions and make the income from state and local bonds taxable as any other income, but this would cause serious dislocations in local finance and would probably force the Federal government to come to the aid of state and local governments. The first income tax in modern times was instituted in England in 1799 by William Pitt as an "emergency measure" to finance the war against Napoleon.

Industrial Unions Labor organizations (unions) which attempt to organize all the workers employed in a given industry, whether skilled or unskilled. In 1935 the major industrial unions broke away from the AFL to form the CIO, since the AFL was dominated by the craft unions, whose membership consisted of skilled workers organized according to their specific crafts. Typical industrial unions are the United Mine Workers, while the building trade unions, the machinists union, the typesetters and the photoengravers are typical craft unions.

Inheritance and Estate Taxes (Death Taxes) Government levy on the share of an estate as it is received by the heir. An estate tax is levied on the entire estate as left by the deceased. The purpose of death taxes is more political and social (the desire to reduce economic inequality and give all people a more equal start) rather than fiscal. The taxes produce only about 1–2% of Federal, and less than 3% of state tax revenues. In order to prevent states from competing among each other in attracting wealthy people by keeping the death taxes low, the Federal government in 1924 agreed to credit up to 25% of the Federal tax on payments of state death taxes. If a state levied no death tax, the full tax went to the Federal government; if it levied a tax higher than 25% of the Federal tax, the estate had to pay the difference to the state in addition to the Federal death taxes. It was thus in the interest of the states to keep their death taxes at 25% of the Federal tax. Death taxes are steeply progressive. Combined Federal and New York State death taxes take about 15% of an estate of $200,000, 30% of an estate of $1 million and almost 80% in the case of $100 million. Minimum exemptions and marital deductions vary widely from state to state. The Federal government and the states also collect "gift taxes" to prevent a person from transferring part of his wealth in anticipation of death. All gifts in excess of $50,000 (within a year) are subject to a steeply progressive gift tax. Gift and death taxes are complex, and experts can often cut the total tax due on large estates by as much as 50%.

Institution An established organization, custom or practice, such as the 40-hour week, the banking, monetary or credit system, labor unions, corporations, collective bargaining, installment buying, securities markets, transportation and communication system, government regulatory agencies, etc. *Institutional framework* consists of the economic, social and political institutions which form part of the economic system. *Institutional economics,* a school of economic thought which was especially influential in the U.S. during the first three decades of the 20th Century. The school assumes that in order to understand the operations of an economic system, it is of primary importance to study the institutional framework. Well-known exponents of the school were John R. Commons, Wesley C. Mitchell and Thornstein Veblen.

Interlocking directorates A method of curtailing competition. If the same men act as directors of competing firms, they can influence the policies of these firms in order to curtail competition. Interlocking directorates are forbidden in the United States. For instance, a banker could not be at the same time a director of the Ford Motor Company and of Chrysler. However, this does not preclude that the same man is a director of a number of non-competing companies. About a third of the directorships of the 250 largest corporations are held by about 400 men, most of whom hold numerous directorships.

Investments The term has a specific meaning in the language of the economists. It refers to the net addition (after allowance for depreciation) to the stock of factories, machinery, transportation facilities and inventories. In popular language, people speak of "investments" when they buy U.S. government savings bonds or 100 shares of U.S. Steel at the New York Stock Exchange. To the economist, purchases of securities do *not* represent "investments." Investments always mean "real capital formation" — "capital" meaning "capital goods," i.e., productive facilities.

Investment bankers See securities underwriters.

Iron Law of Wages A wage theory which was popular during the 19th Century, but is rejected today. The theory is based on the Malthusian "law" that the population will always tend to increase faster than the food supply. If wages are raised above the subsistence level, the population will increase faster than the food supply (because for a while the worker, with more income, will be able to provide better for his children and more of them will survive beyond infancy). In due course there will be more workers than jobs, and the demand for food will exceed the food supply. The higher wages of yesteryear will thus result in increased misery as wages sink again to the subsistence level. By "subsistence level," David Ricardo understood an income adequate for a worker to feed himself and his wife, and to raise two children. Ricardo realized that this is not an absolute amount, but that it is determined partly by the prevailing standard of living.

Joint Demand Most goods are demanded in conjunction with other goods. The demand for gasoline and tires is a "joint demand" with the demand for automobiles. Thus the supply and price of either gasoline, tires, or cars individually affect the supply and price of the two other products.

Juglar Cycles Wave-like fluctuations in business activities, a full cycle lasting about 7–10 years, first observed by Clement Juglar in the 1860's. (See also Kondratieff and Kitchin cycles.)

Kitchin Cycles Wave-like fluctuations in business activities of rather short duration (about 40 months as against 7–10 years for the Juglar cycles), first observed by Joseph Kitchin in 1923. (See also Kondratieff cycles.)

Knights of Labor American labor organization which started in Philadelphia in 1869, originally as a secret fraternal order. By 1878 it had gained national scope, and the secrecy was abandoned in 1881. It supported and helped to win various major strikes, e.g., against the Union Pacific and the Wabash Railroad, but gradually lost out to the American Federation of Labor, and even though it continued to exist until 1917, it had little power after the 1890's. The Knights of Labor attempted to organize all workers irrespective of specific crafts to which they belonged, and irrespective of race and creed. They accepted farmers, small businessmen and foremen as long as they sided with labor against "capitalism." The chief reason for the decline of the Knights of Labor was the fact that the members of skilled crafts did not think that their specific interests were the same as those of unskilled workers, and they preferred their own craft unions.

Kondratieff Cycles Business cycle theory presented in 1923 by N. D. Kondratieff, emphasizing the fact that in addition to the regular business cycle fluctuations (lasting 7–10 years) first observed by Juglar in the 1860's, there are so-called "long waves," extending over a period of about 40 years. Schumpeter attributed the Kondratieff cycles to wave-like changes in technological developments.

Laissez faire A political and economic philosophy based on the premises of the 18th Century Enlightenment. It assumes that just as the physical universe is governed by inherent laws (such as the laws of gravitation) the social system is likewise governed by a system of inherent forces, which, if not disturbed by government interference, will make for "the best of all worlds." Hence the belief of the advocates of laissez faire that "the least governed country is the best governed country," and their demand for "freedom of production" (laissez faire) and "freedom of trade" (laissez passer).

Lawful Money The term was important during the 19th Century, when some money was "lawful" and hence could be used by banks as legal reserves, and other types of money could not be used for this purpose. Today the distinction has disappeared; all coin and paper money is "lawful money"; and the phrase "redeemable in lawful money," which appears on the Federal Reserve Notes, is meaningless. If the holder of a $10 Federal Reserve Note were to demand "lawful money," he could be given either another $10 Federal Reserve Note, or ten $1 Federal Reserve Notes, or five $2 United States notes.

Least-Cost-Substitution Principle One of the basic doctrines in the theory of production. In order to hold the cost of production to the minimum (and thus maximize the profit) an entrepreneur must strive to "substitute" the least expensive factor of production for the more expensive ones. He must strive for the best possible combination of "least-cost factors." If machines prove cheaper than labor because of an increase in wages, machines will tend to be substituted for labor. If this is not done, the overall cost will rise, the competitive position of the business will be impaired and (in theory at least) the general standard of living of the country may decline.

Legal Tender All types of money which can be tendered in payment of taxes and debts. All paper money is legal tender, as well as coins within reasonable limits. Checks are not legal tender. A creditor may thus refuse to accept a check. But if he refuses to accept paper money he has no claim against the debtor for interest on the unpaid debt.

Liberalism The meaning of the word has changed completely during the past 35 years. According to 19th Century usage, liberalism stood for the freedom of the individual from government controls. Liberals believed that the "least governed country is the best governed country." They opposed the conservatives who stood for the maintenance of social institutions. During the 19th Century the liberal parties (at least in Europe) represented business interests. The modern usage of the word developed since the 1930's. Its emphasis is not on a "personal freedom," but on "freedom from want." Modern liberals, as a rule, do not represent business interests, but "the common man" and labor.

Limited Partnership A business organization which, in addition to general partners who are fully liable for all obligations of the business, has one or more additional partners, whose liability is limited to the amount which they have contributed to the business. For instance, when a general partner dies and the firm finds it difficult to pay the deceased partner's share to his widow, the latter is often induced to become a limited partner. She has no voice in the conduct of the business, but shares in the profits.

Liquidity Preference An important concept in Keynesian economics. The degree to which people hold their assets in cash or near-cash rather than in assets which cannot readily be converted into cash. In order to induce them to convert their cash and demand deposits into investments, thus diminishing their liquidity, people must be given an inducement in the form of an adequate rate of interest.

Listed Securities Stocks and bonds which are bought and sold on the floor of one of the stock exchanges (chiefly the New York Stock Exchange). Unlisted securities are traded in the over-the-counter market (*viz.*). There are many more unlisted than listed securities. Only the more important issues are listed.

Lydia Kingdom in what is today Asia Minor. The first coins were made in Lydia some time between 750 and 700 B. C. King Croesus of Lydia was probably the first to produce gold coins.

Macroeconomics The branch of economic theory which developed since the 1930's and deals with "the economics of the nation," as against microeconomics, which deals with "the economics of the firm." Macroeconomics deals almost exclusively with aggregates such as aggregate (total) purchasing power, aggregate income, total employment, the balance of payments equilibrium, the rate of economic growth, etc. National economic planning rests on macroeconomic theories.

Maintenance of Membership A provision in contracts between employers and unions which provides that, after a contract has been signed the individual worker has the right to withdraw from the union during a limited period of time (usually 2 weeks) after which time he may not give up his union membership during the life of the contract without losing his job. The "maintenance of membership" provision was widely used during World War II. It has since been replaced largely by the union shop provision.

Malthusianism The theory popularized by Thomas Malthus (1766–1834) that the population increase always will tend to be greater than the increase in the food supply, so that a segment of mankind will always be close to the starvation level. Malthus regarded this as "a law of nature." Economists built on this Malthusian idea a theory of wages — the so-called "iron law of wages" — which was very popular during the 19th Century. It assumed that an increase in wages above the subsistence level would result in an increase in the rate of population growth, which in turn would lead to unemployment and more starvation. Hence, economists assumed, wages could never rise for any length of time above the subsistence level.

Margin Requirements In buying securities the investor, as a rule, does not have to pay the full purchase price. He has to make only a partial (marginal) payment and can borrow the balance from his broker or a bank. The size of the down payment (margin requirements) is fixed from time to time by the Federal Reserve System under the so-called Regulation "T" (applicable to brokers and securities dealers) and Regulation "U" (applicable to banks). Margin requirements in recent years have fluctuated between 50% and 70%. If margin requirements are increased, the cost of buying stocks increases. Such increases should have a dampening effect on stock prices and may discourage stock speculation.

Marginal Efficiency of Capital An important concept in Keynesian theory. In planning an additional (marginal) investment, the entrepreneur calculates the expected return on the "marginal investment." If he invests an additional (marginal) million dollars, and expects a return of $100,000 from his additional investment, the productivity (efficiency) of his additional (marginal) capital investment would be 10%. According to Keynesian theory the volume of investments is determined by (1) the cost of capital and (2) (and more importantly) by the "marginal efficiency of capital."

Marginal-Factor-Cost A concept employed in the theory of production referring to the cost of additional (marginal) factors of production. If it costs the entrepreneur $100 a week to employ an additional (marginal) worker, the "marginal factor cost" (of this worker) would be $100. The "marginal factor cost" must always be lower than the "marginal revenue product," the value of the goods which the "marginal factor" (in this case the additional worker) produces.

Marginal Physical Product A concept in the microeconomic theory of production which refers to the increase in the physical output resulting from the employment of one additional (marginal) factor of production.

Marginal Propensity to Consume (or Save) Two concepts which are important in Keynesian theory. The Keynesian notion of "propensity" can best be translated (although not exactly) by "tendency" or "inclination." If a consumer receives additional (marginal) income of, let us say, $500 a year, he may either spend the money on additional consumption, or he may save it. The percentage of the additional (marginal) income which is consumed is governed by what Keynes calls the "marginal propensity to consume," the percentage which is saved by the "marginal propensity to save." Keynes assumed that the additional income consumed will tend to be smaller than the "average propensity to consume" (the pecentage of the total income spent on consumption goods). Average propensity to consume and average propensity to save must always be equal to total Disposable Income; and marginal propensity to consume and marginal propensity to save must always be equal to the marginal (additional) income.

Marginal Utility The degree of utility (or satisfaction) derived from the input of an additional (marginal) unit. The concept is important in microeconomic demand and price theory. A man, let us say, owns six shirts. He buys an additional (marginal) shirt. The satisfaction (utility) which he gets from the additional shirt would constitute the "marginal utility." Microeconomic theory assumes that this marginal satisfaction is equal to the price (let us say $5) which the consumer paid for the additional (marginal) unit. It is assumed further that the degree of utility declines with the purchase of each additional unit. In other words, the seventh shirt would provide less utility (satisfaction) and the consumer would hence be expected to pay less than $5 for it.

Mature Economy One of the basic premises of the Keynesian theory (proved wrong by subsequent experience) namely, that in some countries (Keynes thought especially of Britain and the U.S.) production facilities have been fully developed, the normal needs of the consumer have been largely satisfied, and the population growth has slowed down, as a result of which the demand for additional investments tends to be less than the savings, which continue to accumulate. The result would be "idle savings," leading to a corresponding decline in production and employment. To off-set this development, Keynes suggested an increase in government spending (equal to the accumulation of idle savings) — a theory which has served as a justification for huge government deficits and resulting chronic inflation throughout the world for almost 30 years. Actually the Keynesian "mature economy" premise lost its validity with the outbreak of World War II in 1939. Rather than suffering from "idle savings," the world has been plagued by a chronic shortage of investment capital, due to revolutionary technological changes, a tremendous increase in consumer demand in developed as well as underdeveloped countries, and a world wide "population explosion."

Mercantilism The term was coined by Adam Smith in referring to the economic ideas and policies which prevailed during the Age of Absolutism from the 16th to the 18th Century. Mercantilism has been called a "tool of state-making." Its aim was to strengthen the state, not to increase the well-being of the individual. In order to maintain a large army and a strong navy, to pay for the costly court and a large bureaucracy, the state needed money, which in those days consisted of gold and silver. The aim of Mercantilism was therefore to increase the nation's store of precious metals. This required a surplus of exports over imports (with the balance paid in precious metals) which in turn made it necessary to keep domestic prices and wages as low as possible and to curtail domestic consumption. In order to strengthen the state, the standard of living of the masses had to be kept as low as possible. The American Revolution of 1776 was in part directed against the mercantilistic restraints exercised by the British government.

Merger The joining together of one or more individual companies into one new and larger company. The Department of Justice carefully watches for mergers which may result in an impairment of competition.

Microeconomics The branch of economic theory which deals with "the economics of the firm," as against macroeconomics, which deals with "the economics of the nation." Microeconomics is the traditional 19th Century approach. It was not until the 1930's that macroeconomic theory became important. Microeconomics assumes tacitly that the economy of the nation is a mere sum total of the economic activities of millions of firms and individuals. Its two most important issues are the question of price formation, and the distribution of income among the factors of production.

Monopoly From the Greek "monos" (alone) and polein (sell). A market structure in which there is only one seller, e.g., a town which is served by only one railroad. Since monopolies can use their power to raise prices freely, "natural monopolies," resulting from a situation where competition would not be sound for economic or other reason (e.g., two or more phone companies in one city), are subject to government supervision and regulation; "artificial monopolies," created through the co-operation of supposedly competing companies, are prohibited under the Sherman and the Clayton Anti-trust Acts.

Monopsony From the Greek "monos" (alone) and "psonein" (buy). A market structure with only one buyer, who can thus control prices if the seller is compelled to sell. Examples are local grain elevators and cotton gins, especially in former days when the roads were bad and the farmers could not send their produce to the next town. Monopsonies (like monopolies) are subject to government control.

Multiplier An important concept in macroeconomic theory going back to Keynes. Additional (autonomous) spending — resulting either from the mobilization of formerly idle savings, deficit spending by the government financed through the creation of additional credit, or the influx of foreign capital — results in a multiple increase in the Gross National Product as the additional investment filters through the economy in the form of secondary consumption spending. The multiplier is the numerical coefficient which indicates the increase in total income resulting from an autonomous investment. If an autonomous investment of $1 billion produces an increase in the GNP of $4 billion, the multiplier is "4." The multiplier is always the inverse of the "marginal propensity to save."

National Bureau of Economic Research Private research organization, founded by Wesley C. Mitchell, and now headed by Arthur F. Burns. Famous for its extensive research in business cycle statistics and its work on national income data.

National Income (NI) Statistical compilation prepared by the Department of Commerce and the National Bureau of Economic Research. The former bases its calculation on the total payments (in the form of wages, interest, rent and profits) made to the factors of production; the latter, on the aggregate market value of the goods and services received by the public in the course of the year. The two approaches look upon the same process from different points of view, but arrive at the same results (subject to minor statistical differences).

National Income Accounts Statistical aggregates indicating the total production of goods and services, and the total income. The most important aggregates are: Gross National Product (indicating the value of all the goods and services produced); Net National Product (GNP less allowance for depreciation); National Income (total payments to the factors of production); Personal Income (total income received by individuals), and Disposable Income (Personal Income after payment of income taxes). The National Income Accounts were developed gradually since the 1930's to form a basis for macroeconomic planning.

National Income Budget A method of calculating Federal government revenues and expenditures to show the effect of government operations on the economy. The "National Income Budget" omits all Federal loans, includes tax receipts as they accrue (not as they are actually paid) and government orders as they are actually executed and thus affect production and employment in private industry (not as they are authorized by Congress ("Administrative Budget") or as they are eventually paid for ("Cash Budget").

"Near Money" Liquid assets such as savings deposits and short-term government obligations which are technically not considered money (money consisting of currency and demand deposits) but which can readily be converted into money. The Federal Reserve, as a rule, regards time deposits (including savings deposits) as "money" rather than "near money," because of the ease with which time and savings deposits can be converted into demand deposits. It is helpful to think of the stock of money not as a fixed amount, but rather in terms of the "moneyness" of liquid assets, indicating the ease with which the supply of money can be increased.

Negotiable Instruments A legal concept referring to the transferability of assets. Assets can be transferred either by "negotiation" or by "assignment." Only checks, commercial drafts, acceptances, promissory notes and a few other commercial instruments pass by "negotiation" and are thus "negotiable instruments." All other assets pass by "assignment." The most important difference between "negotiation" and "assignment" is the fact that a "negotiable instrument" conveys clear title to the third party. A dishonest merchant sells defective merchandise and takes a promissory note in payment. He then endorses the note to a finance company. The signer of the note is fully liable to the finance company, even though the goods do not live up to the purchase contract. On the other hand, "A" steals a car from "B" and then sells it to "C," the transfer constituting an "assignment" rather than a "negotiation." "B" can recover the car from "C," even though "C" purchased the car in good faith from "A," because "A" did not have good title to the car (which he had stolen) and hence could not transfer a better title than he possessed. On the other hand, a stolen check properly endorsed to an innocent third party could be collected by the third party (unless payment was stopped). The distinction between transfer by "negotiation" and "assignment" goes back to Roman Law. It helps to make checks and other negotiable instruments more freely acceptable.

To meet the requirements of "negotiability" the negotiable instrument must represent an unconditional promise to pay a fixed (or ascertainable) sum of money on a fixed (or ascertainable) date. It must show the names of the maker of the instrument, of the beneficiary (or payee) and of the drawee (or payor).

Net National Product (NNP) Statistical compilation representing the aggregate value (in current dollars) of all the goods and services produced during a given year after deduction of the necessary allowance for depreciation (see Gross National Product).

Normative Discipline A branch of human knowledge which is based on the acceptance of a system of ethical standards, which it applies to everyday life. Normative economics, which was characteristic of medieval economic thought (and is reflected in the modern social encyclicals), accepted as known the ethical norms by which man was to live. It then analyzed social customs and business practices to ascertain whether they conformed to the basic principles. Normative economics thus deals with "what ought to be," while analytical economics tries to discover "what will be."

Oeconomia From Greek word "oicos" (household), meaning the management of the household, or in a wider sense, the production of goods and services for consumption within the household, rather than for sale at a profit (Chrematistike). Economics did not acquire its modern meaning until the 17th Century.

Oligopoly A market structure characterized by a small number of sellers, characteristic of modern industry. E.g., three automobile manufacturers account for about 90% of the total domestic car production. The trend toward oligopoly is due partly to technological factors. It requires vast investments in factories and machinery to turn out modern durable consumer goods. If there were 100 automobile manufacturers competing with each other, none of them would have enough sales to justify the heavy investments. The danger in oligopolies lies in the fact that they facilitate price-fixing agreements and other restraints of trade.

Oligopsony A market structure characterized by small number of buyers; e.g., the demand for Pullman cars or railroad equipment in general, or for automobile parts used by automobile manufacturers. If a manufacturer who has to sell in an oligopolistic market loses one or two major accounts, he may be forced out of business.

Open Market Operations By far the most important tool of the Federal Reserve System's monetary policy to control the volume of credit. Open market operations consist in the purchase or sale of government securities (chiefly Treasury Bills and other short-term obligations) and, to a very minor degree, of commercial paper. By buying in the open market, the Federal Reserve increases the supply of money; by selling, it dries up excess credit. All buying and selling is done by the "Trading Desk" of the New York Federal Reserve Bank, which operates in close cooperation with the Board of Governors and the U.S. Treasury. Basic policies are determined by the Open Market Committee of the Board of Governors, which consists of the seven Governors, the President of the New York Federal Reserve Bank and four other Federal Reserve bank presidents (representing the major areas of the country), with the other seven Federal Reserve bank presidents participating in the deliberations. The Federal Reserve started open market operations on an informal basis during the 1920's. The Federal Open Market Committee was formally established by the Banking Act of 1933. Open Market Operations serve a dual purpose: (1) They form the chief tool of the Federal Reserve to pursue an anti-cyclical (or "full employment" or "maximum growth") policy; and (2), less spectacular but extremely important, they are used to eliminate sharp day-to-day fluctuations in the supply of and demand for credit, which during the 1920's often resulted in violent fluctuations of interest rates, especially in the "call money" market (loans contracted by stock brokers to finance the margin purchases of their clients).

Organic Society There are two basic concepts of society: the organic and the atomistic. Under the organic concept of society the individual is compared to the cell of a body. The cell can survive only as long as the whole body is healthy. A diseased cell can poison the organism. The cells are basically different, each performing special functions as part of the entire system. Under the atomistic concept of society, the individual is compared to a self-contained grain of sand, each a unit unto itself, all more or less alike, and all subject to the impersonal forces of nature. Under the organic concept of society, society (the organism as a whole) is the ultimate entity; under the atomistic, it is the individual (the single grain of sand). During the 19th Century the atomistic concept of society predominated; during the Middle Ages, the organic; and the trend in modern times is again toward the organic viewpoint. Whether a society thinks of itself in atomistic (individualistic) or organic (statist-social) terms has a great deal to do with the type of socioeconomic theories it develops.

Over-the-counter market While most of the important stock and bond issues are "listed" on one of the stock exchanges (chiefly the New York Stock Exchange), the majority of the stock and bond issues are "unlisted." They are traded in the so-called "over-the-counter" market, provided by several thousand securities dealers who stand ready to buy and sell for their own account various unlisted issues in which they "make a market." Daily quotation sheets for unlisted securities indicate which dealer makes a market in a given issue. The over-the-counter dealers are closely supervised by the Securities and Exchange Commission.

Parity The term, meaning equality or equivalence, is used in economics in a number of different connections. Parity prices in agriculture, for instance, refer to the price at which farm products would have to sell to give the farmer the same purchasing power as he possessed in a certain base year. Parity of exchange means the official rate (usually based on the relative price of gold) at which the currency of one country can be exchanged for that of another.

Partial Equilibrium, also known as the Marshallian Equilibrium, after Alfred Marshall who developed it. The partial equilibrium theory deals with the price and quantity sold of just *one* product, assuming that all other factors (outside the supply of, demand for and price of the one product) remain unchanged. In contrast, the General Equilibrium theory of Léon Walras holds that the millions of partial equilibria must be conceived as being interconnected, and that nothing happens in the economy which does not affect a multitude of other economic events.

Partnership A business organization with more than one owner. Partnerships are created through written or oral agreements by two or more individuals, who jointly conduct a business, assume jointly all responsibilities, and share in the profits according to a previously agreed-upon schedule. The partners assume "unlimited liabilities," i.e., if the assets of the business are not adequate to cover all claims, the creditors can seize the private assets of the individual partners. Many stock exchange brokerage houses, law and accounting firms are organized as partnerships.

Perfect Competition A notion which plays an important role in microeconomic theory. Basically, perfect competition assumes that there are so many individual buyers and sellers, that no one of them can affect the price within a given market area. This is the situation in the case of the individual farmer, who can sell his entire crop at the prevailing market price; he can sell no more at a lower price; he can sell nothing at a higher price; and the general market price will not be affected whether he sells his crop or not. Similarly, the individual buyer at a grocery store will not affect the price of coffee in the city, whether he buys coffee or not. He will not be able to get coffee below the established price, and since he can get all he needs at the established price, he will not get more by offering to pay a premium. Microeconomic theory originally assumed perfect competition as the "normal" market structure, and basic microeconomic models are based on perfect competition.

Personal Income (PI) Statistical compilation of the aggregate income received by all individuals in the course of a year, prior to the payment of personal income taxes.

Physiocrats A group of French philosopher-economists who played a fairly important role in France between about 1750 and 1785. They represent the first school of "scientific" economists, in that they assumed the social order (just as the physical universe) to be governed by inherent laws, it being the task of the economist to discover these laws. François Quesnay, the founder and leader of the Physiocrats, thought that his *Tableau Economique* (best translated as "Economic Blueprint") could be compared with Newton's "laws" of gravitation. The Physiocrats assumed further (in the spirit of the Enlightenment) that man lived potentially in the "best of all worlds" (because the world was created by God). Poverty and social tensions, they thought, were due to government interference with the beneficial laws of nature. The slogan for which they are best known is: "Laissez faire! Laissez passer! Le monde và de lui même" ("Freedom of production! Freedom of trade! The world runs by itself").

Planned Obsolescence The attempt of manufacturers to make the goods which the consumer owns look out-of-style, in order to induce the consumer to buy something new even though the old goods are still perfectly usable. The fashion industry has long relied on "planned obsolescence" in order to induce the public to buy new suits, dresses or hats. Since the 1930's "planned obsolescence" has played an increasingly important role in the durable consumer goods industries. The best example are the annual model changes in the auto industry. Since World War II the home building industry has followed a similar policy of "planned obsolescence." There is a good deal of disagreement among economists and sociologists whether planned obsolescence helps to improve the standard of living of the people, or whether it represents economic waste.

Positivism The philosophic notion which goes back to Auguste Comte (1798–1857) that all true knowledge is derived from the analytical study of the material world. Positivism was characteristic of the spirit of "scientific certainty" which prevailed during the second half of the 19th Century. Modern scientists (and modern economists) are far less certain that they can ever attain a full understanding of ultimate reality.

Pragmatic Discipline Pragmatism is a predominantly American philosophical movement of the 20th Century. It assumes that theory should be a guide to action, and that the "truth" of a theory is to be tested by its practical application. Pragmatism has little to say about "ultimate ends." Pragmatic economics, which is characteristic of many aspects of modern economic planning, is predominantly operational, a tool of practical politics. It is not primarily concerned with either ethical values (normative economics) or universal theories (analytical economics).

Preferred stock Certificates of ownership in a corporation, similar to common stock; but preferred stockholders have certain prior claims (prior to the common stockholders) regarding the earnings and assets of the company. Preferred stockholders receive a fixed dividend before any dividends can be paid to the common stockholders. In return for this preferential treatment preferred stockholders, as a rule, surrender their right to participation in the earnings of the company beyond the fixed dividends (although there are exceptions to this rule). There are various types of preferred stocks. *Cumulative preferred:* If a company fails during a given year to pay the stipulated dividend, these dividend arrears must be paid in subsequent years before the common stockholders receive anything. *Non-cumulative preferred* stockholders, on the other hand, have no further claim if no dividend was paid during a given year. However, if preferred dividends have been omitted for a certain time (as a rule five quarterly payments) the preferred stockholders are given the right to elect the majority of the directors, i.e., the control of the company passes from the common to the preferred stockholders. *Participating preferred stock* is entitled to the stipulated dividend before anything can be paid to common stockholders, and then participates with the common stockholders (according to a predetermined schedule) in the remainder of the earnings. *Redeemable or callable preferred stock* may be paid back at the option of the common stockholders (usually at a premium). *Convertible preferred stock* may be converted into common stock at the option of the preferred stockholders.

Progressive Taxes Government levies which increase more rapidly than income, e.g., personal income taxes. In 1962, for example, a man with an income of $4800 (and the usual family deductions) paid only $48 in income taxes, while a man with twice the income paid $1584.

Propensity to Consume (or Save) These concepts play an important role in Keynesian theory, "propensity" (in Keynesian language) meaning about the same as "inclination" or "tendency." An individual can use his Disposable Income (net income after taxes) either for consumption or for saving. The "propensity to consume" indicates the percentage of disposable income which the individual spends on consumption (the balance being saved). The numerical values of the "propensity to consume" (let us say 0.93) and of the "propensity to save" (0.07) must always add up to one. Total savings of the nation must be equal to total investment demand, to prevent the accumulation of "idle savings" (which in turn would lead to unemployment). Keynes assumed (on the basis of the depressed conditions of the 1930's) that in the case of "mature" (fully industrialized) nations total savings tended to exceed investment opportunities. In other words, the over-all "propensity to save" was too high. He therefore suggested a shift of income (through government intervention) from high to low income groups, whose "propensity to consume" was thought to be higher, thus curbing the accumulation of savings on the part of the high income groups. The Keynesian arguments appealed to the equalitarian sentiments of our time and had a profound effect on government policy in striving for greater equality of income. Empirical evidence does not support the original Keynesian assumptions. The relative distribution of spending and saving seems to be determined chiefly by cultural, institutional and cyclical/psychological factors, rather than by the level of income. Even though the per capita income of the American people is about eight times as large as that of the Japanese, the rate of individual savings is much higher in Japan. While real per capita income in the United States increased sharply during the postwar years, the rate of savings remained fairly constant. It fluctuated chiefly with cyclical changes: People saved relatively less in "good" times, and more when the economic situation was uncertain. (See also "marginal propensity to consume [or save]").

Property Taxes Government levies levied on property, either real estate, personal (moveable) property, or intangibles (stocks, bonds and other securities). Property taxes form the backbone of local taxes in the U.S. The difficulty lies in appraising the value of the property. This is particularly true with regard to personal property. The tax assessor is rarely qualified to judge the value of a picture, rug or table silver. One of the controversial issues regarding real estate taxes is the question whether land and improvements should be taxed at different rates, with fairly high rates on land and lower rates on improvements, in the hope that this would encourage the owners to improve their property, thus preventing the development of crowded slums.

Proportional Taxes Government levies in direct relationship to the taxpayers' income or wealth. The same percentage is deducted from a worker's wages for Social Security Taxes, whether he earns $2000 or

$4000. The same property tax rate applies, whether a home is valued at $15,000 or at $30,000.

Proprietorship (Single Proprietorship) A business owned by one man or one woman, who makes all decisions, gets all the profits, and assumes all the risks. Most of the small farms and retail establishments are individual proprietorships. The chief disadvantage of a proprietorship is the fact that the owner assumes "unlimited liability," i.e., if the assets of the business are not adequate to cover all the claims of the creditors, the latter can seize the personal assets of the proprietor: his car, home and furniture.

Protective Motive One of the reasons given by economists to explain the individual's changing tendency to save. In times of economic stress, individuals are likely to increase their rate of savings in order to be prepared for a decline in income or other eventualities. The development of social security and extensive welfare measures which provide the individual with greater economic security, are often cited as a reason for the relatively low rate of individual savings in the U.S. (compared to other countries). (See also speculative motive.)

Public Sector The economy is often divided into the "public" and the "private sector." The former consists of the goods and services produced and/or consumed by the government and government agencies; the latter, of the goods and services produced and/or consumed by private industry and the consumer. In the United States the public sector accounts for about 20% and the private sector for about 80% of total production and consumption.

Purchase Power Theory of Wages The modern theory that wages must be maintained high enough to assure a mass purchasing power level adequate to provide markets for all the goods and services which the economy can produce at the full employment level. The theory thus starts with the macroeconomic concept of full employment, and attempts to adjust wages in order to achieve the full employment goal. The Purchase Power Theory is in conflict with the traditional marginal producmately by the productivity of the workers.
tivity theory of wages, according to which wages are determined ulti-

Rate of Exchange The ratio at which the unit of one currency (e.g. the dollar) can be exchanged for one unit of another currency (pound sterling). The official rate of exchange is usually determined by the relative price of gold in the two countries. In the United States Congress has fixed the price of gold at $35, while the British Parliament has fixed the price at £14.58⅓. The rate of exchange is thus $2.40 = £1.

Rationalism The pursuit of knowledge by reasoning from "self-evident" truths. Economics tends to be a predominantly rational (as against empirical) discipline. Economic theories are based on such "self-evident" truth as the notion of the "economic man," or "economic maturity" of certain nations.

Regressive Taxes A government levy, such as a sales tax on a necessity, which weighs more heavily on the poor than on the rich. The richest Maharaja does not use much more salt than the poorest field worker, and both thus pay about the same salt tax.

Regulatory State A philosophy of government which was developed by the second generation utilitarians—reinforced by practical considerations. While the first generation of Utilitarians at the beginning of the 19th Century saw the cause of human misery primarily in the oppression by the all-powerful state (which induced them to advocate a policy of laissez faire), the second generation saw the cause in the lack of protection of the individual against the oppression by all-powerful economic interests. The regulatory state aims to protect the individual against abuses by powerful private interests. The Federal Trade, Interstate Commerce, Security and Exchange, and many similar Commissions are symptomatic of the spirit of the regulatory state.

"Rent Socialists" The advocates of an economic notion which had its origin with Ricardo, who pointed out that the increase in population as a rule results in a steady increase in the value of land, thus giving the land owner an "unearned gain" at the expense of the other classes of society. The 19th and 20th Centuries produced many advocates of one form or other of "land socialism." Some favored the outright nationalization of all land. Others (e.g., Henry George: *Progress and Poverty*) wanted to tax away the gains derived from increasing land values (due to population growth rather than improvements made by the owner). Some economists recommend that real estate taxes be levied at different rates on the land and on improvements, with the former taxed more heavily than the latter, thus recapturing a large part of the increased value of the land while encouraging improvements. Even though fairly successful in Australia and Pennsylvania, the system is rejected by most orthodox economists and meets with often violent opposition by real estate interests.

Representative Money Paper money which has the legal character of a warehouse receipt. The silver certificates (which are being gradually withdrawn), for example, state that for each $1 certificate there is "on deposit in the Treasury of the United States one dollar in silver, payable on demand." The gold certificates which were withdrawn from circulation in 1933 were another from of representative money. — All other paper money in circulation in the United States is credit money, issued on the basis of the good faith and credit of the issuer, chiefly the Federal Reserve System.

Reserve Requirements Commercial and savings banks are required by law to maintain reserves equal to a certain percentage of their demand and time deposits. Members of the Federal Reserve System must maintain these reserves in cash or as deposits with their respective Federal Reserve Banks. The rates may be changed by the Board of Governors within the limits fixed by Congress, i.e.,

	Demand Deposits	*Time Deposits*
Reserve City banks	10% — 22%	3% — 6%
Country banks	7% — 14%	3% — 6%

By changing the reserve requirements the Board of Governors can increase or decrease the lending capacity of the banking system, and thus counteract cyclical fluctuations.

Savings To the economist, savings represent the difference between income and consumption. If a man has a $5000 income, and he spends for consumption purposes $4800, he "saves" $200. The savings can take the form of paying off the mortgage on the home, of paying life insurance premiums, of buying government savings bond, etc.

Scarcity In the language of the economist all goods and services which are not free (such as air) are "scarce goods" (as against "free goods"). "Scarcity" and "utility" are the two basic forces which, according to the marginal utility theory, determine price.

Scholasticism The predominant philosophy of the Christian Middle Ages. At its fullest development during the 13th Century (especially in the *Summa Theologica* of St. Thomas Aquinas) it represents a balance between faith and intellect. There are two sources of knowledge: (1) revelation and authority and (2) the human mind and sense perception. If revelation and reasoning (or sense perception) appear in conflict, Scholasticism held that revelation and the authority of the Bible or Aristotle are to be trusted, rather than man's mind or senses. Applied to economic thought, Scholasticism developed a system of normative economics based on the notion that the basic (ethical) laws which (should) govern socio-economic relationships are known *a priori,* and that the task of the economist consists in analyzing existing customs and practices in the light of eternal truth to judge whether they conform to the basic standards.

Secular Trend Long-range growth rate of an economy, determined by the growth of the labor force, technological and managerial developments.

Securities Underwriters Investment bankers who purchase an entire stock, bond or debenture issue from a corporation or government, and then undertake to distribute the securities to individual investors. The securities underwriters thus "underwrite" the risk of distributing the securities at a given price. They operate under close supervision of the Securities and Exchange Commission.

Sherman Anti-Trust Act of 1890 Law which declared illegal "every contract, combination in the form of trust or otherwise, or conspiracy, in restraint of trade or commerce among the several States, or with foreign nations." Monopolistic restraints were unlawful throughout the Middle Ages as subversive of public welfare. The Common Law reflects this attitude. The Sherman Anti-Trust Act represents the first important statutory enactment in the United States designed to protect the public against agreements by producers to regulate the flow of goods and services in order to raise prices. The Act was directed in particular against the rapid growth of trusts during the 1880's.

Social Security Taxes A government levy collected from the employer and the worker to pay for old age security and unemployment benefits.

Socialism A socio-economic philosophy which stresses society at the expense of the individual, and collective or public ownership in the place of private property. There are many forms of socialism. The Fabian Socialists, who provided the philosophic arguments for the British Labour Party, believe in the gradual transfer of the privately owned industries to the government. The best-known socialist movement is Marxism. Karl Marx advocated the overthrow of the bourgeois free enterprise society and the establishment of the "dictatorship of the proletariat." Marxian socialism forms the basis of modern communism.

Speculative Motive Keynes explains "liquidity preference" (the desire to stay liquid rather than to invest savings) with two motives: (1) precautionary motive (to be prepared for unexpected eventualities such as sudden unemployment) and (2) speculative motive (to take advantage of declining prices).

Standard Coin Coins whose intrinsic metal value is equal to the face amount. E.g., prior to 1933, a $20 gold coin contained $20 worth of gold. Since gold coins have been withdrawn from circulation, the American monetary system has no more standard coins.

Standard of Value One of the important functions of money is to serve as a unit of measurement. Wheat is measured in bushels, eggs in dozens and the speed of cars in miles, while the cost and price of goods and services are measured in terms of dollars and cents.

Store of Value (also at times referred to as "Store of Purchasing Power). An important function of money. Income earned today can be "stored" in the form of money to be spent at some future date. This may be done either by keeping actual paper money and coins or, more conveniently and safely, by depositing the money in a bank. Chronic inflation impairs the function of money as a store of value. As the dollar depreciates, the "stored up" purchase power diminishes, just as the quantity of wheat diminishes when stored in a rat-infested warehouse.

Subsidiary Coin Coins whose intrinsic metal value is less than the face amount. The United States uses only subsidiary coins since the gold dollars (which were the only standard coin in circulation) were withdrawn in 1933.

Tax Incidence The actual taxpayer can often "shift" the burden of a tax to some other party. The corporation income tax is paid by the corporation, but the latter can shift the burden, wholly or in part, to the consumer by raising prices, or to labor and the supplier of raw materials by reducing wages and the prices paid for raw materials. The term *tax incidence* refers to the final effect of a tax, the place where the burden of the tax ultimately rests; i.e., the individual or group which cannot shift the tax to another party.

Tax Shifting The actual taxpayer can often transfer the burden of a government levy to some other party. The corporation income tax, for example, is paid by the corporation, but the latter can shift the burden of the tax to the consumer by raising prices. In theory, the corporation could also shift the burden to the worker by reducing wages. The former would be called "forward shifting," the latter "backward shifting." In many instances it is impossible to ascertain who actually carries the burden of a tax, since the shiftability of a tax depends upon the relative elasticity of the supply of and demand for a given product or factor of production.

Theory of Games A mathematical theory of price formation developed by Oskar Morgenstern and John von Neumann (*Theory of Games and Economic Behavior,* 1944). It is based on the assumption that all entrepreneurs (players) are striving to maximize their profits. Under conditions of perfect competition or monopoly the individual player can calculate with certainty the best possible combination of price and volume of output. In an oligopolistic market situation, however, (which is typical of the modern economy) the entrepreneur cannot predict which one of a substantial number of possible actions his competitors will take. Yet each action of any of the competitors affects the best possible price-output combination of each "player."

As long as the number of players does not exceed three (three competing firms) and the number of possible policy decisions is not too large, modern probability mathematics and electronic computers can provide the answer as to what will be the best strategy for each player to pursue. On the other hand, if there are half a dozen or more competing firms and the number of possible policies is very large (as is the case in real life), the complexity of the possible strategies is such that it exceeds the grasp of the human mind, the capacity of the computers, and above all the state of our mathematical knowledge. A typical oligopolistic market situation is thus beyond the reach of the Theory of Games. As Morgenstern and Neumann emphasized, a new system of mathematics would have to be developed before we could solve mathematically the problem of price in an oligopoly.

Time Deposits Banks distinguish between (1) "demand deposits," money held by commercial banks in the form of checking accounts, which are payable on demand, and (2) "time deposits," which the banks need not pay on demand. There are two types of time deposits: (1) Savings Deposits, which must be "evidenced by a pass book." Banks may require 30-day notice of withdrawal; but, as a rule, commercial banks wave the requirement and pay savings deposits on demand upon presentation of the pass book. (2) Time Deposits (in the narrower sense) which are covered by a special agreement between the depositor and the bank. These time deposits are payable at a fixed date in the future, "not less than 30 days after the date of the deposit." The "contract" between the depositor and the bank is a negotiable Certificate of Deposit, which means that the depositor can sell the contract (i.e., transfer the time deposit balance) by endorsing the certificate, just as a check is transferred by endorsement. Under the Federal Reserve Regulation "Q" only individuals and non-profit organizations may own savings deposits. Corporations have time deposits evidenced by Certificates of Deposit. Commercial banks are not allowed to pay interest on demand deposits. Interest on time deposits is limited by Federal Reserve regulations. The so-called savings deposits in Savings and Loans Associations represent, from a technical and legal point of view, not "deposits" but "shareholders" accounts. The depositors are actually "owners" of the bank, not "creditors." This distinction can become important in case of bankruptcy.

"Transparency of the Market" A theoretical assumption of the marginal utility theory, according to which all buyers and sellers in a given market are fully aware of how many units of a certain product will be sold at various prices. Interpreted literally, the assumption is clearly unrealistic, although buyers and sellers, as a rule, strive for the best possible understanding of the market forces.

Treasury Bills Promisory notes of the United States Treasury, with a maturity of usually 90 days, which are sold through the Federal Reserve at a discount to the highest bidder. For instance, if a bank bought a $100,000 Bill at $99,500 (payable in 90 days at its par value of $100,000) the bank would earn about 2% annually (4 times $500 equals $2000 on about $100,000 investment). The Federal Reserve uses the weekly sale of Treasury Bills by the Treasury to increase or restrict the liquidity of the banking system, the sale or purchase of Treasury Bills being among the most important instruments of monetary policy in the United States.

Treasury Certificates Short-term obligations of the U.S. Treasury, maturing, as a rule, in about one year.

Treasury Notes Medium-term obligations of the U.S. Treasury, with a maturity of between one and five years.

Turn-over Tax A government levy widely used in some countries (e.g., the German "Umsatzsteuer") which involves a relatively small levy (1–2%) whenever goods pass from the raw material producer to the manufacturer, to the wholesaler and, ultimately, to the retailer. The tax is ultimately paid by the consumer, even though most consumers are not aware of this fact. The corporation income tax in the U.S., to some extent, has a similar effect: Much of the tax burden is passed on to the consumer in the form of higher prices.

Union Shop When closed shop agreements were banned by the Taft-Hartley Act, union shop agreements took their place. These provide that while an employer may hire non-union labor, once employed the worker must join the union as a condition of holding his job. The National Labor Relations Board has ruled that unions may expel members for a variety of reasons, in which case the employer is required to fire the worker. As of 1963 almost 75% of the workers covered by collective bargaining agreements were subject to union shop provisions, while 19 states banned the union shop under so-called "right to work" laws.

Unit Banking System A system of commercial banking in which each local bank is an independent corporation and not merely a branch office of a large bank. Unit banking is characteristic of the United States. Most states prohibit or restrict the opening of branches (the chief exception being California, which has a branch banking system). Most foreign countries have branch banking systems. While the United States has some 13,000 independent banks, in Britain more than 80% of the commercial banking business is done by five big banks, which have thousands of local branches.

Unit of Account One of the minor functions of money. Books are kept not in terms of the quantities of goods and services purchased or sold, but in terms of dollars and cents.

United States Notes See "greenbacks."

Usury Originally the taking of any form of interest. During the past 100–150 years the meaning of the term has undergone a change. It now refers to "excessive interest" charges. What is excessive is defined by law. Usury (the taking of any form of interest) is prohibited in the Old and New Testament.

Utility According to the marginal utility theory, price is determined by two basic factors: utility (the usefulness of goods) and scarcity. No article can have "value" (in the sense that a buyer would be willing to pay for it) unless it is useful (has utility).

Variable Cost Total cost is composed of fixed cost (which does not vary with the volume of output) and variable cost (which varies with the volume of output). Real estate taxes, interest payments on the mortgage, maintenance of the building and depreciation due to obsolescence represent fixed cost. Wages, raw materials, selling cost, electric power and depreciation due to wear and tear make up the variable cost. The distinction is important in Marshallian price theory. Once the plant has been built, a manufacturer can be expected to produce (even at a loss) as long as the selling price is higher than variable cost (thus covering part of the fixed cost). If, however, existing production facilities have to be replaced or expanded to meet existing demand, prices have to be equal to total cost (variable and fixed).

Velocity An important concept in monetary theory. It refers to the number of times a unit of money changes hands, i.e., its turn-over rate. Since a dollar represents purchasing power every time it changes hands, total purchasing power is determined by (1) the quantity of money in circulation (M) and (2) the rate at which the money changes hands (V).

Welfare State The modern welfare state philosophy is based on the assumption that in our modern complex society the individual is no longer able to cope with the multitude of socio-economic problems, such as unemployment, old age, etc. It has thus become the task of the state to look after the welfare of the people. As far back as the 1880's Germany enacted the first welfare state measures, but the widespread development of the welfare state philosophy is largely a result of the Great Depression of the 1930's and of the postwar years. The Employment Act of 1946 is a typical welfare state measure. The welfare state is the opposite of the laissez-faire state, which assumes that it is the individual's duty and right to look after himself.

Workmen's Compensation Insurance Under common law the employer is not responsible for injuries suffered by his workers while at work, unless the employer can be shown to have been negligent. Even in this case the injured worker has to bring legal action to collect damages. — Gradually, beginning in 1908, individual states passed laws requiring employers to carry insurance for the protection of their workers, and by 1948 all states had workmen's compensation laws. Today the cost of the insurance is regarded as part of the cost of doing business, not unlike the social security taxes which the employer has to pay.

Study Questions

CHAPTER 1

1. Discuss the difference between Economics and the Economy.
2. What is the basic difference between normative and analytical economics?
3. Do you regard the modern welfare state (unemployment insurance, farm support program, housing aid, etc.) as a form of normative economics?
4. Discuss some of the basic weaknesses of analytical economics.
5. Is economics an art or a science?
6. Give reasons for the necessity of including institutional factors in the study of economics.
7. What are the advantages of excluding both institutional and cultural factors from the study of economics?
8. Give examples of the interconnection between the prevailing cultural climate and the development of economic institutions.

CHAPTER 2

1. What are the basic questions which any economic system has to answer?
2. Why should leisure be classified as an "economic good?"
3. What considerations determine what goods and services are to be produced? Can there be differences of opinion between the economist and the social planner?
4. The division of income (which determines for whom goods and services are produced) can be based on economic, social and political considerations. Discuss.
5. All economic theories are based on philosophic premises. Show how the change in the prevailing philosophic climate regarding the relationship between the individual and society has influenced economic theory, including the development of macroeconomics.

6. Explain how the prevailing popular estimate of the capacities and nature of man as an individual affects economic theory. Show the change which occurred between the 19th and 20th Centuries.
7. What do we mean by "private property?" Has the nature of private property changed during the past 50 years?
8. Is there a conflict between security and individual freedom? What has been the experience during the past 50 years in the United States?

CHAPTER 3

1. Does the size of the population have a bearing on the prosperity of a country? What is the connection between the size of the population and the prevailing standard of living?
2. What is the relationship between the rate of population growth and the rate of economic development in the developing countries?
3. How does the distribution of the population by age groups affect the rate of unemployment in the United States?
4. Has the rate of population growth in the United States been affected in the past by economic factors (booms and depressions)?

CHAPTER 4

1. Discuss a) Anarchy; b) Laissez faire; c) the Regulatory State; d) the Welfare State; e) Socialism, and f) Totalitarianism.
2. Show how and why the United States gradually developed during the past 50 years from a regulatory to a welfare state.
3. What do we mean by (a) an organic and (b) an atomistic philosophy of society?
4. What do we mean by Absolutism?
5. What do we mean by Mercantilism?
6. What do we mean by Liberalism? Show how the meaning of the word has changed during the past 40 years.

CHAPTER 5

1. Explain why more people throughout the world suffer from nutritional deficiencies today than did 30 years ago.
2. What do we mean by Neo-Malthusianism?
3. What are the reasons for the chronic "overproduction" of farm products in the United States?
4. List the reasons why some economists feel that the farm aid program has been a failure.
5. Give a brief history of the development of the American farm aid program.
6. Describe the change in constitutional philosophy as a result of which the New Deal farm aid program was first held unconstitutional in 1936 and then approved as constitutional a few years later.
7. What is the basic philosophy behind the "parity price" notion?
8. Give some reasons why the "parity price" notion may be unsound from an economic point of view, or why it may be sound.
9. What were the two dramatic changes in American agriculture which occurred during the 1940's and 1950's?

CHAPTER 6

1. What is the basic difference, as far as personal liability is concerned, between the position of a member of a partnership and of a stockholder in a corporation?
2. What are the advantages of a proprietorship (as against a corporation)?
3. What are the advantages of doing business as a corporation?
4. List some corporations which have been created through special legislative charter rather than under existing laws of incorporation.
5. What is the difference between equity capital and borrowed capital?
6. What is the difference between common and preferred shares?
7. What is the difference between bonds and debentures as the terms are used in the United States?

8. Why is a cumulative participating preferred stock more desirable than a non-cumulative non-participating issue?
9. Why is it that an unsecured debenture issue of one company can be a sounder investment than a first mortgage bond of another?
10. What are the two functions of security markets?
11. What is the difference between listed and unlisted securities?
12. What are the problems of "Bigness" as far as American corporations are concerned?
13. Has there been a definite trend toward concentration of economic power during the past 35 years?
14. List some of the forms of restraint of competition which have been used in this country and Europe.
15. Give some of the factors which determine the size and location of business enterprises.

CHAPTER 7

1. In which way is labor different from other "factors of production"?
2. According to 19th Century economic theory, what determined wages?
3. List some of the basic issues involved in present-day labor relations.
4. Give a brief history of the development of the American labor movement.
5. What is the difference between national and international unions?
6. List some of the methods used in decades past by some employers to combat labor unions.
7. What is the basic conflict between craft and industrial unions?
8. What are fringe benefits?
9. How can we ascertain whether wages are adequate to provide the necessary aggregate purchasing power or whether they create an inflationary pressure?
10. Why is it that "above equilibrium" wages will produce unemployment?
11. What do we mean by "guidelines" with regard to wage increases?

12. Why do some unions object to the "guideline" approach?
13. How can hourly wages rise faster than man-hour productivity without producing unemployment?
14. Is there anything wrong with the following argument? Higher wages will make for increased consumption, which will result in increased production. This in turn will reduce the unit cost because the fixed cost can be spread more widely.
15. Why does an increase in wage levels, and especially in minimum wages, tend to affect the employment opportunities of unskilled workers in America more directly than the job opportunities of skilled workers?
16. Is there a connection between the level of wages on the one hand, and mechanization and automation on the other?
17. What do we mean by "featherbedding?"
18. Why would a reduction of the work week from 40 to 36 hours probably not result in a 10% increase in job opportunities?
19. What legal or contractual provisions make for union security?
20. What is the difference between union security and job security?

CHAPTER 8

1. In which way did the role of the consumer according to Mercantilist economic theory differ from his role according to modern economic theory?
2. Does Professor Galbraith in his famous best-seller *The Affluent Society* agree with Adam Smith that "consumption is the sole end and purpose of all production?" What is his view?
3. List some of the basic changes which have occurred during the past half a century in the structure of the American family. How did these changes affect the economy?
4. Is there a connection between the increase in the sale of consumer goods and the fact that more and more American housewives hold jobs?
5. Give some reasons for the sharp increase in the crime rate since the end of World War II.
6. Aggregate personal income rose by well over 150% during the first 20 years after the war. Why did the real per capita income increase at a much slower rate?
7. There has been a change in the distribution of income during

the past 30 years. Which income groups suffered a relative decline, which benefited most? How did the lowest income group fare?

8. How do we define "poverty" in the United States?
9. Explain how changes in the rate of increase in the consumer debt can affect business conditions in general.
10. What is the difference between social and private consumption?
11. List some of the regulatory agencies of the government and show how they are expected to protect the public.
12. Discuss the rise of welfare legislation in the United States.
13. What is OASDI?
14. What is Medicare?
15. How do Social Security taxes affect the consumption pattern?

CHAPTER 9

1. What is the difference between macro- and microeconomics?
2. What is the difference between the public and the private sector?
3. What is the difference between analytical and operational economics?
4. List the four most important macroeconomic goals.
5. Is there a potential conflict between the goals of full employment and of price stability?
6. How did Lord Beveridge define "full employment?" What does the United States government regard as "full employment?"
7. Explain the possible conflict between economic and political rationality.
8. Explain the difference of the economist acting as a "scientist" and as a "social philosopher."

CHAPTER 10

1. List the two major philosophic assumptions regarding the nature of man and the nature of the social order which underlie the economic theory of free enterprise.
2. What is the historical connection between the philosophic premises of free enterprise and the Newtonian revolution?

3. What did the Physiocrats mean with the phrase "laissez faire?" Who or what was to govern the socio-economic order?
4. What is the role of the profit motive in the theory of free enterprise?
5. What is the role of competition in the theory of free enterprise?
6. What is the difference between the type of free enterprise governed by "self-interest" which Adam Smith had in mind, and the "survival of the fittest" philosophy of Herbert Spencer?
7. What is the difference between centralized economic planning and direct controls, and decentralized planning and indirect controls?
8. Does the guideline approach to the determination of prices and wages reflect a trend toward direct or indirect controls?
9. Is it possible to reconcile direct centralized controls and the principle of consumer sovereignty?
10. In which way does the notion of "maximum efficiency" have a different meaning according to the traditional communist view in Russia, and according to the traditional American view?
11. Give some of the arguments used by underdeveloped countries in favor of centralized planning and direct controls.
12. Discuss the basic conflict between centralized controls and the reliance on the price mechanism of the market.
13. What are the basic tools of indirect controls?
14. What is the Quantity Theory of Money?
15. What is the relationship between the quantity of money and the output of goods and services according to modern economic theory?

CHAPTER 11

1. When and where was the coinage of money invented?
2. As far as we know, which nation was the first to use paper money, and when?
3. What are the two basic functions of money?
4. List three other functions of money.
5. What is the most widely used paper money in the United States?
6. How do you define the total money supply?

7. What are the reasons for including (or for excluding) time and savings deposits in the total money supply?
8. Explain what we mean by saying that all forms of money used in the United States are based on credit.
9. Why can't the United States government just "print money?"
10. What is the difference between a branch banking and a unit banking system?
11. What is the FDIC?
12. Who are the member banks of the Federal Reserve System?
13. Explain why there has been a sharp decline in bank investments (chiefly United States government securities) since the end of the war, and an even sharper increase in loans.
14. What do we mean by legal reserves, excess reserves and free reserves?
15. Who determines legal reserve rates?
16. What determines the amount of loans and deposits which the commercial banking system as a whole can create at a given time?
17. The Federal Reserve can increase the lending capacity of the commercial banking system, but does this by necessity lead to an increase in the supply of money?
18. In which way did the Federal Reserve System as constituted in 1913 represent a political compromise?
19. Throughout the world, the position of the central banks has changed during the past 35 years. Explain.
20. Who determines the policies of the Federal Reserve?
21. To what extent is the Federal Reserve System privately owned?
22. Which body determines the monetary policies of the System?
23. To what extent is the Federal Reserve politically independent?
24. What do we mean when we say that the Federal Reserve was originally created to assure the necessary elasticity of the supply of currency?
25. In which way can commercial banks "shift" part of their assets to secure additional liquidity?
26. During the 1920's and 1930's Federal Reserve policy was directed toward which two objectives?
27. Since the end of World War II the Federal Reserve has taken on which two additional tasks?
28. Gold continues to perform which important function?

CHAPTER 12

1. What is the specific meaning of the word "fiscal?"
2. Is there a definite limit on how large the public sector can grow before it threatens to strangle private enterprise?
3. What did President Kennedy have in mind when he spoke of "our obsolete tax system?"
4. What are the reasons that the Treasury has rarely been able to forecast with any degree of accuracy the probable surplus or deficit in the Federal budget?
5. What are the differences between the Administrative, the Cash and the National Income Budgets?
6. What are the basic three sources of revenue of a sovereign government?
7. In which way does taxation and borrowing from the public represent a transfer of purchasing power from the private to the public sector?
8. When does a deficit in the Federal budget result in an increase in the supply of money?
9. Must all deficit spending be inflationary?
10. Assume that the total output of goods and services is more or less at the full employment level, how can the spending of the public sector (either for defense or welfare) be increased without causing inflation?
11. What do we mean by the "purely fiscal" aspects of fiscal policy?
12. What factors (other than purely fiscal consideration) affect fiscal policy?
13. What are the five basic types of taxes?
14. What type of taxes produce the major portion of income of a) the Federal Government, b) the state governments and c) local governments?
15. Distinguish between the "benefit" and the "ability to pay" principles of taxation.
16. Distinguish between progressive, regressive and proportional taxes.
17. What do we mean by "shifting" taxes?
18. What taxes can be shifted?
19. Can excise taxes be shifted more easily if the demand for the product is elastic or if it is inelastic? Explain.

20. Distinguish between the forward and backward shifting of taxes.
21. Which expenditures have risen more sharply since 1945 (both percentage-wise and in actual dollars), Federal expenditures or state and local expenditures?
22. What do we mean by debt ceiling?
23. What is the difference between marketable and non-marketable government securities?
24. What are the two types of short-term government obligations?
25. What do we mean by "shortening" the government debt? What is the effect upon the economy?
26. Why is it that state and local governments are becoming increasingly dependent upon Federal aid?

CHAPTER 13

1. The modern study of business cycle fluctuations is about how old?
2. What is the difference between cyclical and seasonal fluctuations?
3. What do we mean by long-range trends?
4. What two factors influence long-range trends?
5. Explain the difference between those students of the business cycle who try to discover the forces which bring about cyclical changes, and others who try to discover warning signals which indicate an impending cyclical change.
6. What is the difference between exogenous and endogenous forces?
7. Distinguish between the overproduction and the underconsumption theories.
8. Why does modern economic theory follow the underconsumption approach?
9. Why did 19th Century theory tend to follow the overproduction approach?
10. In which way are booms and depressions self-generating and self-liquidating according to the overproductionist viewpoint?
11. Explain the Keynesian underconsumptionist approach.
12. What is the inner link between the "mature society" premise and the underconsumptionist cycle theory?

13. What are the business indicators of the National Bureau of Economic Research?
14. Distinguish between the Kondratieff, Juglar and Kitchin cycles.

CHAPTER 14

1. The sudden interest in the problem of economic growth and development during the 1950's was due to which two reasons?
2. How can one measure economic growth?
3. Why did most 19th Century economists show little interest in the problem of economic growth?
4. Looking back over history, is there any reason to assume that economic growth is more prevalent than economic decline?
5. List the factors which made for economic growth in the United States prior to World War I.
6. Why are even minor changes in the rate of growth important in the long run?
7. Why is a rapid rate of economic growth particularly important for the United States during the 1960's and 1970's?
8. What was apparently the most important factor which contributed to the economic growth of the United States during the 30 years 1930–1960?
9. How can the government stimulate or regulate the rate of growth?
10. What do we mean by the "output-gap?"
11. What is the difference between physical productive capacity and capacity from the economic point of view?
12. How can the fiscal system retard or promote economic growth?
13. Show how the American farm subsidy policy can be expected either to promote or retard economic growth.
14. Why is it helpful to distinguish between economic growth and economic development?
15. Distinguish between the forces which made for rapid economic development in Britain (during the 18th and 19th Centuries), in the United States (during the 19th Century) and in Japan (since the 1850's).
16. Why can it be said that industrialization is the result (not the cause) of economic change?
17. Can economic development be achieved without social change?

18. Why was the Marshall Plan extremely successful in rebuilding Western Europe, while similar foreign aid programs in other parts of the world were either complete failures or produced only very limited results?

CHAPTER 15

1. Define what is meant by a Balance of Payments.
2. What determines how long a country can suffer a balance of payments deficit?
3. Why was it that balance of payments statistics were not systematically compiled until the 1920's and 1930's?
4. Describe Hume's Price-Specie-Flow mechanism.
5. Why is Hume's model no longer realistic today?
6. Have the forces illustrated by Hume's model been eliminated or suspended?
7. Why is it that the modern tendency of stressing domestic economic planning is likely to result in balance of payments difficulties?
8. Why do most underdeveloped countries have balance of payments deficits?
9. What is the relation between rising prices and the rate of economic growth?
10. Why did the United States not have to worry about its balance of payments during the 1930's and 1940's, even though prices rose sharply during the 1940's?
11. Why is it true that the United States did not become "poorer" between 1950 and 1965, even though American gold reserves declined by more than 40% and short-term obligations to foreigners increased by almost 300% as a result of the chronic balance of payments deficit?
12. What do we mean by saying that a nation is "living beyond its means?" Is this phrase subject to different interpretations?
13. How does one measure a nation's international liquidity?
14. What is the difference between a nation's wealth and its international liquidity?
15. Discuss five ways in which a country can cope (temporarily or otherwise) with a balance of payments deficit.

16. Is it correct to say that America's balance of payments deficit is due to our foreign economic aid program?
17. Is it true that the private sector of the American economy shows a surplus in the balance of payments, while the entire deficit is due to the operations of the public sector?
18. What do we mean by "terms of trade?"
19. What do we mean by "flight capital?"
20. If we take into consideration the return on long-term foreign investments, do capital accounts show a surplus or a deficit?
21. How do you explain the more than 50% increase in long-term capital investments abroad between 1962 and 1964?
22. What are the reasons for the outflow of short-term funds, both recorded and non-recorded?
23. List three factors which apparently contribute to the deficit in the American balance of payments.

CHAPTER 16

1. What do we mean by the international division of labor?
2. Distinguish between an "absolute" and a "comparative" advantage.
3. Indicate the possible conflict between the free trade policy of the 19th Century and the "full employment" goal of the 20th Century.
4. What do we mean by the "Theory of the Periphery?"
5. Show the reasons why foreign trade is important for the American economy, and why it is relatively less important than in the case of Britain.
6. In which way does the mobility of capital affect the flow of trade?
7. Explain how booms and depressions can be "exported."
8. How does the "full employment" policy affect the balance of trade and thus the balance of payments?
9. Distinguish between the different types of credit granted by the World Bank, the International Monetary Fund and the International Development Association.
10. Explain the nature of the "supplementary drawing rights" to be created by the International Monetary Fund.

11. What will be the likely effect on foreign trade and the domestic price level, if a nation stresses the idea that "defence is more important than opulence?"
12. Describe ad valorem, specific, mixed, compound, and compensating duties.
13. Compare the American insistance on a most-favored-nation clause and the European general and conventional tariff system.

CHAPTER 17

1. How would you define national income accounts?
2. Why was it not necessary during the 19th Century to compile national income accounts?
3. To what extent do the national income accounts represent a "photograph" of the economy?
4. The Department of Commerce and the National Bureau of Economic Research use two different methods of calculating the national income data. What is the difference?
5. What is the difference between the Gross National Product and the Net National Product?
6. What is the difference between Personal Income and Disposable Income?
7. All national income accounts of the United States grew rapidly during the postwar years. Why did the GNP grow more rapidly than Disposable Income?
8. In which way do the basic assumptions on which the national income data are based differ from one country to another, e.g., between the United States and Soviet Russia?
9. If a man marries his housekeeper does this increase or decrease the GNP? Why?

CHAPTER 18

1. What is the difference between direct and indirect economic intervention?
2. What are the three implied premises on which indirect economic intervention is based?

3. What do we mean by "compensatory spending?"
4. In order to achieve an economic balance at the full employment level, government spending (G) according to the theory of compensatory spending must always be equal to what?
5. What do we mean by the 45° line?
6. What do we mean by the ordinate and the abscissa?
7. Why must all points on the 45° line be equidistant from the vertical and horizontal axes?
8. Do we have an inflationary or deflationary situation if the sum of C + I + G is larger than the full employment equilibrium?
9. If total spending exceeds total income, how is the difference accounted for?
10. Why did 19th Century economic theory fail to recognize the danger of "excessive saving" which plays such an important role in Keynesian theory?
11. What do we mean by the marginal propensity to save?
12. Why does modern economic theory assume that the marginal propensity to save increases faster than disposable income?
13. How does the notion of over-saving justify public spending?
14. What does Professor Samuelson mean by the Paradox of Thrift?
15. Why was there no such paradox during the 19th Century?
16. What do we mean by the multiplier?
17. What do we mean by the acceleration principle?

CHAPTER 19

1. Show (with the help of the quantity theory of money model) how modern economic theory proposes to achieve full employment and a maximum rate of economic growth (without inflation or a balance of payments deficit) through the proper monetary and fiscal policies.
2. Which agency is responsible for monetary policy?
3. Which agency is responsible for fiscal policy?
4. What are the three tools at the disposal of the Federal Reserve to regulate the supply of money?
5. Why does the Federal Reserve rely less on discount rate changes than it did in the past?
6. What do we mean by open market operations?

7. What do we mean by changes in the reserve requirements?
8. What do we mean by changes in the margin requirements?
9. What do we mean by legal, excess and free reserves?
10. What do we mean by the velocity of money?
11. Has it happened that the banking system has substantial free reserves yet does not increase its loans and investments?
12. Can Federal Reserve policy assure an increase in bank loans and thus an increase in deposits?
13. What do we mean by the built-in automatic stabilizers of the fiscal system?
14. What do we mean by a flexible budget?
15. What is the connection between compensatory spending and a flexible budget?
16. Why can fiscal policy not be governed exclusively by economic considerations?
17. What tax policy will tend to curb saving?
18. What tax policy will tend to curb consumption?
19. From a purely economic point of view, should developing countries tax income or consumption?
20. Will the effects of fiscal policy be more far-reaching in the long run or as an anti-cyclical tool?
21. What will be the effect on the economy if the government covers its deficit by selling savings bonds to the public?
22. What will be the effect if the government sells long-term bonds to savings banks, insurance companies and corporations?
23. What will be the effect if the government finances its deficit by selling Treasury Bills to the Federal Reserve?

24. *The effects of monetary and fiscal policies*

Monetary and fiscal measures can either increase the supply of money and credit (that means, have an inflationary effect); or they can decrease the supply of money and credit (and thus have a deflationary effect); or they can have no effect on the supply of money and credit. Figure out what will be the effect of the following measures:

1) Increase of legal reserve requirements of member banks.
2) Lowering of the discount rate.

3) Increase of margin requirements.
4) Purchase of U. S. Treasury Bills by the Federal Reserve.
5) Purchase of U. S. Gov't bonds by a corporation from a commercial bank.
6) Purchase of U. S. Savings Bonds by an individual:
   a) immediate effect.
   b) effect over period of 3–6 months.
7) Reduction of surtaxes on income compensated by an increase in sales taxes.
8) Reduction in tariffs and increase in higher bracket income taxes.
9) Redemption of U. S. Government bonds.
   a) if held by the Federal Reserve System.
   b) if held by a commercial bank.
   c) if held by an individual.
   (Remember that the Federal Government can reduce its total debt, i.e., redeem bonds, only when it has a surplus of revenues over expenditures.)
10) Enlargement of the public works program.
   a) while the budget is balanced (consider what will be the effect over a period of 6–12 months).
   b) while the government has a deficit.
11) Switch from a public works program to direct relief.

CHAPTER 20

1. Distinguish between macro- and microeconomics.
2. Are agencies of the United States government ever confronted with microeconomic problems?
3. Give some of the dangers resulting from a one-sided emphasis upon either the macro- or the microeconomic view.
4. What was the scholastic approach to the problem of prices?
5. What was the mercantilistic idea of what should determine prices?
6. What is the price theory of the modern planned economy?
7. What is the basic premise of the traditional microeconomic theory of price based on the notion of equilibrium?
8. Who argued that prices are determined by cost?

9. Who argued that prices are determined by demand?
10. How did Alfred Marshall reconcile the two conflicting views of cost and demand by introducing the element of time?
11. What do we mean by fixed cost?
12. What do we mean by variable cost?
13. When are prices determined by demand?
14. When are prices determined by total cost?
15. What do we mean by imperfect competition?
16. What is a monopoly, a monopsony, an oligopoly and an oligopsony?
17. Given nine possible market situations. Which four permit rational predictions regarding price and the volume of output?

CHAPTER 21

1. What does the economist mean by the term "supply?"
2. In which way does the term "demand" as popularly used differ from the more specific use of the term by the economist?
3. What two forces determine supply?
4. If prices decline, what will be the effect on (a) the immediate supply and (b) long-term supply?
5. What will be the effect of rising production cost and stable prices on the level of employment?
6. Why is a curve which slopes upward from left to right likely to be a supply curve?
7. In the language of the economist, is there a difference between "supply" and the "supply schedule?"
8. If there is a change in supply, will this involve a movement "on" the supply curve, or "of" the supply curve?
9. What does the economist mean by demand?
10. What are the two factors which determine the price from the demand side?
11. What do we mean by diminishing utility?
12. What are free goods and what are economic goods?
13. How is it possible for a free good to become an economic good?
14. What do we mean by marginal utility?
15. What do we mean by the transparency of the market?

16. Which point on the supply and demand curves determines the price?
17. If prices are increased through a price support program, what will be the effect upon the quantity demanded?
18. How can we raise the price even though the demand schedule remains unchanged?
19. Why are rent controls likely to produce a disequilibrium between the quantity of housing demanded and supplied?
20. What do we mean by elasticity of supply?
21. Why is the immediate supply curve a vertical line?
22. What do we mean by elasticity of demand?
23. Why is the demand for necessities relatively price-inelastic?
24. If the price declines and total sales increase, what can we assume regarding the elasticity of demand in this particular price range?
25. Why is it important for a businessman to know whether the demand for his product is elastic or inelastic?
26. If the demand schedule is drawn as a straight horizontal line, what can be said about the degree of elasticity?
27. What is the basic difference between the partial and the general equilibrium?

CHAPTER 22

1. What are the two factors involved in the theory of production?
2. What are the three premises which underlie the theory of production?
3. Why is the traditional theory of production not applicable to a socialist, or to a predominantly self-sufficient household economy?
4. Distinguish between the technological and the economic aspects of production planning.
5. What are the two basic notions on which the economic theory of production rests?
6. What is the marginal revenue product?
7. What is the marginal factor cost?
8. What do we mean by least-cost-substitution?

9. Why is the optimum output from the production point of view not necessarily the same as the optimum output from the market point of view? Which one will be decisive in a market economy?
10. Distinguish between the popular use of the term "distribution" and the use of the term by the economist.
11. What is the Marxian theory of distribution?
12. What do we mean by derived demand?
13. Why in a market economy is the reward paid to the factors of production ultimately determined by the consumer?
14. What do we mean by joint demand for the factors of production?
15. How can a union increase the income of its members if the marginal productivity of the workers is lower than that of competing factors of production?
16. Is it possible in the long run to reduce the reward to one factor of production (let us say interest) below the equilibrium level, while paying other factors of production (e.g., wages) above equilibrium rewards?

CHAPTER 23

1. What determines wages according to the following wage theories?
   a) Scholastic theory
   b) Mercantilist theory
   c) Classical theory
   d) Marxian theory
   e) Marginalist theory
   f) Purchase power theory
2. Explain the basic conflict between the 19th Century marginalist theory of wages and the 20th Century purchase power theory.
3. Which of the six wage theories reflects normative thought?
4. Which reflects most clearly the microeconomic scientific approach?
5. Why does the modern purchase power theory of wages reflect the macroeconomic approach?

6. If we speak of wages being in equilibrium what does this mean according to
   a) the marginalist theory?
   b) the purchase power theory?
7. If the work week is reduced from 40 to 35 hours, and the hourly wages remain unchanged, what will be the effect?
8. What will be the effect if the work week is reduced but total take-home pay remains the same?
9. Would you base your arguments on the marginalist or the purchase power theory of wages, if you were
   a) a union leader, or
   b) an employer?

CHAPTER 24

1. What is the difference between the medieval meaning of the word usury and the modern meaning?
2. Give some of the medieval arguments against usury.
3. Give some of the arguments which have been made to justify the charging of interest.
4. What is the difference between the "abstinence," "time preference" and "liquidity preference" explanations of interest?
5. What do we mean by the equilibrium theory of interest?
6. List two factors which affect a man's propensity to consume.
7. What do we mean by the term marginal efficiency of capital?
8. What factors affect the marginal efficiency of capital?
9. Modern economists assume that low interest rates stimulate the purchase of durable consumer goods. Why would this argument have been rather meaningless 50 years ago?
10. How important are interest charges in relation to total production cost?
11. Does empirical evidence confirm the widely held notion that low interest rates stimulate the economy and high interest rates retard it?
12. In which way do interest rates have an anti-cyclical effect, according to the traditional theory?
13. Why is it that modern economists are opposed to the idea of

permitting rising interest rates to put a brake on economic expansion?

14. Knut Wicksell distinguished between the "natural rate" and the "market rate" of interest. What is the difference? What will be the effect if the "market rate" for any length of time is maintained below the "natural rate?"

CHAPTER 25

1. What is the difference between "contract rent" and "economic rent?"
2. Nineteenth Century economists, especially the classical school, saw a basic difference between "land," on the one hand, and the other factors of production on the other. What was this difference?
3. In which way did the peculiar position of land lead the classical economists to develop a theory of rent which differed fundamentally from their theories of wages, interest and profit?
4. Was there any connection between the fact that the classical economists lived in England at a time when the enclosure movement had virtually come to an end and the population had been increasing rapidly, and the type of rent theory which they developed?
5. How did a different general outlook (the optimism of the Physiocrats on the one hand, and the pessimism of the Ricardian school on the other) lead to different rent theories?
6. What have the philosophic notions of (a) the "bountifulness of nature" and (b) the "niggardliness of nature" to do with different theories of rent?
7. Distinguish between rent as "price-determining" and rent as "price-determined."
8. Explain why according to classical theory, the rent on marginal (the poorest) land must be zero.
9. Why did the Marginalists choose to disregard the notion that land is price-inelastic, which formed the basis of the Ricardian theory?
10. What is the basic emotional and rational appeal of the so-called land-socialists?

11. What are the arguments in favor of taxing land (especially urban real estate) and improvements at different rates?

CHAPTER 26

1. Discuss four different ways of figuring "profits."
2. Show how profits are affected by bookkeeping procedures especially regarding depreciation and depletion.
3. Is there a rule-of-thumb relationship between the rate of profit on a business investments and the rate of return on government bonds?
4. What accounts for the spread?
5. What do we mean by opportunity cost?
6. Historically speaking, what has been the attitude toward profit in most civilizations?
7. What do we mean by "place utility" and "time utility?" How have the two notions been used to justify profit?
8. Do many Americans feel that the government can and should control the profits of large corporations?
9. What is a "reasonable profit," according to popular opinion?
10. What is the basic difference between the Ricardian and the Marginalist theories of profit?
11. What will happen if the rate of profit in a given line of business (or in a given country) is (a) abnormally high or (b) abnormally low?
12. Show how the significance of profit in the economy changes depending upon whether we postulate "consumer sovereignty" or the "irrationality of consumer demand."
13. If profits are eliminated, what can serve as a rational basis for efficient economic planning?
14. In which way do profits prevent waste?
15. What is the role played by profits in communist economic theory?
16. What is the role of profits in a mixed economy?
17. Discuss some U.S. Government business ventures not governed by profit considerations.
18. Since Adam Smith, free enterprise theory has postulated the profit motive as the driving force in the economy. Explain.

19. What is the relationship between profits and full employment?
20. What is the connection between the rate of profits and the rate of capital investments?
21. What is the effect of profit differentials between various countries on the international flow of capital?

Sources of Statistical and Other Current Information

Statistical Abstract of the United States. A national data book and guide to sources, published annually (since 1879) by the U.S. Department of Commerce, Bureau of the Census. More than 1000 pages of statistical data on virtually every aspect of economic life in the United States.

The World Almanac, published annually by the *New York World-Telegram.* About 900 pages of factual data on economic, political and other developments in the U.S. and abroad. Contains lists of leading consumer magazines, major newspapers, foundations, public trusts and funds, associations and societies. A handy table of weights and measures.

The Economic Almanac, published annually by the National Industrial Conference Board, New York. Some 600 pages of statistical data. Contains an alphabetical list of designations of government and international agencies and a glossary of terms.

Survey of Current Business, published monthly by the U.S. Department of Commerce, Bureau of Foreign and Domestic Commerce. Probably the best single source for current information on general business conditions, commodity prices, trade, wholesale and consumer prices, employment and wages, balance of payments and fiscal data. Each issue contains a number of articles on topics of current interest such as the balance of payments, tourist expenditures, etc.

Federal Reserve Bulletin, published monthly by the Board of Governors of the Federal Reserve System, Washington, D.C. The best source of information for current data on monetary, banking and credit developments, both national and international. Also contains fiscal data and statistics on production and prices.

Monthly Labor Review, published monthly by the Department of Labor, Bureau of Labor Statistics, Washington, D.C. The best source on current information on all aspects concerning labor. Also contains special articles and a "Chronology of Recent Labor Events."

Agricultural Statistics, published annually by the Department of Agriculture. Provides some 600 pages of statistical data dealing with every aspect of agriculture.

Economic Report of the President, published twice annually (in January and July) by the U.S. Government Printing Office, Washington, D.C. The report reflects the economic and political views of the White House. The data (and to some extent the underlying economic theories) are furnished by the President's Council of Economic Advisors. The "Report" provides the official economic forecasts of the government and reflects the trends in economic thinking and planning in the United States.

Economic Indicators, prepared monthly by the Council of Economic Advisors. It contains a brief summary of economic, monetary and fiscal statistics.

Facts and Figures, published annually by The Tax Foundation, New York. It provides the best source of information (in compact form) on federal, state and local finance.

International Financial Statistics, published monthly by the International Monetary Fund, Washington, D.C. It contains current financial data on the more than one hundred members of the Fund.

Yearbook of International Trade Statistics, published annually by the Statistical Office of the United Nations. Presents detailed trade statistics for more than a hundred countries, some of them going back to 1930.

Annual Report of the International Monetary Fund contains an annual survey of the most important developments in the field of international finance.

Pick's Currency Yearbook, compiled annually by Franz Pick and published by the Pick Publishing Corporation, New York. A unique compilation (not otherwise readily available) on "free" ("black") markets in foreign exchange and precious metals throughout the world. ("In monetary matters, governments everywhere either must hide the truth, or lie. . . .")

Bibliography

CHAPTER 1 The Nature and Scope of Economics

Boulding, Kenneth E.: *The Skills of the Economist* (Cleveland, H. Allen, 1958)

Burns, Arthur F.: *The Frontiers of Economic Knowledge* (Princeton, Princeton University Press, 1954)

Chandler, Lester V.: "The Scope of Economics" from "A Preface to Economics" (New York, Harper & Brothers, 1947), p. 1–16

Committee for Economic Development: — "Economic Literacy for Americans" (New York, 1962)

Encyclicals — *"Rerum Novarum," "Quadrogesimo Anno," "Mater et Magistra"* (Paulist Press, 180 Varick Street, New York 14, N.Y.)

Hutchison, Terence W.: *The Significance and Basic Postulates of Economic Theory* (New York, M. Kelley, 1960)

Keynes, John Neville: *The Scope and Method of Political Economy* 4th Ed. (New York, Kelley & Millman, 1955)

Knight, Frank H.: *On The History and Methods of Economics* (Chicago, University of Chicago Press, 1956)

Knight, Frank H.: "Social Economic Organization" from "The Economic Organization," (New York, Kelley & Millman, Inc., 1951) p. 3–22

Marshall, Alfred: "Definition of Economics" in Anderson, Gitlow and Diamond (Eds.) "General Economics: A Book of Readings" (Homewood, Ill., Richard D. Irwin, Inc., 1959) p. 3–4

Morgenstern, Oskar: *The Limits of Economics* (Translated by Vera Smith) (London, W. Hodge & Co., 1937)

Robbins, Lionel: *An Essay on the Nature and Significance of Economic Science* 2nd revised edition (London, Macmillan & Co. Ltd. 1935)

Robbins, Lionel: "The Economist in the Twentieth Century" (London, Macmillan & Co. 1954)

Stigler, George J.: "The Theory of Competitive Price" (New York, The Macmillan Co., 1942) Chapter 1

Wallich, Henry C.: "Is Economics a Science?" in Anderson, Gitlow and Diamond (Eds.) "General Economics: A Book of Readings" (Homewood, Ill., Richard D. Irwin, Inc., 1959) p. 4–10

Weisskopf, Walter A.: *The Psychology of Economics* (Chicago, University of Chicago Press, 1955)

CHAPTER 2 The Cultural Framework

Galbraith, John Kenneth: "The Affluent Society" (Boston, Houghton Mifflin, 1958)

Hayek, Friedrich von: *The Road to Serfdom* (Chicago, University of Chicago Press, 1944)

Hayek, Friedrich von: "Individualism and Economic Order" (London, Roubledge & K. Paul, 1949)

Knight, Frank H. & Merriam, Thornton W.: "The Economic Order and Religion" (New York, Harper & Brothers, 1945)

Kolko, Gabriel M.: *Wealth and Power: An Analysis of Social Class and Income Distribution in the United States* (London, Thames and Hudson, 1962)

Mises, Ludwig von: "Human Action; A Treatise on Economics" (New Haven, Yale University Press, 1949)

Myrdal, Gunnar: *Challenge to Affluence* (New York, Pantheon Books, 1963)

Petit, Thomas A.: "Freedom in the American Economy" (Homewood, Ill., Richard D. Irwin, Inc., 1964)

Wilhem, Roebke: A *Humane Economy: The Framework of the Free Market* (Chicago, Henry Regnery Company, 1960)

CHAPTER 3 Population Trends

Anderson, Gitlow and Diamond (Eds.) "General Economics: A Book of Readings" (Homewood, Ill., Richard D. Irwin, Inc., 1959.) Two articles on "Population Growth and Poverty" by Thomas Robert Malthus and Kingsley Davis, p. 26–39.

Myrdal, Gunnar, "Population, a Problem for Democracy" (Cambridge, Mass., Harvard University Press, 1940)

Political and Economic Planning, "World Population and Resources," Research Study, (London, 12 Upper Belgrave Street, 1959)

Veblen, Thorstein, "The Instinct of Workmanship and the State of the Industrial Arts" (New York, Macmillan Co., 1917)

CHAPTER 4 Economics and Politics

Drucker, Peter Ferdinand: "The End of Economic Man. A Study of the New Totalitarianism" (New York, The John Day Company, 1939)

Drucker, Peter Ferdinand: "The New Society; the Anatomy of the Industrial Order" (New York, Harper & Brothers, 1950)

Keynes, John Maynard: "The End of Laissez-faire" 2nd Ed. (London, L. and V. Woolf, 1926)
Mises, Ludwig von: "The Anti-capitalistic Mentality" (Princeton, Van Nostrand, 1956)
Orwell, George: "Nineteen Eighty-Four" (New York, Harcourt, Brace, 1949)
Wallich, Henry C.: "The Cost of Freedom" (New York, Harper & Row, 1960)

CHAPTER 5 Agriculture

Committee for Economic Development, "An Adaptive Program for Agriculture" (New York, 1962)
Committee for Economic Development, "Toward a Realistic Farm Program" (New York, 1957)
Higbee, Edward: "Farms and Farmers in the Urban Age" (New York, Twentieth Century Fund, 1963)
McCabe, Ralph: "Agriculture's Role in the 1960 Decade," (Food and People) U.S. Congress Joint Economic Committee, Subcommittee on Foreign Economic Policy, Washington, 1961.
Schultz, Theodore W.: "Agriculture in an Unstable Economy" (New York, McGraw-Hill Book Company, Inc., 1945)
Schultz, Theodore W.: "The Economic Organization of Agriculture" (New York, McGraw-Hill Book Company, Inc., 1953)
Schultz, Theodore W.: "Transforming Traditional Agriculture" (New Haven, Yale University Press, 1964)

CHAPTER 6 The Organization for Production

Berle, Adolf A. and Means, Gardiner C.: "The Modern Corporation and Private Property" (New York, The Macmillan Company, 1933)
Boulding, Kenneth E.: "Principles of Economic Policy" (Englewood Cliffs, N.J., Prentice-Hall Inc., 1958)
Cheit, Earl F.: "The Business Establishment" (New York, John Wiley & Sons, Inc., 1964)
Dimock, Marshall E.: "Business and Government," 4th ed. (New York, Holt, Rinehart and Winston, Inc., 1961)
Taussig, F. W.: "Large-Scale Production" from "Principles of Economics," 3rd ed. Vol. 1 (New York, Macmillan Company, 1921), p. 48–66

"Wall Street 20th Century" (A republication of the Yale Daily News' Wall Street 1955), (The Investment Association of New York, 1960)

CHAPTER 7 Labor and the Union Movement

Cartter, Alan M.: "Theory of Wages" (Homewood, Ill., Richard D. Irwin, Inc., 1959)

Committee for Economic Development: "Union Powers and Union Functions: Toward a Better Balance" (New York, 1964)

Committee for Economic Development: "The Public Interest in National Labor Policy" (New York, 1961)

Grgeory, Charles: "Labor and the Law" (New York, W. W. Norton & Co., Inc., 1958)

Reynolds, Lloyd: "Labor Economics and Labor Relations" (Englewood Cliffs, N.J., Prentice-Hall, 1959)

CHAPTER 8 The Consumer

Burns, Arthur F.: "Looking Foward" (New York, National Bureau of Economic Research, 1951)

Clark, Lincoln H.: "Consumer Behavior, The Dynamics of Consumer Reaction" (New York, New York University Press, 1954)

Harris, Seymour E.: "Economics of Social Security" (New York, McGraw-Hill Book Company, Inc., 1941)

CHAPTER 9 Four Macroeconomic Objectives

Burns, Arthur F.: "Prosperity without Inflation" (New York, Fordham University Press, 1958)

Haberler, Gottfried: "Inflation, Its Causes and Cures" (Washington, D.C., American Enterprise Association, 1960)

Hansen, Alvin H.: "Economic Policy and Full Employment" (McGraw-Hill Book Company, 1947) see esp. pages 233–47: "Inflation Risks under Full Employment."

CHAPTER 10 Free Enterprise and Economic Planning

Clark, John Maurice: "Alternative to Serfdom" (New York, Vintage Books, 1960)

Clark, John Maurice: "Guideposts in Time of Change" (New York, Harper and Row, 1949)
Hayek, Friedrich von: "Freedom and the Economic System" (Chicago, University of Chicago Press, 1939)
Knight, Frank H.: "The Ethics of Competition" (New York, Harper & Brothers, 1935)
Knight, Frank H.: "Freedom & Reform: Essays in Economics & Social Philosophy" (New York, Harper & Brothers, 1947)
Lee, Baldwin: *Capitalism and Economic Systems* (New York, McGraw-Hill, 1959)
Mises, Ludwig von: "Planning for Freedom" 2nd ed. (South Holland, Ill., Libertarian Press, 1962)
Schumpeter, Joseph A.: "Capitalism, Socialism and Democracy" (New York, Harper and Brothers, 1947)
Shultz, George P. and Aliber, Robert Z. (Editors): "Guidelines. Information Controls and the Market Place" (Chicago, The University of Chicago Press, 1966)
Slichter, Sumner H.: "Modern Economic Society" (New York, Henry Holt & Co., Inc., 1928) Chapter III

CHAPTER 11 The Monetary and Banking System

American Economics Association: "Readings in Monetary Theory" (Philadelphia, Blakiston Co., 1951)
Bell, James Washington, and Spahr, Walter Earl (Eds.): "A Proper Monetary and Banking System for the United States," (New York, The Ronald Press, 1960)
Committee for Economic Development: "Money and Credit: Their Influence on Jobs, Prices and Growth," The Report of the Commission on Money and Credit (paperback) (New York, Prentice-Hall Inc., 1961)
The Federal Reserve System After Fifty Years, Hearings before the Committee on Banking and Currency, House of Representatives (Washington, D.C., U.S. Goverment Printing Office, 1964)
Hazlitt, Henry: "What You Should Know About Inflation" (New York, D. Van Nostrand Company Inc., 1960)

CHAPTER 12 The Fiscal System

Heilbroner, Robert L., and Bernstein, Peter L.: "A Primer on Government Spending" (New York, Random House Inc., 1963)

Mosher, Frederick C., and Poland, Orville F.: "The Cost of American Governments: Facts, Trends, Myths" (New York, Dodd, Mead & Company, 1964)

Musgrave, R. A., and Peacock, A. T. (Eds.): "Classics in the Theory of Public Finance" (New York, Macmillan Co., 1958)

Pechman, Joseph A.: "Federal Tax Policy" (Washington, The Brookings Institution, 1966)

Stans, Maurice H.: "The Need for Balanced Federal Budgets" *Annals of the American Academy of Political and Social Science,* 1959

The Tax Foundation: "Facts and Figures" (New York, published annually)

CHAPTER 13 Cyclical Fluctuations

Clark, John J., and Cohen, Morris (Eds.): *Business Fluctuations, Growth, and Economy Stabilization; A Reader* (New York, Random House, 1963)

Fellner, William J.: "Trends and Cycles in Economic Activity" (New York, Holt, Rinehart and Winston, Inc., 1956)

Haberler, Gottfried: "Prosperity and Depression" (Geneva, League of Nations, 1941)

Mitchell, Wesley C.: "Business Cycles and Unemployment" (New York, McGraw-Hill, 1923) (see especially pages 5–18.)

CHAPTER 14 Economic Growth

Committee for Economic Development: "Economic Growth in the United States: Its Past and Future" (New York, 1960)

Denison, Edward F.: *The Sources of Economic Growth in the United States and the Alternatives Before Us* (New York, Committee for Economic Development, 1962)

Kendrick, John: "Productivity Trends in the United States" (Princeton, Princeton University Press, 1961) (A study by the National Bureau of Economic Research)

Landsberg, Hans H.: *Natural Resources For U.S. Growth* (Baltimore, Johns Hopkins Press, 1964)

Myrdal, Gunnar: "Rich Lands and Poor, the Road to World Prosperity" (New York, Harper & Brothers, 1957)

Owen, Wilfred: *Strategy for Mobility* (Washington, Brookings Institution, 1964)

Rostow, W. W.: "The Stages of Economic Growth" (Cambridge, Harvard University Press, 1964)

CHAPTER 15 The Balance of Payments

Committee for Economic Development: "The International Position of the Dollar" (New York, 1961)
Committee for Economic Development: "National Objectives and the Balance of Payments Problems" (New York, 1960)
"Finance and Development — The Fund and Bank Review" — A quarterly publication of the International Monetary Fund and the Bank for Reconstruction and Development (Washington, D.C.)
Haberler, Gottfried: "The Theory of International Trade," (London, William Hodge & Co., 1936)
Jacobsson, Per.: "The Market Economy in the World of Today" (Philadelphia, The American Philosophical Society, 1936)
Mikesell, Raymond I.: "U.S. Private and Goverment Investment Abroad" (Eugene, Oregon, University of Oregon Book, 1962)
Ohlin, B.: "Interregional and International Trade" (Cambridge Mass., Harvard University Press, 1933)
Rist, Charles: "The Triumph of Gold" (translated from French by Philip Cortney) (New York, Philosophical Library, 1961)
Triffin, Robert: "Gold and the Dollar Crisis" (New Haven, Conn., Yale University Press, 1960)
Viner, Jacob: "International Economics" (Glencoe, Ill., The Free Press, 1951)

CHAPTER 16 International Trade

Allen, William R. and Allen, Clark Lee (Eds.): "Foreign Trade and Finance. Essays in International Economic Equilibrium and Adjustment" (New York, the Macmillan Company, 1959)
American Economic Association: "Reading in the Theory of International Trade" (Philadelphia, The Blakiston Company, 1949)
Chamber of Commerce of the United States: "Foreign Commerce Handbook" (Washington, D.C., United States Chamber of Commerce)
Graham, F. D.: "The Theory of International Values" (Princeton, Princeton University Press, 1948)
Haberler, Gottfried: "The Theory of International Trade" (New York, Macmillan Company, 1937)

Meade, J. E.: "Trade and Welfare" (London, Oxford University Press, 1955)

Ohlin, Bertil: "Interregional and International Trade" (Cambridge, Harvard University Press, 1953)

Viner, Jacob: "Studies in the Theory of International Trade" (New York, Harper & Bros., 1937)

Woytinsky, W. S. and Woytinsky, E. S.: "World Population and Production: Trends and Outlook" (New York, Twentieth Century Fund, 1953)

CHAPTER 17 National Income Accounts

Department of Commerce: "Survey of Current Business" (a monthly publication) The July issue, as a rule, contains complete National Income figures for the preceding year. See also Supplements for 1954 and 1957.

Kuznets, Simon S.: "National Income: A Summary of Findings" (New York, National Bureau of Economic Research, 1946)

Ruggles, Richard and Nancy D.: "National Income Accounts and Income Analysis" (New York, McGraw-Hill Book Company, Inc., 1956)

CHAPTER 18 The Theory of Macroeconomic Intervention

Carskadon, Thomas R. and Soule, George: "USA in New Dimensions" (New York, The Macmillan Company, 1957)

Harris, Seymour H. (Ed.): "The New Economics" (New York, Alfred A. Knopf, Inc., 1947)

Keynes, John Maynard: "The General Theory of Employment, Interest and Money" (London, Macmillan & Co. Limited 1936)

CHAPTER 19 The Tools of Economic Intervention

Committee for Economic Development: "Fiscal and Monetary Policy for High Employment" (New York, 1962)

Committee for Economic Development: "Reducing Tax Rates for Production and Growth" (New York, 1962)

Goldenweiser, E. A.: "Monetary Management" (New York, McGraw-Hill Book Co. Inc., 1949)

Lewis, Welfred Jr.: "Federal Fiscal Policy in the Postwar Recessions" (Washington D.C. The Brookings Institution, 1962)

Morgenstern, Oskar: *"On the Accuracy of Economic Observations"* 2nd Ed. (Princeton N.J., Princeton University Press, 1963)

CHAPTER 20 Price, the Basic Issue of Microeconomics

Leftwich, Richard H.: "The Price System Resource Allocation" 2nd ed. (New York, Holt, Rinehart and Winston, Inc. 1960)

Morgenstern, Oskar, and von Neumann, John: "Theory of Games and Economic Behavior" (Princeton, Princeton University Press, 1953) Chapter 1

Roche, John Ward, and James, Gomer Rhidian: *"Getting and Spending: An Introduction to the Market Economy"* (London, Institute of Economic Affairs, 1963)

CHAPTER 21 Supply, Demand, and Price

Bye, Raymond E.: "Interaction of Supply and Demand" in Epstein, Ralph C. and Butler, Arthur D. "Selections in Economics" Vol. 2 (Buffalo; Smith, Keynes and Marshall, 1958)

Chamberlin, Edward H.: "The Theory of Monopolistic Competition: A Re-orientation of the Theory of Value" (Cambridge, Mass., Harvard University Press, 1956)

Stigler, George J.: "The Theory of Price" Revised Ed. (New York, The Macmillan Co., 1952)

CHAPTER 22 The Theories of Production and Distribution

American Economics Association: "Readings in the Theory of Income Distribution" (Philadelphia, Blakiston Co., 1946)

Davenport, Herbert J.: "Value and Distribution. A Critical and Constructive Study" (Reprint; New York, Augustus M. Kelley, 1908)

Stigler, George J.: "Production and Distribution Theories, The Formative Period" (New York, The Macmillan Company, 1941)

CHAPTER 23 Wage Theories

Douglas, Paul H.: "The Theory of Wages" (Reprint; New York, Augustus Kelley, 1947)

Miller, Herman P.: "Income of the American People" (New York, John Wiley & Sons, Inc., 1955)

Taylor, George W. and Pierson, Frank C.: "New Concepts on Wage Determination" (New York, McGraw-Hill Book Co., Inc., 1957)

Woytinsky, W. S. and Others: "Employment and Wages in the United States" (New York, Twentieth Century Fund, 1953)

Wright, David McCord (Ed.): "The Impact of the Union" (New York, Harcourt, Brace & Co., 1951)

CHAPTER 24 The Changing Role of Interest

Cassel, Gustav: "The Nature and Necessity of Interest. A Theory of Wages, Interest and Profits" (1899) (Reprint, New York, Augustus M. Kelley)

Fisher, Irving: "The Theory of Interest" (1930) (Reprint, New York, Augustus M. Kelley)

Ritter, Lawrence S.: "Money and Economic Activity. A Selection of Readings in the Field of Money and Banking" (New York, Houghton Mifflin Company) First Ed. (1952) Chapter 8; Second Ed. (1961) Chapter 7

Wicksell, Knut: "Interest and Prices" (translated by R. F. Kahn) (London, Macmillan & Company, Limited, 1936)

CHAPTER 25 The Theory of Rent

Bye, Carl R.: "Developments and Issues in the Theory of Rent" (New York, Columbia University Press, 1940)

George, Henry: "Progress and Poverty" (New York, Appleton Century, 1879)

Ricardo, David: "The Principles of Political Economy and Taxation" (New York, Everyman's Library, E. P. Dutton & Co., 1911)

CHAPTER 26 Profit as a Dynamic Force

Kierstead, B. S.: "Capital, Interest, and Profits" (Oxford, Basil Blackwell & Mott, Limited, 1959)

Knight, Frank H.: "Risk, Uncertainty, and Profits" (Boston, Houghton Mifflin Co., 1921)

National Industrial Conference Board: "Wages, Prices and Profits" (New York, 1949)

Index

Abscissa, 306, 366
Ability-to-Pay Principle, 199, 440
Absolutism, 26–27, 440
Accelerator Principle, 320–21, 441
Accord of 1951, 441
Acton, Lord, 79
Advantage
  absolute, 264
  comparative, 264–5
Agency Shop, 109, 441
Agriculture
  Agricultural Adjustment Acts, 57
  agrobusiness, 59
  changing nature in US, 59
  declining farm population, 60
  farm aid policy, 54–8, 61–5
  increased productivity, 59
  modern neglect of, 52
  overproduction in U.S., 53
  parity prices, 57
  production controls, 57
  technological revolution, 58
American Federation of Labor (AFL), 95–6, 98, 441
Analytical discipline, 5, 7–12, 441
Anarchism, 43, 442
Anti-trust Laws
  Clayton Act, 84–86, 95
  Sherman Act, 84–85
Aristotle, 20, 409, 427
Atomistic philosophy of society, 25–26, 442
Automatic stabilizer, 334
Automation, 102

Balance of Payments
  and full employment, 268
  as economic barometer, 248
  as economic goal, 135
  deficit, 249, 253
  definition, 442
  development of statistics, 184
  effect of domestic policies, 331

Balance of Payments (*cont'd*)
loss of gold, 235
role of gold, 249–53
soft credits, 271
theories and policies, 249
Banking
art of commercial banking, 166–67
branch, 164, 481
commercial banking system, 163–4
unit, 164, 443
Banks
lending capacity, 165–6, 169
management, 166–7
member and non-member banks, 164–5
national and state banks, 164
Benefit Principle, 199, 443
Berle, Adolf A., 80
Beveridge, Lord, 138
Bill of Rights, 44
Birth Rate, 38, 115–6
Boehm-Bawerk, Eugen von, 385
Bonds, 71–3, 443
"Bread-and-Butter Issues," 93
Bretton Woods Agreement, 255, 270
Budget (Federal)
administrative, 188, 441
capital, 189, 443
cash, 188, 444
flexible, 336, 454
national income, 188, 467
Burns, Arthur F., 12, 225, 466
Bureau of Labor Statistics, 294
Business Cycle
causes, 213–9
cyclical fluctuations, 315
definition, 211–2, 443
Dewey-Dakin cycles, 214–5
endogenous, 215, 450
exogenous, 212, 451
forecasts, 227
history of, 211
importance of, 215
indicators, 225–6
international implications, 227
Juglar cycles, 212, 460
Kitchen cycles, 226, 460
Kondratieff cycles, 226, 460
overproduction theories, 216–222
phases, 216
statistical-empirical approach, 225–6
sunspot theory, 214
underconsumption theories, 218, 222–5
"Buy-American" Act, 281

Capital
equity and borrowed, 71
goods, 444
need for investments, 40
Capitalism, 444

Cartels, 86
Central Banks
  history of, 169
  independence of, 170, 324
Chamberlin, Edward H., 355
Check-off system, 109, 444
Chrematistike, 444
Clark, John Bates, 385
Classical School
  price theory, 376
  rent theory, 419–20
  wage theory, 396–7
Clayton Act of 1914, 84–86, 95, 445
Closed shop, 108, 445
Co-determination, 445
Coins, 478
Commercial Banking System
  assets & liabilities, 165
  lending capacity, 165, 169
Compensatory spending, 303, 337, 445
Competition
  as balancing mechanism, 145
  imperfect, 346, 353, 355, 457
  monopolistic, 355
  perfect (pure), 353–4, 470
Compulsory unionism, 108
Congress of Industrial Organization (CIO), 98, 446
Constitution
  commerce clause, 45
  welfare clause, 45
Consumer
  borrowing, 120–1
  credit controls, 177
  irrationality, 432
  rationality, 372–3
  role of, 111–2
  sovereignty, 113, 432
Consumption
  and growth, 118
  and saving, 118
  new philosophy, 113
  public and private, 122
Controls (economic), 146–7
Convertibility, 446
Corporation
  creation, 70
  description, 69, 446
  financing, 70
  limited liability, 69
  perpetual life, 69
  private and public, 70
Cost
  fixed, 352, 454
  of living, 293
  of production, 352, 364–5
  variable, 352, 481
Credit Controls
  direct and specific, 325
  indirect and general, 326
Currency
  devaluation, 255–6
  stability, 135

Danbury Hatters Case, 95, 447
Debentures, 71, 73, 447

Debt
ceiling, 203
federal, 202–5
management, 340
"shortening" of, 205
Deflation, 310
Deficit Spending, 447
Depletion, 447
Demand
aggregate, 371
curve, 368–9
derived, 391, 447
elasticity of, 379–81
joint, 391, 460
marginalist theory of, 362, 372–5
schedule, 367
Deposits
demand, 160
derived, 168
primary, 167
time and savings, 160, 479
Depreciation, 291, 447
Dewey-Dakin cycles, 214
Diagrammatic
analysis, 308
presentation, 306
Diminishing
returns (law of), 389
utility, 370
Discount rate, 177, 327, 448
Distribution
based on relative productivity, 390–1
theories of, 389–90
Disposable Income, 284, 289–291, 314–5, 448
Due Process of Law, 448
Duties
ad valorem, 276–7
countervailing, 279
mixed, compound, compensating, 277
specific, 277

Economic
development, 242–5
direct controls, 146
forces, 15
goods, 21, 448
indirect controls, 151–4, 300
intervention, 299, 322
laws, 15, 144–5
man, 449
planning, 146–7
rent, 417, 449
Economic Growth
and deficity spending, 238
and employment, 235
and taxes, 238–41
causes of, 236–7
changes in rate of, 234
impediments to, 241
in the U.S., 233
Economics
analytical, 7–11
and politics, 42
art or science, 11–12
definition of, 4–5

Economics (*cont'd*)
macro, 132–3, 462
micro, 132, 465
normative, 5–7
pragmatic, 5, 12–13
scope of, 13–16
Elasticity
of demand, 378–80
of money, 449
of supply, 377–8
unitary, 379–80
Embargoes, 281
Empirical Approach, 8, 449
Employment
full, 136–9
wage cost and rate of, 401
Encyclicals, 450
Enlightenment, 27, 450
Equilibrium
general (Walrasian), 381, 455
particial (Marshallian), 380, 470
price, 451
Equipment Trust Certificates, 74
Epistemology, 450

Fabians, 451
Factors of Production, 22–3, 452
Family, 114–6
Fair Labor Standard Act, 107
Farm
aid, 54–8, 61–5
credit, 55
family, 59
policy (New Deal), 56
population, 60
Featherbedding, 102, 106, 452
Federal
budget, 184, 188
Communication Commission, 46
debt, 202–5
Deposit Insurance Corp. (FDIC), 164–5, 453
Intermediate Credit Bank System, 56
Land Bank System, 56
Trade Commission, 46, 86, 123
Federal Reserve
Board of Governors, 172
clearing system, 174
functions, 173–5
government influence, 170, 324–5
history, 169–70
member banks, 164, 172
monetary policy, 170–2, 175–7, 325–31
notes, 160, 453
Open Market Committee, 329–31
reserve requirements, 165–166, 168–9, 177, 328–9, 476
structure, 172–3, 177

Fiscal
  aims of policy, 194–5
  limitation of policy, 343
  meaning of term, 185, 453
  policies, 332–40
Flight capital, 454
Flow chart, 300–1
Food and Drug Administration, 123
Foreign exchange rates, 180
Foreign trade restrictions, 257, 280
  importance, 260–1
  theory (Keynesian influence), 265–7
Franklin, Benjamin, 20
Free enterprise philosophy, 142
Free entry, 354
Freedom
  economic, 30
  of contract, 30
Fringe benefits, 100, 454
Full employment, 14–15, 135–136, 302, 454

Galbraith, John Kenneth, 22, 113, 315, 432
General Agreement on Tariffs and Trade, 282
George, Henry, 421
Gold
  and foreign exchange rates, 180
  and international price equilibrium, 179
  and international trade, 268
  and money supply, 178
  as medium of exchange, 181
  clause cases, 31
  coin, 157
  "Cross of . . . ," 171
  loss of gold, 255
  role of, 177, 255
Gold Standard, 249–53
  decline of, 250–52
  role of, 249–50
  vs. economic planning, 252–253
Goods
  economic or scarce, 371
  free, 372
Granger Movement, 54
Great Society, 24
Greenbacks, 160, 456
Gompers, Samuel, 95
Government
  revenues, 189–90
  spending, 192–3, 201–2
"Guideline" theory ("Guideposts"), 102–3, 333, 456

Hard money, 170
Harrod, R. F., 16, 220
Hawley-Smoot Tariff, 279
Hawtry, R. G., 220
Hayek, Friedrich von, 219
Hobbes, Thomas, 26, 142

Holding Companies, 87, 456
Hughes, Chief Justice Charles Evans, 30
Hume, David, 179

Import quotas, 280
Income
  disposable, 117, 290–1, 448
  distribution of, 117
  national, 285–7, 289–90, 466
  personal, 290–1, 471
Individual
  nature of, 26–28
  relation to society, 25–26
Industries
  location, 87–88
  size, 87–89
Inflation
  causes, 309–10
  gap, 308–9
Inherent rights, 29
Injunctions, 96
Input-output model, 382
Institutional framework, 15, 93, 450
Interest
  and capital formation, 414
  equilibrium theory, 412
  justification of, 409
  tool of economic planning, 414
Interlocking directorates, 87, 458
International
  Bank for Reconstruction and Development (World Bank) (IBRD), 270
  Development Assoc., 271–2
  division of labor, 263
  Monetary Fund, 181, 256–7, 270
  monetary system, 270
International Trade
  absolute and comparative advantage, 264–5
  arguments for protection, 272–5
  division of labor, 263
  how to overcome deficits, 269
  importance of, 260–1
  import restrictions, 280–1
  Keynesian influence, 265–7
  role of gold, 268
  terms of trade, 275
  theories and policies, 262–5
  U.S. policy, 282
Interstate Commerce Commission, 123
Investment bankers, 75
Investments
  definition, 459
  in cyclical theory, 218–20
Iron Law of Wages, 9, 397

Jevons, William Stanley, 214

Job security, 100, 105–107
Johnson, President L. B., 118
Joint demand, 391
Juglar, Clement, 212, 460

Keynes, John Maynard, 9–10, 12, 101, 224–5, 265, 315, 339, 436
Kitchin, Joseph, 226, 460
Knights of Labor, 95, 460
Knodratieff, N. D., 226, 460

Labor
  changing position of, 97–8
  exploitation of, 93
  factor of production, 93
  productivity of, 36, 102
  psychological aspects, 94–5
  relations, 92
  scarcity of, 353–6
  spreading of work, 106
Laissez faire, 43–4, 461
Landrum-Griffin Act, 100
Law of Poverty, 9
Least-cost-substitution principle, 387–8, 461
Legal tender, 461
Leisure, 20
Leontieff, Wassily W., 382
Lewis, John L., 98, 105
Liberalism, 29, 461
Liquidity
  preference, 412, 462
  ratio, 167
Lock-outs, 96
Locke, John, 27, 29
Lydia, 157, 462

Macroeconomics
  definition, 132–3, 346–7, 462
  objectives, 131–5
  theory, 300–5
Maintenance of membership, 462
Malthus, Thomas R., 8–9, 37, 222–3, 397, 463
Margin requirements, 176–7, 463
Marginal
  factor cost, 387–8
  physical product, 464
  propensity to consumer or save, 464
  revenue product, 387–8
  utility, 464
Marginalist
  demand theory, 372–3
  wage theory, 398
Marshall, Alfred, 5, 254, 265, 351, 376, 381
Marshall, Chief Justice John, 69
Marx, Karl, 223–4, 397
Mature economy, 10, 313, 315, 317, 464
Medicare, 47, 127–9

Means, Gardiner C., 80
Meany, George, 107
Mercantilism, 345, 348, 350–1, 396, 465
Merger, 465
Microeconomics
  definition, 132–3, 346–7, 465
Mill, John Stuart, 265, 421
Mitchell, Wesley C., 225, 466
Mixed economies, 345
Monetary policies, 170–2, 175–177, 325–31
Money
  creation of, 162, 167–9
  credit, 161
  definition, 157
  functions of, 158–9
  guarantor of solvency, 160
  hard and soft, 170–1
  importance of, 161
  in the U.S., 159–61
  lawful, 461
  medium of exchange, 158
  nature of, 157
  paper, 168
  representative, 475
  standard of deferred payments, 158
  standard of value, 158
  store of value, 159
  supply of, 160
  unit of account, 159
Monopoly, 79–82, 356, 465
Monopolistic competition, 355–356
Monopsony, 356, 466
Morgenstern, Oskar, 11, 358
Mortality rate, 38
Most-favored-nation clause, 278
Multiplier, 318–9, 466

National
  Bureau of Economic Research, 225–6, 285–6, 466
  Income, 284, 286–9, 466
  Income accounting, 284, 291, 466
  Labor Relations Act of 1935, 30, 97
  Labor Relations Board (NLRB), 97
National product
  gross, 284–5, 287–8, 291–2, 456
  net, 284, 288–9, 302, 318
Natural law, 144
Near money, 467
Negotiable instrument, 467
Neumann, John von, 11, 358
Newton, Sir Isaac, 142–3
Normative discipline, 5–7, 468
Norris-LaGuardia Act of 1932, 97

Obsolescence, 471
Oeconomia, 468

Old Age Survivor and Disability Insurance (ASDI), 126
Oligopoly, 83, 356–7, 468
Oligopsony, 356–7, 468
Open market
  committee, 173
  operations, 177, 329, 468
Opportunity cost, 426
Ordinate, 306, 366
Organic philosophy of society, 24–5, 469
Output gap, 238
Overpopulation, 37, 39
Overproduction, 216–22
Over-the-counter market, 469

Paradox of
  thrift, 316
  value, 372
Parity
  definition, 470
  farm prices, 57–8
Partnership
  general, 68, 470
  limited, 68, 462
Peoples' capitalism, 78
Perfect competition, 353–56
Personal income, 284, 288, 290
Physiocrats, 418–9, 471
Pigou, A. C., 219
Place utility, 428
Planning
  and personal freedom, 149
  centralized, 146–7, 149–50
  decentralized, 146, 151–54
  in Russia, 148
Population
  overpopulation, 37–9
  problems in U.S., 39–41
  trends and economic prosperity, 34–7
Positivism, 471
Poverty, 118–9
Pragmatic discipline, 12–13, 472
Prebisch, Raul, 274
Price formation, 353
Price index
  consumer, 293–5
  weighted, 296
  wholesale, 294
Price-specie-flow mechanism, 179
Price theories
  determined by cultural framework, 349
  mercantilistic, 348–50
  microeconomic, 351–2
  modern "general welfare," 350
Private pension plans, 126
Products homogeneous and differentiated, 354
Production
  cost of, 352, 365
  theory of, 385–8
Profit
  and degree of risk, 426

Profit (*cont'd*)
  and depreciation, 425
  and full employment, 435
  basis of price calculation, 433
  classical theory, 429
  definition, 424
  marginalist theory, 430
  measure of, 436–7
  motive, 144–5
  philosophic conflict, 432
  public attitude, 427
  ratio, 167
  regulating volume of production, 430
  squeeze, 438
Propensity to consume and save
  average, 314
  definition, 472
  marginal, 314
Property
  private, 29–32
  rights, 29, 31
Proprietorship, 68, 474
Protectionism, 272–3
Protective motive, 474
Proudhon, Pierre Joseph, 29
Public sector, 474
Purchasing power (aggregate), 371
Pure Food and Drug Acts, 46

Quantity theory of money, 179–80, 331

Rate of exchange, 474
Rationalism, 8, 475
Reciprocal trade agreements, 279
Regulation "T" and "U," 326
Regulatory
  agencies, 123
  state, 45, 475
Rent
  contract, 417, 446
  differential, 419
  economic, 417, 449
Reserve requirements, 165–6, 169, 177, 328, 476
Reserves
  excess, 166, 451
  free, 165, 169, 454
  required, 166, 328
Restraints of trade (types of), 83–7
Reward-for-abstinence theory, 411
Reuther, Walter, 105–6, 316
Ricardo, David, 265, 389, 397, 419, 430
Right-to-work laws, 109
Robinson, Joan, 355
Robinson-Patman Act, 123
Roosevelt, President Franklin D., 13, 31, 180
Round-about production process, 386
Rousseau, Jean Jacques, 27, 142

Safety ratio, 167
Samuelson, Paul A., 316
Saving, rate of, 119
Savings
  and investments, 305
  definition, 476
  excess, 311, 316
  idle, 304, 457
Say, J. B., 222
Scarcity, 362, 364, 368, 476
Scholasticism, 394–5, 428, 476
Schumpeter, Joseph, 219, 421
Secular trend, 477
Securities and Exchange Commission (SEC), 46, 123
Securities
  effect of taxation, 76
  listed and unlisted, 78, 462
  markets, 74, 78
  registration statements, 76
  type of, 71
  underwriters, 75, 477
Self-equilibrating forces, 297, 299
Self-evident truth, 8–9
Shaftesbury, Earl of, 27
Shay's rebellion, 54
Sherman Anti-Trust Act of 1890, 84–5, 95, 477
Silver certificates, 160–2
Smith, Adam, 272, 372, 434
Social Security Act of 1935, 115, 125
Socialism, 48, 477
Soil Conservation Act of 1936, 57
Spreading the work, 106–7
Speculative motive, 477
Standard of value, 158, 478
Stabilizers (built-in automatic), 334
State and local finance, 205–6
Stock market, 77
St. Thomas Aquinas, 20
Stackelberg, H. von, 355
Store of value, 478
Strike-breakers, 96
Sun-spot theory, 214
Supplementary unemployment insurance, 125–6
Supply
  changes in, 367
  factors determining, 365
  schedule, 366

Taft-Hartley Act of 1947, 100, 108
Tax
  cost of collecting, 195
  incidence, 200, 478
  shifting, 200–1
Taxation
  and economic planning, 195
  and growth, 239–41
  constitutional basis, 198
  limits, 191
Taxes
  ability-to-pay principle, 199

Taxes (*cont'd*)
benefit principle, 199
consumption, 197
corporation income, 44, 196, 334
excise, 197, 201, 451
federal, 196–8
income, 196–7, 457
inheritance and estate, 197, 458
on business activities, 197
personal income, 196–7, 334
progressive, 199, 472
property, 196, 473
proportional, 200, 473
regressive, 199, 475
social security, 197, 477
state and local, 198
turnover, 480
Tariffs
ad valorem, 276
American system, 277–8
complex, 279
conventional, 278
countervailing, 279
general and conventional, 277
mixed, compound and compensating, 277
most-favored-nation clause, 278
multiple, 278
protective, 276–7
revenue, 276
simple and complex, 278–9
specific, 277
Terms of trade, 275
Theory of
games, 358, 478
the periphery, 274
Time
preference, 411
utility, 428
Totalitarianism, 48
Transparency of markets, 347–355, 480
Treasury
bills, certificates, notes, 480

Unemployment
causes of, 136–8
frictional, 139
insurance, 47, 125, 335
supplementary insurance, 125–6
Union
bread-and-butter issues, 96
craft, 98, 447
exemption from anti-trust laws, 86
industrial, 98, 458
security, 107–8
shop, 108–9, 480
Unionism
anti-union measures, 96–7
compulsory, 108–9
in the U.S., 93
modern issues, 99–100

Unionism (*cont'd*)
  size of union movement, 99
Unit of account, 159, 481
Underconsumption, 216, 218, 222
Underdevelopment, 318, 339
Unearned income, 286
Unlimited liability, 69
United States
  Department of Commerce, 285–6, 294
  Department of Justice, 350
  notes, 160, 162, 163, 481
  Tariff Commission, 279–80
U.S. Government
  bonds, 204
  budget, 188–90
  concentration of power, 202
  debt, 202–5
  savings bonds, 204
  size, 185–6
  spending, 186–7
  taxation, 187
Utility
  definition, 481
  diminishing, 370
  measuring of, 373
  role in demand theory, 364, 368, 373

Velocity, 331, 481
Voluntary cooperation, 333
Voltaire, Francois Marie, 144

Wages
  and rate of employment, 401
  determined by, 402
  iron law of, 9
  minimum, 30
Wage theories
  classical, 396
  conflicting, 101, 108
  equilibrium, 102
  marginalist, 398
  Marxian, 397
  mercantilistic, 396
  purchase power, 404–5, 474
  scholastic, 394–5
War on poverty, 47, 119
Walras, Leon, 381, 420
Welfare
  general, 350–1
  state, 46, 124, 482
Wilson, President Woodrow, 28
Workman's compensation, 47, 124, 482
World bank, 270

Yellow dog contracts, 96